CHINA IN THE INDIAN OCEAN

One Ocean, Many Strategies

CHINA IN THE INDIAN OCEAN

One Ocean, Many Strategies

Cdr M.H. Rajesh

United Service Institution of India, New Delhi

PENTAGON PRESS

China in the Indian Ocean: One Ocean, Many Strategies
Cdr M.H. Rajesh

First Published in 2018

ISBN 978-93-86618-36-8

Disclaimer: The views expressed in this book are those of the author and do not necessarily reflect those of the United Service Institution of India or any other organisation.

Published by
PENTAGON PRESS
206, Peacock Lane, Shahpur Jat
New Delhi-110049
Phones: 011-64706243, 26491568
Telefax: 011-26490600
email: rajan@pentagonpress.in
website: www.pentagonpress.in

Printed at Aegean Offset Printers, Greater Noida, UP.

To those on watch in the Indian Ocean

CONTENTS

FOREWORD

The strategic implications of China's increasing footprints in the Indian Ocean Region have engaged governments, think tanks and analysts. The Indian Ocean's importance in the Chinese calculus has been on the rise ever since China opened up in the 1970s and became a net oil importer in the 1990s, due to markets and resources in its littorals. The military gravitas of this becomes evident when one considers China's arms transfers to the region and antipiracy patrols which have been a regular feature since 2008. The roll-out of the Belt and Road Initiative in 2015 has articulated this more coherently with regional infrastructure initiatives including ports, power, roads and rail projects. These projects cannot be seen from an economic prism alone, as they tend to have serious strategic spill overs.

China's rise and related events in the Indo-Pacific has been an area of focus for the USI of India. This work by Commander M.H. Rajesh, a Research Fellow at the USI, is a timely one in that genre that covers the economic and strategic aspects of China's presence in the Indian Ocean. Using a broad overview of the Belt and Road Initiative as a 'grand strategy', he connects the dots through multiple regional events related to China. The initial chapters on the South China Sea, the Maritime Forces of China and the Indian Ocean provide the reader a generic context to that presence. The rest of the chapters are more specific as well as granular in their approach, commencing with the China Pakistan Economic Corridor. He incisively discerns some patterns in China's presence, packaging those as strategies of access, resources and networks –all in separate chapters. That should help the reader quickly capture the essence of China's approach to the region. That is one seminal contribution of this work; the other significant effort has been to seamlessly weave economy with strategy and to weave continental and maritime strategies to present a cohesive picture.

We are also perhaps at a point of history when the Indian Ocean is returning to the centre stage of geopolitics after a prolonged period of hiatus. As economies along the IOR littorals grow, naturally, the importance of the region too shall grow. Both India and China too have regained some of their lost glories in their modern avatars and are seeking deserving status. The Indian Ocean has in effect, become that arena where these powers will interact, in addition to their unsettled continental borders. This work is also important from that perspective.

The canvas of this book has necessarily been a wide one to encompass a whole range of nested issues. It often extends beyond the littorals of the Indian Ocean, touching the global nodes of China's maritime network, which help a reader understand the broader maritime geopolitics. From energy politics in the Middle East to ethnic strife in Myanmar and the connectivity initiatives in Africa, the book covers multiple factors that block by block go into building the strategies adopted by China in the Indian Ocean.

It is hoped that this seminal work will not only engage the reader, but will contribute to a body of contemporary understanding about the Indian Ocean and China.

New Delhi **Lt Gen PK Singh, PVSM, AVSM (Retd)**
Oct. 2017 Director, USI

PREFACE

My interest in this subject was triggered during my tenure as a submarine captain in 2009. China had just commenced its presence in the Indian Ocean as a part of the anti-piracy patrols. The interest continued through my subsequent desk job; mid-way through which, my service was kind enough to spare me for a sabbatical at the United Service Institution of India. This book is a result of my research during that period.

The USI provided me the most conducive environment for research. It facilitated few field visits to East Asia and provided me with opportunities to interact with scholars and think tanks in India and abroad. My seniors at USI, Lt Gen P.K. Singh, Director, and Maj Gen B.K. Sharma, Head of Research and CS3, were pillars of support, giving me complete intellectual freedom. Rear Admiral Sudarshan Y. Shrikhande guided me to stay the course through my research. I cannot thank him enough for the sustained encouragement on strategy, geopolitics and professional matters over a decade! Jabin Jacob, M.V. Rappai and Sanjay Pulipaka, who have walked the path before, went through several ideas of this book and suggested improvements. I am grateful to them.

Lt Gen SL Narasimhan and Rear Adm Monty Khanna shared their erudite views over some subjects in this book. I am thankful to both these soldier scholars for encouraging me.

Prof. William C. Kirby and Prof. Peter K. Bol, at Harvard, have never known me, but their fascinating 15-month online course 'China X' opened my eyes to China. My colleagues at the USI have been a great source of encouragement. Of these, Cmde Lalit Kapur and Dr Roshan Khanijo were extremely helpful during my work. Dr Leena Srivasatava went through a part of my work and gave valuable suggestions. I am grateful to her. Prem Reuben, Pradeep Nair, Jabin Jacob and Sanjay Kannoth went through the ideas in the book diligently and suggested crucial course corrections. I would have drifted ashore without you. Stubborn errors that remain are entirely mine!

Brig Sri Kumar and Brig Sanal Kumar were sources of encouragement. R.S. Sunil, Prakash Gopalan, Chetan Chandegave and Anirudh Chauhan gave valuable insights. C.P. Vinod, Ranjan Bhattacharya, Vivek Sharma and Saurabh Rastogi have been a great support. I express gratitude to them.

I am indebted to my parents, Rajam and Haridasan, and mother in law Ponnamma Nair for supporting me through this work. Along with Radhika, Renjitha, Hari and Anu they have tolerated my absence. Prof Rajan Gurukkal, Late Mr NBN and Mr PCN as great teachers were indulgent, inspired and shaped my views. I owe them immensely.

My daughter Gayathri read through parts of the draft and edited them. Hope her generation finds this work interesting. Lastly, my beloved wife Priya has been a pillar of support through this work as she has been with my other endeavours. I thank her deeply.

Views expressed in this work are personal and not of any organisation. I have tried to acknowledge all those who have helped me and cite all sources used in the work. If anything has been missed out, it is an oversight.

New Delhi **Cdr M.H. Rajesh**

Sep. 2017

LIST OF FIGURES

List of Tables

ABBREVIATIONS

A2AD	Anti-Access Area Denial
AAGC	Asia-Africa Growth Corridor
ABSDF	All Burma Students' Democratic Front
ACD	Asia Cooperation Dialogue
ADB	Asian Development Bank
ADMM+	ASEAN Defense Ministers' Meeting Plus
AEI	American Enterprise Institute
AESA	Active Electronically Scanned Array
AEW	Airborne Early Warning
AFRICOM	United States Africa Command
AIIB	Asian Infrastructure Investment Bank
ALP	Arakan Liberation Party
AP	Adhaalath Party
APEC	Asia-Pacific Economic Cooperation
ARF	ASEAN Regional Forum
ARRND	Agreement on Rapid Response to Natural Disasters
ASBM	Anti-Ship Ballistic Missiles
ASEAN	Association of Southeast Asian Nations
ASW	Anti Submarine Warfare
AWACS	Airborne Warning and Control System
BBIN	Bangladesh, Bhutan, India, Nepal (BBIN) Initiative
BCIM-EC	Bangladesh, China, India, Myanmar Economic Corridor
BIMSTEC	Bay of Bengal Initiative for Multi-Sectoral Technical and Economic Cooperation
BNP	Bangladesh Nationalist Party
BOT	Build-Operate-Transfer

BPC	Bangladesh Petroleum Corporation
BRF	Belt and Road Forum
BRI	Belt and Road Initiative
CAGP	Central Asian Gas Pipeline
CAREC	Central Asia Regional Economic Cooperation
CASCF	China-Arab States Cooperation Forum
CBMs	Confidence-Building Measures
CDB	China Development Bank
CENTCOM	United States Central Command
CGPCS	Contact Group on Piracy off the Coast of Somalia
CHEC	China Harbour Engineering Company
CHISREP	China Ship Reporting System
CICA	Conference on Interaction and Confidence-Building Measures in Asia
CICT	Colombo International Container Terminals Ltd
CITIC	China International Trust Investment Corporation
CMC	Central Military Commission
CMI	Civil-Military Integration
CNF	Chin National Front
CNPC	China National Petroleum Corporation
COPH	China Overseas Port Holding Ltd
COSCO	China Ocean Shipping (Group) Company
CPB	Communist Party of Burma
CPC	Communist Party of China
CPEC	China-Pakistan Economic Corridor
CS	Continental Shelf
CSSC	State Shipbuilding Cooperation
DDG	Destroyer, Guided Missile
DKBA	Democratic Karen Benevolent Army,
DRP	Dhivehi Rayyithunge Party
DWP	Defence White Paper
EAMF	Expanded ASEAN Maritime Forum
EAO	Ethnic Armed Organisations
EAS	East Asia Summit
ECRL	East Coast Rail Line
EEZ	Exclusive Economic Zone
EGAT	Electricity Generating Authority of Thailand
ELINT	Electronic Intelligence

ESPO	Eastern Siberia-Pacific Ocean
ETIM	East Turkistan Islamic Movement-
EW	Electronic Warfare
FFG	Frigate, Guided Missile
FOCAC	Forum on China-Africa Cooperation
FoN	Freedom of Navigation
FSU	Former Soviet Union
GCC	Gulf Cooperation Council
GDP	Gross Domestic Product
GFC	Global Financial Crisis
GFZL	Gwadar Free Zone Ltd
GITL	Gwadar International Terminals Ltd
GMS	Greater Mekong Sub-region
GMSL	Gwadar Marine Services Ltd
HADR	Humanitarian Aid and Disaster Relief
HADR	Humanitarian Assistance and Disaster Relief
HP	Hutchison Port
ICBC	Industrial and Commercial Bank of China
IGAD	Intergovernmental Agreement on Development
IMB	International Maritime Bureau
IMF	International Monetary Fund
INSTC	International North–South Transport Corridor
IONS	Indian Ocean Naval Symposium
IOR	Indian Ocean Region
IORA	Indian Ocean Regional Association
ITLOS	International Tribunal for the Law of the Sea
JCC	Joint Coordination Committee
JCPOA	Joint Comprehensive Plan of Action
JEC	Joint Economic Commission
JIDD	Jakarta International Defence Dialogue
JL	Ju Lang
JP	Jumhooree Party
KIO	Kachin Independence Organisation
KKH	Karakoram Highway
KLIP	Kuala Linggi International Port
KLO	Kamatapur Liberation Organisation
KNLA	Karen National Liberation Army
KNLA-PC	Karen National Liberation Army-Peace Council

KNPP	Karenni National Progressive Party
KPK	Khyber Pakhtunkhwa
LAPSSET	Lamu Port-South Sudan-Ethiopia-Transport
LCS	Littoral Combat Ship
LNG	Liquefied Natural Gas
LPD	Amphibious Transport Dock
LPH	Landing Platform Helicopter
LSCI	Liner Shipping Connectivity Index
LST	Landing Ship, Tank
LTE	Low Tide Elevations
MDA	Maldives Development Alliance
MDP	Maldivian Democratic Party
MEA	Ministry of External Affairs
MITT	Myanmar International Terminal Thilawa
ML	Main Line
ML1	Main Line 1
MNDAA	Myanmar National Democratic Alliance Army
MOGE	Myanmar Oil and Gas Enterprise
MOOTWs	Preparing for Military Operations Other Than War
MSR	Maritime Silk Road
NATO	North Atlantic Treaty Organisation
NCA	Nationwide Ceasefire Agreement
NDB	New Development Bank
NER	North Eastern Region
NHPC	National Hydroelectric Power Corporation
NLD	National League for Democracy
NMSP	New Mon State Party
NSC	NATO Shipping Centre
NSCN-IM	National Socialist Council of Nagaland (IsakSwu, Muivah)
NSCN-K	National Socialist Council of Nagaland (Khaplang)
NSR	New Silk Road
OBOR	One Belt One Road
OEM	Original Equipment Manufacturer
OMTE	Outline of Military Training and Evaluation
OPEC	Organization of the Petroleum Exporting Countries
ORBAT	Order of Battle (List of Units)
PACOM	United States Pacific Command
PAPF	People's Armed Police Force

PB	Political Bureau of the CPC Central Committee
PBC	People's Bank of China
PBSC	Politburo Standing Committee
PLA	People's Liberation Army
PLAAF	People's Liberation Army Air Force
PLAGF	People's Liberation Army Ground Forces
PLAN	People's Liberation Army Navy
PLANAF	People's Liberation Army Naval Air Force
PLARF	People's Liberation Army Rocket Force
PLASAF	People's Liberation Army Second Artillery Force
PLASSF	People's Liberation Army Strategic Support Force
PMS	Preparation for Military Struggle
PNLO	Pa-Oh National Liberation Organisation
PNS	Pakistan Naval Ship
POK	Pakistan-Occupied Kashmir
PPM	Progressive Party of Maldives
PRC	People's Republic of China
PRC	Piracy Reporting Centre
PSA	Port of Singapore Authority
PSA	Port of Singapore Authority
PSC	Production Sharing Contract
RCEP	Regional Comprehensive Economic Partnership
RCSS	Restoration Council of Shan State
ReCAAP	Regional Cooperation Agreement on Combating Piracy and Armed Robbery against Ships in Asia
RMA	Revolution in Military Affairs
SAARC	South Asian Association for Regional Cooperation
SADC	Southern African Development Council
SAM	Surface to Air Missile
SAR	Search and Rescue
SASAC	State Owned Assets Supervision and Administration Commission
SCO	Shanghai Cooperation Organization
SCS	South China Sea
SDR	Special Drawing Right
SEATO	Southeast Asia Treaty Organization
SGRF	Oman's State General Reserve Fund
SHADE	Shared Awareness and Deconfliction

SIPRI	Stockholm International Peace Research Institute
SKRL	Singapore Kunming Rail Link
SLD	Shangri-La Dialogue
SLFP	Sri Lanka Freedom Party
SLOCs	Sea Lines of Communication
SLORC	State Law and Order Restoration Council
SLPA	Sri Lanka Ports Authority
SOA	State Oceanic Administration
SOE	State Owned Enterprise
SPDC	State Peace and Development Council
SREB	Silk Road Economic Belt
SSB	Submarine Ballistic, Ballistic Missile Submarine
SSBN	Submarine Ballistic Nuclear, Ballistic Missile Submarine, Nuclear-powered
SSG	Guided Missile Submarine
SSGN	Guided Missile Submarine, Nuclear-powered
SSK	Hunter-Killer/ASW Submarine
SSN	Attack Submarine, Nuclear-powered
SSPP	Shan State Progressive Party
STOBAR	Short Take-Off and Barrier-Assisted Recovery
TAPI	Turkmenistan-Afghanistan-Pakistan-India
TEU	Twenty-Foot Equivalent Unit
ULCC	Ultra Large Crude Carriers
ULFWSA	United Liberation Front of West South Asia
UN	United Nations
UNCLOS	United Nations Conventions on the Laws of the Sea
UNFC	United Nationalities Federal Council
UNFGG	United National Front for Good Governance
UNLFW	United Liberation Front of Western South East Asia
UNP	United National Party
UREC	Union Resources and Engineering Company
USSR	Union of Soviet Socialist Republics
UWSA	United Wa State Army
VLCC	Very Large Crude Carriers
WPNS	Western Pacific Naval Symposium
WTO	World Trade Organization
YCEG	Yunnan Construction and Engineering Group

CHAPTER 1

INTRODUCTION: CHINA IN THE INDIAN OCEAN—ONE OCEAN, MANY STRATEGIES

This is a book about China's maritime strategy in the Indian Ocean. Ever since China opened up four decades ago, it has sought markets, resources and political alliances across the globe. This quest has taken it across the Indian Ocean more than the others, due to resources and markets and since other littorals were geopolitically crowded spaces with comparatively developed economies and established security structures. A major ocean in the world whose littorals promise scope for rapid economic growth is the Indian Ocean. It is also devoid of deep strategic and security structures unlike the Atlantic and the Pacific. With such an allure, the Indian Ocean has been high on China's agenda for economic growth and influence. China has step by step set a new strategic normal in the Indian Ocean with submarine deployments, acquisition of bases, deployment of ships for anti-piracy, arms sales and patterns of investments. This has been an incrementally rising trend for over a decade that can alter the politics of this ocean and its littorals.

I have written this at the end of a two-year sabbatical at the United Service Institution, India's oldest think tank that deals with security. It tries to cover the broad contours of Chinese actions in logical segments while maintaining the central plot of China's Strategy in the Indian Ocean. This work has relied on information gleaned from Chinese White Papers, study of its investments in Indian Ocean littorals, trends in domestic, regional and international politics, data on arms sales etc., and then connecting those dots to paint the larger picture. This in a way is a narrative of that rise from empirical evidence, than a theoretical explanation of that rise pivoting on international relations theories. At the same time, broad insights from scholars and geostrategists such as Mackinder and Mahan have tempered that narrative. A vast set of contemporary inputs such as books, articles, white papers, public lectures, etc., have been perused. Several Chinese initiatives mentioned in the book are dynamic in nature, altering according to ground realities. However, patterns broadly remain the same.

I have commenced with the approach of studying the Indian Ocean initiatives by looking at the internal changes in China. The Belt and Road Initiative (BRI) was announced around the time this research commenced. China also released its vision document about that grand scheme. It was sensed that the Belt and Road and its vision expressed the general course adapted by that nation, laying a road map for the future. Hence that was deemed the 'grand strategy' explaining some of the economic underpinnings that could explain Chinese actions in the region. 'Politics is a concentrated expression of economics', stated Lenin. This could be especially true with China which is a Marxist Leninist state. On that count, this book presumes that Chinese economic plans are closely linked to strategy and will in fact drive its strategy. Quite often one segregates them into separate silos. I believe that these two domains need to be looked at as one seamless entity- this is the first fusion of silos that I have attempted. Yet, a chapter has been devoted to hard power, where the Chinese naval development over the years has been curated and contextually explained. In the organisation of the chapters itself, the various sub-strategies have been branded into themes. They commence by articulating a grand strategy and attempt to take the reader through themes of hard power, revisionism of law, creation of alliances, quest for access, swapping debt for strategic equity, creation of footholds and maritime networks, and need for resources. Though the belief is that the economy will eventually drive strategy, this work recognises the Daedalian way in which they are entwined.

The vantage spot from where that strategy is narrated is India that occupies a central position in an ocean named after it. China's rise obviously evokes caution and occasional alarm in India, like when it chose to supply submarines to Bangladesh or dock them across straits in Sri Lanka. China is a rising global power, a neighbour with an unsettled border, an Asian co-traveller, and an opponent that handed out a debacle five decades ago. It is also the political opposite of a democracy as an authoritarian state, a competitor for resources and markets, a development model to emulate, and a manipulator of its neighbourhood—all at the same time—to India. I concede that a Chinese narrative will have a mixed view that mirrors the above impressions. Unlike many other countries in the world which react to China's rise from a distance, India with such a proximate location has no such luxury. It shares a 3,488 km border which both countries have been trying to settle through a bilateral political process. This is an ongoing process whose progress has been slow, tardy, yet unbroken. It is also a border that has, despite the differences, been calm thanks to matured statecraft from both nations.

Such a six-decade old continental reality had a new maritime parallel, when China decided to step up its activities in the Indian Ocean. Something that had been anticipated for long in the strategic circles is occurring now. The economic foray now has a matching muscle in the military and it is finding bases, clocking sea time in the Indian Ocean and finding friends on the way. Before I set about seeking answers to China's intentions in the Indian Ocean, I was confronted with some other interesting questions. They were:

- How is China evolving as an economic and military power?
- What is the rationale behind the Belt and Road Initiative?
- How are the Chinese building their maritime forces and how have they evolved?
- What is happening in the South China Sea (SCS) and why is it important?
- What are the security contours in the Indian Ocean?
- What are the specifics of their Indian Ocean activities in the sub regions in the IOR?
- Is there a way to connect the dots and arrive at a pattern in their actions?
- What are the implications of China's actions in the Indian Ocean?

This book attempts to answer some of these questions. As far as possible, they are in an order where each theme is fitted into one chapter. Some questions like its energy initiatives had to be answered in many chapters, since access lay in one sub region and source in another sub region. The order of chapters has been arranged in the logical manner of the questions. This first chapter, which you are reading now, is a broad overview of the book introducing the reader to the work.

The second chapter describes the Belt and Road Initiative—a major Chinese plan—which not only comes close to a grand strategy but the tenets of which connect the chapters of this book like a thread. Since the central theme of the book is about oceans, the Maritime Silk Road (MSR) has been the chosen cynosure in BRI over its continental plan, though an attempt has been made to compare it with the Silk Road Economic Belt (SREB), its land counterpart.

This is a second fusion of silos; breaking maritime and continental silos to see them as one whole edifice.

The third chapter is about the evolution of China's maritime hard power. China's maritime strategy has been evolving and its naval power and presence has been growing. These changes have been in response to new domestic realities, the status of Taiwan, the South China Sea, the increasing share of trade in the GDP and international factors such as relations with the US. It describes how the Party's navy has created three-and-a-half fleets to deal with four specific roles such deterrence, anti-access, trade protection and territorial sovereignty.

The fourth chapter examines China's actions in the South China Sea, especially in the light of the Hague Tribunal's verdict. The South China Sea connects the Pacific to the Indian Ocean through the Malacca and other adjacent straits. That marginal sea is not only crucial to China's access to the Indian Ocean, but it is also a sea where the effect of its rise has been immediately felt. Unlike the East China Sea, the SCS is far enough not to intimidate the US or its treaty allies directly. China has therefore chosen a space where it can challenge the existing order to achieve its two-ocean strategy. The actions of China in the South China Sea have economic reasons, geopolitical underpinnings, legal factors and history—all entwined into an intricate problem. The historic revisionism, scant regard for law and finlandised bilaterals forebode what is in store ahead from the rising power for the rest of the world.

The fifth chapter is about the Indian Ocean. The central canvas of this book is that geostrategic space. Common sense says that oceans are only the medium and that continents will always dominate the oceans so long as men live on land. Yet when we take away that medium, the veritable economic exchanges that enrich the continents cease to exist. The Indian Ocean is that important medium for China. The focus of that chapter is to analyse the economic and political character of its littorals and examine the present and future security structures therein. After all, a Chinese strategy will shape and get shaped by the realities therein!

From the sixth chapter, the book changes tack to a description of the relevant regions within the Indian Ocean. The first among them is about Pakistan—China's only ally. It describes the various facets of the China Pakistan Economic Corridor, which is a flagship project in the Belt and Road Initiative. Pakistan has been a major factor in China's Strategy in the region. The contours of those relations were explained as an 'axis' till the CPEC.[1] The chapter tries to argue that this erstwhile transactional relation that focussed exclusively on India is expanding to a broader alliance where an economic weft has been laid over a strategic warp deepening that relation. The jury is out on the success of the CPEC and some say that 80 per cent of the CPEC is being considered as a write-off by China.[2] This is an interesting development that needs to be recorded and watched, especially its maritime terminus at Gwadar, which, according to me, is likely to emerge as a Chinese base in the foreseeable future.

The seventh chapter is about the 'footholds' that China is crafting for itself in the Indian Ocean and the maritime 'networks' of ports and shipping that it is creating globally. The rubric of footholds is about countries like Sri Lanka, Maldives and Bangladesh, which are neither large enough to be attractive markets nor are connected to China geographically unlike some others. They are not even countries with major resources that China hankers after. Yet, they have been important in China's Indian Ocean plan, providing ports and prospective bases in crisis. The transfer of complex and potent platforms like submarines also creates naval ecosystems in the Bay of Bengal which China can plug and play into. The maritime network that China is creating is also discussed in the same chapter, which includes port building, port acquisition, port operations, shipbuilding and shipping operations. This is described as a global phenomenon to put such regional developments in perspective. Perhaps, the global spree of maritime asset acquisition by the Chinese and Hong Kong companies has not got the attention it deserves, with too much attention being on Gwadar, whose future is a foregone conclusion.

Chapter Eight is about access to the Indian Ocean. There are six nations in the region that can assist China gain access to the Indian Ocean, of which one—Pakistan—has been covered in Chapter Five. Myanmar, Thailand, Indonesia, Malaysia and Singapore are the other five. Of these, Myanmar is in a different league altogether, given that it provides the shortest access from China to the Indian Ocean, something China has recognised and has deeply invested in through oil and gas equities, pipelines and the refining industry. This is besides the resources Myanmar promises- especially metals and minerals, and its hydropower potential. Such connectivity is enabled through a deft balancing of ethnic armed organisations against the core of the Barmars. Singapore, due to its very close alliance to the US, has become a bone of contention. It is a crucial cog in the US rebalance, accentuating China's Malacca vulnerability.

The recently concluded Belt and Road Forum had two notable absentees from China's neighbourhood. One was India which boycotted the forum over infringement of sovereignty. The other was Singapore, whose head of state was not invited for myriad reasons. A delegation however attended. China is creating alternate maritime, economic and financial centres mimicking and rivalling Singapore in Malaysia at the crucial Malacca straits. Indonesia and Thailand are the other two nations crucial for access to the IOR. The former is too large to ignore or to subsume into its orbit easily, whereas the latter has been wooed through big ticket military transfers like submarines and frigates. The various investment and political dynamics between these nations and China are discussed in this chapter. The pipeline, rail and canal options being considered for access by China are also elaborated in this chapter.

The ninth chapter is about China's quest for resources which is influencing its IOR strategy. Africa and the Middle East loom large in China's quest for resources—the former for oil, minerals, metals, investments, and the latter for oil and investments. The island nations of Mauritius and Seychelles are discussed in the same chapter as they assist China further in its Africa policy. The odd man out in this chapter is Australia, which is a major trade and investment destination for China, yet politically in the opposite pole as a vibrant, liberal democracy.

Chapter Ten, the final chapter, draws up a conclusion from the preceding nine chapters and sums up the book, but only after looking at some global trends in energy, climate, technology, military and politics. A study of any strategy that ignores those broader trends of the globe is bound to be an incomplete one.

NOTES

1. Andrew Small, *The China-Pakistan Axis: Asia's New Geopolitics* (Oxford University Press, 2015).
2. Tom Miller, *China's Asian Dream: Empire Building along the New Silk Road* (Zed Books, 2017).

CHAPTER 2

Belt and Road Initiative as a Grand Strategy

This chapter examines the Belt and Road Initiative (BRI) as a grand strategy that connects several dots and assists in painting a picture of China's Maritime Strategy in the Indian Ocean.

A grand strategy can be simply put as steps across multiple domains using all resources, including the military, to achieve a national objective. Economy and security are the two major pillars of that structure. Another related domain that looms large in this context is critical infrastructure megaprojects. Ports, rail, roads, dams and power projects alter geographies and effect geopolitics. To define China's grand strategy, the 'objective' or 'aim' of that strategy needs some analysis.

Historical and cultural interpretations on China abound in Chinese strategic concepts like ***zhongguo*** or 'middle kingdom', i.e., being the centre of the universe, and ***tianxia/tianming***, or a 'mandate to rule all under heaven'. However, a more palpable and contemporary understanding of what China wants to achieve had to be culled out for the purposes of this book. This is the 'China Dream', which has been the defining concept of President Xi Jinping's tenure. The Belt and Road Initiative is a project that aims to deliver the tangibles of the 'China Dream'.

President Xi first used the term during his visit to the National Museum of China, as the General Secretary of the Communist Party of China (CPC) in 2012, where he said, "*Nowadays, everyone is talking about the 'China Dream', in my view, to realise the great renewal of the Chinese nation is the greatest dream for the Chinese nation in modern history.*"[1] *Xinhua*, which covered the event, stated that according to Xi, "*The 'China Dream' has conglomerated the long-cherished aspiration of Chinese people of several generations, represented the overall interests of the Chinese nation and Chinese people, and has been a common expectation of every Chinese.*"

It is evident from Xi's statement that he was himself invoking an idea which had been in existence for some time. The origin of this idea has been attributed to many sources. However, when the General Secretary of the CPC and the President-designate echoed that vision, the term took on a different dimension altogether. Ever since Xi's address at the National Museum on November 29, 2012 the term acquired legitimacy, and has been repeated often in official communiqués and also attributed to the President so much so, that the *Xinhua* website has a separate section called the '*China Dream*', which serves as a repository of various manifestations of that idea, which in internet terms can be termed as 'crowd sourcing of ideas'.[2]

Though the '*China Dream*' has not been articulated in precise terms, the broad contours of that idea, in Xi's own words, envisage a moderately well-off society by 2021 and a fully developed nation by 2049. Both years are significant—being the hundred-year anniversaries of the Chinese Communist Party and the Chinese nation, respectively. Together, these are called the '***two centenaries***' *for* which targets have been set that need to be achieved by the nation. These aims were clarified by Xi in his address at the museum, where he quoted liberally from Mao, and the famous poet Li Bai. As reported by *Xinhua*, Xi said, "*I believe that by the time when the Communist Party of China marks its 100th founding anniversary, the goal to complete the building of a moderately prosperous society in all respects will be inevitably achieved. When it comes to the 100th founding anniversary of new China, the goal of building an affluent, strong, civilized and harmonious socialist modern country will certainly be fulfilled, and the dream of great renewal of the Chinese nation will inevitably be accomplished.*"[3]

There are alternate views of the dream as expressed by the China scholar David Shambaugh in his famous article, 'Coming Chinese CrackUp', in the *Wall Street Journal*. Shambaugh amongst other issues, states, "*Mr. Xi's real 'China Dream' has been to avoid the Soviet nightmare. Just a few months into his tenure, he gave a telling internal speech ruing the Soviet Union's demise and bemoaning Mr. Gorbachev's betrayals, arguing that Moscow had lacked a 'real man' to stand up to its reformist last leader.*"[4] Shambaugh is a renowned China scholar and his article did indicate a sense of desperate measures being taken by Xi, not to let China go down the Soviet road. With the BRI, China seems to be integrating economic spaces, contributing to economic growth and preventing disintegration of the state, which was partly responsible for the Soviet collapse.[5]

Xi has also identified that prosperity is extremely essential for China and highlighted that in the 'Dream'. Various analysts have indicated that political reform is not a part of the '*China Dream*'. Rather than any large-scale reform, Xi has chosen to refine the existing order, weeding away corruption. In order to achieve the levels of prosperity that President Xi aspires to, China requires changing its economic model from a 'foreign direct investment-manufacture-export' model to spreading its economic networks beyond its borders, and absorbing other nations into its value chain. This is ever so critical with the slowing down of growth as the old model is not delivering, as indicated by slowing growth rates which have settled at single digits.

The settling of the Chinese GDP growth rate to its reduced single-digit level at below seven percent has been explained as the ***new normal*** by its leadership. This according to the Guardian[6] is "*a clever bit of messaging by China's leaders, who must explain to the country's 1.4 billion citizens why the economy will no longer be growing by 10% a year*". When a country that grew at double digits for thirty years slows down, there must be a new way to prosper. The Belt and Road Initiative is that next big idea that can sustain that new normal to which the Chinese have reconciled to. This initiative is a tool by which hitherto untapped markets and resources can be amalgamated into one seamless Sino-centric network that China can control to maintain the new normal.

The contours of China's grand *Belt and Road Initiative* (BRI), also called the *One Belt One Road* (OBOR), emerged in the form of a white paper at the Boao Forum just as research for this book commenced in 2015. Clearly, the document provided the ambitious vision China had laid for itself for its future. The significance of such an articulation was immediately seized, and therefore the BRI has been placed as the first chapter of this book.

The rationale for such a positioning was because it was felt that whatever China did in the neighbourhood could now be linked and branded as the BRI plan. Such a 'passage plan', in maritime parlance, provides a reference line both to the student of politics and the reader, to which they can readily relate. China's Maritime Strategy in the Indian Ocean, which is the central theme of the book, is expected to be an offshoot of the BRI and in turn influences the BRI based on ground realities and possibilities. The BRI brand has been tenaciously built over these two years by China. It was evident that the projects that China would undertake hereafter, were going to be under that rubric, unless it was a purely strategic exchange such as nuclear cooperation or an arms deal.[7] Just as the book was nearing completion in mid-2017, the initial phase of the BRI rollout culminated with the Belt and Road Forum[8]—a summit (BRF).[9]

This author is of the view that the forum is a meetup, whereas the initiative refers to the actual projects on ground. This was a summit in Beijing attended by 60 countries of which 29 representatives were heads of states. The heads of several international organisations, including the UN, the World Bank, the WTO, and the IMF, were in attendance. There were announcements of a 14.5 billion USD infusion to the Silk Road Fund, a loan corpus worth 36.2 billion USD to the China Development Bank and 18.8 billion USD for the China EXIM bank, and 8.7 billion USD for humanitarian projects. There was also a joint statement on the Belt and Road Initiative which was signed by a few nations. India abstained from this forum, details of which are highlighted in this chapter.

The *BRI* has therefore attracted the attention of scholars and statesmen alike. Converting the recall value of the Ancient Silk Road, China has proposed a Sino-centric idea of physical networks spanning continents and oceans. Apart from its physical vastness, the idea spans a gamut of domains, from economics to culture.

Physically, the Belt and Road Initiative has two segments. To the north is the land route that cuts across Eurasia, called the Silk Road Economic Belt (SREB). To the south there is the sea route called the Maritime Silk Road (MSR), commencing from the Chinese Coast passing through South East Asia into the Indian Ocean and touching several ports en route before terminating in Europe. This chapter will try to examine the historic premise, economic rationale, dynamics of maritime transportation, geopolitical implications and responses to the Maritime Silk Road idea. The chapter will also examine the areas of concern and possible areas of convergence between India and China regarding the One Belt One Road as it traverses the Indian Ocean.

Historical Overview

It was the Western demand for riches of Asia, like China's silk and India's spices, that inspired the network of roads and ports across Eurasia and the Indian Ocean. Silk and spice were light, highly valued and non-perishable goods, making them ideal drivers of global commerce. During that phase of history, India and China together shared over 80 per cent of the global GDP.[10] The world is again reaching a point of time when Asia is taking centre stage. The routes existed from 200 BC to around 1500 AD and came to be collectively called the Silk Route. The credit for the nomenclature of these routes as the *Silk Route* goes to Ferdinand Richtofen,[11] a German geographer who published his work in 1877 after an extensive exploration of this region. This ancient route weakened due to a tumultuous power shift along its alignment, when the Ottoman Empire displaced the Byzantine Empire. This forced the Western world to discover a direct sea route to India being a destination, as well as a significant transit hub, reducing the relevance of this network after 1500 AD.[12] The southern maritime route, the predecessor of the present Maritime Silk Road, offered far less terrestrial friction, could carry larger loads and faced lesser political uncertainties. It was also more multimodal, where predictable monsoon winds aided sea-based transportation across Indian Ocean. The oceanic route handed goods over to a contiguous overland route which traversed across Egypt and onwards to the Mediterranean coast. Across the Mediterranean, the maritime mode clutched in again. The ease, economy of scale and multimodality remain key factors in maritime transportation. To date, 90 per cent of global trade in volume[13] is being carried via sea and therefore maritime transportation plays a significant role in global prosperity and growth. Just as the old Silk Road was extinguished due to tumultuous power shifts induced by the rise of the Ottomans, the new Silk Road is emerging at a time when the global system is undergoing power shifts induced by several factors, of which China is a singularly important one.

Contemporary Silk Route

The idea of the new Silk Road was mooted by Chinese President Xi Jinping for the first time in September 2013 at the Nazarbayev University in Kazakhstan-saddling China and Central Asia, as the Silk Road Economic Belt (SREB). This set the stage for the 'land route'. The location is important, as Kazakhstan is key to China's land routes into Eurasia. It was a month later, in October 2013, during a visit by President Xi[15] to Indonesia, that the 21st century Maritime Silk Road was announced during his address to the Indonesian parliament. The location was again significant; as Indonesia, an archipelagic nation is strategically located on the Maritime Silk Road between the Pacific and Indian Oceans. The exact contours of the Maritime Silk Road were released 18 months later through a vision document in March 2015 on the side-lines of the Boao Forum (the Asian equivalent of Davos), where leaders from industry and corporates meet informally[16] (Refer Appendix for the full version of the vision document). It is called the '*Vision and Actions on Jointly Building Silk Road Economic Belt and 21st-Century Maritime Silk Road*' and was issued by the National Development and Reform Commission, Ministry of Foreign Affairs, and the Ministry of Commerce of the People's Republic of China, with State Council authorisation.[17] The vision document was released as the First Edition-2015, which indicates the open-ended architecture of an evolving idea. No maps accompanied the document. The 5600-word text is in eight parts and covers the principles, framework, cooperation priorities, mechanisms, internal regions, and the formalities that a document of this nature must articulate.

It is an omnibus document that covers a wide gamut including infrastructure, trade and finance, culture and education—to list a few. The vision has been broad and its physical scope large. It states that "*the 21st-Century Maritime Silk Road is designed to go from China's coast to Europe through the South China Sea and the Indian Ocean in one route, and from China's coast through the South China Sea to the South Pacific in the other*". Whereas the land route is articulated as "*The Silk Road Economic Belt focuses on bringing together China, Central Asia, Russia and Europe (the Baltic); linking China with the Persian Gulf and the Mediterranean Sea through Central Asia and West Asia; and connecting China with Southeast Asia, South Asia and the Indian Ocean*".

The two specific areas where India is directly affected and involved in BRI are the Bangladesh-China-India-Myanmar (BCIM) Corridor and the China-Pakistan Economic Corridor (CPEC). Both these sub-constructs have been described as 'closely related' to the One Belt One Road idea. An analysis of the vision document indicates that the One Belt One Road is an open-ended project in scope and participation, with no rigid contours except that they all lead to the Middle Kingdom. It articulates the contours in a broad manner without too much specifics. It connects most present projects and the multilateral and bilateral organisations that involve China. The vision document gives an overall impression that it is a process of re-branding and interweaving of what China has been doing already, or its future engagements in a variety of domains under one single umbrella, giving the Chinese economic and foreign policy engagement a new direction.

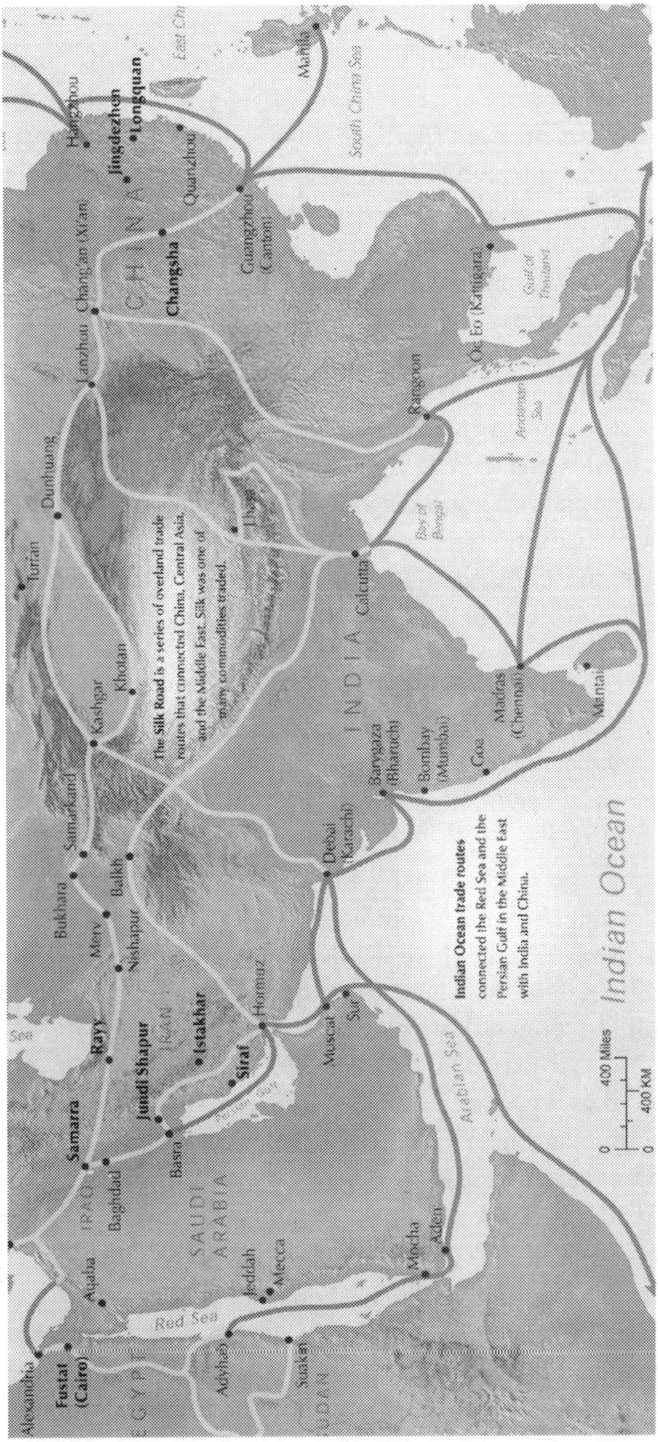

Figure 2.1. Old Silk Road

(*Source:* Adapted from Oriental Institute, University of Chicago)[14]

BRI—An Economic Perspective

Signs of a New Economic Order. The address to the Indonesian parliament also indicated the emergence of a new financial order, by proposing the Asian Infrastructure Investment Bank (AIIB) to finance infrastructure construction and promote regional interconnectivity and economic integration.[18] In fact, Xi was the first foreign head of state to address the Indonesian parliament. That he chose to announce the formation of an alternative to the US-dominated Asian Development Bank (ADB) and the World Bank in such a setting abroad, underlines the Chinese intentions unambiguously. The announcement of a new bank heralded a new financial architecture in the globe. This financial measure was necessary, since an idea however grand and appealing, cannot be put to practice without financial muscle. The World Bank or ADB dominated by the US and Japan couldn't be expected to fund a Chinese Idea. After all, there has been a brewing sense of discomfort over Western financial institutions across Asia. The AIIB was one instrument to put money where the vision was. Further, as a separate vehicle exclusively for the Silk Road Projects, President Xi, in Nov. 2014, pledged USD 40 billion for the Silk Road Fund. This was at the Asia-Pacific Economic Cooperation (APEC) meet. It was amplified at the APEC meet that the Silk Road funds will be used "*to provide investment and financing support to carry out infrastructure, resources, industrial cooperation, financial cooperation and other projects related to connectivity for countries along the Belt and Road*[19]". The first investment from the Silk Road Fund was to Pakistan's Karot Hydroelectric Project.[20]

The signs of the alternate economic order just did not end with banks and funds. The Boao Forum where the BRI was rolled-out is itself a 'Davos with Chinese characteristics'. The emergence of mega free trade agreements like the Regional Cooperation for Economic Partnership (RCEP), the acceptance of Yuan as part of the IMF's SDR[21], the establishment of the Xiangshan Forum as a parallel to the Shangri La dialogue on security, etc., have been steps in that direction. The BRI therefore needs to be seen in that broader context of alternate architectures.

The One Belt One Road vision document makes a direct reference to the 2008 Global Financial Crisis (GFC) highlighting the effect and lessons learned from that crisis.[22] The crisis, according to China, not only exposed the weakness of the existing global economic structure, but also deeply affected China, since it was dependent on a 'Foreign Direct Investment-Manufacture-Export' model. Such a model of growth had also become unviable as its economy grew, leading to rising incomes. As China's economy grew, it reached that phase of growth where it would have fallen into what some economists call the 'middle income trap' where such a growth model is unviable. Only 13 nations[23] have ever escaped the quagmire of a middle income trap with innovation, ingenuity and bold reforms—something that China knows too well.

Multiple economic transitions are therefore underway in China. Boosting domestic consumption and encouraging services over manufacturing is one. In manufacturing, the transition is to low volume high value products, shifting the high volume low value production to the neighbourhood, absorbing them into a Sino-centric value chain.[24] Another factor is the large foreign exchange reserves that China holds. Years of export over imports and a high savings rate have made it the highest holder of foreign exchange reserves. China tided over the GFC 2008, by investing massively in infrastructure. This created the infrastructure building capacities which are currently idle. If we combine these with large infrastructure deficits in Asia and Africa, the resultant idea is the Belt and Road Initiative.

Creating critical infrastructure such as transportation networks including ports, rail and road, power projects, etc., are prerequisites for that idea. With the largest foreign exchange reserves and idling infrastructure capacity, China is in an ideal position to implement such a plan. This is the trajectory that most Asian Tiger economies also followed when they shifted manufacturing to China, at similar points of their growth trajectory when China was opening up. This in a nutshell is understood as the economic rationale behind One Belt One Road. The flipside is that if countries are to be coupled economically, as the BRI envisions, there have to be structured studies on how the new model can be mutually beneficial for all nations. Economists need to jointly examine its viability in the context of present trade imbalances, which is already in China's favour. Equally important are the strategic underpinnings of such a plan.

Transportation and Connectivity Perspective

The connectivity between global economies is facilitated by a complex transportation system over air land and sea. Since the One Belt One Road is focusing on networks, where transportation modes play a major role, a comparison between the modes of transportation is in order. On land there are options of road, rail and pipelines, whereas over sea, there are options of ships and pipelines. The cost of each mode varies, and can go as high as

60 per cent of the cost of the product in cases like Liquefied Natural Gas. A modern container ship can carry 18,000 twenty-feet containers. If lined up, these containers will be more than 100 kilometre-long. Possibilities of such economies of scale tilt the balance heavily in favour of maritime transport. The economics of road, rail and maritime transport is best understood by a graph (Fig 4.1) from the book *Geography of Transport Systems* by Jean Paul Rodrigues.[25] On the X axis, we have distances and on the Y axis, we have costs. The value of D1 is between 500-750km and D2 is approximately 1500km. The graphs C1, C2 and C3 indicate road, rail and marine mode of transportation, respectively. The commencing points of C1,C2,C3 show the terminal costs, which shows that the terminal costs or costs incurred in infrastructure and handling at terminals are highest for maritime (C3), followed by rail (C2), whereas road is the cheapest (C1). Thus, road transportation is the cheapest for smaller distances. Rail transport is the cheapest for distances between 500 and 1500km. However, for distances greater than 1500km, maritime transport works out to be the cheapest mode.

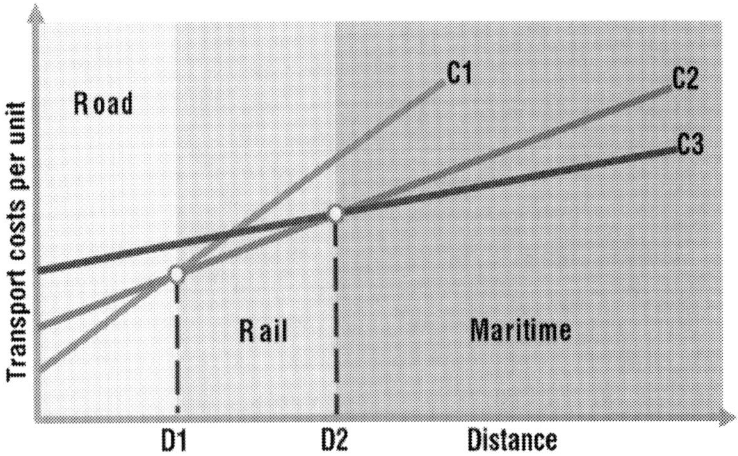

Figure 2.2. Cost Comparison of Transportation Modes
(*Source:* Geography of Transport Systems[26] (p. 113))

Simplifying the transportation debate to land-versus-sea mode based on costs alone can be misleading. Even though the two modes may appear to be competing with each other, in reality, the sea and land modes of networks are highly complementary. In the world of multimodal transport driven by containerisation, one physical network cannot survive without the other. Ships and oceans provide economy of scale between continents, whereas land modes provide last mile delivery. Without continental networks to hinterlands, the maritime network will be idle. Therefore, the Maritime Silk Road and Silk Road Economic Belt are viewed as highly complementary and interdependent constructs. This is highly significant, since most mental maps often segregate them into two water tight silos, whereas they are to be examined as seamless multimodal entities!

A brief note on the land routes is also in order at this juncture. The SREB has created a flutter through mega rail connectivity projects across Central Asia. The Chinese obsession with railways is on a rise since the inaugural run of a train from Yiwu in China to Madrid.[27] This has opened a new interest in continental transportation pivoting on rail networks. The Madrid run was later followed by trains from China to Hamburg and London. This has led to a view that trains, which are at the forefront of continental transportation domain, have re-emerged as the vanguard of geo-economics.

This is a déjà vu moment in geopolitics, with strong security connotations. A hundred years ago, the Eurasian region underwent a similar railway enthusiasm. Traditionally, water transport offers the least friction and highest haulage efficiency and as a result, remains most economical for long distances. However, with the industrial revolution, the advent of the steam engine brought in a new wave of enthusiasm about railway lines, especially transcontinental railway lines. The Trans-Siberian line in 1905 and the Berlin to Baghdad line, which was finally commissioned in 1940, were two such endeavours that caught imagination. This forced the renowned geographer and strategist Mackinder to wonder in 1904, whether the Colombian epoch of maritime powers was over. His 'heartland theory' of Eurasia being the geographical pivot of history was partly borne out of a confidence that he reposed in railways to move goods in peace and armies in war, quickly from one area to another. The other relevant facts were that the heartland being far away from shore lines could never be attacked by ships, which were the vanguard of any emerging power intending to spread its tentacles across the globe. He saw the heartland as being invincible from ships, and rail replacing ships in the transportation problem (or armies replacing navies!). It also serves to reckon that he was British, from an imperialist maritime power and an island, whose main enemies were continental Germany and Russia. Today, as we see similar Chinese enthusiasm for high speed rail networks, it may be worth wondering if Mackinder's prediction ever became reality. In the author's view, it did not, since maritime networks developed at an exponential rate as compared to rail networks. Newtonian friction after all favoured water transport.

The SREB is about a Eurasian land bridge connecting Europe and China.

According to Professor Jean Paul Rodrigues in his ***Geography of Transport Systems***, the idea of a Eurasian land bridge was offered by the erstwhile USSR in the 1960s; however due to geopolitical uncertainties, the project did not find traction. Professor Rodrigues states that the main challenges to its success were multinational cooperation, security, change of gauge and economics. He cites security threats to the line in Kazakhstan, parts of Siberia and Western China. Regarding the economic viability of this mode, he argues that since there are no double stack services, such a long line can be uneconomical at more than 3000km.[28] This is exacerbated by shorter trains. He also argues that even though the time taken from China to Germany can be 15 days, the final run within Europe can add up to 21 days which adds up to be comparable to the time taken via sea. The high trade imbalance also leads to a lack of backhaul opportunities to Asia, which affects all modes of container traffic. Despite these impediments, the Eurasian land bridge offers opportunities. In the grand Eurasian Rail Dream, the Russian paranoia of maintaining a separate gauge for its rail lines that still remain since the Soviet times, could pose a road block. The wagons have to be shifted from one network with a specific width to another network with a different width. One will have to wait and see how the SREB will overcome these legacy problems and alter the dynamics in this region.

A Maritime Economic Perspective

There are certain maritime trends significant to networks that need to be discussed in context. Martin Stopford, one of the foremost analysts of maritime economics, has identified the ***west line***, which is a fictional line that depicts the shift of centres of maritime activity across the globe in history. The 'centre' commenced 5,000 ago from the Indian Ocean.[29] Today, it has traversed three-fourths of the globe and is hypothetically located in East Asia. The future progression of this line is westwards to the Indian Ocean, where the centre of maritime economy will eventually shift. That six out of seven corridors planned in the One Belt One Road go westwards, shows that the thrust is along the grain of 'westline'. India too is setting the stage for the shift with 'Sagarmala', its own internal initiative. Stopford, the doyen of maritime economics after an analysis of the 5,000-year trajectory of the west line, lists three major lessons which are relevant to a maritime transportation system.

- The first is the central part that shipping has played in the global economy. The locus of west line has also been the economic centre of gravity of the globe.

- The second is that the *basics of economics of the maritime business have not changed, all that much, over the years.*
- The third is that *shipping prospers during periods of political stability.*[30] The relevance of security to shipping has also been highlighted by Jean Paul Rodrigues, another prominent scholar of transportation.[31]

A maritime economic perspective as gleaned from the *west line* indicates that shipping will always remain significant to global economy and political stability in international relations which also enable prosperous and peaceful shipping. With 90 percent of volume and 70 percent of value of global trade[32] passing via sea, this is a significant precondition for global growth.

Maritime Geographic Trends

Whilst the west line explains chronological shifts, there are significant geographic trends of shipping. Since the earth is a sphere, the shortest distance around the sphere is along a great circle like the equator.[33] Therefore, the equatorial circumnavigation route serves as the main trunk route of the global shipping network. This east–west line that connects the Panama, Suez Canals and Malacca straits is ideally served by large ships that offer an economy of scale. However, the canal sizes pose a limitation. The recent increase of the size of the Panama Canal has made this option more viable. This trunk line connects ports that serve as 'hubs' from where 'spokes'—the North–South pendulum routes and the inter-ocean pendulum routes—serve the outlying ports. Transportation to the hinterland with gateways and corridors through intermodal options becomes critical for regionalised ports to efficiently adapt to these wider geographic trends.[34]

What the Maritime Silk Route or an Indian port-based development initiative, 'Sagarmala', has to achieve is an integration to this global pattern of maritime trade and also has to complement that trend for success.[35] The largescale maritime infrastructure investments that China is undertaking across the globe, amounting to over USD 46 billion in over 40 ports, over the past seven years, needs to be contextualised in this framework. Investments in Colombo, Hambantota, Cristobel, Balboa, Malacca Gateway, Melaka and Piraeus are some significant investments that follow that rule.[36] An oddity in such investment has been Gwadar, far away from such a network, with no active hinterland or even a rail line or a pipeline to evacuate the voluminous commodities and merchandise that ships unload.

The question naturally arises if the 'String of Pearls' construct was different from the Silk Road. It was a report in 2007 by M/s Booze Hamilton, a US defence research consultancy, that gave the sobriquet '***String of Pearls***' to the ports that the Chinese were committed to financially, in the region during that period. This was the early understanding of the Chinese pattern of investments in the Indian Ocean. Though they appeared commercial in nature, the assumption that any deep financial commitment would eventually be associated to security was indeed valid in this situation as later events proved. It is no secret that the host nations in the IOR that absorb Chinese assistance have deep political fissures and are economically weak. The prospect of repayment or higher interest rates could draw the host nation into a vortex, where the lender could extract concessions. The investments also provide an opportunity to the Chinese to familiarise themselves with the IOR which will be useful in a crisis. With the major oil and mineral reserves lying in the West across the Malaccas, the Chinese Flag has followed trade, as the ships and submarine visits later confirmed. The significant shift today has been that though the initial investments that China made appeared piecemeal, it has now been packaged under the rubric of the Maritime Silk Road. The concerns raised by that original report very much remain in this author's view.

Security Perspectives

Having examined the maritime perspective, it is necessary to discuss the security and geopolitics of the BRI/Maritime Silk Road. Maritime Security or peace over maritime routes is a prerequisite for maritime commerce. This has been highlighted by the very history of Silk Route and studies of the west line. Therefore, even when the overall rationale of the One Belt One Road is rooted economically, there have been serious questions whether the One Belt One Road will limit itself to economy or whether it is a strategic initiative with security underlays. The historic trend has been that such an ambitious network will always be accompanied by security collaterals even if it has not been articulated in the vision document.

I argue that the Belt and Road Initiative is a grand strategy around which multiple domain strategies will evolve, including the military and maritime strategies. A military strategy is always a subset of an economic strategy, especially, in a Leninist state like China, where civil, military, economy and strategy are a seamless continuum under the ideological edifice of Marxism and Leninism. Politics is the most concentrated expression of economics as per that ideology, and military power is essentially a political tool. This has never been different for other powers either, irrespective of ideology.

The Chinese initiatives in the Indian Ocean and China's recent emphasis on the oceans in the Defense White Paper, make its intentions unambiguous—which is to use the oceans the way great powers have used them to advantage. Mahan has indeed influenced Chinese thought on the use of sea power. Scholars such as Toshi Yoshihara and James Holmes have elucidated this phenomenon well in their work *Chinese Naval Strategy in the 21st Century—The Turn to Mahan*.[37] In fact, the popular Chinese television series,[38] *TheRise of Great Powers* (***DaguoJueqi***) have the oceans as a consistent theme across the entire serial. At the same time, the Chinese focus on railways and continental routes across the Eurasian heartland is highly reminiscent of Mackinder's concept of control of the heartland. A combined infusion of both and land and sea into a national conscience is attributable to hegemonic ambitions. Robert Kaplan sums up the likely effect brilliantly citing Mackinder in his article in *Foreign Affairs*.[39] He cites Mackinder who stated in his 1904 article, "The Geographical Pivot of History", thus—'*Chinese, should they expand their power well beyond their borders, 'might constitute the peril*[40] *to the world's freedom just because they would add an oceanic frontage to the resources of the great continent, an advantage as yet denied to the Russian tenant of the pivot region*'. Despite such an advantage of warm water coast over the Russian Empire a hundred years ago, the maritime geography of Western Pacific induces several constrictions in its ambition such as Malacca Straits. The intent of the SREB and MSR infrastructure built for commerce and investment purposes can change quickly, if Napoleon's proverbial giant decides to awaken.

The flag has invariably followed trade in history. It appears either in the form of alliances or direct military presence providing security guarantee. The Chinese Defense White Paper of 2015,[41] which followed a month after the One Belt One Road vision document, was therefore, of interest. The opening statements link both the papers to the '*China Dream*', the common fount of both visions. The DWP states—"*In their endeavor to realize the Chinese dream of great national rejuvenation, the Chinese people aspire to join hands with the rest of the world to maintain peace, pursue development and share prosperity*". This is the theme of the BRI too. The paper also articulates "*safeguarding the security of China's overseas interests and support for national economic and social development*" as a ***strategic*** role. Apart from such direct support of commerce and economy, the covert 'behind the scenes' financial coercion, or a greater, more muscular, use or threat of use of force, could become the reality one day. Regimes that do not fit snugly into the Chinese commercial architecture would find it harder with such an inclusion in the DWP. There is a promise of "*far sighted planning for a favourable strategic posture*". There is another area where the paper states that due to "*international turmoil and the security of* *overseas interests concerning energy and resources, strategic SLOCs, as well as institutions, personnel and assets abroad, has become an imminent issue".* Overseas bases like Djibouti have quickly followed.

There is a mention of "*reorientation from theatre defense to trans-theater mobility*". Whilst this stresses on mobility across land theatres, it also is another expression for expeditionary warfare across seas. The DWP makes the following statement about the oceans, where the MSR is relevant, "*The traditional mentality that land outweighs sea must be abandoned, and great importance has to be attached to managing the seas and oceans and protecting maritime rights and interests*".[42] This is one of the salient take-away from this White Paper. It also has carefully chosen the word 'maritime power' in the following statement in the DWP: "*...strategic support for building itself into a maritime power*". A ***maritime power*** is different from a naval power. Maritime is a much broader term that applies to all facets of oceanic ventures, such as merchant shipping, shipbuilding industry, fishing fleet, ports, *entrepôts*, bases, etc. On the other hand, the term naval power has a narrower connotation and applies only to maritime military aspects. It is relevant to note that China has now overtaken South Korea in shipbuilding in terms of orders, though in value Korea retains a marginal edge, which could also get eclipsed by 2018.[43] The DWP states that "*...faithfully fulfilling China's international obligations, the country's armed forces will continue to carry out escort missions in the Gulf of Aden and other sea areas as required, enhance exchanges and cooperation with naval task forces of other countries, and jointly secure international SLOCs*".[44] This can be construed as complementary to the BRI interests.

It is important that such protection, as envisaged by China, does not lead to new geopolitical tensions in the region. Therefore, 'confidence building measures' become important with neighbours. Peace and prosperity are key to mutual development. There is a requirement to progress and utilise the Bilateral Maritime Dialogue which was first held in Feb 2016, between India and China, for building greater trust and transparency.[45] Similar such arrangements, either on a multilateral or bilateral basis along the routes, are critical for countries to interact peacefully as efforts are made to safeguard commerce. The BRI, in addition has the potential to divide the region into those with it and against increasing security risks. The detailed study of China's Maritime Forces is in Chapter Three of this book.

India's Response

As a nation, whose sovereign territory has been used to plan one arm of the BRI without consultations, the Indian response has been one of deep concern which has been articulated at various forums and through official communiqués. The Indian position on the One Belt One Road initiative has been that it is China's national initiative with little negotiations with others[46] or structured bilateral discussions.[47] There has also been a view that there is insufficient information regarding the idea.[48] They are valid views that require redressal and cooperation between India and China, which will be the world's two largest economies in twenty years' time. Despite such a view by India, a closer examination reveals that several projects closely related to the BRI/One Belt One Road, like those related to Bangladesh, China, India, Myanmar Corridor (BCIM), are being jointly examined by parties including India and China.[49] The third meeting of the BCIM was recently held at Kolkata in April 2017.

The clearest Indian response was publicised in May 17, when responding to a query on participation of India in the OBOR/BRI Forum. The official spokesperson of the Ministry of External Affairs (MEA) said that the Indian vision of connectivity is about "***universally recognised international norms, good governance, rule of law, openness, transparency and equality***. Such connectivity should not cause ***unsustainable debt burden for communities; balanced ecological and environmental protection and preservation standards; transparent assessment of project costs***".[50] The most prominent reason for India not participating in the Forum has been cited as the China-Pakistan Economic Corridor, where "***no country can accept a project that ignores its core concerns on sovereignty and territorial integrity***".[51] It also has requested a ***meaningful dialogue*** with China ***on its connectivity initiative.*** The complete response is placed at Appendix 2. The response makes it amply clear that Indian concerns go beyond CPEC with lack of bilateral negotiations, transparency, and debt burden all looming as major sore points besides infringements upon sovereignty through the Chinese project.

In a later chapter of this book a financial analysis of the CPEC reveals that China's best ally, Pakistan, has been served an economically burdensome deal, which serves as a harbinger of what others could expect. The Sri Lankan port of Hambantota, where a strategic equity has been extracted in the form of a large tract of land, presumably for a Special Economic Zone, is another example of loans being swapped for strategic long-term equity.

Being a vibrant democracy, there is also a view in India, that its position on the BRI, is incorrect and that India should have 'joined' the BRI. This notion needs some deconstruction. Firstly, the BRI is not a 'treaty' or an MoU with specific deeds that can be 'signed', but an amorphous amalgam of projects involving Chinese banks, enterprises, government loans and critical infrastructure projects. The Indian cooperation in the AIIB, NDB and climate change shows that India has thrown in the hat in where needed, and stayed away from other projects that are not in its interest. The BCIM is such a project, which has been on the anvil for long since India found common cause in that project. Since the BRI in its CPEC avatar infringed upon the sovereignty of India, political support has shrunk for the eastern leg of BRI, which is the BCIM. Questioning sovereignty leaves very little manoeuvring room to any nation. Yet, it is felt that there are several doors that are still ajar, as far as cooperation between India and China is concerned, including with regards to the BRI. In any bilateral exchange such as this, there is also a sweet spot on the negotiation curve after which returns start diminishing for both sides. Hence, there has to be constant evaluation of this bilateral thread between China and India.

The global attitudes to the BRI too have undergone changes with noticeable shifts in the positions of some countries from the time the BRI was announced in 2015, and to the time the Forum was held in May 2017. There have been leadership changes in the USA, and its allies facing China's rise in the Western Pacific were told to pay more for security architectures. In a twist of events, the USA and Japan, two nations that did not form of part of the AIIB, also decided to participate in the Forum. Similarly, India, which has concerns with the BRI is a party to several multilateral forums like the BRICS and the SCO, which issue joint statements in support of the BRI. This is an area that needs careful navigation in the future.

Areas of Concerns and Divergence

A project such as this exists within the framework of the Sino-Indian bilateral relationship. The contours of that relationship invariably affect the BRI. The specific areas of concern and divergence between India and China, which have a bearing on the BRI, are listed below:

- A major project related to the One Belt One Road is the China Pakistan Economic Corridor (CPEC). This, project, worth approximately USD 50 billion, plans to connect Kashgar in Xinjiang with Gwadar in the Indian Ocean. The CPEC passes through the Indian State of Jammu and Kashmir, portions of which are illegally occupied by Pakistan.[52] This is a matter of grave concern to India, which has been conveyed to China.

- India and China have an unsettled border over which a war was fought in 1962, which affects public perceptions. However, to the credit of both nations, the border has been more or less tranquil and the settlement process is being taken forward through special representatives. There is no denying that this unsettled issue has a bearing on bilateral relations. It is felt that China has been delaying a solution to the border problem to keep India unsettled. Settling of the border issue would increase trust between both nations.
- The third concern is regarding arms sales by China. This has two aspects: the first is the quantitative aspect and other is the qualitative aspect.
  - A closer examination of the pattern of arm sales by China indicates that quantitatively 70 per cent of China's arms sales to countries in the Indian Ocean Region are to three maritime neighbours[53] of India—namely, Pakistan, Myanmar and Bangladesh. Since the Maritime Silk Road touches each of these countries, there are concerns that this strategy is entwined with economics.
  - The nature of these weapons that China sells to these countries is also a matter of concern. The sale of lethal platforms like submarines to states in region has the potential to affect stability in the Indian Ocean Region. Unlike other oceans, the maritime security in the Indian Ocean Region is biased to non-traditional threats emerging from fragile states. The threats of piracy and terrorism have funnelled into the sea from such states. It took 30 global navies, including India and China, ten years to combat piracy which threatened global commerce. The naval need of this region are platforms that can aid security of trade and safe seas for basic economic activities. The sale of submarines therefore raises deep questions whether strategy has ruled over regional stability, which is most essential for the common prosperity of this region. The sale of such weapons increases these nations' dependence on China for their supply, repair and replacement for prolonged periods, i.e. over 30–40 years.
- Even though the protection of trade, either by utilising own assets or through a security alliance, is deemed a legitimate aspiration, certain maritime developments have been of concern to India. The presence of Chinese submarines at the nodes of the Maritime Silk Road—in Pakistan and in Sri Lanka—though legitimate, evokes questions if the Maritime Silk Road idea would limit itself to economics alone.[54] In fact, the berthing of the Chinese submarines has been a feature in

all nations where there is a large-scale investment by China or a loan that the nation finds hard to pay. Sri Lanka, Pakistan and Malaysia have all received Chinese submarines for port visits and Bangladesh has been supplied with submarines. This has vindicated the Indian position that the '***unsustainable debt burden***' of ten imposes strategic penalties to the debtor nation. If flag follows trade, submarines have followed loans, as far as China is concerned.

- In the Indian Ocean Region, the greatest emerging threat to maritime commerce is from terrorism. The Al Qaeda[55] almost took over a Pakistan navy frigate and the ISIS[56] has attacked naval and merchant ships. One of the most significant uses of the sea for terror happened in 2008 in India, when the Lashkar-e-Taiba carried out an attack on its maritime capital, Mumbai. Recently, India's attempts to bring a perpetrator of this terror attack to book were repeatedly blocked by China in the UN. Being 'two major nations in Asia and world', India and China need to fight terror together, in letter and spirit, without any other political factors affecting it.
- The case of water, with most rivers in Asia having origins in Tibet, is also a cause of concern. China being a upper riparian with plans for mega geo-engineering projects like dams and the South-to-North water transfer schemes, leaves serious questions in a future where climate change will accentuate water scarcity.

Areas of Convergence

It is felt that these concerns and divergence do not prevent cooperation. Being the two oldest civilisations and neighbours, as well as emerging powers of the world, there have been examples of cooperation even amidst divergence between India and China. Their economic cooperation in the formation of the New Development Bank (NDB)[57] and the Asian Infrastructure Investment Bank (AIIB)[58] are successful examples where both nations have already cooperated. Prolonged negotiations to address interests of both parties were key to successful cooperation in these examples. Politically, climate change has been an area where India and China have had a convergence. Here again, there is a renewed opportunity to strengthen the commitments together, as President Trump has officially withdrawn from the Paris Treaty ceding political space to both nations to lead actions on a front that needs global attention. Another area of convergence has been Afghanistan. There are other areas too where the Indian and Chinese interests can converge in the future under the ambit of the One Belt One Road.

- ***Sagarmala*–the Indian Ports Initiative.** India launched the *Sagarmala* project[59] in March 2015, which is a port-based development model to spur a new phase of growth. India's share of coastal shipping and inland waterways in the transportation segment is below the global optimum. In order to develop ports, adjacent zones and inland waterways, India intends to spend USD 10 billion.[60] With the infrastructure capacities available in China for building economic zones and ports, this could be an area of convergence.[61] This infrastructural initiative can not only give opportunities to infrastructure companies but will also ensure better connectivity to new Indian markets. The development of ports under project *Sagarmala* would interact with the Maritime Silk Road in many ways. For example, in Sri Lanka, where China has invested deeply, which is a transhipment hub to Indian markets.
- **Cooperation in Infrastructure Projects.** Asia requires close to USD 10 trillion worth investment in infrastructure in the next 10 years to meet developmental requirements. For its part, India has been in the process of creating several regional transportation networks. Some of them can link up, or act in concert with the BRI. They are:
  - A North–South access to Central Asia from the Iranian port of Chahbahar, which has the potential to connect landlocked Central Asia to the sea.
  - The Turkmenistan-Afghanistan-Pakistan-India (TAPI) pipeline.
  - The trilateral highway between India, Myanmar and Thailand.
- ***Mausam*—Cultural Initiative.** The third is the Indian initiative named '*Mausam*', which is a purely cultural and historical initiative. *Mausam*, which means 'season' in Arabic, connects maritime Asia by a predictable wind system, the *Monsoon*. It is this weather phenomenon that enabled the original maritime route. Since culture and history are part of the One Belt One Road, convergence can be explored in this domain.
- **Other Indian Projects.** Just as China is trying to transform its economic model from the Foreign Direct Investment-Manufacture-Export model to one that is driven by domestic consumption and the services sector, India is currently transforming itself through several initiatives. Some of the initiatives could be complimentary and can serve both economies.
  - **Make in India**[62] is an initiative that gives a fillip to manufacturing, and is one of the flagship projects of the government. It aims to

encourage the manufacturing segment to spur growth of the Indian economy. It invites investors to a hundred percent Foreign Direct Investment in all segments (except in defence, space and media). Given that Indian products can be competitively priced, they can form an integral part of the global value chain. India is turning to manufacture, just as China is reforming its manufacture-based economic model. This potentially, can be an area of convergence.

- **Digital India**[63] is an initiative to improve online infrastructure by increasing internet connectivity. Digital India focuses on specific areas, namely broadband highways, universal access to mobile connectivity, public internet access, e-governance, electronic delivery of services, electronics manufacturing and information technology for jobs. Each of these areas cuts across multiple domains of expertise which will require global partnerships leading to convergence and opportunities. China's hardware and India's software capabilities have the potential to be complimentary capabilities, which can be exploited.
- **Smart City** projects which seek innovative ideas for city infrastructure.[64] Broadly, they includes 'smart' innovative solutions to streamline basic amenities such as water, electricity, waste management, mobility, e-governance, education, health, security and housing. They envisage 'keel up' green field projects as well as 'smart' overlays to legacy infrastructure to develop a sustainable urban ecosystem. Given that China has tremendous experience in infrastructure, and is reviewing its growth model, there will be lessons to share in this field especially since environmental impact is deemed to be an important factor in "smart cities".
- **Skill India**[65] a programme to increase the skill sets of citizens. Compared to developed nations, India lacks skilled work force. This initiative aims to ensure that the young workforce is re-skilled for employment and entrepreneurship. Chinese experience in skill-building could quickly add value to Indian plans in skilling its populace.
- **Startup India** is an initiative to prime and encourage the entrepreneurial ecosystem in India through funding and tax incentives. India could study the trajectory of China, in this field as well.

These transformations cover a wide swathe of infrastructure and industry. They open up prospects for partnerships with India from across the globe including China. Given the vast experience and expertise of China in infrastructure, as well as in high-end technology areas, participation in these projects could be mutually beneficial for both nations.

Other Regional and International Responses

Revival of the US Silk Road and the Asia-Africa Growth Corridor. It is also important to note that there was another ***Silk Road*** of US origin in the recent past. A little after the world took notice of the ***String of Pearls,*** came the American *New Silk Road* (NSR), announced by Secretary of State Hillary Clinton, to rebuild Afghanistan in Oct 2011.[66] The focus was on Central Asia, however, from the West, which was Afghan-centric. The TAPI pipeline was a critical component of the NSR. The State Department communiqué had this to say about the idea:[67] "*With multiple transitions underway in Afghanistan, the United States and its allies can bolster peace and stability in the region by supporting a transition to trade and helping open new markets connecting Afghanistan to Central Asia, Pakistan, India and beyond. Countries in the region know they have more to gain economically by working together than by being isolated. Promoting connectivity in a region that is the least-economically integrated in the world is challenging, but the benefits can be transformative. This is why the United States is promoting the New Silk Road initiative linking Central and South Asia in four key areas*". The key areas as per the above communiqué were regional energy markets, trade and transport, business and people-to-people connectivity, customs and border operations. There is an uncanny similarity between the NSR and BRI, even though their origins and contexts are different. The fact that the same brand has been used by two nations in different geographic context shows the power of the brand. It is also relevant to note that the 'pivot' or rebalance to East Asia took place subsequent to the announcement of the New Silk Road.

Sensing the infirmities in the NSR, there has been a renewal of efforts by the US to revive the New Silk Road. In a budget request in May 2017, the New Silk Road as well as the Indo-Asia Pacific Economic Corridor (linking South Asia to South East Asia) have been included, with a role for India.[68] This along with the Asia-Africa Growth Corridor (AAGC), which is an India–Japan initiative to connect Asia to Africa, is expected to offer some choice to countries in the region to the Chinese idea.[69] These three constructs to enhance connectivity along with respective national plans, including India's plans mentioned earlier, should give the much-needed choice to the countries within the region which have presently swung towards the only narrative that they repeatedly hear from China. This will also fill the wide gap between infrastructure needs and funding in the region. It is also expected that the US, Japanese and Indian expertise can offer competing alternatives and values which will benefit the region. Since both the NSR and AAGC have been announced in India, it is important that India lives up to the expectations that others would have of it. With China having made the first move in a major connectivity initiative, there is an opportunity to learn from the experience of the BRI to create a better, equitable, sustainable, democratic alternative. It is also pertinent to note that both Japan and USA had sent senior representatives to the Belt and Road Forum, which indicates shifting winds of geopolitics that demand trimming the sails accordingly.

Conclusion

The One Belt One Road is seen in India as a Chinese national initiative, whereas China positions it as an international initiative. Hence, there is a perception gap on the One Belt One Road. If this gap is to be bridged, there is a requirement for China to reach out and negotiate with India and, given the open and democratic nature of the polity, be seen to be doing so. This has been expressed by Indian officials in open forums. Whilst there are concerns, there is also a view in India that there are elements in the One Belt One Road that are useful for India. Some areas like ***Sagarmala*** are areas of convergence and have been mentioned previously in the chapter. Once a *reach out* occurs, the convergences and divergences need to be deliberated by experts in both nations through a structured dialogue. There indeed is that trust deficit between nations, which needs to be bridged by constant engagement at all levels between both nations. One significant way to build trust is through military-to-military cooperation through joint exercises and interoperability.

The ambition, vastness of the vision and energy devoted by China are sufficient evidence to qualify the Belt and Road Initiative as the grand strategy of China, something that fuses multiple domains, and vectors them to achieve goals of economic growth and national rejuvenation. It borders on fashioning itself as a hegemon without exactly fighting the current one in a 'new type of great power relationship' arrangement- a term that has fallen into disuse due to the US discomfort with such overt expressions. It formalises the multiple layers covering infrastructure, economy, finance and culture across continents and oceans with a central theme in pursuit of China's grand plan for itself.

Yes, there are public goods present in that plan, but there is a price to pay for public goods too as debtor nations.

Coming to the brasstacks of the BRI, historically, maritime routes provide better economies of scale when compared to land routes, but they act in concert with land networks. Therefore, the Silk Road Economic Belt and the Maritime Silk Road are highly complementary constructs. The freight by Eurasian rail line will offer an alternative to the costlier airfreight and not replace sea freight through the Indian Ocean. It is true that India has serious geopolitical concerns regarding the One Belt One Road. However, there is also precedence of cooperation between India and China where interests converge. India and China are 'two major powers in the region and world' which have legitimate aspirations regarding their own futures. Given the constructive relations between the two neighbours, there is a need to mutually address the concerns and divergences as well as to capitalise the convergences for which sufficient statecraft exists within both nations. To cite Prime Minister Modi, "*successful revival of the ancient trade routes require not only physical connectivity and requisite infrastructure, but even more important, a climate of peace, stability, mutual trust and respect, support for mutual prosperity and free flow of commerce and ideas*".[70] The key to cooperation therefore, remains as the building of trust between both nations.

Western fatigue with globalisation and free trade has raised the spectre of protectionism again. Under such circumstances, if the Asian century is to be realised, there has to be a mutual accommodation and trust between the two large nations within Asia. Both nations, though at different points of the growth curve, have deep domestic compulsions to sustain growth.

What is crucial to the context of this book is that six out of seven belts and roads of the BRI are headed to the west and among them the southern routes, both continental and maritime, pass via the Indian Subcontinent or the Indian Ocean. India's geographic location astride these routes and the economic opportunities it offers, makes India a critical factor to the success of the BRI. The economy of scale will be favourable to the MSR and that is where the Indian Ocean will be critical, as Chinese SLOCs will straddle the Indian Ocean carrying energy, raw material, finished products for markets and products under process in value chain. The infrastructure that China is creating in the Indian Ocean appears tailored to meet the grand strategy of the Belt and Road Initiative. It leads to and creates markets, enables extraction of resources and generates maritime footholds in the Indian Ocean. It smoothens Chinese access to its west, eventually reaching European markets.

It offers some alternatives that mitigate the Malacca dilemma not only through securing access routes but also by attempting to create new ones and perhaps those that will fragment the existing global network creating new nodes of production. The protector and guarantor of security and eventual success of the Maritime Silk Road is the PLA Navy. This is something which has been expressed lucidly as a stress of '***maritime over land***' in the 2015 Defense White Paper. Therefore, the next chapter, the 'Strategy of Party's Maritime Force', examines the evolution of the Chinese maritime strategy, the organisation and the force structure of a navy capable of supporting this grand strategy. That is the hard power behind the vision. Power, after all, flows through the barrel of the gun.

NOTES

1. "Xi Pledges 'Great Renewal of Chinese Nation'," *Xinhua*, English.news.cn, accessed July 29, 2015, http://news.xinhuanet.com/english/china/2012-11/29/c_132008231.htm.
2. "My Chinese Dream - Chinese Dream", Special Report - *English.news.cn*, accessed July 29, 2015, http://www.xinhuanet.com/english/special/chinesedream/mychinesedream.htm.
3. "Xi Pledges 'great Renewal of Chinese Nation'," *Xinhua, English.news.cn*."
4. David Shambaugh, "The Coming Chinese Crackup," *Wall Street Journal*, March 6, 2015, sec. Life, http://www.wsj.com/articles/the-coming-chinese-crack-up-1425659198.
5. Johannes F. Linn, "Economic (Dis)Integration Matters: The Soviet Collapse Revisited" (The Brookings Institution, October 2004), http://www.brookings.edu/views/papers/200410linn.pdf.
6. "China's 'New Normal' Sees Government Apply Brakes to Accelerating Economy," *The Guardian*, accessed June 12, 2015, http://www.theguardian.com/business/2015/apr/08/china-new-normal-government-economy-growth.
7. Many strategic projects including nuclear cooperation arms sales etc. despite its high value and impact continue outside the purview of the BRI rubric, for e.g. in Pakistan outside the CPEC's ambit.
8. Also called 'The Forum' in this book.
9. BRI is the chosen term in this book to define the Belt and Road Initiative also called as OBOR, BRF, BRAF, etc. MSR and SREB are considered as two branches of BRI.
10. "The Economic History of the Last 2000 Years: Part II - The Atlantic," accessed November 11, 2015, http://www.theatlantic.com/business/archive/2012/06/the-economic-history-of-the-last-2000-years-part-ii/258762/.
11. The Silk Road, Journal of the Silk Road Foundation, Vol. 5, No.1, Summer 2007 accessible at http://faculty.washington.edu/dwaugh/publications/waughsrjournal_v5n1_2007.pdf
12. "The Silk Road and Arab Sea Routes," accessed July 30, 2015, http://people.hofstra.edu/geotrans/eng/ch2en/conc2en/silkroad.html.
13. Kevin Cullinane, *International Handbook of Maritime Economics* (Edward Elgar Publishing, 2011).
14. "Silk Road and Indian Ocean Traders: Connecting China and the Middle East," The Oriental Institute of the University of Chicago, accessed August 20, 2017, https://oi.uchicago.edu/museum-exhibits/special-exhibits/silk-road-and-indian-ocean-traders-connecting-china-and-middle-east.

15. "Chronology of China's Belt and Road Initiative," *Xinhua, English.news.cn*, accessed July 30, 2015, http://news.xinhuanet.com/english/2015-03/28/c_134105435.htm.
16. "Vision and Actions on Jointly Building Silk Road Economic Belt and 21st-Century Maritime Silk Road," accessed July 30, 2015, http://www.fmprc.gov.cn/mfa_eng/zxxx_662805/t1249618.shtml.
17. "Vision and Actions on Jointly Building Silk Road Economic Belt and 21st-Century Maritime Silk Road," accessed July 30, 2015, http://www.fmprc.gov.cn/mfa_eng/zxxx_662805/t1249618.shtml.
18. The Indonesian President Jokowi's idea of a Indonesia as a "Maritime Axis" closely followed heels in his election manifesto in May 2014 as reported by Brookings, http://www.brookings.edu/research/articles/2014/11/indonesia-maritime-liow-shekhar accessed on 16 Jun 15
19. "China to Establish $40 Billion Silk Road Infrastructure Fund," *Reuters*, November 8, 2014, http://www.reuters.com/article/us-china-diplomacy-idUSKBN0IS0BQ20141108.
20. "China's Silk Road Fund Makes First Investment in Pakistan's Hydropower Project," *Xinhua, English.news.cn*, accessed July 30, 2015, http://news.xinhuanet.com/english/2015-04/21/c_134167533.htm.
21. The Special Drawing Right (SDR) is an international reserve asset, created by the IMF in 1969 to supplement its member countries' official reserves.
22. "Vision and Actions on Jointly Building Silk Road Economic Belt and 21st-Century Maritime Silk Road."
23. "The Middle-Income Trap," *The Economist*, accessed May 31, 2017, http://www.economist.com/blogs/graphicdetail/2012/03/focus-3.
24. Maritime Silk Road an Indian Perspective, MH Rajesh, B.K. Sharma and Dr Nivedita Das Kundu, *China's One Belt One Road: Initiative, Challenges and Prospects* (Vij Books India Pvt Ltd, 2016).
25. Jean-Paul Rodrigue, Claude Comtois, and Brian Slack, *The Geography of Transport Systems*, 3 edition (Abingdon, Oxon: Routledge, 2013).
26. Ibid.
27. Ishaan Tharoor, "Map: The World's Longest Train Journey Now Begins in China," *The Washington Post*, November 21, 2014, http://www.washingtonpost.com/blogs/worldviews/wp/2014/11/21/map-the-worlds-longest-train-journey-now-begins-in-china/.
28. Jean-Paul Rodrigue, Claude Comtois, and Brian Slack, *The Geography of Transport Systems*, 3 edition (Abingdon, Oxon: Routledge, 2013).
29. Martin Stopford, *Maritime Economics 3e*, 3 edition (London: New York: Routledge, 2008).
30. Ibid.
31. "Maritime Transportation: Drivers for the Shipping and Port Industries - Transport Research International Documentation - TRID," accessed November 22, 2015, http://trid.trb.org/view.aspx?id=1085868#.
32. Cullinane, *International Handbook of Maritime Economics.*
33. It is a circle on the surface of a sphere which lies in a plane passing through the sphere's centre. As it represents the shortest distance between any two points on a sphere, a great circle of the earth is the preferred route taken by a ship or aircraft.
34. Dr PK Ghosh "Daunting Realities: Territorial Disputes and Shipping Challenges to China's Maritime Silk Road" has appeared in the *Global Asia Journal*, Vol 10, No. 3 Fall 2015. https://globalasia.org/article/daunting-realities-territorial-disputes-and-shipping-challenges-to-chinas-maritime-silk-road/
35. "Maritime Transportation: Drivers for the Shipping and Port Industries - Transport Research International Documentation - TRID."

36. "How China Rules the Waves," accessed April 24, 2017, https://ig.ft.com/sites/china-ports.
37. James R. Holmes and Toshi Yoshihara, *Chinese Naval Strategy in the 21st Century: The Turn to Mahan* (Routledge, 2012).
38. *The Rise of the Great Powers (TV Mini-Series 2006–)*, accessed June 9, 2017, http://www.imdb.com/title/tt2802874/.
39. "The Geography of Chinese Power," *Foreign Affairs*, accessed August 1, 2015, https://www.foreignaffairs.com/articles/china/2010-05-01/geography-chinese-power.
40. Mackinder used a racist expression 'yellow peril' which has been removed by this author in text
41. China's Military Strategy, The State Council Information Office of the People's Republic of China, May 2015, Beijing Accessed November 13, 2015, http://eng.mod.gov.cn/Database/WhitePapers/.
42. China's Military Strategy, The State Council Information Office of the People's Republic of China, May 2015, Beijing Accessed November 13, 2015, http://eng.mod.gov.cn/Database/WhitePapers/.
43. "China to Eclipse South Korea in Most Export Industries by 2018," Report Says - *Korea Real Time,* WSJ, accessed August 1, 2015, http://blogs.wsj.com/korearealtime/2014/10/30/china-to-eclipse-south-korea-in-many-exports-by-2018-report-says/.
44. China's Military Strategy, The State Council Information Office of the People's Republic of China, May 2015, Beijing Accessed November 13, 2015, http://eng.mod.gov.cn/Database/WhitePapers/.
45. "Inaugural India-China Maritime Affairs Dialogue," accessed March 10, 2016, http://www.mea.gov.in/press-releases.htm?dtl/26317/Inaugural+IndiaChina+Maritime+Affairs+Dialogue.
46. "India Wrinkle on China Silk," *The Telegraph*, accessed August 2, 2015, http://www.telegraphindia.com/1150721/jsp/frontpage/story_32798.jsp.
47. "Transcript of Media Briefing by Foreign Secretary in Beijing on Prime Minister's Ongoing Visit to China," May 15, 2015, accessed November 22, 2015, http://www.mea.gov.in/search-result.htm?25245/Transcript+of+Media+Briefing+by+ Foreign+ Secretary+ in+ Beijing+ on+ Prime+ Ministers+ongoing +visit+to+China+may+15+2015.
48. "India Okay with BCIM, Wants Details on China Maritime Silk Road," *Times of India-Economic Times*, accessed November 13, 2015, http://articles.economictimes.indiatimes.com/2014-06-30/news/50974672_1_maritime-silk-road-msr-bcim.
49. "BCIM: Can India Be a Driving Force?," *The Diplomat*, accessed November 13, 2015, http://thediplomat.com/2015/01/bcim-can-india-be-a-driving-force/.
50. "Official Spokesperson's Response to a Query on Participation of India in OBOR/BRI Forum," accessed July 11, 2017, http://mea.gov.in/media-briefings.htm?dtl/28463/Official+Spokespersons+ response+to+a+query+on+participation+of+India+in+ OBORBRI + Forum.
51. Ibid.
52. "Modi Told China, Pakistan Economic Corridor Unacceptable: Sushma," accessed November 13, 2015, http://www.business-standard.com/article/news-ians/modi-told-china-pakistan-economic-corridor-unacceptable-sushma-115053100668_1.html.
53. Calculated by author from "SIPRI Arms Transfers Database," www.sipri.org, accessed November 13, 2015, http://www.sipri.org/databases/armstransfers.
54. "China, Sri Lanka, and the Maritime Great Game," *Foreign Policy*, accessed November 13, 2015, https://foreignpolicy.com/2015/02/12/china-sri-lanka-and-the-maritime-great-game-silk-road-xi-port/.
55. Syed Shoaib Hasan, Saeed Shah, and Siobhan Gorman, "Al Qaeda Militants Tried to Seize

Pakistan Navy Frigate," *Wall Street Journal*, September 16, 2014, sec. World, http://www.wsj.com/articles/al-qaeda-militants-tried-to-seize-pakistan-navy-frigate-1410884514.

56. *Reuters*, "Isis Affiliate Claims Responsibility for Rocket Attack on Egyptian Navy Ship," *The Guardian*, July 16, 2015, sec. World news, http://www.theguardian.com/world/2015/jul/16/egypt-rocket-attack-sinai-province-isis-navy-ship.
57. "BRICS Bank Opens for Business in China - IBNLive," accessed November 13, 2015, http://www.ibnlive.com/news/world/brics-bank-opens-for-business-in-china-1023400.html.
58. "India Joins Asian Infrastructure Investment Bank," *The Times of India*, accessed November 13, 2015, http://timesofindia.indiatimes.com/business/india-business/India-joins-Asian-Infrastructure-Investment-Bank/articleshow/47874916.cms.
59. "Sagarmala: Concept and Implementation towards Blue Revolution," accessed August 20, 2015, http://pmindia.gov.in/en/news_updates/sagarmala-concept-and-implementation-towards-blue-revolution/.
60. "Sagarmala Project: Government to Spend Rs 70,000 Crore on 12 Major Ports, Says Nitin Gadkari," *The Economic Times*, accessed November 11, 2015, http://economictimes.indiatimes.com/news/economy/infrastructure/sagarmala-project-government-to-spend-rs-70000-crore-on-12-major-ports-says-nitin-gadkari/articleshow/49229434.cms.
61. "Keynote Address by Prime Minister at India-China Business Forum in Shanghai" May 16, 2015, accessed November 22, 2015, http://mea.gov.in/Speeches-Statements.htm?dtl/25247/Keynote_Address_by_Prime_Minister_at_IndiaChina_Business_Forum_in_Shanghai_May_16_2015.
62. "Home - Make In India," accessed November 13, 2015, http://www.makeinindia.com/home.
63. "Digital India, MyGov.in," accessed November 13, 2015, https://mygov.in/group/digital-india/.
64. "SmartCities.gov.in," accessed November 13, 2015, http://smartcities.gov.in/.
65. "Skill India Portal," accessed November 13, 2015, http://skillindia.gov.in/.
66. "The New Silk Road?," *The Diplomat*, accessed June 26, 2015, http://thediplomat.com/2011/11/the-new-silk-road/.
67. Bureau of Public Affairs Department Of State. The Office of Website Management, "U.S. Support for the New Silk Road," December 7, 2011, http://www.state.gov/p/sca/ci/af/newsilkroad/.
68. "US, India To Revive 'New Silk Road' Seen As Counter To China's Belt And Road Project," *NDTV.com*, accessed June 8, 2017, http://www.ndtv.com/india-news/us-india-to-revive-new-silk-road-to-counter-chinas-belt-and-road-obor-project-1697632.
69. Dipanjan Roy Chaudhury, "India, Japan Come up with AAGC to Counter China's OBOR," *The Economic Times*, May 26, 2017, http://economictimes.indiatimes.com/news/economy/policy/india-japan-come-up-with-aagc-to-counter-chinas-obor/articleshow/58846673.cms.
70. "Transcript of Prime Minister's Interaction with Chinese Media Organizations," accessed November 22, 2015, http://mea.gov.in/interviews.htm?dtl/24011/Transcript_of_Prime_Ministers_Interaction_with_Chinese_media_organizations.

CHAPTER 3

STRATEGY OF HARD POWER: THE PARTY'S MARITIME FORCE, ITS FOUR ROLES AND THREE-AND-A-HALF FLEETS[1]

Introduction

The previous chapter discussed the grand strategy of China and posited it as the Belt and Road Initiative. This chapter is about the Maritime Military Strategy of China and how it has evolved over time to address various political needs creating suitable inventories in the process.

With rising contestations regarding maritime sovereignty in the Western Pacific and widening footprints in the Indian Ocean, the Chinese navy is the cynosure of analysts. It is therefore timely to review some of the major factors that influence its naval build-up. A primer on the basic roles and types of fleets[2] was deemed necessary to complement the enormous volume of information on the subject. This chapter has been written to serve as that primer about *some* cardinal motivators and elements of Chinese maritime power, to enable a reader to place them in a broader political context.

Navies are built for certain roles that a nation expects they may have to perform. If the British built a fleet with global reach to protect their colonies in an age of imperialism, the US built its fleet in a Mahanian framework for a decisive battle far from its shore. The Soviets went about creating a fleet that focused on a denial of the use of seas and deterrence against its Cold War capitalist rival—the USA. Several factors influence a process of building sea power. Alfred Thayer Mahan, its most influential proponent, stated it more precisely as geographical position, physical conformation, extent of territory, number of population, national character, character and policies of government.[3]

Considering Mahan's factors, China is also additionally unique as a Marxist–Leninist state, where its armed forces are also the Communist Party's own, a matter which has been hoisted in the title of the chapter. As the precedence to such a condition, we have a Soviet example to examine. Though the communist ideology favoured a militia, the Soviets were pragmatic and created an armed force comprising of professionally trained soldiers. China did not make that 'distasteful compromise'[4] as the Soviets did in creating professional armed forces at the early stages of state formation. The armed forces (the PLA) have been groomed to be the ultimate arbiter of the Party's power, and continue to be precariously balanced between the two tenets—a tenet that power flows from the proverbial barrel and another that the party controls the gun. Whilst the former tenet gives it a unique status in polity, the latter implies that professionalism will remain subservient to ideological correctness. Needless to say, there is a contradiction in this style of functioning termed as the 'red versus expert' problem that pervades all professions.

The ground forces (termed the Army in most nations)[5] have a direct role in the sustenance of the Party's power, as illustrated by their role in the Cultural Revolution, the Tiananmen episode and regular presidential exhortations for the army's loyalty to the Party, whereas technically intense forces like the Navy, Air and Rocket Forces can only play indirect roles with limited scope for constabulary role in their form and function. However, the indirect role of the Navy is significant to the Party since the protection of sea lanes, markets and resources remains critical to the continued prosperity that ensures the Party's legitimacy. Mahan had articulated this use of sea power when he stated that 'the *necessity of a navy, in the restricted sense of the word, springs, therefore, from the existence of a peaceful shipping, and disappears with it*'.[6]

This chapter postulates that over the last thirty years of reforms, the Chinese Navy has evolved to become a force that serves four major roles: first is a nuclear-deterrent role, second is a counter-intervention role,[7] the third role is that of protecting its global commercial interests and a fourth emerging role is furtherance of its recent maritime claims. The fleets it is creating for the first three roles are along traditional patterns barring some innovations like the shore-based Anti-Ship Ballistic Missiles (ASBM) for use against US aircraft carrier groups. However, the fleet for the fourth role is getting shaped differently. This fleet is a mix of civil, paramilitary and military elements which is reminiscent of Mao's People's War idea of blurred lines between the civil and the military. Accordingly, in a recent move, it has unified its several maritime constabulary forces[8] under the banner of the Coast Guard. This step has been taken to unify command, avoid working in silos and give multiple agencies a single direction. The timing of this unification,[9] at a time of several ongoing maritime contestations, is significant.[10] It uses its fishing fleet[11] as a first line of aggression. It has also mandated certain military specifications to civil ship construction through the 'The Technical Standards[12] for New Civilian Ships to Implement National Defense Requirements'[13] inspired by the Falkland experience.[14] Therefore, there is a '*hybrid navy*' getting prepared to operate civil ships in tandem with a strong conventional fleet to achieve its national goals.

Background

Prior to commenting on fleets individually, some historical background is essential. Navies and maritime commerce share a symbiotic relation. China as a civilisation, did not find it necessary to trade with external powers via sea—it deemed to have it all as illustrated by Qianlong's condescending reply to Macartney's mission at the turn of the 18th to the 19th centuries.[15] Even the famous maritime forays by Zheng He, six hundred years ago, were episodic seven forays lasting just three decades, where diplomacy was deemed more important than commerce. Significantly, these maritime forays occurred just as the overland Silk Road network became witness to the rise of Timurlane. The maritime endeavour petered out as the powerful literati figured them to be superfluous excursions that drained the exchequer.[16] China soon paid a price for ignoring the seas when imperial adventurers from the West carved away littoral enclaves imposing unequal treaties during China's so-called 'century of humiliation'.

Unlike its Marxist–Leninist predecessor, the former USSR, China was far more reluctant in embracing military modernisation in general and sea power in particular. Navy building demanded a commensurate military industrial complex and high capital investment. The navy relies on material over men. These were antithetical to both Marxist and People's war ideals, retarding navy building.[17] Nations also take time to become technologically mature to build a navy.

The civil war which gave birth to China was a largely a continental affair far from the littorals. Mao had resorted to the philosophy[18] of the People's War that not only used the population effectively but also drew the battle away from the prosperous coast where the Imperialists and Nationalists were in their elements. The strategy got perfected during the *Long March*, steering the people's army into deep rural interiors, avoiding the coast and cities in a strategic retreat.[19] The aim was to lure a superior enemy into a rustic lair and decisively engage him at a place and time of communist choosing.

A brilliant land strategy as that could not be adapted easily into a maritime avatar. In the maritime domain, technology and material play a more significant role than land. The dictum of people over material can't be transposed over sea as in land. The medium of sea is contiguous and homogenous that didn't offer urban–rural fissures crucial for the success of the People's War. Besides, the world over, navies require professional manning and are not amenable to manning by a cobbled militia disbanded after an episodic class struggle. Therefore, the Maoist analogy of soldier as a fish swimming in the sea of people, ironically befitted land than water!

Given the circumstances that he was in, Mao had literally ignored the navy, barring the maintenance of a coastal force to prevent a nationalist invasion from Taiwan. However, the realist in him ordered a response to the Soviets by paving the foundations of a subsea nuclear deterrent. The first naval role as a deterrent is therefore, the oldest one addressed here, canonised by Mao himself. The Ballistic Missile Submarine (SSBN) fleet emerged from this order. The Maoist era was therefore a period of naval stasis, barring the developments on the submarine front. Though divorced from the Soviets by 1960s, the Chinese Navy remained an emaciated Soviet replica belonging to the 'young school' of naval strategy. The civil war trend of avoiding cities continued even after the Nationalists were vanquished. It reached a paranoid proportion when the coasts were deemed vulnerable to counter value nuclear strike and the industries were shifted to interior China in what was known as the third-front strategy. This affected shipbuilding, a key element in the maritime military industrial complex[20].

China's naval awakening commenced only in the 1980s, a few years after Deng Xiaoping's tectonic economic reforms. These reforms had increased maritime commerce, increasing the need for a stronger, long-legged navy. The man behind the awakening was Liu Huaqing, an Army General, who laid the foundations of the modern navy in the 1980s and oversaw its fruition through his continued elevation up the Chinese hierarchy onwards to the Central Military Commission culminating in becoming the last military member of the Standing Committee of Politburo.[21] The Navy finally found continued Party sponsorship through Liu. It was also around Liu's time as Naval Chief that China made its departure from an idealistic People's War to a pragmatic

Local War idea. Local wars got enshrined as a Military Strategic Guideline—the highest written strategy—only later in 1993. The Maoist maritime reluctance melted away and a naval build-up followed, beefed up by the burgeoning industrial complex. Apart from a *local war* idea, the prime maritime motivators initially remained three.

The ***first*** was the nuclear deterrence carried forward from Mao's period. The ***second*** was preventing US interference in the Taiwan Crisis. The ***third*** was the traditional role of the navies to protect trade, which by then had come to occupy a substantial portion of the GDP. Post-Tiananmen and Soviet breakup, Chinese nationalism had been on the rise as an aid for party legitimacy. The maritime territorial contests, an essential element of nationalism, emerged as the ***fourth*** motivator and required a new fleet. A fleet built keel-up for deterrence, denial and commerce protection is insufficient for a calibrated escalation to keep contestation at the desired thresholds. Therefore, this fleet had to be different with small, less intimidating naval vessels, the Coast Guard and civilian ships such as the fishing fleet playing a key role with the other premium fleets donning the role of guarantor at a short call away. After a brief background on how these roles evolved, each role and the fleet created by these roles are described in greater detail.

Roles and Fleets

The roles and associated fleets are described below:

- **Role One Fleet One: The Ballistic Missile Submarine Fleet**: Mao had shunned technology, talking of the atom bomb as a *paper tiger*[22] in an interview in 1946. However, from the First Taiwan Crisis he grasped the role of nuclear weapons in enforcing deterrence. By 1959, he exhorted that he would build a nuclear submarine even if it were to take a thousand years.[23] Considering the importance that China gave to building the SSBN,[24] the foremost role of the Navy continues to be deterrence and the foremost fleet that the Chinese navy maintains is its fleet of SSBNs. The first of the class of SSBNs, the Xia class, was commissioned in the early 1980s. However, this appeared to be a short-lived experimental programme with only two hulls of which one was reportedly lost. The Xia class was followed by the Jinclass, in which large scale design changes to the propulsion systems were undertaken. Unlike other naval inventories, the SSBN is a platform built around the nuclear missile it delivers with a complex command and communication chain. In China's case these missiles were JL1 on board the Xia and JL2 on the follow-on Jin class. It is speculated that China is on the verge of deploying the Jin class submarines with JL2 missiles in them.[25,26,27] This would not only see closure to the six-decade-old Mao's directive but also see a significant political and cultural step of delegating an enormous responsibility of activating the nuclear button shared between a young seagoing captain and a political commissar. China eventually plans to deploy a fleet of eight boats of this class.[28]

- **Role Two, Fleet Two. The Anti Access/Counter Intervention Fleet**: The second motivator to the Chinese naval build-up is to stop external intervention in a future Taiwan scenario. The roots of this aspiration lie in the Third Taiwan crisis in 1996 which was a watershed moment in the naval build-up. The only force that can intervene in Taiwan's favour in that scenario is the US Carrier Battle Group. To avoid a replay of the last crisis which humbled China, it wants to counter an intervention and deny access to a superior force. The anti-access area denial or counter-intervention inventory is aimed at meeting this requirement. It accelerated the process commenced by Liu Huaqing who was by then a member of the Standing Committee of PB. Subsequently, Taiwan has been declared a 'core' issue and has been reinforced by an anti-secession law in 2005 which threatens military action in case of a breakaway. This fleet derives its roots from the young school of naval strategy. It was Theophile Aube, the French naval minister, who is credited in the modern times for the creation of the '*jeuneecole*' or 'young school' of naval strategy.[29] Unable to match British ship sizes and firepower, he created an asymmetric fleet of small and fast torpedo boats that could outmanoeuvre the battleship fleet. The Young School's Cold War Soviet avatar improvised the idea with an impressive line-up of missile boats and submarines. Small, stealthy and eminently suited against US carrier battle groups, they offered asymmetry with disproportionate effect. Communist China faced the asymmetric predicament initially viz. the USA, followed by the Soviets post-Sino-Soviet split coming a full circle, with the USA again emerging as a rival. The initial Chinese inventory came from the former USSR and therefore the seeds of the Young School were intrinsic in the inventory itself. Post-Sino-Soviet split, China rapidly advanced building submarines and missile boats reaching a build rate of up to six submarines a year in the 1960s. China expanded its Missile Boat inventory from 20 to 200 and its submarine inventory from 35 to 100 between the 1970s and the late 1980s.[30] This according to Ellis Joffe, was one of the best in the world by the early 1980s.[31] Opposing fleets tailored for a large scale decisive battle with an equal, faced a tactical dilemma and required creative measures to offset that asymmetry.[32] The major platforms that enable denial are described below:

– **Submarines.** Having assembled and licence-produced the Whiskey and Romeo classes from 1953 and developed a conventional design, the Ming class based on Soviet Romeos in 1971, the Chinese graduated to designing and building a nuclear submarine. By 1974, the PLAN launched the Han-class nuclear attack submarine. The renewed friendship with Russia enabled the import of the Kilo-class boats which were a quantum leap in design with hydro-dynamic and stealth features. They were quickly followed by the Song and Yuan-class submarines. The Yuan submarines, which are similar to the Kilo class,[33] have already been chosen for export to Thailand and Pakistan.[34] Around this period, China also launched the next generation of the Shang-class nuclear attack submarines. The Shang class has improvised propulsion configuration from its predecessor, the Han class.

– **Missile Boats.** As far as missiles boats were concerned, China finalised a light aluminium-hulled Australian catamaran design to create the Hubei class which it now deploys and builds in large numbers. China also has a large number of cruise missiles, which offer an asymmetric advantage in its inventory since defending against them is disproportionately costly. The cruise missile offers a 9:1 cost advantage viz. its defence mechanism.[35]

– **Land-based platforms.** Apart from sea-based platforms, China has also created land-based assets against an incoming fleet. They include the following:

- **Anti-Ship Ballistic Missile (ASBM).** These include land-based missiles, especially the Anti-Ship Ballistic Missile, which can target incoming ships. They are the DF21 missiles with a range of 1500 km and the futuristic DF26 missiles with a range of 2500 km.
- **Shore-based Strike Aircraft.** Strike aircraft such as the Sukhoi 30Mk2 can be effectively used against an intervening fleet. The impending transfer of the S400 air defence missiles from Russia[36] could also serve as a layer of defence against incoming strike from an aircraft carrier.

- **Role Three, Fleet Three:** Apart from a 'Young School', there is a long-legged fleet that China has developed. By the early eighties, it had dawned on China that a denial navy will be woefully inadequate for its unravelling economic model. Trade as a percentage of the GDP was rising, eventually peaking in the first decade of the 21st century (Refer Figure 3.1). Ittons markets and resources lay farther than what its brown water fleet could protect. The obsession with coastal defence against a nationalist invasion and People's War was abandoned to first embrace an 'offshore defence' and later an 'open sea protection' strategy. Reflecting a continental mooring, it set the island chain-based milestones to craft a suitable inventory. Liu's plan for the Chinese navy was to achieve control in what is called the 'First Island Chain' by 2000, which is a line joining the Aleutians, Kurile, Taiwan, Philippines Archipelago and North West Borneo. The second milestone was control of the Second Island Chain over a line that joins Bonin, Mariana, Guam and Palau, by 2020 (Refer Fig 3.2). The third goal was to create a Global Navy by 2050. It commenced gaining sea legs by round-world cruises, inducted a range of modern Western technologies like the marine gas turbine, sonars and helicopters, using the window opened up by Sino-US rapprochement.[37] By 1993, China had become a net oil importer from the Indian Ocean Region, playing a crucial factor in maritime awakening. However it forays were limited till 2008 when regular anti-piracy patrols gave it a reason to remain present in the Indian Ocean under the broad rubric of *New Historic Missions,* a Hu Jintao catchphrase. This was a directive to the PLA to rise up to new missions that commensurate with new national goals and a foreign policy.[38] The long-legged fleet it has developed to meet new roles has three components: heavier multirole destroyers, lighter frigates and today, it also boasts of the second largest fleet of replenishment tankers in the world. The new addition to this fleet is the aircraft carrier.
  - **Destroyers.**[39] The destroyers have evolved from the first indigenous Luda class built 40 years ago to state-of-the-art Luyang-III class which has become the present fleet standard. In that process it has experimented with varying displacement, propulsion systems, stealth hull forms, sensors, combat management systems and weaponry. The stealthy Luyang-III Destroyers at 7000 tons pack an indigenous diesel and gas turbine propulsion, active phased array radar, 64 slot vertical launch

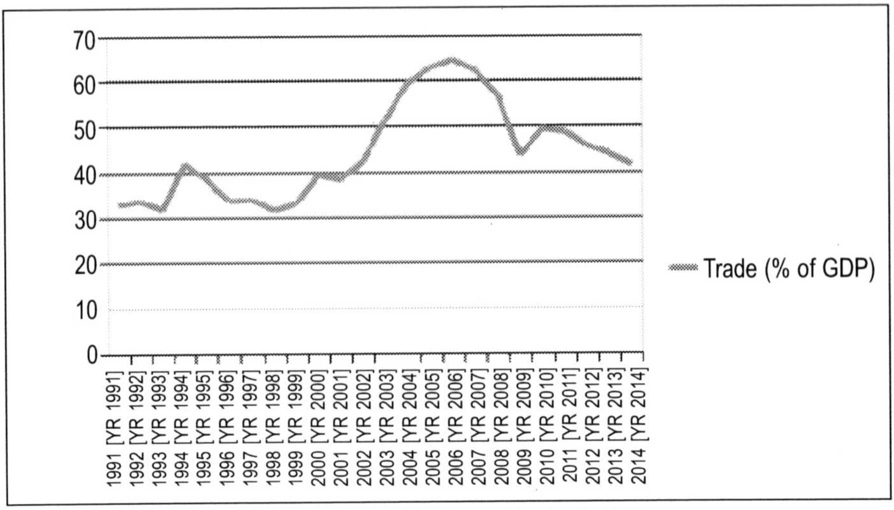

Figure 3.1. PRC Trade as % of GDP Data
(*Source*: World Bank)

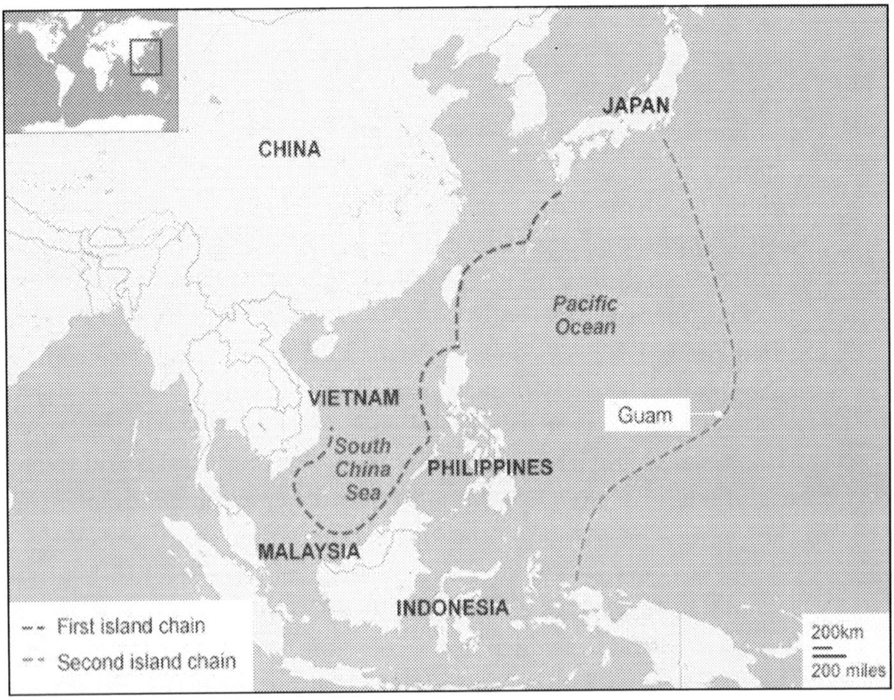

Figure 3.2. First and Second Island Chain
(*Source*: BBC Images http://news.bbcimg.co.uk/news/special/2015/newsspec_12190/media/700x500island_chains_201409-lr_1.jpg)

system, surface-to-air missile range of 150 km and a cruise missile range of 290 km. Just as in the case of submarines, a mid-course import of the Sovremenny class infused a fillip to design and operational experience. The future destroyers are getting heavier with the Type-55 being built at the Jiangnan yard, reportedly at 10,000 tons-plus displacement. This is a trend that is also being reflected in Japan and the USA which have increased their destroyer displacement above 10,000 tons with the Atago class and the Zumwalt class, respectively.

- **Frigates.**[40] The frigates too have evolved over a period commencing with the Jianghus in the 1980s. The types of frigates have stabilised with the standard Jingwei-II and Jiangkai-II frigates with a displacement of approximately 2000 tons and 4000 tons, respectively. There are 10 hulls of Jiangwei-II and 18 of the Jiangkai-II in commission. The lighter of the two, the Jiangwei class, is exported to Pakistan,[41] has inspired designs in Myanmar[42] and perhaps is on the shopping list of Bangladesh.[43]
- **The Liaoning Aircraft Carrier**. The latest addition to the fleet is the aircraft carrier. China's ambition to acquire an aircraft carrier was revealed in the 1970s when an Australian carrier *Melbourne* was purchased as scrap for study. After purchasing two ex-Soviet carriers[44] and converting them into casinos,[45] China purchased a Kuznetsov-class carrier, the *Varyag*, inherited by Ukraine post-Soviet breakup in 1998, and rechristened it as *Liaoning*. As a classic case of civil–military interface, the carrier was purchased by a Hong Kong-based entrepreneur, Xue Zengping.[46] After nearly 20 months under tow, accentuated first by Turkey's refusal of permission to cross the Bosphorus straits and later by a tow rope break, it was docked in Dalian in March 2002. As the refit commenced in 2005, China set up a ski ramp on land to train its pilots in Wuhan.[47] In 2010–11, the ship underwent sea trials. On September 25, 2012 the PLAN commissioned the ship. By November 2012, the Shenyang J15, the carrier-borne fighter plane, had made touchdowns and landings. Given the complexities of carrier operations, the process of integration was hastened with the Brazilian navy's help, since Brazil had experience in carrier operations.[48] The *Liaoning* carries upto 24 J-15 fighter aircraft and 6 Z-8 and 4 Ka-31 helicopters. It is fitted with 4 FL-3000N SAMs in 18-cell launchers. It is powered by steam turbines,

and has 4 shafts driving it. Manned by a crew of 2000 it displaces 59,439 tons at full load.[49] China in April 2017 launched its second carrier, with increased flight deck space.[50] It does not differ very much from the Liaoning and will have conventional propulsion systems. The present inventory uses short take-off and barrier-assisted recovery (STOBAR) concept of air operations. This precludes the use of a catapult, which can launch heavier aircraft like the Airborne Early Warning aircraft into the air with higher payloads and ranges. It will take some time before the Chinese carrier operations mature to the level of other nations due to the complexities involved.

- **Replenishment Ships.**[51] A significant indicator of strategic maritime intent is the number of replenishment tankers. China has three major classes of replenishment ships: Fuqing, Fusu and Fuchi class. The first is the Fuqing class, a tanker commissioned in 1980. Chinese navy operates two out of the four ships built in this class. A limitation of these vessels is the absence of a helicopter deck. The only ship of the Fusu class with the PLAN is with the South Sea Fleet. The latest class is the Fuchi class, which is slightly smaller than the Fusu, and is the premier class that China has. It has six of these ships distributed across its fleets, with two more being built. Just as with its other classes of ships, in 1992, China purchased a Russian tanker, christened the *Qinghai Hu*. This is the largest ship after the aircraft carrier in the Chinese fleet at 38,000 tons. The pattern of a mid-course Russian infusion permeates most classes. It emerges from this pattern that China in its initial maritime build-up, made several classes on its own during the Sino-Soviet split. When the Soviet Union collapsed making top-notch ex-Soviet manpower and material available to China, it used the opportunity to fine tune its designs and subsequently arrive at the stabilised classes.

Role Four, Fleet Three-and-a-Half: The fourth role is that of safeguarding its nationalist claims. If the Chinese naval strategy and People's War were on divergent trajectories earlier, it is now dealing with this new role where its naval strategy has its perigee with the 'People's War'.

- **Corvette Class.** China has in recent times added a new ship, the Jiangdao class, to its fleet. Eighteen of this class are already in commission and up to 30 hulls could be built. The inclusion of this smaller ship in the fleet, which at 1500 tons is lighter than the frigate and heavier than a missile boat, is seen as a move to involve itself proportionally for territorial claims and to have larger footprints at a cheaper price. Heavier, more potent combatants could be intimidating and lead to disproportionate reactions from adversaries, whereas smaller ships are cheaper and less provocative. Three in the series are anti-submarine variants, with towed array and advanced sonars. This class has reportedly been exported to Bangladesh[52] and Nigeria.[53]

– **Coast Guard and Civil Vessels.** Corvettes are not alone in the contestation in the South China Sea. There is a layer of paramilitary and civilian maritime forces that has been carefully groomed to further the Chinese aims. The fishing fleet forms the first layer. The Chinese Coast Guard forms the second layer and the corvette could form the third layer. The Coast Guard ship sizes have been rising in that region displacing upto 5000 tons—which are as heavy as a normal destroyer. In a separate, yet related move, China has also passed a law that all its civil ships will adhere to some military specifications at the building stage itself.[54] China has also reorganised its myriad maritime organisations[55] into one single entity under the Coast Guard.[56] This creates a civil military hybrid fleet that has precedence in Soviet Admiral Gorshkov's[57] ubiquitous fishing fleet which was netting not just fish, but enormous dual-use oceanic data. Therefore, it is this hybrid fleet—part-military-part-civil fleet—which will probably be the one that it could rely on in the South China Sea contestation.

PLANAF. The air arm of the navy is a fairly large fleet, larger than the air forces of several modern nations. It has an estimated 25,000 personnel and 800 aircraft which are organised into eight divisions that serve the three fleets of China.

- **Shore-based strike.** The front line aircraft of the PLANAF is the 24 Su30MKK2 aircraft purchased from Russia in 2004 and cloned as the J16. It is armed with Kh31 missiles. It has the M400 SAR for surveillance. It uses the WS10A Taihang Chinese engines which are earmarked for the J15 A also. Apart from Sukhois, the PLAN operates the J7A as a fighter bomber with the South Sea Fleet. It also operates the J10A fighters in the 4th Division as the Sukhois. These strike aircraft are aimed at the A2AD Taiwan intervention scenario.
- **Carrier-based strike.** China has developed the J15 flying Shark, a carrier-based aircraft. This is based on the Russian Su 27/33. This is a STOBAR-category short take-off from ski jumps and has a barrier-assisted recovery. It uses the Russian AL31F engine, and eventually

uses the Chinese WS10A Taihang engine. It could carry the YJ62 missile. Buddy refuelling extends its ranges. Carrier-borne strike aircraft are heavily dependent on AEW aircraft. However, without catapults and larger deck space, heavier propeller aircraft cannot operate from the carriers. At the moment, China plugs this gap using the Russian KA31 AEW helicopter. China may use a Z8-based helicopter version and a Y7 based propeller version for future generations of the AEW.

- **Helicopters.** China uses Harbin Z-9C, Kamov Ka-28, Changhe Z-8 ASW helicopters and Kamov Ka-31 AEW helicopter. The Changhe Z-18 helicopter has been used from the *Liaoning*.
- **Maritime Reconnaissance Aircraft.** The KJ 200 is the premiere aircraft with Airborne Warning and Control System (AWACS) and AESA. It is based on the Ilyushin Il-76 transport aircraft and is operated by the Air Force. The Harbin SH-5 multipurpose amphibian has an ASW configuration. The Shaanxi Y-8 has an ASW configuration as well as an ELINT configuration.

Other Related Factors. China in the recent past has also introduced the aircraft carrier as well as several large amphibious vessels into its inventory. The aircraft carrier is presently being integrated with the fleet and adds to national pride, as fleets also serve that purpose. China has also commenced building the follow-on carrier class, a slightly heavier one with configuration similar to the *Liaoning*. The carrier could be used against smaller navies fulfilling roles three and four, as described in the chapter. China has also built its amphibious war vessels especially the Yuzhao class, with which it can place boots on littoral grounds in large numbers. These have roles in a Taiwan crisis (Role two) and in territorial contests (Role four).

The graph below illustrates the inventory of the Chinese navy in 1990 compared to 25 years later, and the number of new inductions during the intervening period (Refer Fig. 3.3). The missile boat strength which has not been shown in the graph stands at 86 presently, a large reduction from 200 in the 1990s.[58] However, qualitatively, these boats have improved their firepower.

Shipbuilding. An equally important facet is the shipbuilding industry. That is the fount of a good navy. Shipbuilding therefore has been deemed a strategic sector in China from 1982 and today China is the largest shipbuilder in the world. Predominantly, China's shipbuilding has occurred in three centres—Shanghai, Liaoning and Jiangsu—since 1999.[59] Though there are several yards

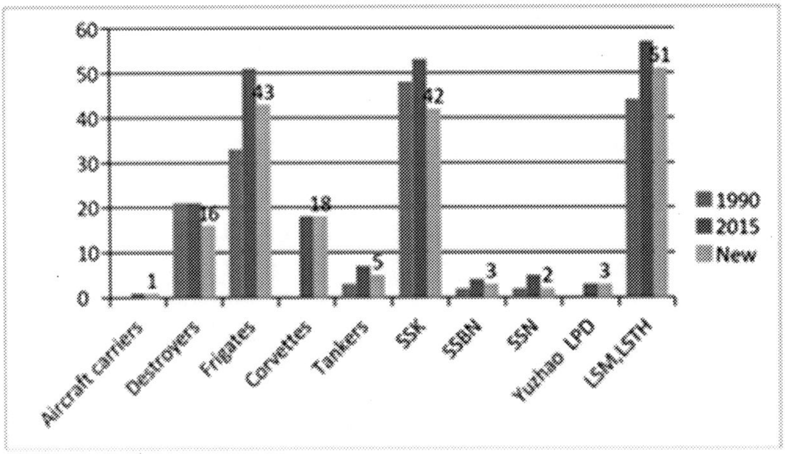

Figure 3.3. PLAN Orbat 1990-2016, without Missile Boats
(*Source*: Jane's Fighting Ships, 1990 and 2015)

that build merchant ships in China, warships in China are built by two major state-owned conglomerates that compete with each other. They are the China State Shipbuilding Cooperation (CSSC) and the China Shipbuilding Industry Corporation (CSIC). They operate in two geographic zones, i.e. North/West and South/East of China. These are administered by the State Council through the State Owned Assets Supervision and Administration Commission (SASAC). However, the military production of these shipyards is under the GAD of the PLA and not under the State Council. The nuclear submarines are built only in the Bohai yard. Dalian builds larger hulls like aircraft carriers. Submarines are built in the Wuchang yard in Wuhan as well as in Jiangnan. The details are available in the Table 3.1.

Table 3.1. Major Shipbuilding Centres of PRC-PLAN with Type of Ships[61]

Group	Shipbuilding companies of China		Ships
	Location	**Yard**	**Ships**
China State Shipbuilding Corporation-South and East	Shanghai	Hudong-Zhonghua	Frigates, LST
		Jiangnan	Destroyers, SSK
	Guangdong	COMEC[60]	
		Huangpu	Frigates
China Shipbuilding Industry Corporation-North and West	Liaoning	Bohai Shipbuilding	SSN, SSBN
		Dalian Shipbuilding	DDG, AC, Tankers
	Hubei, Wuhan	Wuchang Shipbuilding	SSKs SSA

Along with shipbuilding, it is appropriate to examine the build rate of ships which provides an insight into industrial competence. China's rates are highly impressive with up to 16 missile boats and 10 corvettes being built per year. The build rates of ships along with decommission rates are tabulated below in Table 3.2.

Table 3.2. Build Rate Large PLAN Unit

	FFG	DDG	SSK	LST	SSN
Build Rate Large Shipsper every two years	4	3	4	2	1
Decommisson rate Rate 2012/13 only	8	8	3-6	2	

Table 3.2. Contd.

	SSBN	Tanker	LPD	Corvette	Missile Boat
Build Rate Large Shipsper every two years	1	1	1	10	16
Decommisson rate Rate 2012/13 only	1	-	-	-	

Source: Jane's Fighting Ships.[62]

Organisational Changes

So far, this chapter talked of the hardware and motivators behind the hardware. The organisational structure that enables the Chinese state in using this force is equally important. There have been several major organisational changes in the Chinese Defence Organisation recently which have a direct bearing over the PLA Navy and its Maritime Strategy. These changes have been crafted to bring the Navy to the fore in what was predominantly a structure dominated by the ground forces. December 31, 2015, will go down in history as a point of inflection in the transformations of the PLA. On that day it rolled out a series of far-reaching changes to its military, beginning with the institution of a Ground Forces (Army) Headquarters with a separate chief.

This singular step of an Army HQ and a Chief for Ground Forces needs some deconstruction. Till that day, the Army had never had a Chief or a headquarters since other services were deemed branches under the Army. This organisational gap among other issues was behind the explicit exhortation '***the traditional mentality that land outweighs sea must be abandoned***' in the Defence White Paper 2015.[63] By whittling down the Army, China was in effect upgrading the other forces, including the Navy, to an equal status—a telling message on its recognition of realities. The Second Artillery, a force that had controlled conventional and strategic missiles, was renamed the

People's Liberation Army Rocket Force (PLARF) and was also upgraded from a 'branch' to a 'service'. A new force, the PLA Strategic Support Force, was also formed that day which under its ambit controls space operations and information warfare including cyber, psyops and electronic warfare.[64] This is a very significant shift to winning 'informationised' local wars.

A fortnight later, On February 1, 2016, the 'four departments',[65] which were behemoths under the Central Military Commission—China's highest military body—were broken into fifteen nimble smaller organisations under it, consisting of six departments, six offices and three commissions. The formation of the Theatre Commands, in that instalment, added a new dimension to warfighting where, from an army-oriented military region-based organisation, China switched to geographically oriented five multiservice combat commands. This too affects the maritime strategy seriously since the way in which China would have applied military force in a service-oriented framework before the change has given way to a synergised cross-domain application of force. The most telling effect of this occurred a year later in mid-2017 when its Southern Theatre Command, with the most modern assets and bases under the South Sea Fleet, was placed under a Naval Officer, along with the Army and Air Force assets. A little later, the reforms also brought in the Joint Logistics Support Force which provides financial, victualling, uniform, medical services, etc.

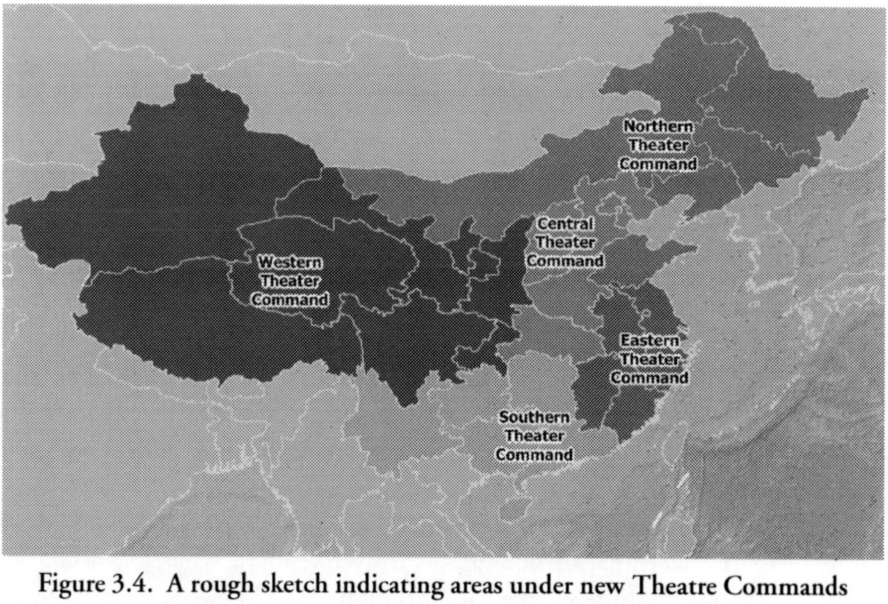

Figure 3.4. A rough sketch indicating areas under new Theatre Commands (based on the China Brief, Jamestown Foundation[66])

Signals that alluded to these reforms had been available slightly earlier. As per Xi's address at a meeting on reforming the armed forces in Beijing from November 24–26, 2015, they aimed to establish a three-tier system where the CMC will serve as the first tier of structure, the Battle Zone Commands/ Troops Command system as the second functional tier and an Administration System that runs from the CMC through various services to the troops as the third tier.[67] It appears that China is trying to replicate the US-style Theatre Command System for operations that runs parallel to the service-oriented administrative structure that ensures professional management of services. Xi stated whilst inaugurating the new Command Structure that this is *'a strategic decision made by the CPC Central Committee and the CMC with an eye to realizing the Chinese Dream and the Dream of a Strong Military. The establishment of the five theatre commands and their joint operational institutions is of great and far-reaching significance in ensuring the PLA to be capable of fighting and winning battles and effectively safeguarding China's national security'*.[68]. Certain other exhortations by President Xi reveal what is expected of the theatre commands; he stated that the new commands must:[69]

- *'Focus on **combat readiness**, and the various military services pursue their own construction and development*
- *Unswervingly follow the **absolute leadership of the CPC** over the military and carry out the orders and instructions of the CPC Central Committee and the CMC to the letter*
- *Devote themselves to **studying how** to fight wars, research the principles of winning modern warfare, speed up the formulation of the theatre commands' strategies, perfect their combat plans, and focus on joint training, so as to obtain initiatives in future warfare*
- *Strengthen **joint command, joint operations and joint support** within the theatre commands, and organize troops to complete daily combat-readiness and military operations'* (emphasis by the author)

These changes have benefitted the maritime forces in many ways:

- The manpower cuts which were a central part of this change has affected the Navy the least. When cuts were 40 per cent from the Army and 30 per cent from the Air Force, only 10 per cent was cut from the Navy.[70]
- The creation of theatre commands infused jointness by taking the combat commands out of the army hierarchy. The first non-army Theatre Commander is Vice Admiral Yuan Yubai, A former North Sea Fleet Commander elevated to head the Southern Theatre

Command in 2017.[71] He will have the South Sea Fleet under him which is the most modern fleet and commands bases with nuclear submarines. This fleet also got combat experience in Vietnam in 1974 and 1988. In all probability, this Fleet will spearhead any operation in the South China Sea and the Indian Ocean. This has indicated that theatre concepts are being put into practise in a rational manner, possibly with a lead service in respective theatres like the Navy in the Southern Theatre which has a predominantly maritime role.

- Slightly earlier to the 2015 reforms, in 2013, the five separate maritime law enforcement entities termed as the five ***dragons*** have been united into a single body under the State Oceanic Administration.[72]
- There will be an eventual formation of up to one lakh marines by converting two amphibious divisions and one armoured brigade to deal with expeditionary roles.
- The formation of the PLASSF is with stress on Pysops, EW and Cyber Warfare, which can affect operations.

Conclusion

This chapter tried to briefly describe some basic factors that influence the roles and fleets of the Chinese maritime forces. The types of inventory and resultant fleets have been segregated based on the broad rationale of force building for easier understanding.

During the Mao era, there was a maritime stasis barring submarines, including the nuclear ones. That stasis has given way to a discernible vigour, articulated in the 2015 Defence White Paper as "the traditional mentality that land outweighs sea must be abandoned". The Chinese Defence White Paper 2015 has been discussed in relation to the Belt and Road Initiative in Chapter 2. The White Paper is also placed in Appendix 3 for reference. The defence white paper had a significant change in name calling it 'China's Military Strategy' explicitly, issued at a time when 'disputes over land territory are still smouldering'.

Overall, the PLAN is a navy that has grown quickly in the past twenty-five years to its present form, fuelled by widening economic and political interests. The maritime roles envisaged and the force being created befits the Grand Strategy of Belt and Road, which demands protecting China's expanding economic and strategic interests farther from the shores- along the trajectory of the Maritime Silk Road (MSR). The Maritime Silk Road provides more basing options for China as much as it fuels the need for a long-legged fleet.

The **first** role of that navy continues to be deterrence enabled by its SSBN fleet and associated command systems. Speculation is now rife about its operational deployment. The turn of events in the Third Taiwan Crisis placed anti-access and area denial back on the pedestal. Taiwan is a core issue and this defines the **second** role around which a strong fleet of submarines, missile boats, land-based aircraft and missiles have evolved. The opening up of the economy brought to the fore the need of a navy that had roles beyond the Taiwan straits. For this **third** *open sea* protection role, a fleet of destroyers, frigates and tankers has been built. This fleet along with submarines has shown its regular presence in the Indian Ocean since 2008. The base in Djibouti[73] and the alliances it forges with its allies such as Pakistan, have sustenance of this fleet in mind. Rising nationalism has necessitated a **fourth** role, where China wants to act giving an adequate scope for calibrated escalation, keeping a threshold in purview. This has resulted in a hybrid half-fleet with civil–military elements. This takes the navy through a full circle, reminiscent of the People's War with blurred lines of division between the civil and the military.

The territorial claims, counter claims, island building and an ambiguous nine dashed line over water with no modern legal basis have led to tensions and some fast-paced developments in the Western Pacific. This is a critical maritime space for the world with trillions of dollars worth of traffic. This chapter underlines some basic aspects of China's maritime power-building and places it in that context—especially the hybrid fleet approach. The civil–military interface dynamic is important to note, since such a practice in the Western Pacific will find a parallel in the Indian Ocean as footprints and interests increase over time.

At the operational end of the spectrum, similar type of ships and fleets may not act independently in tight silos, but in concert with other fleets. For example, submarines—a tool for denial—have appeared in the Indian Ocean along with a regular presence of a Chinese Task Group in the Gulf of Aden since 2008. Nations also designate and station their fleets geographically as China has done, dividing them into North, East and South Sea Fleets under its newly created theatre commands. Yet, such a geographic and administrative segregation or an operational deployment will rely on the basic elements of sea power, some of which has been contextualised here as the three-and-a-half fleets of the Party. What is also significant is that a professional armed force might also find the ideological oversight, as practised in China increasingly, as a burden.

The reorganisation of the PLA is the largest in scope within any major armed forces since the Goldwater-Nichols Act of USA in 1986. For a conservative organisation like the military, such changes will take some time to settle and become effective. Some challenges to jointness will continue to remain—like disjointed land and maritime frontiers in certain cases. The Theatre Command that faces its Indian Ocean neighbours on land is the Western Theatre Command, whereas the Command that will protect access to the Indian Ocean is the Southern Theatre Command. It must be assumed that the coordination between them will be done at the Central Military Commission.

As a part of its Indian Ocean hard power strategy, the anti-piracy missions since 2008 have institutionalised China's naval presence in the Indian Ocean of up to three ships at any given time. By shifting the schedules through delayed departure from or by advanced arrival in IOR, or by sending a group on a goodwill visit after or before patrol, on occasions, China has shown the capacity to substantially increase its presence in the Indian Ocean. China has also acquired a base in Djibouti[74] besides gaining strategic equities in various ports in the region. Gwadar is one such prospective Chinese naval base. There has also been a qualitative change in deployment with submarines routinely being deployed in the IOR.[75] They have also docked submarines in ports of debtor nations in IOR such as Pakistan[76] and Sri Lanka,[77] as well as Malaysia.[78] Bangladesh[79] has received two Ming-class submarines; Pakistan[80] and Thailand[81] have signed deals for Chinese submarines. These deals cement a long military and technical relationship which China can tap into in the Indian Ocean Region. These nations are also important cogs in the BRI plan, close to the crucial choke points in the IOR. This signals a change in the quality of the Chinese naval deployment which is on an upward trajectory in the Indian Ocean apart from commercial port operations in which China is emerging as a major global player.

A significant indicator of the Chinese geopolitical and maritime behaviour are the incidents in the South China Sea. If China has to enter the Indian Ocean it has to traverse the South China Sea. Currently, it is in the business of tightening its vice-like control of that sea with island building, reclamation and claims over vast swathes of sea through the nebulous nine dashed line. The lessons from the South China Sea today are important to the Indian Ocean. The next chapter deals with them.

NOTES

1. Part of this chapter was published by the author in an article "The Party's Maritime Power: Four Roles and Three-and-a-Half Fleets". China Report 53, no. 1 (February 2017): 46–58. doi:10.1177/0009445516677363. The author is grateful to China Report for providing permissions to use it in this Chapter.
2. This commentary restricts the scope of the term 'fleet' to the type of inventory and not the geographical distribution of ships into the South, East and North Sea Fleets.
3. A.T. Mahan, *The Influence of Sea Power Upon History, 1660-1783*, n.d. Kindle Edition
4. "Making of Soviet Strategy", Condoleezza Rice, Peter Paret, Gordon A. Craig, and Felix Gilbert (eds), *Makers of Modern Strategy from Machiavelli to the Nuclear Age* (Princeton University Press, 2010).
5. The People's Liberation Army is the generic name for all military services, with suffixes discerning them as Ground Forces, Navy, Air Force, Rocket (Missile) Force, etc.
6. Mahan, *The Influence of Sea Power Upon History, 1660-1783*. p.4, Kindle Edition
7. Also termed anti-access area denial (A2AD) and sea denial.
8. "Dragons Unite," *The Economist*, March 16, 2013, http://www.economist.com/news/china/21573607-protect-its-maritime-interests-china-setting-up-civilian-coastguard-dragons-unite.
9. Lyle J. Goldstein, *Five Dragons Stirring Up the Sea: Challenge and Opportunity in China's Improving Maritime Enforcement Capabilities* (PN, 2010).
10. "Taming the Five Dragons? China Consolidates Its Maritime Law Enforcement Agencies," *The Jamestown Foundation*, accessed May 15, 2016, http://www.jamestown.org/programs/chinabrief/single/?tx_ttnews%5Btt_news%5D=40661&cHash=c3c1a5 a4ce04d29db680c8a092843afd.
11. "Why China Is Arming Its Fishing Fleet," *Stratfor*, accessed June 23, 2016, https://www.stratfor.com/analysis/why-china-arming-its-fishing-fleet.
12. "China Prepares Its 172,000 Civilian Ships for War," *The Diplomat*, accessed July 3, 2015, http://thediplomat.com/2015/06/china-prepares-its-172000-civilian-ships-for-war/.
13. "New Rules Mean Ships Can Be Used by Military," accessed May 13, 2016, http://english.chinamil.com.cn/news-channels/china-military-news/2015-06/18/content_6546905.htm.
14. Gabriel Collins and Grubb, Michael, *A Comprehensive Survey of China's Dynamic Shipbuilding Industry-Commercial Development and Strategic Implications*, n.d.
15. "Qinglong's Letter to King George," accessed June 23, 2016, http://academics.wellesley.edu/Polisci/wj/China/208/READINGS/qianlong.html.
16. John King Fairbank and Merle Goldman, *China: A New History, Second Enlarged Edition* (Harvard University Press, 2006).
17. For details on PLA trajectory after Mao, read Ellis Joffe, *The Chinese Army after Mao* (Weidenfeld and Nicolson, 1987).
18. As per Science of Military Strategy, 2008 Edition, the People's War is a philosophy and above strategy in the pecking order.
19. "The Geopolitics of China: A Great Power Enclosed," *Stratfor*, accessed June 23, 2016, https://www.stratfor.com/analysis/geopolitics-china-great-power-enclosed.
20. Collins and Grubb, Michael, *A Comprehensive Survey of China's Dynamic Shipbuilding Industry-Commercial Development and Strategic Implications.*
21. Detailed account of Liu's role in James R. Holmes and Toshi Yoshihara, *Chinese Naval Strategy in the 21st Century: The Turn to Mahan* (Routledge, 2012).
22. Mao Tse-tung, *Selected Military Writings of Mao Tse-Tung* (Praetorian Press Llc, 2011). The

actual words of Mao were *"the atom bomb is a paper tiger which the U.S. reactionaries use to scare people. It looks terrible, but in fact it isn't. Of course, the atom bomb is a weapon of mass slaughter, but the outcome of a war is decided by the people, not by one or two new types of weapon*". Talk with the American Correspondent Anna Louise Strong, August 1946.

23. John Wilson Lewis and Litai Xue, *China's Strategic Seapower: The Politics of Force Modernization in the Nuclear Age* (Stanford University Press, 1996), p. 18.
24. An SSBN is nuclear powered ballistic missile capable submarine.
25. "China Deploys First Nuclear Deterrence Patrol," *The Diplomat*, accessed December 28, 2015, http://thediplomat.com/2015/12/china-deploys-first-nuclear-deterrence-patrol/.
26. Stephen Saunders, *Jane's Fighting Ships, 2014-2015* (Jane's Information Group, 2015).
27. "Inside the Ring: China's Nuclear Missile Submarine Patrols Give New Strike Capability," *The Washington Times*, accessed December 28, 2015, http://www.washingtontimes.com/news/2015/dec/9/inside-the-ring-chinas-nuclear-missile-submarine-p/.
28. Saunders, *Jane's Fighting Ships, 2014-2015.*
29. Geoffrey Till, *Seapower: A Guide for the Twenty-First Century* (Routledge, 2013).
30. Joffe, *The Chinese Army after Mao.*
31. Ibid.
32. The US has a tactical concept termed the *Joint Concept for Access and Manoeuvre in the Global Commons (JAM-GC)* to deal with an asymmetric threat from China. In the long-term, the US has a *third offset* strategy for the military–industrial complex to invest in innovations to deal with asymmetric threats.
33. "Essay: Inside the Design of China's Yuan-Class Submarine," *USNI News*, August 31, 2015, https://news.usni.org/2015/08/31/essay-inside-the-design-of-chinas-yuan-class-submarine.
34. "China to Provide Eight Submarines to Pakistan by 2028," *IHS Jane's 360*, accessed September 17, 2016, http://www.janes.com/article/63293/china-to-provide-eight-submarines-to-pakistan-by-2028.
35. Dennis M. Gormley, Andrew S. Erickson, and Jingdong Yuan, *A Low-Visibility Force Multiplier: Assessing China's Cruise Missile Ambitions* National Defense University, (LULU Press, 2015), p. 77.
36. *Sputnik*, "Game Changer: China Will Soon Have S-400 Air Defense Systems Defending Its Skies," accessed August 7, 2017, https://sputniknews.com/military/201702151050707023-china-s400-production-stage-analysis/.
37. Similar navies had absorbed imported versions of these quite early.
38. Mulvenon, *China Leadership Monitor*, No. 27 1 Chairman Hu and the PLA's "New Historic Missions" James Mulvenon.
39. Saunders, *Jane's Fighting Ships, 2014-2015.*
40. Ibid.
41. Ibid.
42. Ibid.
43. Andrew Detsch, "With Pricey Naval Revamp, Bangladesh Can't Afford to Fail," *The Diplomat*, accessed August 8, 2017, http://thediplomat.com/2013/11/with-pricey-naval-revamp-bangladesh-cant-afford-to-fail/.
44. "China's First Aircraft Carrier Anchors In 'Fun Zone'," *The Washington Post*, accessed August 7, 2017, https://www.washingtonpost.com/archive/politics/1999/01/25/chinas-first-aircraft-carrier-anchors-in-fun-zone/66c78e76-fe65-4436-b4f0-447b66d28829/?utm_term=.a9c6a137f9a7.
45. "Bed, Breakfast And Bombing Runs: China Turns Soviet Aircraft Carrier Into Hotel," *WIRED*, accessed August 7, 2017, https://www.wired.com/2011/12/china-aircraft-carrier-hotel/.

46. "Chinese Government Still Owes Me US$120m for Buying It an Aircraft Carrier, Says PLA Veteran," *South China Morning Post,* accessed May 13, 2016, http://www.scmp.com/news/china/diplomacy-defence/article/1931060/chinese-government-still-owes-me-us120m-buying-it.
47. "Chinese Carrier-On-Land Facility Adds Destroyer," *USNI News,* January 26, 2015, https://news.usni.org/2015/01/26/chinese-carrier-land-facility-adds-destroyer.
48. "PLAN Officers to Train on Brazilian Aircraft Carrier," Jamestown, accessed August 7, 2017, https://jamestown.org/program/plan-officers-to-train-on-brazilian-aircraft-carrier/.
49. Saunders, *Jane's Fighting Ships, 2014-2015.*
50. "China Military Online," accessed May 13, 2016, http://english.chinamil.com.cn/.
51. Saunders, *Jane's Fighting Ships, 2014-2015.*
52. Ibid.
53. "Nigeria to Receive Chinese OPVs Later than Planned," *defenceWeb,* accessed September 17, 2016, http://www.defenceweb.co.za/index.php?option=com_content&view= article&id=43360:nigeria-to-receive-chinese-opvs-later-than-planned&catid=51:Sea&Itemid=106.
54. "China to Explore Civilian Ships' Great Potential for National Defense," accessed March 25, 2016, http://eng.mod.gov.cn/TopNews/2015-06/12/content_4590018.htm.
55. Lyle J. Goldstein, *Five Dragons Stirring Up the Sea: Challenge and Opportunity in China's Improving Maritime Enforcement Capabilities* (PN, 2010).
56. "Dragons Unite."
57. "Sergey Georgyevich Gorshkov, Soviet Admiral," *Britannica.com,* accessed September 17, 2016, https://www.britannica.com/biography/Sergey-Georgyevich-Gorshkov.
58. Saunders, *Jane's Fighting Ships, 2014-2015 and 1990-91.*
59. Collins and Grubb, Michael, *A Comprehensive Survey of China's Dynamic Shipbuilding Industry-Commercial Development and Strategic Implications.*
60. CSSC Offshore & Marine Engineering (Group) Company Limited (COMEC), formerly Guangzhou Shipyard International Company Limited (GSI).
61. Collins and Grubb, Michael, *A Comprehensive Survey of China's Dynamic Shipbuilding Industry-Commercial Development and Strategic Implications.*
62. Calculated by author; Data from *Jane's Fighting Ships.*
63. "Full Text: China's Military Strategy," accessed August 7, 2017, http://eng.mod.gov.cn/Press/2015-05/26/content_4586805.htm.
64. "Chinese Military Launches Two New Wings for Space and Cyber Age," *South China Morning Post,* accessed January 3, 2016, http://www.scmp.com/news/china/diplomacy-defence/article/1897356/chinese-military-launches-two-new-wings-space-and-cyber.
65. General Staff Department, General Political Department, General Logistics Department and General Armaments Department.
66. "The PLA's New Organizational Structure: What Is Known, Unknown and Speculation (Part 1), Jamestown," accessed August 26, 2017, https://jamestown.org/program/the-plas-new-organizational-structure-what-is-known-unknown-and-speculation-part-1/.
67. "Xi Urges Breakthroughs in Military Structural Reform," accessed January 3, 2016, http://eng.mod.gov.cn/DefenseNews/2015-11/26/content_4630715.htm.
68. "President Xi Announces Establishment of PLA Theater Commands - China Military Online," accessed February 1, 2016, http://english.chinamil.com.cn/news-channels/2016-02/01/content_6884075.htm.
69. Ibid.
70. "The Radical Plan to Turn China's People's Liberation Army into a Modern Fighting Force," *South China Morning Post,* accessed September 30, 2015, http://www.scmp.com/news/china/

diplomacy-defence/article/1854534/radical-plan-turn-chinas-peoples-liberation-army.

71. "Admiral to Head PLA's Southern Theatre Command," *South China Morning Post*, January 19, 2017, http://www.scmp.com/news/china/policies-politics/article/2063649/admiral-named-head-plas-southern-theatre-command.
72. "Dragons Unite."
73. Jeremy Page, "China Builds First Overseas Military Outpost," *Wall Street Journal*, August 19, 2016, sec. World, http://www.wsj.com/articles/china-builds-first-overseas-military-outpost-1471622690.
74. "China Opens First Overseas Base in Djibouti," accessed August 12, 2017, http://www.aljazeera.com/news/2017/08/china-opens-overseas-base-djibouti-170801104040586.html.
75. "China Deploys Submarine in Indian Ocean Region Even as India-China Standoff Continues," accessed August 12, 2017, http://indiatoday.intoday.in/story/china-submarine-in-indian-ocean-region-india-china-standoff/1/993606.html.
76. "Chinese Nuclear Submarine At Karachi Could Have Spied On India's Warships," *NDTV.com*, accessed August 12, 2017, http://www.ndtv.com/india-news/chinese-nuclear-submarine-seen-at-karachi-too-close-for-comfort-1645798.
77. "Chinese Submarines in Sri Lanka Unnerve India: Next Stop Pakistan?," Jamestown, accessed August 12, 2017, https://jamestown.org/program/chinese-submarines-in-sri-lanka-unnerve-india-next-stop-pakistan/.
78. Atul Aneja, "As Maritime Silk Road Takes Root, China Docks Submarine in Malaysia," *The Hindu*, January 10, 2017, sec. International, http://www.thehindu.com/news/international/As-Maritime-Silk-Road-takes-root-China-docks-submarine-in-Malaysia/article17017569.ece.
79. "Why This Indian Neighbour Decided to Buy 2 Submarines From China," *NDTV.com*, accessed August 12, 2017, http://www.ndtv.com/world-news/bangladesh-prime-minister-sheikh-hasina-defends-decision-to-buy-2-chinese-submarines-1724293.
80. "Chinese Nuclear Submarine At Karachi Could Have Spied On India's Warships."
81. "Thailand Approves $393-Mln Purchase of Chinese Submarines," accessed August 12, 2017, http://in.reuters.com/article/thailand-china-idINKBN17Q15O.

CHAPTER 4

THE STRATEGY OF SECURING SEA LINES: THE SOUTH CHINA SEA

Four hundred years ago in the South China Sea (SCS), a Portuguese carrack, the *Santa Catarina*, laden with riches was seized by the Dutch. Both nations were at war during that period. The seizure of this ship led to a prolonged legal defence of this act by a jurist named Hugo Grotius. From this defence emanated a legal concept about the oceans, termed '*mare liberum*' or concept of the open seas. The essence of the concept is that seas are open to use by all, antithetical to the Portuguese principle of '*mareclausum*' or closed seas. A similar debate has been replayed 400 years later in the same sea, in courtrooms in the Netherlands in a curious rhyme of history; it is also about similar principles of law.

In July 2016, a tribunal, in the faraway The Hague, delivered its award over several features and an ambiguous line over water in the South China Sea—an issue that had been brewing for several years between China and other nations.[1] The appellant to the arbitral tribunal—a redressal forum of the United Nations Conventions on the Laws of the Sea (UNCLOS), was the Philippines. The UNCLOS is the law that governs matters pertaining to the judicious use of the sea by nations. The tribunal award brought a much-needed legal clarity over several matters. The award went against China, in favour of the Philippines. Nevertheless, considering the hard, *historical* position taken by China, the heat and dust over the SCS is unlikely to settle anytime soon. This chapter tries to place some relevant aspects of that case and gauges some of its impacts.

The South China Sea

The South China Sea is a marginal sea in the Pacific Ocean that washes the shores of the South East Asian nations and China (Refer Fig 4.1). It has several reefs and shoals, which make it rich in fish and easy-to-extract resources. Nations that abut that sea, i.e. China and the ASEAN nations, are significant engines of global growth. They are also steeply into trade; 90% of their trade happens via these waters. This is especially true of China, which is the foremost trading nation in the world.[2]

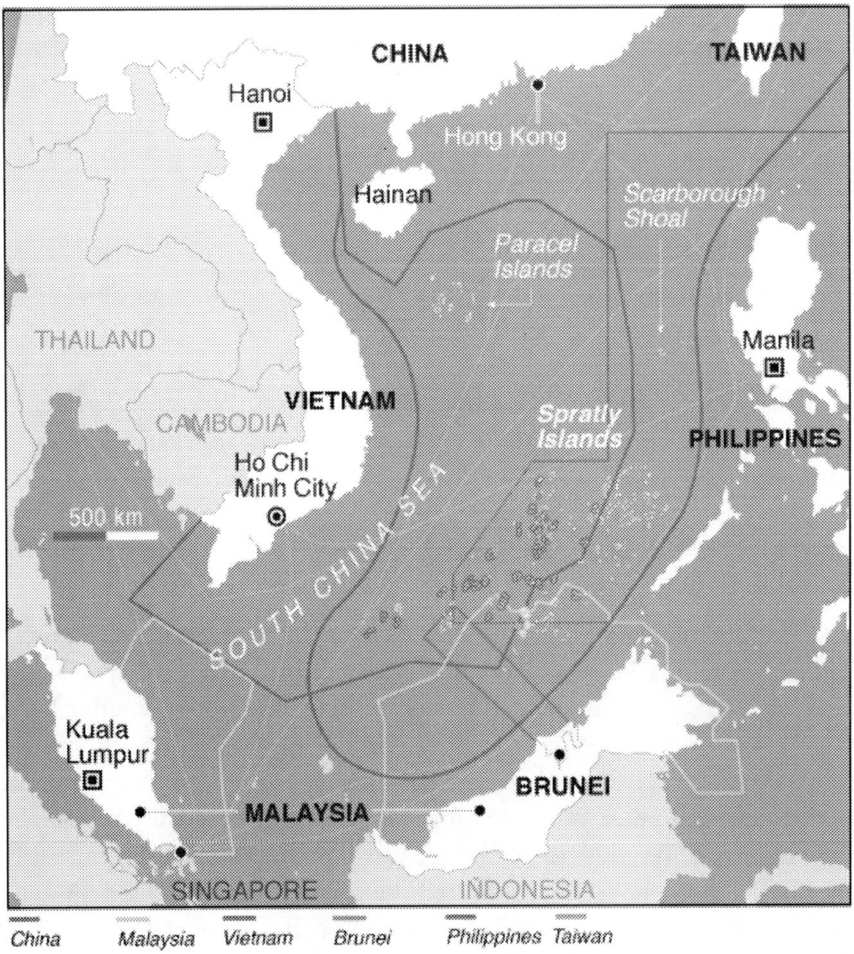

Figure 4.1. The Map of the SCS

(*Source:* http://blogs.voanews.com/state-department-news/2012/07/31/challenging-beijing-in-the-south-china-sea/)

The SCS is also an important maritime conduit to the world with substantial traffic of up to 60,000 ships per annum, to and from the Malacca Straits—a vital choke point. It connects the Indian and Pacific Ocean economic system, which has markets at one end and resources at the other. Any disturbance to this Indo-Pacific system can upset the global economy.

China, along with India, was the leading economic power of the globe with China peaking in 1820[3] and declining thereafter till reforms commenced in the 1970s. It faced a 'century of humiliation' from colonisers who came through the sea and carved up enclaves, or like Japan, which colonised China. The People's Republic of China (PRC), which is its modern avatar, is extremely conscious of this maritime underbelly. So much so, that the Long March was directed away from the coast as a part of its people's war philosophy. Albeit, that was an astute move by Mao, to avoid the strength of the imperialists and capitalists on the littorals and to lure them deep into the rural interiors.

The Disputes over the SCS

The SCS has over two hundred land features in separate groups, most of which are presently being contested. They belong to the Pratas, Paracel and the Spratly Island groups, Scarborough and James Shoals and the Macclesfield Bank. China, Vietnam, Indonesia, Taiwan, the Philippines, Brunei and Malaysia are involved in bilateral and multilateral disputes over the various features or the entitled seas around them. Among all the disputes, the Spratly Islands group involves the most number of claimants including China, Malaysia, the Philippines, Taiwan and Vietnam. Paracels, the northern group of islands, is disputed between China, Taiwan and Vietnam.

Over and above the contests over these small features, there is a unique claim from China known as the 'nine-dashed line'. The Spratly Islands lie within the so called nine-dashed line. This is a Chinese cartographic feature which dates back to a 1947 map produced during the Nationalist rule. The political rivalry between the Communists and Nationalists has only made matters more complex as the records and rationale behind the line are held with Taiwan.[4] The modern version of this nine-dashed line did not surface till 2009. That year, China submitted the present avatar of the nine-dashed line in its *note verbale* to the UN, in response to a continental shelf claim by Vietnam and the Philippines.[5] Over the years the 'dashes' that constitute the line have varied both in numbers and positions.[6] Two dashes in the Gulf of Tonkin Bay were deleted, as China settled that portion of the claim with Vietnam, whereas an additional dash was added near Taiwan. China, since

2012, has also issued passports with a map which includes the nine-dashed line,[7] as if to tattoo this map into domestic and international consciousness.

But there is one problem. The UNCLOS ***does not*** recognise such a line over water. Hence, the SCS disputes have two main issues: national ownership of land features within the nine-dashed line, as well as the legality and interpretation of the infamous nine-dashed line. There are obviously certain geopolitical reasons too for such a claim, which will also be covered in this chapter.

The Laws of the Sea

The UNCLOS is the successor of the laws of the ocean, first articulated as *mare liberum,* which was mentioned at the beginning of this chapter. The concept got refined over a period, resulting in the ***cannon shot*** or the 'three mile rule' – based on distance from the shore where coastal states had sovereign rights. Growing marine activities demanded a constant revision of these rules. The UNCLOS conferences that commenced in 1958 were held to meet this requirement. The convention took thirty-six years of negotiations to finally come into force in 1994. China and all the parties involved in the SCS disputes are signatories of the UNCLOS. The most notable country that is not a signatory to the UNCLOS is the USA. The USA adheres to the principles of the UNCLOS but is not a party due to its reservations with regard to the UNCLOS's Seabed Convention. Some tenets of the UNCLOS relevant to the dispute are as follows (Refer Fig 4. 2):

- A country's entitlements over sea stem from its ownership of adjacent land. This is the doctrine of "*la terredomine la mer*" or that the *land dominates the sea.* In simpler terms, an entitlement over the seas doesn't accrue without ownership of land.
- The extent and rights of entitlement over sea varies in dimension and scope from 12 nm territorial rights to 350 nm economic rights for a continental shelf claim.
- Land features such as rocks, drying heights, reefs and islands may confer entitlements to the adjacent sea. To limit such claims, they have to qualify certain criteria such as its natural condition, capability to sustain habitation or economic life. For example, rocks above high water that do not fulfil these criteria do not confer economic rights up to 200 nm, but only to a 12 nm territorial sea around them.
- Small features such as rocks that are visible only during low water [Low Tide Elevations (LTE)], do not provide entitlement over the sea, nor can they be appropriated by occupation.

- The UNCLOS had also accounted for *historic claims* during its formulation. Pre-existing rights to resources were considered, but not adopted by the convention. Such rights were extinguished with provisions of the Exclusive Economic Zone (EEZ)/Continental Shelf (CS) in the UNCLOS.
- The UNCLOS defines an archipelagic regime exclusively for states that exist as a group of islands, such as Indonesia and the Philippines. They have provisions for an archipelagic baseline and internal waters inside them (Refer fig 4.2). The archipelagic regime also has a qualifying criterion in terms of a ratio between land and water.[8]
- The degrees of freedom of passage vary, depending on the nature of waters, i.e., internal, territorial, straits, and high seas.

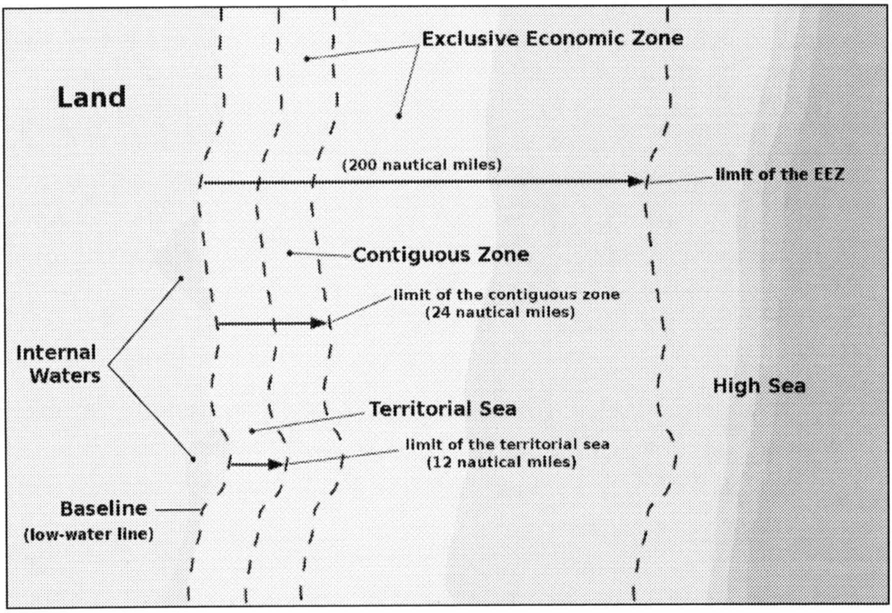

Figure 4.2. UNCLOS Maritime Zones[9]

(*Source:* By Antonioptg (Own work) [CC BY-SA 4.0 (http://creativecommons.org/licenses/by-sa/4.0)], via Wikimedia Commons)

The UNCLOS also provides for various dispute resolution mechanisms. States could choose one or more designated organisations for settling disputes, including the International Tribunal for the Law of the Sea (ITLOS), the International Court of Justice or Arbitral Tribunals.

A Brief History of Disputes

There are several reasons for the SCS disputes. First, the nations in the region were decolonised post-World War II and they emerged with incipient perceptions about their entitlements and inadequate maritime capacities. Oceans were a new frontier for the new states and maritime capacities and awareness increased only with economic growth. The UNCLOS negotiations enhanced this process. One trigger was the discovery of oil in the Spratly Islands in the 1970s. The presence of reefs and shoals also meant that the area was abundant in fish—a significant source of protein for the countries in the region. China is the top fish producer globally, producing ten times as much as India, the second largest producer.[10] In the late 1990s, the tiger economies of South East Asia and then China, grew phenomenally, relying on trade as well as energy flows through the SCS. As the significance of the SCS grew, the disputes also turned bitter.

China and North Vietnam fought a bitter naval battle over the Paracel Island group in 1974, resulting in a Chinese control over these islands. In 1988, China clashed with Vietnam over the Johnson Reef, killing 64 Vietnamese soldiers.[11] The disputes got even more accentuated, once the UNCLOS came into force in 1994, with the Philippines becoming an archipelago and claiming several features. By 2002, astute diplomacy yielded a declaration of conduct in the SCS between the ASEAN and the PRC, which provided some mechanisms to ease tensions. Fifteen years later, they have agreed to prepare a framework for the rules of conduct at the Guiyang meet in May 2017.[12] The delay is a measure of the complications involved.

Most nations in the SCS commenced the building up and reclamation the features in their possession. Some of this infrastructure development was with a military perspective to create garrisons and airfields and some were to improve habitability. In retrospect, they also altered the natural state of the features reclaiming a total of approximately 3,300 acres, of which 3,000[13] acres was accounted for by the Chinese. One chief incentive of the build-up was an expectation to alter the natural features to increase the entitlements of the surrounding seas.

As an aside to the territorial disputes, Freedom of Navigation (FoN) became another flashpoint in the SCS. The FoN operations are a US initiative that routinely challenges national claims beyond the UNCLOS the world over, including those of the US allies. The EP3 Aircraft incident in 2001 in the Hainan Island[14] and the USNS *Impeccable* incident in 2009[15] added a new dimension to the SCS. Not only was the SCS a hotbed for territorial disputes, but also became a zone where differing interpretations of the UNCLOS between the US and China regarding freedom of overflight and navigation through the EEZ started playing up. These are also signs of a shift in balance of power, triggering the US pivot to Asia in 2011.

Arbitration

The territorial disputes kept simmering till early 2013 when the Philippines chose the arbitration route, through the Permanent Court of Arbitration at The Hague. This is an intergovernmental body established by treaty in 1899, which has administered a majority of the UNCLOS arbitrations to date.

What was notable in the case was that the Philippines, instead of directly taking the matter of history and ownership of the contested features, took the route of interpretation of the UNCLOS as the core matter of the case.[16] This was an astute strategy, primarily since the tribunal has no mandate to award sovereignty or delineation. Two core questions from the Philippines comprised the legality as per the UNCLOS of '*Historic Rights and the 'Nine-Dash Line'* and the '*Status of Features*' in the Spratly Islands. From these two core questions emerged the *lawfulness of Chinese actions*. It also raised the issues of *aggravation of the dispute* and *harm to the environment* in its submission.[17]

China abstained from the arbitration, instead indicating its views and non-acceptance of arbitration through position papers.[18] Yet, the hearing proceeded, as according to the UNCLOS, "*absence of a party or failure of a party to defend its case shall not constitute a bar to the proceedings*". The tribunal initially decided on the admissibility and jurisdiction of the case in October 2015 and awarded the final verdict against the nine-dashed line in July 2016. As expected, China rejected the verdict.[19]

The Award

The award of the Tribunal on the core issues, was as follows:[20]

- ***Historic Rights and the 'Nine-Dash Line'.***
  - ***'Nine-Dash Line'.*** The scope of entitlement is defined by the UNCLOS. Claims in excess by China are invalid regarding the nine-dashed line.
  - **Comments.** An entitlement over sea originates from the ownership of land. The waters in contest are more than 350 miles away from the Chinese mainland, beyond the maximum zone of entitlement (i.e. the Continental Shelf). Therefore, the Chinese entitlement

around the Spratly Islands, if any, would emerge from the ownership of features within it and not the dashed line over water. China has not yet explained the dashed line, clarifying any of the following likely meanings of that line, listed in order of severity over the freedom of seas.[21]

- * As a national border with sovereign rights over features, water and subsoil within that line
  - Its effect—Severely challenge the UNCLOS and global order.
- * As a line to indicate that all or some features within it, belong to China. An argument, put forth by scholars like Wu Shicun, head of National Institute for South China Sea Studies.[22]
  - Its effect—Challenging the UNCLOS and regional order.
- * As an indication of certain historic non-exclusive rights, short of sovereignty.
  - Its effect—Challenging the UNCLOS and regional order. It is here that the historical aspect of the claim becomes relevant.

- ***History and UNCLOS***. The Tribunal award stated that during the formulation, the UNCLOS had considered historic rights, but they were not adopted. These rights are deemed to be subsumed and extinguished within the EEZ rules. It then stated that though Chinese navigators and fishermen historically made use of the islands, there was no evidence that it historically exercised exclusive control over these waters or their resources. The tribunal, therefore, concluded that there is no legal basis for China to claim historic rights or exclusive rights to resources within sea areas of the nine-dashed line.
- **Comments**. Under the UNCLOS I, historic rights could be claimed in respect of historic *bays* and historic *waters*.[23] Both pertain to sovereignty over sea areas, with certain well-defined quantifiable as well as subjective criteria, qualifying them as either territorial sea or internal waters. In these cases, a claimant has to establish notoriety and continuous, effective control, besides an acquiescence of foreign states in the exercise of that authority.[24] In distinguishing between historic water, title and rights, there is an interpretation that historic 'water' or historic 'title' are about sovereignty whereas historic 'rights' are a lesser set of rights.[25]

- ***Status of Features***. The tribunal considered the features next. As described earlier, an island, rock or a low tide elevation accrues different entitlements over water. The principal test for the feature was its capacity in the natural state to *sustain human habitation or an economic life of their own.* The conclusion of the tribunal from present and historic evidence was that none of the Spratly Island features were islands.

  - ***Implications and Comments.*** This meant that none of the Spratly features generated an EEZ or continental shelf claim, irrespective of ownership by ***any*** nation, thus freeing up a very large area for global commons. To illustrate the effect of the verdict—if they were awarded the status of 'islands', then a theoretical island with a negligible area, or a 'point island', would generate 1,25,600sq nm of EEZ (3.14×200×200 nm^2); the same feature if classified as a rock would generate 452 sq nm of territorial seas (3.14×12×12 nm^2).[26] The verdict also meant that certain sea areas were part of the Philippines EEZ since they were not within the 'possible' entitlement of China. Additionally, since no EEZ would be generated by the Spratly Islands, the Chinese claims on the restrictions on the freedom of navigation within an EEZ would also be invalid around those features.

- ***Other Awards.*** The three other awards, which were highly relevant to the Philippines, that emerged from the above core awards were:
  - China had violated the Philippines' sovereign rights in its EEZ and the Chinese law enforcement vessels had unlawfully posed a serious risk of collision when they physically obstructed the Philippine vessels.
  - China had caused severe harm to the coral reef environment and violated its obligation to preserve and protect fragile ecosystems and the habitat of depleted, threatened, or endangered species.
  - China had aggravated the dispute, by reclaiming land and carrying out construction activities during dispute resolution.
- Apart from the core and subsidiary awards, it also clarified that Low Tide Elevations (LTE) cannot be appropriated by occupation, which discourages that route to expand national claims. This could affect the Subi Reef, the Hughes Reef and the Mischief Reef which have been found to be LTEs, where China is presently building artificial features.
- A tabular summary of awards is placed in Table 4.1.

Responses

International responses were along expected lines, mostly in a measured and diplomatically acceptable tone. Even domestic responses within the affected nations were muted and controlled.

- **China.** The Chinese response to the tribunal award was by portraying it as '*a political farce under the pretext of law*'. Post-arbitration, it stated that the award is *null and void* with no *binding force* and that China *has neither accepted nor recognized it.* The entire event offered some indications of the Chinese scheme. It had already crafted a response, one alluding to the existence of internal waters in the SCS taking the archipelagic/historic route for legitimising what is within the nine-dashes.[27] A white paper was also released with copious historic details and accompanying infographics reinforcing its historic claim. Both responses fell short in their content to counter the logic of the verdict apart from hardening the historical route to the claim. In an attempt to gain support, China also incorrectly interpreted the joint Russia-India-China statement[28] as a measure of Indian and Russian support.[29] Pakistan and Taiwan were the notable supporters of China.
- **India.** The Indian statement mentioned the following:[30]
  - It expressed support to the freedom of navigation, overflight and unimpeded commerce.
  - It encouraged respect for international law and the UNCLOS.
  - India sought resolution of disputes using peaceful means without the use of force or threats and sought self-restraint in not complicating disputes.
- **The Philippines.** The dynamics in the Philippines also underwent a change. Its new President Duterte had been busy at home with a questionable severity on the crackdown on drugs. It also risked a fallout with its ally, the USA, with sound bites touching the nadir of civility. The mood was to mend equations with China and the chief interlocutor, ex-President Fidel Ramos, engaged in negotiations to normalise relations with China. The official Philippine reactions were also restrained.[31] This appeared a case of domestic compulsions driving the China policy in a different direction away from its earlier path that had led it to the tribunal. The Philippines was then undertaking a severe law and order crackdown initiated by the new President that bordered on human rights violations. Amidst pressures regarding this crackdown, he needed friends, and found a ready one in China. Hanoi, too clamped down on anti-China protests.[32]

- President Trump's China policy will also be crucial to the South China Sea. Unlike the previous Presidents who used economy as a balancer in relations, Trump has been overtly critical of the Chinese monetary policies which according to him hurt the US business. He has shown lesser interest in managing the globe putting US allies in the region in some doubt about a continued support from the US. However, his phone call to the Taiwanese President broke several conventions, much to the chagrin of China. In a tweet supporting his phone call in early December 2016, he equated this call to China's currency policy, tariffs on US goods and the Chinese military build-up in the South China Sea. His response to the capture of the US drone by China was ambivalent. He initially accused the Chinese of 'stealing' a captured US drone, but soon tweeted indifferently—'let them keep it!'!' President Duterte, who had given less importance to the tribunal verdict thus far, also warmed up to the new US leadership. Amidst these mixed signals and events, a new policy is yet to become discernible. The Trump administration's first FoN patrol, as per reports, occurred in May 2017 with the USS *Dewey* at the Mischief Reef.[33] Even with this FONOPS, the messaging has been mixed, with very little official communication from Washington.[34] Such ambiguities have also had political impacts. One such impact is that some of the US's close allies like Japan have considered joining the Belt and Road Initiative, sensing the shifting grounds.[35] This is a remarkable shift compared to Japan's position two years back. It had promised USD 110 billion in aid to Asia when the AIIB was inaugurated with a corpus of USD 100 billion.[36]

A Geopolitical Perspective

It is essential to examine in retrospect as to why China is undertaking contrarian actions after signing the UNCLOS in 1996. Its late maritime and national resurgence, geography and historical actions in the continent, partly answer that puzzle. It appears that just as it had created a continental buffer around a Han core by annexing Xinjiang, Tibet and Inner Mongolia in the initial days of the PRC, it is currently in the process of creating a maritime buffer zone in the SCS. Though it is a geographic buffer, it is a vital area called a political *core,*[37] albeit in unofficial parlance, due to several reasons.

- The SCS holds reasonable reserves of oil and gas. However, this is not such a voluminous treasure to risk poor relations in the entire neighbourhood, says Tom Miller in the book, *China's Asian Dream*. At 11 billion barrels, it can barely meet the Chinese needs for a few years, given China's consumption.[38]

- As the largest consumer of fish in the world, with a depleting fish stock in the Chinese EEZ, the SCS is a source of food and livelihood for China.
- The US Pivot to East Asia, partially in response to the SCS events, has accentuated that insecurity. The basing plan of the Littoral Combat Ships in Singapore and those of the Marines at Darwin in Australia, are two specific events of the pivot.
- These disputed areas are next to the Hainan Island which is the main naval base with nuclear submarines and latest ships of the navy. The control of the SCS will provide greater defence in depth, preventing threats from approaching close to the Chinese coast.
- The SCS is extremely vital to China's trade and energy flows. This is especially important to sustain the legitimacy of the Communist Party with the '*new normal*' of slow economic growth. Even a minor disturbance to trade flows can cause severe imbalance, with a political price to pay. The criticality of it came about when the Malacca Dilemma was reinforced by President Hu Jintao in 2003.[39] A greater control of the SCS is vital to mitigate that dilemma.
- Of all explanations of the SCS issue, Robert D. Kaplan puts it most accurately. The SCS, he says, is the vital area leading to the Malacca Straits enabling a *two ocean strategy*. Kaplan also finds a parallel. He equates it to the Caribbean Sea which was critical to the US's Two Ocean presence with the construction of the Panama Canal.[40] Tom Miller of Gavekal too believes that shipping routes are the real reason for China's SCS policy and endorses this in his book..[41]
- The Maritime Silk Road, which has now come to formally represent the Chinese intentions to expand their tentacles westwards, has underlined the need for a greater control of the SCS. The interesting irony is that as Kaplan compares China's actions in the South China Sea to a two-ocean strategy induced by the making of the Panama Canal, the reality today is that container terminals at Balboa and Cristobal at either end of Panama are operated by Chinese firms[42] and China is contemplating a parallel canal in Nicaragua,[43] rivalling the Panama Canal. This is apart from Panama itself switching recognition to China from Taiwan.[44] Much water seems to have flown in the canal!

- There are several military initiatives by China in the South China Sea which are a cause of concern:
  - China has built air strips and radar stations on the three features of the Spratly Islands (Fiery Cross, Subi and Mischief) and the Woody Island in Paracel islands, which additionally has a SAM battery. Spratly airfields have hanger facility for 24 combat aircraft whereas the Woody Island can house 16 combat aircraft. China test-fired a cruise missile also from the Woody Island. The militarisation has continued unabated, during and after the verdict, with the Woody Island serving as a template for the rest of the Chinese ventures. As far as the other nations' airfields are concerned, Vietnam constructed the Spratly Island airfield in 1976,[45] the Philippines built one on the Thitu Island in 1978, Malaysia built one in 1983 on the Swallow Reef and Taiwan built the Itu Aba in 2006.[46]
  - The previous chapter also discussed the fleet that China is building, with new types of ships like the Jiangdao-class, which are cheaper to build and which can bolster the constabulary role of the PLA Navy. The Jiangdao-class ships are being built in large numbers and can act in concert with the Coast Guard and other civilian vessels including fishing vessels.
  - This is a new phenomenon wherein civilian ships are the first line of action. Here it is important to note that the law regarding shipbuilding standards is being amended for a better civil–military interface.[47] Such a new law envisages the use of a maritime 'militia', where civilian ships built to specifications can contribute to maritime security initiatives.
  - The State Oceanic Administration has multiple ocean-related security agencies which have been merged for a better management of oceans.[48]
  - The domestic maritime safety law is being amended for the first time after the UNCLOS came into force.[49]

Steps to Control the Buffer

China has used a dual-pronged approach to control this buffer, the SCS. On the one hand, China is purporting that the waters within the 'nine-dash line' are internal waters based on a historic claim. This route, utilising a historic claim to provide rights over such a vast area of sea is very rare, and is presently being adopted by China. Chinese statements reiterate the *historic* claim in an effort to give a fillip to its 'rights' over these waters.[50] In fact, the Chinese post-tribunal response invokes history over twenty times, whereas the UNCLOS mentions history just twice, that too in a text ten times as voluminous. This revisionist tendency is extremely dangerous for a global maritime order created over a period based on the UNCLOS. China's aim appears to convert the SCS into a zone where it has higher degree of control than what is allowed by the UNCLOS. Among the maritime zones within the ambit of the UNCLOS, 'internal *waters*', offer the highest degree of navigational control.[51] They are usually landwards of 'baseline' or within the boundaries of an archipelago.[52] The geography of contested waters in the SCS cannot legally become internal waters to China since:

- It is not landwards of any Chinese baseline.
- The creation of an archipelagic base line is an exclusive privilege of an *archipelagic* state[53] such as Indonesia or Philippines, unlike China with a continental mainland.
- The tribunal has also ruled that the Spratly Islands do not fulfil the stringent, quantifiable archipelago criterion as per the UNCLOS on their own, even if the features were deemed as a single entity.

Yet, the three significant post-tribunal Chinese responses on the *sovereignty* and the award of the Tribunal by Chinese Foreign Minister Wang Yi[54], the Government[55] and the White Paper,[56] describe the SCS as *internal* waters!

China's reclamation and building process in the Spratlys group is being carried out on the Subi Reef, Fiery Cross Reef, Mischief Reef, Johnson Reef, Hughes Reef, Gaven Reefs and Cuarteron Reef, whilst, the creation or claim over features provide measurable methods of control; however, these claims would not be as extensive as those of historic waters and will be restricted by the UNCLOS. These claims would however, superimpose over the claim to buttress the issue that the waters within the 'nine-dash line' are internal waters.

Therefore, while the tribunal has rejected the historic claim being made by China, China has not accepted that verdict and has continued to stick to its views. China has also occupied various features in the SCS through reclamation, thus providing a fallback option for claims which will be supported by ground realities as possession is nine tenths the law![57] That must explain the logic of island building.

Implications of the Award

The most significant implication of the award is that it clarified several issues to a wider audience, hitherto not available from a legal perspective.

- To the affected parties it has offered a legal respite. The Tribunal established the right of the Philippines to seek redressal even though China was not party to the arbitration.
- It established that making historic claims based on a modern narrative was illegal. It has clarified that *"there was no legal basis for China to claim historic rights to resources within the sea areas falling within the 'nine-dash line'."* Further, the tribunal has awarded that such rights were considered and deemed extinguished when the EEZs were decided.
- By awarding that the subject features are not islands but rocks and low tide elevations, it has freed huge water space for use as global commons.

This award serves as a precedence and reference to further resolutions of disputes in the region. However, since this award did not judge on sovereignty, it leaves that question open for resolution between the affected parties. Here, China's insistence of a bilateral approach to resolution takes a leaf off the bourgeoisie rule-book to diminish the power of collective bargaining, especially considering the power differential between China and the individual nations involved in the dispute.

The verdict has affected China's claim to adherence to the rule of law and peaceful development. Even though it abstained and rejected the verdict as a "farce", it reacted throughout the proceedings through position papers, public hearings across nations and newspaper advertisements in a communication campaign.

As a cue for the road ahead for the world, it is good to recall that power in global politics will remain diffused in the future.[58] This is also one reason why adherence to law becomes all the more important. Such an international society, where the law runs the writ, will devolve less power to hegemons and prevent blatant infringements. Archaic concepts like buffer zones have proven to be part of problem rather than the solution. The efforts must be towards a rule-based, equitable cooperative construct to emerge as we transition to a new order. It would be ideal and augur well for China as a responsible global power to scale down the actions and take lead in a cooperative, oceanic regime based on rule of law with all stakeholders. That would assuage some of its own insecurities as much as those of the others.

The award will positively affect the rule of law for oceans. So far, members of the Security Council including the USA have shown little respect to previous arbitrations,[59] whereas, middle powers have amicably settled issues by arbitration irrespective of the size of the countries involved, as in the case of the India–Bangladesh Settlement.[60] China has portrayed the Philippines action as a proxy initiative by the USA. It is relevant here that the USA, a non-party to the convention, was not allowed to be a part of the Tribunal hearings. It is time that the USA became a party to the UNCLOS and strengthen the regime in a world which is becoming increasingly multipolar. As Bill Hayton states, the irony of it all is that China has ratified the UNCLOS but doesn't adhere to it, whereas the US has not ratified but adheres to most of its provisions!

The Chinese internal situation is presently marked by a powerful President, an anti-corruption campaign which has shaken its polity, an economic slowdown and a painful transition of the economic model to a service and domestic consumption-oriented one. Such a transition makes any nationalist issue sensitive. The SCS can become a rallying point for the Chinese domestic constituency. Despite etching the 'nine-dashed line' on public consciousness through passports, China has so far clamped down on public response.[61] It can ill-afford any popular uprisings, as previous experiences indicate that such events quickly spin out of control and attain a different scale and direction.

The SCS has so far not been officially elevated to the status of a core[62] issue unlike Taiwan, Tibet and Xinjiang. Yet its responses evoking historical rights and reclamation of features are signs that the issue is far from over. The 'verdict' was one window of opportunity, to tone down the rhetoric as a first step to an eventual settlement. It remains to be seen how far China would push the envelope in the matter, as the 'nine-dashed line' has become too well known for it to be easily erased from public memory and hence could remain. However, the PRC can alter its interpretations to suit the verdict for non-exclusive rights such as those over Scarborough Shoals or the joint development route that it seeks as per the UNCLOS.[63]

Some Scenarios

China's choices in this regard could be the following:

- As a future global power that accords high priority to the rule of law within China, the award by the Tribunal offers an opportunity to shape the world where it is a major stakeholder. That means giving up of the planned maritime buffer and some accentuation of its perceived insecurity. This can be balanced by a cooperative maritime regime under ASEAN mechanisms. This option may not be easy to settle into for China. A powerful President may be able convince the security czars of the benefits of such an option. The main challenge will be to explain the 'nine-dashed line' in a manner to suit its domestic law and the international law.

- China can disregard the Tribunal awards and continue with island building, with or without withdrawing from the UNCLOS. This is the most dangerous option that can destabilise the whole region. This is an aggressive measure that China can ill-afford and may avoid, considering the deep stakes in the global economic system that relies on order.
- China can hold on to the features it presently controls but stop the ocean geo-engineering projects. This will win it diplomatic manoeuvring room in the region. China would have, in any case, achieved partial strategic success with the build-up. This could be its most likely plan of action.

Conclusion

Whatever be its choice, it appears that the issue is far from over, considering the stakes involved. India and the world must encourage the parties to resolve disputes through peaceful means without use of force and for them to exercise self-restraint based on the principles of the UNCLOS. For a stable order, law needs to be upheld above short-term politics. As China's sphere of influence is expanding, its actions in the SCS have also hardened over time. As far as the Indian Ocean is concerned, the SCS is vital for access between oceans and a smooth flow of commerce in the Indo-Pacific system. It is therefore vital for all IOR nations with an annual trade flow worth USD 5 trillion.

The Dutch seizure of the Portuguese carrack *Santa Catarina* in the South China Sea, four hundred years ago, provided the world with a liberal law of the sea. However in this unfortunate rhyme of history, China wants to unlearn those hard-learned lessons of law through the dashed line about which China itself has very little clarity!

Table 4.1. Submissions and Tribunal Awards (Summarised from the Award)

No.	Submission by The Philippines	Tribunal Award
1	The Maritime Claim of China may not extend beyond what is permissible in the UNCLOS	Scope of entitlement is defined by the UNCLOS. Claims in excess by China are invalid.
2	China's claims to sovereign rights, jurisdiction and to 'historic rights', especially within the 'nine-dash line' are contrary to the UNCLOS.	Pre-existing rights to resources were considered, but not adopted by the convention. Such rights were extinguished with provisions of the EEZ/CS in the UNCLOS. There is no legal basis for China to claim 'historic rights' to resources within the sea areas falling within the 'nine-dash line'.
3	Scarborough Shoal has no entitlement of EEZ/CS	Scarborough Shoal is a rock. Rocks have no entitlement of EEZ/CS.
4	Mischief Reef, Second Thomas Shoal, and Subi Reef, being low-tide elevations (LTE) have no entitlements	They are LTE and therefore with no entitlement; further. They are not features that are capable of appropriation by occupation.
5	Mischief Reef and Second Thomas Shoal are within the EEZ/CS of the Philippines	They are LTE and therefore with no entitlement. Further, they are within the EEZ of the Philippines.
6	Gaven Reef and McKennan Reef (including Hughes Reef) are low-tide elevations	They are LTE and therefore with no entitlement.
7	Johnson Reef, Cuarteron Reef and Fiery Cross Reef have no entitlement to EEZ/CS	They are rocks. Rocks have no entitlement for EEZ/CS.
8	China has unlawfully interfered with the sovereign rights of the Philippines with respect to its EEZ and CS	China has violated the sovereign rights with respect to the EEZ/CS of the Philippines under the UNCLOS.
9	China has unlawfully failed to prevent its nationals and vessels from exploiting the living resources in the exclusive economic zone of the Philippines.	China has unlawfully breached its obligations under the UNCLOS and failed to prevent its nationals and vessels from exploiting the EEZ of the Philippines.
10	China has unlawfully prevented Philippine fishermen from pursuing their livelihood in the Scarborough Shoal.	Fishermen from the Philippines (like those from China) had traditional fishing rights at Scarborough Shoal and China has interfered with these rights in restricting access.
11	China has unlawfully violated its obligations under the Convention to protect and preserve the marine environment at Scarborough Shoal, Second Thomas Shoal, Cuarteron Reef, Fiery Cross Reef, Gaven Reef, Johnson Reef, Hughes Reef and Subi Reef	China has caused severe harm to the coral reef environment and violated its obligation to preserve and protect fragile ecosystems, as well as the habitat of depleted, threatened, or endangered species under the UNCLOS.
12	China has unlawfully occupied and carried out construction activities on Mischief Reef.	China has unlawfully breached Articles under the UNCLOS. As a low-tide elevation, Mischief Reef is not capable of appropriation by occupation.
13	Chinese law enforcement vessels have manoeuvred in a dangerous manner, causing serious risk of collision to Philippine vessels navigating in the vicinity of Scarborough Shoal	Chinese law enforcement vessels had unlawfully created a serious risk of collision when they physically obstructed Philippine vessels violating Collision Regulations and, as a consequence, breached Article under the UNCLOS.
14	China has unlawfully aggravated the case since the commencement of arbitration	China has unlawfully aggravated the dispute by dredging, artificial island-building, and construction activities and destroyed evidence of the natural condition of features in the SCS that formed part of the Parties' dispute.
15	China shall respect the rights and freedoms of the Philippines under the Convention	Both Parties are obliged to comply with the UNCLOS.

NOTES

1. Award of PCA Case Nº 2013-19. In the Matter of the South China Sea Arbitration - before - an Arbitral Tribunal Constituted Under Annex VII to the 1982 United Nations Convention on the Law of the Sea- between -the Republic of the Philippines- and -the People's Republic Of China accessible at https://pca-cpa.org/wp-content/uploads/sites/175/2016/07/PH-CN-20160712-Award.pdf.
2. "WTO, 2015 Press Releases - Modest Trade Recovery to Continue in 2015 and 2016 Following Three Years of Weak Expansion accessed September 8, 2016, https://www.wto.org/english/news_e/pres15_e/pr739_e.htm.
3. For a quick look of the historic GDP shares refer graph at "Hello America," *The Economist*, August 16, 2010, http://www.economist.com/node/16834943. For historic Global GDP refer works of Angus Maddison at Groningen University. url http://www.ggdc.net/maddison/oriindex.htm
4. Bill Hayton, *The South China Sea: The Struggle for Power in Asia* (Yale University Press, 2014).
5. "Full Text: China Adheres to the Position of Settling Through Negotiation the Relevant Disputes Between China and the Philippines in the South China Sea," *Xinhua, English.news.cn*, accessed September 9, 2016, http://news.xinhuanet.com/english/china/2016-07/13/c_135509153.htm.
6. Limits in the Seas, No. 143 China: Maritime Claims in the South China Sea, United States Department of State Bureau of Oceans and International Environmental and Scientific Affairs
7. "China Stamps Passports with Sea Claims," accessed August 8, 2017, https://www.ft.com/content/7dc376c6-3306-11e2-aabc-00144feabdc0.
8. "Preamble to the United Nations Convention on the Law of the Sea," accessed June 12, 2017, http://www.un.org/depts/los/convention_agreements/texts/unclos/part4.htm.
9. "UNCLOS-En.png (1200×750)," accessed August 10, 2017, https://upload.wikimedia.org/wikipedia/commons/c/c8/UNCLOS-en.png.
10. "India Ranks No. 2 in Fish Production – but No. 1 China Is Ten Times Bigger," *The Telegraph*, accessed June 12, 2017, http://www.telegraphindia.com/1140909/jsp/frontpage/story_18816197.jsp.
11. "Spratly Islands Dispute Defines China-Vietnam Relations 25 Years after Naval Clash," *South China Morning Post*, August 10, 2017, http://www.scmp.com/news/asia/article/1192472/spratly-islands-dispute-defines-china-vietnam-relations-25-years-after.
12. Laura Zhou, "China and Asean Agree to Draft Code of Conduct in South China Sea," *South China Morning Post*, May 18, 2017, http://www.cnbc.com/2017/05/18/china-and-asean-agree-to-draft-code-of-conduct-in-south-china-sea.html.
13. Ely Ratner, "Course Correction," *Foreign Affairs*, June 13, 2017, https://www.foreignaffairs.com/articles/2017-06-13/course-correction.
14. Elisabeth Rosenthal With David E. Sanger, "U.S. Plane in China After it Collides with Chinese Jet," *The New York Times*, April 2, 2001, sec. World, https://www.nytimes.com/2001/04/02/world/us-plane-in-china-after-it-collides-with-chinese-jet.html.
15. "U.S. Accuses the Chinese of Harassing Naval Vessel," *The New York Times*, March 9, 2009, sec. Asia Pacific, https://www.nytimes.com/2009/03/09/world/asia/09iht-ship.3.20710715.html.
16. Hayton, *The South China Sea.*
17. For details read https://pca-cpa.org/wp-content/uploads/sites/175/2016/07/PH-CN-20160712-Award.pdf
18. Position papers available at http://www.fmprc.gov.cn/nanhai/eng/snhwtlcwj_1/

19. For details of statement by PRC at http://www.fmprc.gov.cn/nanhai/eng/snhwtlcwj_1/t1379492.htm
20. "PCA Case Nº 2013-19. In the Matter of the South China Sea Arbitration Before an Arbitral Tribunal Constituted Under Annex VII to the 1982 United Nations Convention on the Law of the Sea Between the Republic of the Philippines and the People's Republic of China Registry: Permanent Court of Arbitration PH-CN-20160712-Award.pdf," accessed July 18, 2016, https://pca-cpa.org/wp-content/uploads/sites/175/2016/07/PH-CN-20160712-Award.pdf.
21. Refer Limits in the Seas, No. 143 China: Maritime Claims in the South China Sea, United States Department of State Bureau of Oceans and International Environmental and Scientific Affairs
22. Hannah Beech, "Just Where Exactly Did China Get Its Nine-Dash Line From?," *Time*, July 19, 2016, http://time.com/4412191/nine-dash-line-9-south-china-sea/.
23. Historic Bays: Memorandum by the Secretariat of the United Nations, United Nations Conference on the Law of the Sea, document A/CONF.13/1 Source : http://legal.un.org/diplomaticconferences/lawofthesea-1958/docs/english/vol_I/4_A-CONF-13-1_PrepDocs_vol_I_e.pdf
24. Juridical régime of historic waters, including historic bays, Extract from the Yearbook of the International Law Commission 1962 , vol. II
25. For detailed discussion read Limits of the Seas, No 143, ibid
26. Hayton, *The South China Sea.*
27. "Statement of the Government of the People's Republic of China on China's Territorial Sovereignty and Maritime Rights and Interests in the South China Sea," accessed July 17, 2016, http://www.fmprc.gov.cn/mfa_eng/zxxx_662805/t1379493.shtml.
28. "Joint Communiqué of the 14th Meeting of the Foreign Ministers of the Russian Federation, the Republic of India and the People's Republic of China," accessed August 10, 2017, http://mea.gov.in/bilateral-documents.htm?dtl/26628/Joint_Communiqu_of_the_14th_Meeting_of_the_ Foreign_Ministers_of_the_Russian_Federation_the_Republic_of_India_and_the_Peoples_ Republic_of_China.
29. "India with Us on Verdict, Says China," *The Hindu*, accessed July 17, 2016, http://www.thehindu.com/news/national/india-with-us-on-verdict-says-china/article8850469.ece.
30. Statement on Award of Arbitral Tribunal on South China Sea Under Annexure VII of UNCLOS http://www.mea.gov.in/pressreleases.htm?dtl/27019/Statement+on+Award+of+Arbitral+ Tribunal+on+South+China+Sea+Under+Annexure+VII+of+UNCLOS
31. "Philippines Urges 'restraint and Sobriety' after South China Sea Ruling," *The Economic Times*, accessed July 20, 2016, http://economictimes.indiatimes.com/default-subsec/defence/philippines-urges-restraint-and-sobriety-after-south-china-sea-ruling/articleshow/53172579.cms.
32. "Hanoi Clamps down on Protests against China after Ruling," *Taipei Times*, accessed July 20, 2016, http://www.taipeitimes.com/News/front/archives/2016/07/18/2003651263.
33. Tom Mitchell and Demetri Sevastopulo, "US Navy Conducts First Operation in South China Sea under Trump," *Financial Times*, May 25, 2017, https://www.ft.com/content/6662b665-07d2-304c-b25b-51d1748b1c83.
34. "The US Conducts the First South China Sea Freedom of Navigation Operation of the Trump Era, But It Was 'Off the Record,'" *Lawfare*, May 25, 2017, https://lawfareblog.com/us-conducts-first-south-china-sea-freedom-navigation-operation-trump-era-it-was-record.
35. hermes, "Japan Open to Joining Belt and Road Push," Text, *The Straits Times* (June 6, 2017), http://www.straitstimes.com/asia/east-asia/japan-open-to-joining-belt-and-road-push.

36. "Japan Unveils $110 Billion Plan to Fund Asia Infrastructure, Eye on AIIB," *Reuters*, May 21, 2015, http://www.reuters.com/article/2015/05/21/us-japan-asia-investment-idUSKBN0O617G20150521.
37. China's Assertive Behaviour Part One: On "Core Interests" Michael D. Swaine
38. Tom Miller, *China's Asian Dream: Empire Building along the New Silk Road* (Zed Books, 2017).
39. "China's 'Malacca Dilemma'," *The Jamestown Foundation*, accessed August 2, 2015, http://www.jamestown.org/single/?no_cache=1&tx_ttnews%5Btt_news%5D=3943.
40. Robert D. Kaplan, *Asia's Cauldron: The South China Sea and the End of a Stable Pacific* (Random House Publishing Group, 2014).
41. Miller, *China's Asian Dream.*
42. "Hutchison Ports PPC – Balboa," *Hutchison Ports*, accessed June 13, 2017, /en/ports/world/panama-ports-company-port-of-balboa-ppc-balboa/.
43. Suzanne Daley, "Lost in Nicaragua, a Chinese Tycoon's Canal Project," *The New York Times*, April 3, 2016, sec. Americas, https://www.nytimes.com/2016/04/04/world/americas/nicaragua-canal-chinese-tycoon.html.
44. "Panama Establishes Ties with China, Ditches Taiwan in Win for Beijing," *Reuters*, June 13, 2017, http://www.reuters.com/article/us-panama-china-idUSKBN194054.
45. The group is named after this island
46. "Airpower in the South China Sea," *Asia Maritime Transparency Initiative*, accessed July 25, 2017, https://amti.csis.org/airstrips-scs/.
47. "New Rules Mean Ships Can Be Used by Military - China - Chinadaily.com.cn," accessed May 6, 2016, http://www.chinadaily.com.cn/china/2015-06/18/content_21036944.htm.
48. "Dragons Unite," *The Economist*, March 16, 2013, http://www.economist.com/news/china/21573607-protect-its-maritime-interests-china-setting-up-civilian-coastguard-dragons-unite.
49. "Proposed Changes to China's Maritime Safety Law and Compliance with UNCLOS," *Lawfare*, February 21, 2017, https://www.lawfareblog.com/proposed-changes-chinas-maritime-safety-law-and-compliance-unclos.
50. "Infographics: White Paper on Settling Disputes with Philippines," *Xinhua, English.news.cn*, accessed July 17, 2016, http://news.xinhuanet.com/english/photo/2016-07/13/c_135509723.htm.
51. Internal waters are landwards of Base line. Archipelagic states, which are only five in the world, can have internal waters depending upon their archipelagic baseline.
52. Article 47(1).
53. Article 47(1).
54. "Remarks by Chinese Foreign Minister Wang Yi on the Award of the So-Called Arbitral Tribunal in the South China Sea Arbitration," accessed September 9, 2016, http://www.fmprc.gov.cn/mfa_eng/zxxx_662805/t1380003.shtml.
55. "Full Text of Chinese Government Statement on China's Territorial Sovereignty and Maritime Rights and Interests in S. China Sea," *Xinhua, English.news.cn*, accessed September 9, 2016, http://news.xinhuanet.com/english/2016-07/12/c_135507754.htm.
56. "Full Text: China Adheres to the Position of Settling Through Negotiation the Relevant Disputes Between China and the Philippines in the South China Sea," *Xinhua, English.news.cn.*
57. "'Beati Sunt Possidentes' (Blessed Are Those in Possession): A Leitmotif for Chinese (& Pakistani) Statecraft," April 10, 2017, http://www.vifindia.org/article/2017/april/10/beati-sunt-possidentes-blessed-are-those-in-possession.
58. "Global Trends 2030," accessed November 12, 2015, http://www.dni.gov/index.php/about/organization/global-trends-2030.

59. Graham Allison Diplomat The, "Of Course China, Like All Great Powers, Will Ignore an International Legal Verdict," *The Diplomat*, accessed July 17, 2016, http://thediplomat.com/2016/07/of-course-china-like-all-great-powers-will-ignore-an-international-legal-verdict/.
60. "Kerry Praises India's Approach to Solve Maritime Disputes, Says No Military Solution to S China Sea Issue," *Latest News & Updates at Daily News & Analysis, DNA*, August 31, 2016, http://www.dnaindia.com/world/report-kerry-praises-india-s-approach-to-solve-maritime-disputes-says-no-military-solution-to-s-china-sea-issue-2250702.
61. Lucy Hornby, "Beijing Censors South China Sea Protest," *Financial Times*, July 18, 2016, http://www.ft.com/cms/s/0/2e3ec4fe-4c8c-11e6-8172-e39ecd3b86fc.html#axzz4EuVQQHL0.
62. Ibid.
63. Tim Daiss, "China, Philippines Reportedly Set to Agree on Joint South China Sea Oil Exploration," *Forbes*, accessed July 25, 2017, http://www.forbes.com/sites/timdaiss/2016/10/18/china-philippines-oil-deal-underway-in-south-china-sea-says-report/.

CHAPTER 5

THE STRATEGIC SPACE IN FOCUS: THE INDIAN OCEAN AND ITS SECURITY[1]

Introduction

Profits from trading in the Indian Ocean trade once attracted global powers to its shores, motivating the oldest recorded guide to the mariner in history-*The Periplus Maris Erythraei.*[2] It was about maritime voyages and trade in the Indian Ocean littorals. The secret behind the Indian Ocean's prosperity was a natural phenomenon called the monsoon, which assured rhythmic reversal of winds offering tremendous predictability to the sailor, the merchant and the farmer alike, forming a deep and sophisticated economic system along the ocean's rim. The Indian Ocean economic and cultural system had become the cynosure of Rome in the West as much as to Nanjing in the East two millennia ago. However, that network was partially overland across Middle East and North Africa. Parts of it were called the Silk Road which ended with the discovery of a direct sea route to India from Europe. The 400-year interregnum in history after Vasco da Gama's arrival on the Malabar coast of India altered the Indian Ocean's history. From being a destination of yore, the Indian Ocean today plays a major role as the connector of the Atlantic and Pacific Oceans which have been the twin hubs of global economic activity. History seems to be turning a full circle with littoral nations in the Indian Ocean Region (IOR) again emerging as drivers of growth.

Ninety years before Vasco da Gama discovered that sea route to India, Ming China had evinced a brief interest in Indian Ocean through Zheng He's seven voyages from 1405 to 1433 AD. This quickly waned when the literati banned further maritime activities. Six hundred years later, the Middle

Kingdom has revoked its interest in Indian Ocean again. This increasing interest in the Indian Ocean today is driven by China's vision about its own future, where the Indian Ocean plays a pivotal role, with an accompanying strategy tailored to achieve it. They have been broadly discussed in the previous chapter regarding the BRI. Signs of that strategy are evident in the Navy it is creating as well as in the rationale of actions in the South China Sea. The strategic space in question in this book is the Indian Ocean. Any Chinese plan has to eventually interact with certain realities in the Indian Ocean. The aim of this chapter therefore is to provide an overview of the Indian Ocean from a security perspective. Specific Chinese interests with respect to separate geographic areas in the Indian Ocean have been described in detail in the subsequent chapters.

From a geographic perspective, the Indian Ocean is the third largest ocean. A significant feature of this ocean are the choke points that control access to it. Four major choke points are the Suez Canal connecting the Red Sea to the Mediterranean through Egypt; the Bab el Mandeb controlling access to the Red Sea between Djibouti, Somalia, Eritrea and Yemen; the Strait of Hormuz which controls access to the Persian Gulf between Iran, UAE and Oman and the Strait of Malacca which allows access from the Pacific Ocean between Indonesia and Malaysia. China has developed very good relations with each nation that lies on these choke points. The Indian Ocean is a critical conduit between the Pacific and the Atlantic, which are the two larger oceans.

Countries in the IOR are not a homogeneous group by any yardstick. There are no strongly held economic and security architectures in place in the Indian Ocean. Politically, the Indian Ocean does not have a NATO-like alliance system or mutual treaties which the US has put in place in the Pacific with Japan and Korea or the Taiwan Relations Act. However, the US with its presence in the region has been intervening in the littoral states to maintain a status quo in the balance of power. The Indian Ocean nations barring a few were colonised and gained independence only in the early half of the 20th century.

Economy, Energy and Trade in the IOR with Relation to China

Some of the fastest growing economies are in the Indian Ocean region. India is the fastest growing major economy whereas Myanmar tops the growth rate globally. Six out of top 10 growth rates are from the IOR littorals.[3] Two dozen IOR littoral nations have had a growth rate beyond 3 per cent, with 10 nations growing at 5 per cent growth. South Asia is growing at 7.4 per cent.[4] Therefore, the IOR littorals are important to China for trade and investments, especially under the renewed synergy infused by the BRI.

For a trading nation such as China, where 90 per cent of volume and 70 per cent of value of trade traverse by sea,[5] the sea lanes are extremely important. Despite China's humongous success from trade, there are deep geographic vulnerabilities such as the Malacca and other choke points which are an important factor in the Indian Ocean that worries China. China's economic and political initiatives in the region have strong connections with the maritime vulnerabilities of the Indian Ocean.

Coming to maritime initiatives by China, it is to the top shipbuilder with 35 per cent of building output; it is also the top manpower supplier.[6] Overall, 11 per cent of global shipping and 17 per cent of global container volumes are being carried by Chinese hulls.[7] By 2030, it will overtake Greece as the top owner.[8] 6/10 top container routes have had China at one end.[9] However, they are mostly in the Pacific Ocean. 32 out of top 50 container ports were being fully or partially owned by China and handled 67 per cent of containers.[10] Since 2010, it has invested 45 bn in 40 ports globally.[11] Just one stealthy acquisition of M/s Terminal Link of the French giant CMA CMG gave it 49 per cent ownership in 15 ports across the globe including ones in the US and at the either ends of the Panama Canal. The list of ports with stakes by China in the Indian Ocean is as under.[12]

Table 5.1. List of Indian Ocean Ports in which Chinese Firms have a Stake

Firms	Port
Hutchison Port (HP)[13]	HP Westports, Kuala Lumpur, Malaysia, HP MITT, Yangon (Tilawa), Myanmar, HP KICT, HP Pakistan, Karachi, Pakistan, HP Sohar, Oman, HP Dammam Saudi Arabia, HP Dar Es Salaam, Tanzania, HP Ajman, United Arab Emirates.
Others[14]	Colombo (CICT), Hambantota, Maday Island (Kyuakphyu), Gwadar, Darwin (Landbridge Group), New Castle,[15] Melbourne (China Investment Fund),[16] Ashdod,[17] Singapore[18] (3 berths, COSCO-PSA 49 per cent), Port Said East, Suez Canal Container Terminal (COSCO 20 per cent) Bagamoyo,[19] Port Klang,[20] Carey Island,[21] Meleka,[22] I-Havan Maldives, Beira Mozambique, Doraleh, Djibouti.

Coming to maritime traffic, in iron ore, China is the largest mover, being the top importer and producer.[23] In 2015, 70 per cent of iron ore headed to China, of which 54 per cent went from Australia whereas 20 per cent went from Brazil.[24] China's trade created a whole new class here in 2011 called the Vale Max—the 400000DWT [25] giant ore carrier, double the size of its predecessor – designed to make transportation across the Indian Ocean cheaper whereby the Brazilian ore became competitive with Australian ore. China will soon own roughly forty-five out of seventy of these mammoths which traverse the Indian Ocean.[26] These are long-term contracts lasting decades. So, China's appetite drives demand, forcing changes in ship sizes, which in turn affect ports and berth requirements which require fresh investments, which China is in a position to create. In dry bulk metals like copper, nickel and zinc, China's demand is roughly half the global demand. Hence half of those ships that ply will have something to do with China.

The Indian Ocean is also rich in resources, especially hydrocarbons. Over 50 per cent oil and natural gas reserves are in the Indian Ocean littorals. As much as 40 per cent of global offshore oil production is from the Indian Ocean.[27] Therefore, nations not only traverse the Indian Ocean for trade, connecting its littorals as well as linking both oceans, but it is also a very important source of energy for China and other nations.

While China definitely has an edge in dry bulk and container transportation, what matters most to China as far as the Indian Ocean is concerned is sources as well as the transportation of oil and gas. Roughly, 30 per cent of the global shipping tonnage is Oil/Gas.[28] China is the largest energy consumer since 2011 and is the largest oil importer since 2015. Its oil import dependency is around 57 per cent which can increase to 76 per cent by 2035.[29] Of this oil, the Middle East provided 52 per cent, Africa 22 per cent and South America 9 per cent in 2014.[30] Since distances are large; South American oil mostly traverses by VLCCs to China via the Indian Ocean. This means that more than 80 per cent of China's oil has traversed the Indian Ocean. Knowing the significance of carrying oil in its own ships, China targets to carry 80 per cent of its oil in its own ships by 2030.[31]

Coming to LNG, China has a 30 per cent import dependency which will grow to 42 per cent by 2035.[32] Qatar, Algeria, Yemen, Oman, Equatorial Guinea and Nigeria were the sources of gas that has traversed the Indian Ocean Region. That meant around 30 per cent of LNG has traversed Indian Ocean.[33] Gas and oil markets behave slightly differently; gas being highly rigid with high transportation costs, long-term investment in liquefaction and regasification infrastructure and options for pipelines/LNG. Such rigidity encourages long-term political relations. Roughly, 85 per cent Liquefied Natural Gas (LNG) for China is sourced from the IOR and 90 per cent of its LNG traverses the IOR to reach China. Barring the LNG from Algeria, Papua New Guinea, Nigeria and Guinea, all of its LNG sources are in the IOR (Ref Fig 5.1). This is apart from the natural gas pipeline from Myanmar to carry equity gas to Yunnan.

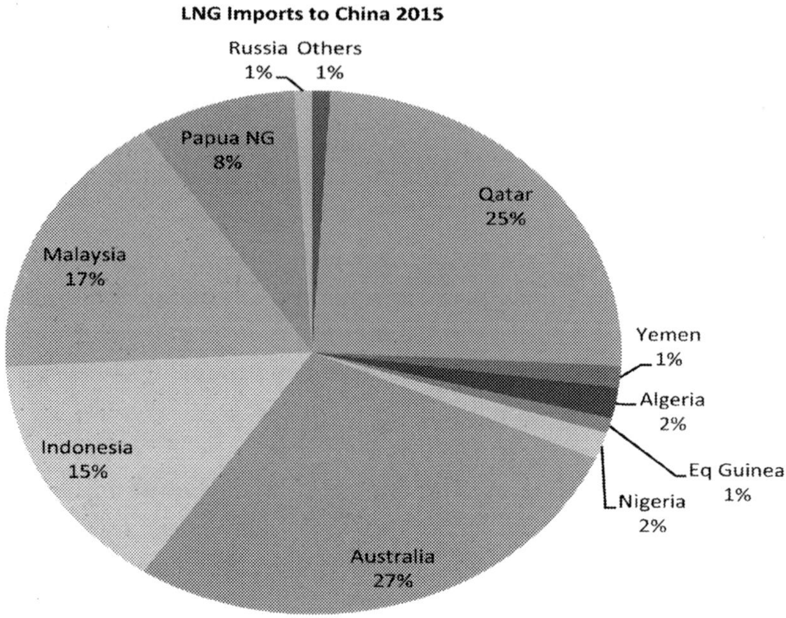

Figure 5.1. LNG Imports of China 2015[34]
(*Source:* BP Statistical Review of World Energy, 2016)

Therefore, both in the case of oil as well as LNG, China's dependence on the IOR is only going to increase and not decrease in the times to come. So, energy is a major vulnerability for China in the IOR which affects its view of the region as well as its engagements in the region.

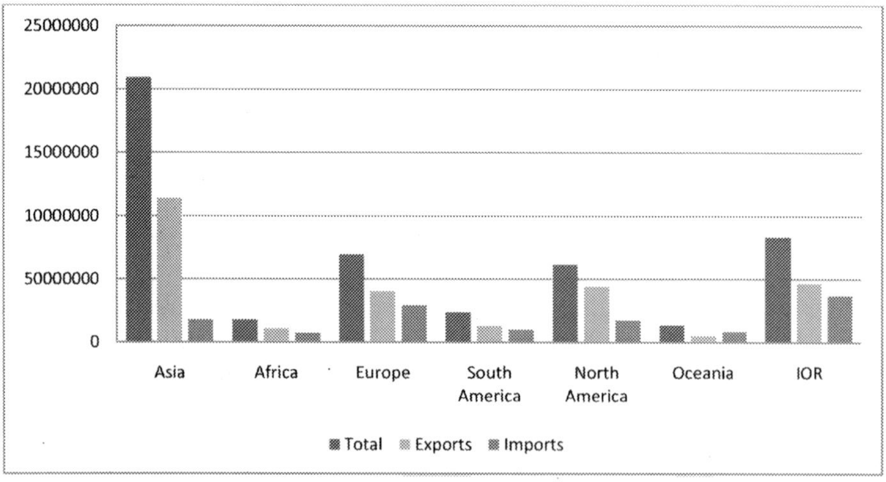

Figure 5.2. Region-wise Trade, China 2015 (in 10000 USD)
(*Source:* Statistical Yearbook of China, 2015)

When one considers China's regional trade figures for 2015 from the Statistical Year book of China published by the National Bureau of Statistics,[35] the Indian Ocean Littoral nations as a group are next only to Asia[36] as a group in the total trade carried out by China. The graph above has been compiled to illustrate that fact. The yearbook does not give the Indian Ocean figures for trade, and the same have been calculated by the author. This indicates the commercial relevance of the IOR to China (Ref Fig. 5.3).

China has also invested deeply in the region, which will now see an increase with the BRI project. The total country-wise investment, trade and arms sales done by China in the IOR are illustrated in the graph below. China has close to USD 446 billion worth cumulative investment in the region as per the data available in the American Enterprise Institute (AEI) database on China's trade. China has undertaken cumulative arms sales worth USD 37 billion as per the data taken from the Stockholm International Peace Research Institute (SIPRI) and has over USD 831 billion worth of trade annually in this region as per the data from the National Statistics Bureau of China. Some notable features are that Australia, Malaysia, and Singapore are top trading partners; China has cumulatively invested heavily in Australia and Indonesia, whereas Pakistan has seen more cumulative arms sales than investment. This is a trend that the CPEC is expected to reverse. Myanmar and Bangladesh, in India's neighbourhood, have also received a large volume of arms in the IOR.

Security Scenario in the IOR

Having briefly looked at why the IOR is crucial for China's growth from the trade, resources and energy perspectives, the security scenario needs elaboration. The IOR nations are diverse in economic, political, religious, cultural or strategic outlook and, therefore, building a collective, consensual, pan-ocean idea of security is a challenge in the region. This is true for the littoral nations trying to build a pan-ocean community as much as any other non-resident power which has to influence this strategic space. Such an external power interaction will have to also base itself on some accepted global trends that affect the region. Some regional and pan-ocean organisations do exist; however, a pan-ocean indigenous maritime security regime is yet to evolve in the IOR. The ongoing anti-piracy campaign in the region highlights some lessons for the future. As this chapter was being written, the 25th Anti-Piracy Mission by China was on in the Indian Ocean, a process that gave China a reason to be present in IOR almost on a permanent basis. The origin of the piracy problem and its scope give some pointers to the future if such a security structure were

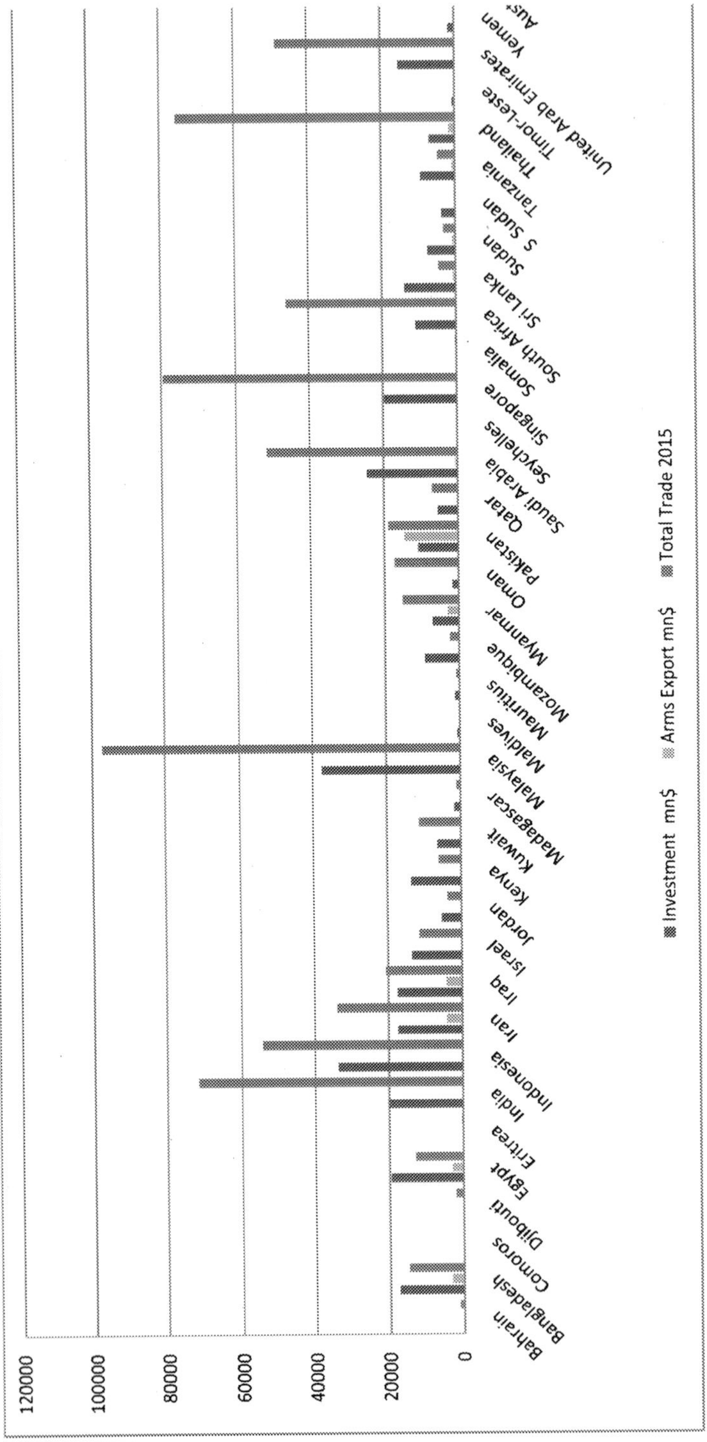

Figure 5.3. Trade Investments and Arms Sales

(*Source:* AEI Database, SIPRI, and China Statistical Yearbook)

to evolve in the IOR. This chapter also examines the global trends for the future, the diversity, prospective structures, their motivators and certain specific recommendations to improve maritime security in the IOR region.

Defining the Indo-Pacific. A discussion on the Indian Ocean today will be incomplete without discussing the Indo-Pacific construct. Rory Medcalf articulates that at the simplest level of understanding, the "Indo-Pacific" label means recognising that the accelerating economic and security connections between the Western Pacific and the Indian Ocean is creating a single strategic system.[37] It is a maritime system with markets at one end and sources at the other—balanced by geopolitics. If the line or ends get disturbed, the world gets affected! A cursory glance at the Indo-Pacific indicates that it is a very large construct which any single power will find hard to manage. So, there has to be a 'core' Indo-Pacific where all the significant activities are taking place. This paper considers that the limit of that core should be approximately 12,000nm. This is because the earth is round and navigationally, beyond half the earth's circumference being subject to factors like canal sizes, etc., ships have the option to go the other way round; therefore, the Indo-Pacific becomes less relevant at that geographic limit. There are some geographic disrupters of the idea too, such as opening up of routes through the Arctic Ocean or a canal that China is planning in Nicaragua. If they fructify, the traffic along this system could change a little! The Indo-Pacific has certain distinct regional security complexes with diverse identities. Barry Buzan identifies them as the South African Complex, the Horn of Africa Complex, the Middle East Complex, the South Asia Complex and the East Asia Complex.[38] One of the key arguments of this chapter is that since the region is too large, security capacities will remain distributed within these complexes. Whilst that is the way Buzan sees it, China, while dealing with Indian Ocean, follows its own logic. The Indian Ocean nations have been grouped and placed in subsequent chapters of this book to suits China's logic as estimated by the author.

Pacific and IOR—Key Differences. If an Indian Ocean security perspective is to be developed, differences between the IOR and the Western Pacific are important factors to consider. An Indian Ocean perspective to security structures could reflect this difference. Some key differences are stated below:

Table 5.2. Pacific and IOR- Key Differences

Factor	**Indian Ocean**	**Pacific**
Diversity	High	Low
GDP	Low	High
Flash Points	Fragile states, Terror, Land	Evolved states, Territorial disputes, Sea
Climate Change Effect	High	Low
US Presence	May wane	Resident power
Structures	Multilateral Evolving	ASEAN-based and Mini-laterals
Maritime Security	Evolving (IORA/IONS)	Better (ADMM+, EAMF, EAS), WPNS
Security Objectives	Liberal	Realist
Resources	Source of Oil	Consumer of Oil
Trade	Markets	Manufacturers
Demography	Young	Ageing

Source: Author.

Global Trends Affecting IOR Structures. The backdrop for a future Indian Ocean regional security mechanism will be set by certain salient predictions regarding the Indian Ocean. The dominant themes to be considered are:

- The rise of its Asian and African littorals at a historic pace.[39]
- The future of the power structure as a distributed one rather than a centralised hegemon in power.[40]
- Demography which will play a major role, especially the youth bulge, and its impacts on productivity, migration and security.[41]
- Quest for resources, especially for energy, metals, food and water.[42]
- Climate change and its impacts on the Indian Ocean littorals and on all human endeavours.[43]

Diversity—An Intrinsic Factor in the IOR. The Indian Ocean littoral is home to 38 countries of myriad hues and a large number of equally diverse and relevant hinterland nations like Afghanistan. They are diverse in races, cultures, religions, economic structures and strategic outlook, with a limited common ground to bind them together. The African littorals have clear demarcations with the prosperous Southern Africa economically distinct from the rest of East Africa. The Horn of Africa has been a hotspot for many years and is being addressed by a separate security structure. The Persian Gulf has a high-value dynamic of its own. South Asia, South East Asia, the Indian Ocean Islands and Australia are other separate sub regions. Fifty percent of the prospective failed states are within the IOR littoral. In GDP terms, four out of the top 20 (India, Indonesia, Australia, Saudi Arabia), and three out of the bottom 20 (Comoros, Madagascar, Seychelles) are from the Indian Ocean.

Per capita GDP distribution is even more stark, with four out of top 10 (Qatar, Singapore, Kuwait, and UAE) and three out of bottom 15 nations (Comoros, Madagascar, Mozambique) being there in the region. The average Qatari is 200 times richer than the average Malagasy.[44] There are five religions and several races along its shores. Yet, at close to 9 trillion US dollars, the region commands 11 per cent of the global GDP which lends it a heft of its own.[45] This diversity and a lack of shared threat perception make the creation of regional structures, like that Europe's NATO, difficult to envisage in the IOR. Therefore, overlaying the effect of Chinese strategy is a creative challenge over such a diverse grouping.

Layers in the Security Structure. The search for objectives of a regional security architecture involves major security threats that are being faced by the IOR. For the purposes of this chapter, a broader concept of security—beyond a military sphere—has been adopted. Therefore, this study about regional security structure essentially has two separate layers:

- The first is a global realist layer, linked to 'realpolitik', where any rising power will be balanced by other powers, either by internal security investments or by alliances. The new mental maps of Indo-Pacific, US rebalance, Belt and Road Initiative, RCEP, are all linked to this economic and security balancing process.[46] Those structures (security investments/alliances) could be exclusive in nature. The key driver of this layer will be assessing and calibrating to the rise of China, the future of US power and their relation to various other regional and middle powers.
- The second layer comprises a wider gamut of liberal, non-traditional domain of security for which there is a wider scope for participation in the IOR. This layer will deal with prevention of a non-traditional crisis and as 'first responders' post-crisis, and under the existing international law and UN statutes. This layer will be privileged as an inclusive construct where external powers like China and the US could be included.

Therefore, future IOR structures will have both traditional realist layers that focus on balance of power, and the liberal inclusive structures that focus on non-traditional security. Both the layers will invariably influence each other. This is analogous to the events in the Pacific, where a liberal economic construct coexists with a realist, intensely rivalrous construct which constantly balance each other out. A classic case, where a change in the geopolitical balance can affect developmental initiatives, is illustrated in the following case. One early event linked to the BRI was the formation of the AIIB by China. Japan initially abstained from joining the AIIB and promised USD 110 billion in lieu for infrastructure—USD 10 billion more than China's USD 100 billion infusion in the AIIB.[47] Two years later, the tables had turned by 2017 due to a variety of reasons. Japan not only took part in the Belt and Road Forum, but was actively considering joining the Belt and Road Initiative by mid-2017.[48]

Objectives. The salient objectives of the Indian Ocean security architecture are explained as follows:

- **Ensure Safe Maritime Commerce in the IOR.** Most IOR nations belong to the undeveloped global south of the economic divide. These nations cannot achieve their true potential without an unhindered maritime transport that enables 90 per cent of the global trade in volume. Therefore, the dividends of a stable maritime order are a strong ***common motivator*** to bind the littorals. The unique feature of the IOR is its nature as a maritime superconduit that connects the Atlantic and the Pacific. Therefore, the security of the IOR is of a ***local*** as well as a ***global*** interest. This motivates extra-regional powers to own a stake in the security of the IOR. Coalition operations against piracy in the western Indian Ocean are proofs of this tendency-something that China has used wisely to gain a toehold in the IOR. The major threat to maritime commerce could be a conventional confrontation in the IOR, piracy and terrorism.
- **Aid in Ocean Resource Management.** One of the major security operations of the non-traditional realm in the Indian Ocean has been the ongoing Anti-Piracy Operations. These operations have been going on for the past decade with billions being spent by the global powers. A closer look at the piracy problem indicates that what lay at the heart of the Somali trouble was the loss of fishing as a livelihood due to dumping of toxic waste off the Somali coast by other nations.[49] Predictions indicate that food, energy and water are likely to be major resources that will be contested in the future.[50] Therefore, one objective of the collective structure should be to complement the existing international structures that ***arbitrate and motivate*** order in the race for resources.
- **Develop Capacities to deal with Disasters/Environment/Climate Change.** Climate change raises sea levels, makes wet places wetter and dry places drier. The rise of sea levels impacts the IOR littorals directly. Global warming leads to depletion or relocation of fish stock,

loss of arable land and contamination of existing water resources forcing large scale migration.[51] The low-lying Bangladesh and Maldives will be affected by the rising sea levels. If oil catapulted the Middle East to centre stage of the global politics in the last century, water shortage could be the theme of the future in the already dry Middle East. Though the rich and the poor nations will be affected, there is a distinct link between climate change vulnerability and GDP which makes the poorer countries more vulnerable to climate change.[52] The Indian Ocean has some of the poorest countries in the world. Here, the recent pull-out by the USA has ceded some precious space to China which is only eager to assume that space. However, it is a stark reality that while China itself is weaning away from coal, it is infusing billions into Pakistan for coal projects. A detailed discussion of this factor is in the chapter on Pakistan. Other than such predicted changes, unpredictable natural disasters such as earthquakes, tsunamis, floods and droughts are better managed collectively. Therefore, an acceptable objective of the structure should be to ***collectively deal*** with the effects of disasters and climate change. China has been on the toes on this count. It leverages its continuous presence in Indian Ocean for anti-piracy missions to be active in missions such as the recent floods in Sri Lanka in May 2017[53] or the airlift of drinking water to Maldives in 2014.[54]

- **Prevent Use of Oceans for Terrorism.** The Indian Ocean has witnessed several serious terror incidents. In a recent incident, terrorists attempted to hijack a frontline Pakistan Navy Frigate, the PNS *Zulfiqar*. A successful hijack could have resulted in catastrophic consequences for the entire region. In 2008, terror strikes in Mumbai were carried out by terrorists via the sea route from Karachi. The attacks on the USS *Cole* and MV *Limberg* were carried out by terrorists at sea. There is a need to ***address the threat of terrorism*** through collective security structures. The sceptre of the Al Qaeda has been active at sea, and the ISIS could follow suit if unchecked. The Task Force 50 that operates in the IOR has been formed with the aim of '***war on terror***'. China's record on this critical aspect of terror in the IOR does not auger well, India had requested the UN for action against Pakistan for releasing Zaki Ur Rahman Lakhvi, a mastermind of the Mumbai terror attack which happened via sea, under the 1267 sanctions regime. This was blocked by China in June 2015.[55] A related event played out in December 2016 when China blocked India's attempt to designate Masood Azhar as an international terrorist under the 1267 regime. Masood is the head of the Jaish-e-Mohammad, a banned organisation, and has had personal links with the Al Qaeda and Osama bin Laden and was associated with the hijacking of the Indian Airlines flight IC-814 in 1999 to Kandahar and the Pathankot attack in 2016.[56] China has been blocking these to protect its only ally, Pakistan, which is a significant partner in its Indian Ocean Strategy.

- **Management of Trans-Ocean Crime.** The opium producing regions of the world, namely the Golden Triangle, which comprise Myanmar, Laos and Thailand, and the Golden Crescent involving Iran, Pakistan and Afghanistan, lie on the Indian Ocean Rim. Drug trafficking has a close link with terrorism.[57] The trafficking of humans and small arms are another menace in the oceans which requires collective redressal, since they are transnational crimes that exploit the open oceans. ***Cooperative management of trans-ocean crime*** must be an objective of these structures. Several armed ethnic organisations in the Golden Triangle in the littorals of the Bay of Bengal are involved in drug cultivation and trafficking. The region also suffers from drug menace, especially opium which is cultivated there, and proliferation of methamphetamine.[58] China has deep influence over some of these large EAO groups through the Wa Army. However, just as it does with terror in Pakistan, it just turns the other way and uses these insurgent groups to exert pressure on the Myanmar government to protect China's access to the Indian Ocean through Myanmar, in which it is deeply committed.
- **Creation of Critical Infrastructure.** The IOR littorals also need critical infrastructure like ports, power projects, rail, roads, etc. China has the economic and industrial capacity to fill the void. They have been discussed partially in the second chapter and in some detail in subsequent chapters.

Existing Structures and their Contribution to Security. Major countries/regional organisations in the IOR that currently observe a security role through their presence, which may continue in the future, are as follows:

- **Role of the USA.** The present collective security framework exists under the UN umbrella and US pre-eminence. The US has three unified command structures—namely, AFRICOM, CENTCOM and PACOM and three fleets: the Fifth, Sixth and Seventh Fleets which focus on the Indian Ocean (Refer Fig 5.5). Considering the recent creation of the Africa Command, and the relevance of the Middle East in the overall US strategy, the Western Indian Ocean will continue to be of interest to the United States. With lesser reliance on Middle Eastern oil, the interest in the region will slowly wane and shift to Africa. The US base at Diego Garcia is a critical asset in its Indian Ocean Strategy. The rebalance to Asia has underlined that the Western Pacific is becoming a greater priority to the US. The US has treaty obligations in the Western Pacific with South Korea and Japan as well as obligations arising out of the Taiwan Relations Act. The Rise of China, the situation that it has created in the South China Sea and the belligerence of North Korea which directly threatens its treaty allies, means that the US could turn its gaze more to the East in the future.

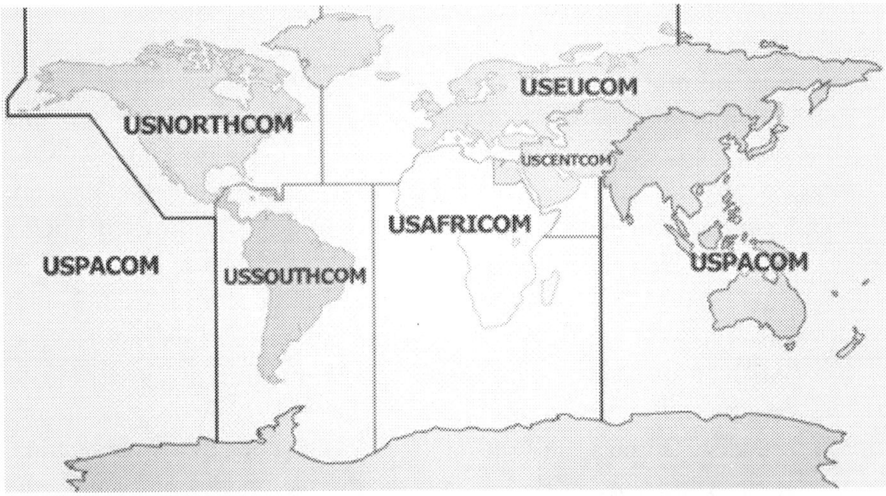

Figure 5.4. The US Geographic Commands in the Indian Ocean
(*Source*: US Army (http://www.army.mil/info/organization/) [Public domain], via Wikimedia Commons)

- **African Organisations.** The African Littorals have three organisations that are relevant to the IOR. Along the littorals, the regional organisation in the southern half, the Southern African Development Council (SADC), has 15 members. It focuses on the prosperous southern portion of Africa. In the north, there is the Intergovernmental Agreement on Development (IGAD), which has 7 members. None of these organisations have a security element in their charter. However, the most prominent African organisation, the African Union, has a

Standing African Force. This is an evolving concept which conducted its first military exercise in early Nov 2015.[59] This development is of interest for security in Africa, though it will be some time before a maritime element could emerge out of this regime. However, the appearance of a "security regime" in Africa is indeed inspiring. The US AFRICOM deals with the security of all of Africa except Egypt, with a headquarters in Germany and major base in Djibouti. It is in the same port city that China set up its first foreign base. Details of China's Africa Initiative are in Chapter Nine.

- **Persian Gulf.** The littoral adjacent to Africa, the Persian Gulf Region, has an important organisation, called the Gulf Cooperation Council (GCC), with 6 members. It has a clear aspiration for security with a joint military force named the *Peninsular Shield Force* which took part in the 1991 Gulf War and also intervened in Bahrain during the uprising there in 2011.[60] The GCC has the economic capacity to invest in a force and is one of the largest defence spenders ahead of Russia, France, or the rest of the Middle East put together.[61] Due to deep ties in this region, the United States has been the principal provider of security to the Persian Gulf region, with the CENTCOM forward HQ based in Qatar and the US Fifth Fleet located in Bahrain. Recently, there have been severe cracks in the GCC. These are being primarily led by Saudi Arabia against Qatar, which maintains warm relations with Iran, Israel, the Taliban and allegedly with the Al Nusra. Besides, Qatar also maintains relations with the Muslim Brotherhood which is an Islamist group which is known for its opposition to dynastic rule. These have threatened the GCC. The US policy under President Trump against the Iran deal has deepened the fissures. China, at the same time, maintains a three-pronged policy of keeping the Arab League, Iran and Israel on separate tracks, engaging them economically.[62] The Arab League also encompasses nations in Africa. This is a policy that has worked well under the US security umbrella, since the burden of realpolitik has been borne by them. It remains to be seen what the future will unravel for this volatile region as the power shifts occur. China's role in the Middle East is elaborated in Chapter Nine.
- **South Asia.** The most significant organisation in the subregion is the South Asian Association for Regional Cooperation (SAARC) with Bhutan, India, Maldives, Nepal, Pakistan, Sri Lanka and Afghanistan as members. This association promotes economic and socio-cultural

development in the region. SAARC has an Agreement on Rapid Response to Natural Disasters (ARRND), with an excellent disaster management knowledge portal.[63] It does not have a security regime or a standing force. However, from the maritime perspective, the three littoral members—India, Sri Lanka and Maldives—have an NSA-level security dialogue on maritime security.[64] This is a structure separate from the SAARC; yet, it is of significance considering the strategic location of the three states astride important shipping lanes. China's relations with these states have been discussed in separate chapters. China has an ongoing annual Maritime Cooperation Dialogue with India.[65]

- **South East Asia.** There are two South East Asian organisations which contribute to the security objectives of enhancing regional security in the IOR . They are listed below:
  - **Bay of Bengal Initiative (BIMSTEC).** The Bay of Bengal Initiative for Multi-Sectoral Technical and Economic Cooperation (BIMSTEC) involves Bangladesh, India, Myanmar, Sri Lanka, Thailand, Bhutan and Nepal. This has a separate working group focusing on Counter-Terrorism and Transnational Crime[66] and Environment and Natural Disaster Management, both of which are led by India. BIMSTEC also has an initiative in place to deal with climate change which is led by Bangladesh. In the absence of cooperation for connectivity through Pakistan to Afghanistan, Iran and Central Asia, this is critical to India's Act East policy, wherein connectivity to the east is being enhanced along IOR littorals.
  - **ASEAN.** At the Eastern Limits of the IOR, constructs become ASEAN-centric and get truly Indo-Pacific. The ASEAN is the *literal and figurative fulcrum* of the Indo-Pacific idea, to borrow the word "fulcrum" from President Jokowi who used it for Indonesia. The ASEAN derives its security perspective from the ADMM-Plus Committee which has five IOR states—namely, Indonesia, Malaysia, Myanmar, Singapore and Thailand— with two additional IOR states, Australia and India, as observers.[67] With China, Japan, the Russian Federation and the United States, this body is structured aptly for security initiatives. The ASEAN brings to the IOR, the South China Sea experience of maritime security and serves as a vital link of the Indo-Pacific. The ASEAN nations have been beneficiaries of prosperity enabled by maritime

commerce. This contributes to the cause of maritime security in the IOR. The ASEAN experience also reminds us that organisations take a long time to evolve a security regime. The ADMM took shape 40 years after the inception of the ASEAN.[68] Compared to the IOR structures, the ASEAN has an evolved maritime outlook which has assisted formations of indigenous maritime cooperation between India, Malaysia, Singapore and Indonesia to prevent piracy. Now, this trend has to spread westwards. Again, Medcalf[69] tells us that the 'gathering of leaders that founded the East Asia Summit on December 14, 2005 in Kuala Lumpur is the moment the contemporary Indo-Pacific was born'. Since the ASEAN is the basic building block of structures in that region, the Indo-Pacific character is intrinsic to it. The South China Sea disputes, with China on one side and the close economic and political relations that China shares with many nations in this group on the other, have caused fissures in this group. Yet, 15 years after a declaration regarding the code of conduct, there has finally been an agreement to prepare a framework for rules of conduct at the May 2017 ASEAN Meet concluded in Guiyang.[70]

- **Ocean-Themed Groupings – IONS and IORA.** The Indian Ocean also has two organisations that have a pan-oceanic character. These are the Indian Ocean Regional Association (IORA) and the Indian Ocean Naval Symposium (IONS). Since the objective of this chapter is to consider organisations with the potential for enhancing security structures in the IOR, a closer analysis of these two pan-oceanic structures is deemed necessary.
  - **IORA.** The rationale behind forming the IORA was to unite the littoral nations on the basis of the shared Indian Ocean identity for '*socio-economic co-operation and other peaceful endeavours*'.[71] The organisation was established in 1997 and comprises 21 members and seven dialogue partners to date. It incrementally included maritime security in its agenda in the last five years. Member countries of the IORA form a USD 9 tn grouping, whereas its Pacific equivalent, the APEC, is a 30tn USD grouping. As South Asia and Africa grow between 6–7 per cent, one has to be optimistic about the IORA. One should deem the IORA as a prospective 'APEC'. China has engaged itself with IORA as a dialogue partner since 2000. The IORA in its Jakarta session in

2017 raised itself to Summit level with several heads of state in attendance.

- **IONS.** The IONS was established in 2008 to increase maritime cooperation among navies of the Indian Ocean Region by providing an open and inclusive forum for the discussion of regionally relevant maritime issues and to develop a common understanding for possible cooperative endeavours in the future. The IONS has 22 members and four observers including China.[72] It was inspired by the Western Pacific Naval Symposium, with which it shares nine members.

• **Comparisons – the IOR, IONS and IORA.** An analysis of the membership of the two groupings reveals the inclusive nature of their composition:-

- **Inclusiveness vis-à-vis the IOR.** The Indian Ocean has 38 nations in its littorals that include the UK and France as a consequence of their Indian Ocean territories. 22 nations are members in both the IONS and IORA. That makes the IONS–IORA constructs fairly inclusive with 70 per cent membership of the IOR littoral nations. China, the US and Japan are either observers or dialogue partners in these forums. China has been vying for a full membership in this grouping. Djibouti, Eritrea, Iraq, Sudan, Israel, Jordan, Qatar, Bahrain and Kuwait are neither members of the IORA nor the IONS presently.
- **What the IORA and IONS exclude.** Maldives, Myanmar, Pakistan, Saudi Arabia, Timur-Leste are members of the IONS but are not members of the IORA. Maldives and Myanmar are working towards IORA membership.[73] On the other hand, Comoros, Kenya and Yemen are members of the IORA, but not of the IONS. Both the IONS and IORA do not have a total overlap in membership and roles. Therefore, the IONS and IORA will have to coexist as two distinct organisations with overlapping roles.
- **IORA and Maritime Security.** A review of the evolution of the IORA through a study of its annual communiqué indicates that the IORA has incrementally included security in its ambit of concerns.[74] Though it is essentially an economic grouping, there is a growing recognition that economic growth requires a stable security situation in the IOR. The task of ensuring security commences from a political consensus between members. The

political mandate is executed through the Coast Guards or Navies of the region. The organisation that embodies this aspiration is the IONS. Meaningful maritime security requires a closer liaison between the two organisations which was articulated by the IORA Perth Communiqué of November 2013 seeking "*information-sharing and other activities with both civilian and non-civilian dimensions*".[75] This idea needs to be fleshed out and taken forward to its logical end.

- **Indo-Pacific Connects—Trans-Ocean Groups.** There are many organisations that already have an Indo-Pacific character today. The ASEAN, ARF, ADMM+, EAMF and EAS are in the cusp between the IOR and the Pacific. Similarly, the APEC– IORA and the IONS–WPNS, the intra-ocean blocks, have common members. This informally furthers the Indo-Pacific idea. These are areas that offer a sharing of perspective and cooperation between India and China. They are tabulated below:

Table 5.3. Existing Organisations with an Indo-Pacific Character

ARF		ASEAN		ADMM+EAS+EAMF		IONS - WPNS	APEC – IORA
Pacific	**IOR**	**IOR**	**Pacific**	**Pacific**	**IOR**	**Common nations**	
13	12	5	5	10	8	9	7

Lessons from Piracy for future IOR Structures. A major crisis in the recent times in the IOR has been piracy. Its genesis and subsequent containment offers some insights regarding what the future security structures should be. Piracy annually cost the world USD 2–6 billion, shared by the industry and state as per the analysis of studies by the centre, *Ocean without Piracy*.[76] Piracy was finally controlled by several task forces and surveillance centres.[77]

- The task forces, which carried out anti-piracy missions, were as follows:
  - US Navy's Task Force 151.
  - Additional tasking to Task Force 150 (Global War on Terror TF).
  - Operation Atalanta by the EU.
  - Operation Ocean Shield by the NATO.
  - Independent deployments by Russia, Malaysia, Japan, China and India. Of this, the Chinese anti-piracy escorts have completed their 25th Deployment.
  - A host of private security firms with armed guards on vessels.
- The monitoring mechanism includes the following:

- Contact Group on Piracy off the Coast of Somalia (CGPCS) in New York.
- The Shared Awareness and Deconfliction (SHADE) initiative meetings in Bahrain.
- Regional Cooperation Agreement on Combating Piracy and Armed Robbery against Ships in Asia (ReCAAP) in Singapore.
- Piracy Reporting Centre (PRC) of the International Maritime Bureau (IMB) in Malaysia.
- Maritime Security Centre, Horn of Africa, London.
- NATO Shipping Centre (NSC), London.

The effort brought together at least 30 navies from across the globe with coordination centres spread halfway across globe on a yet unfinished business. The lessons that can be gleaned from this event towards an IOR structure are as follows:

- A failed state on land and an abuse of the sea can wreak havoc on the global commons.
- Resolving a similar problem in the future can involve a fairly large force (anti-piracy fleets were probably the largest deployment since WW II).
- It can take a long time to push back such a scourge.
- Therefore, there is a need to constantly monitor continental events that can spill over to the sea, even from distant shores.

The Future Structure of the IOR. From the above sections in this article, the following conclusions can be drawn regarding the future security structures of the IOR:

- **Distributed Architecture.** As Asia and Africa rise economically, there will be a need for indigenous maritime security structures to evolve and deal as the first responders to any challenge. Regional organisations in the IOR have the potential to initiate subregional maritime security regimes. Enhancing maritime awareness in existing constructs is the best way to contribute to Maritime Security than any de novo structures. A distributed architecture such as the expanded ASEAN Maritime Forum is a good model which can provide maritime security. The creation of a political consensus regarding the relevance of safe sealanes is the first step in this direction. Given the political diversity of the IOR, a pan-region organisation where countries find a shared traditional threat appears as a tall order. This problem cannot be wished away or simplified. Once a consensus becomes reality, the

IOR–IONS duo can provide the 'maritime layer' to the existing constructs. Funding and capacity-building are the two cornerstones which will dictate this process. The littorals have to take the lead in this regard.

- **Addressing the Issue of Scale.** The effort to deal with piracy throws some light on the scope and scale of the problem, given the size of the IOR. The search and rescue (SAR) efforts for the MH370[78] have reiterated that large scope. Given this scope, a monolithic, homogenous IOR structure of security appears ambitious. The mandate and capacity will remain in diffused littoral organisations within regional security complexes. The littoral organisations have to contribute collectively to the IOR maritime security, where the whole tends to be larger than the sum of its parts as far as a pan-ocean structure is concerned. A trilateral like the India-Maldives-Sri Lanka Maritime Dialogue and the recently commenced India–China Maritime dialogue is the way ahead.
- **Relevance of Inclusive Structures.** The United States will remain the preeminent power in the IOR, and will continue to play a critical role in the near term. However, there are signs of fatigue in its global management. The result of the recent US elections has only underlined that tendency. What happens to the Middle East with lesser US involvement is worth pondering. Japan and China are already based in Djibouti. The UK has returned to the east of Suez after 40 years to a base in Bahrain. Resident middle powers like India, Australia, Indonesia and South Africa remain at pole positions in the IOR littorals. China, Japan and Korea play a key role in both oceans for sustaining their economies. Russia has regained its global relevance in Syria, coupled with predictions of a positive economic growth rate in 2017. Under such a multipolar circumstance, an inclusive structure will bring greater benefits than an exclusive approach to the IOR structures. The IORA and IONS possess that inclusive nature.
- **Funding and Governance.** It is these countries, endowed with political will and economic heft – India, Indonesia, Australia and South Africa –which have to take the lead for the funding and collective governance of the IOR security structures. When we consider the Indo-Pacific, the triangular relations between India, China and US become extremely critical to the region. A greater mutual accommodation of each other's concerns will augur well for the Indo-Pacific.

- **Looking Out for the Next Somalia.** The root of any maritime problem will remain on land as illustrated by the piracy off-Somalia. It was a failed state on land that led to the abuse of the sea which seeded the piracy trouble that the world is still dealing with. If one scrapes the surface of the scourge of terrorism at sea, the conclusions could be similar. Most states in the fragile state index are in the IOR. They are the ones which need some hand-holding in capacity building. Any IOR security structure will have to constantly monitor and respond to the emerging situations in these littorals constantly.
- **IORA–IONS: The Maritime Layer of Choice.** Given their pan-oceanic character and inclusiveness, the IORA and IONS together have the potential to contribute to Maritime Security. The following measures could enhance their role:
  - **Funds and Initiative.** The emerging IOR powers—namely, India, Australia, Indonesia and South Africa—will have to infuse greater energies to create a consensus, generate funds and build the capacity to take the IORA–IONS construct forward.
  - **IORA–IONS as Maritime Twins.** It is important that both organisations exist as interrelated but separate entities since the membership and mandates do not have total overlap. However, there should be greater linkages between these organisations if the spirit of the IORA's Perth Communiqué is to be taken forward.
  - **Next Way Points.** The following 'way points' are recommended for the IORA–IONS construct.
    - Raising the annual meeting to a biennial summit with the heads of state. The first summit took place in Jakarta in March 2017.
    - A Humanitarian Aid and Disaster Relief (HADR) table-top exercise followed by an actual exercise.
    - The creation of a central web-based IOR portal for sharing assets for HADR, similar to the SAARC's disaster knowledge portal.[79]
    - A central data fusion centre of white shipping in the IOR.
    - Sharing of intelligence and domain expertise between members.
  - **Role of the Coast Guards.** Since non-traditional security occupies a high share of the spectrum of problems in the IOR, the Coast Guards have a major role as domain specialists of that arena. Whilst an Asian Coast Guard conclave exists, there is 'forum-gap' in the IOR which requires to be filled either under the IONS or separately as a stand-alone entity.

- **Safe Commerce as a Motivator for Consensus.** Collective security is mostly about creating a political consensus. A good maritime order which facilitates commerce can serve as a strong motivator for consensus between the IOR nations, which are placed on the bottom of the growth curve. The economic rationale of the IORA can progress only if peace prevails in the oceans, which facilitates 90 per cent of the trade. The IORA and IONS can serve as maritime connectors between the many littoral organisations creating a pan-ocean consensus about maritime security. Upgrading the IORA meets to summit-level meetings will assist in generating a political consensus.

Conclusion

When the other chapters in this book look at China's multiple manoeuvres to gain an advantageous position in the IOR, this chapter was deemed necessary to understand some basic facts about the IOR—the strategic space in question. The Chinese dependence on the IOR in broad terms, including investments, trade, energy and arms sales were discussed along with the regional dynamics of the IOR in this chapter. From the next chapter onwards, the book will move to the specific facets of that strategy.

From a historical perspective of maritime commerce, Martin Stopford in his book *Maritime Economics* describes the ***west line***, a fictional line that tracks the historic trajectory of global centres for maritime commerce. According to him it commenced its westward journey five thousand years ago from the north-western shore of the Indian Ocean.[80] History has pushed it across three-fourths of the globe and it hypothetically hovers over the Western Pacific today. The natural progression of the west line is to the Indian Ocean, where the centre of maritime economy will eventually shift. The locus of the west line progresses in tandem with the locus of the economic centres of gravity of the globe. That augurs for the IOR a unique economic gravitas in the future. China appears to be well aware of that fact! Maritime Security, an enabler of peaceful commerce, is a prerequisite for that shift in the centre of gravity. The challenge before us today is to forge a peaceful condition amidst the interplay of a wide spectrum of factors to usher that line of prosperity into the IOR.

The US will remain the pre-eminent power in the IOR, and will continue to play a critical role in the near term. What happens to the Middle East as the US power wanes is worth pondering- Japan and China are already in Djibouti. The UK has returned to the Indian Ocean after a hiatus of several decades. For an indigenous structure, India, Australia, Indonesia and South

Africa have to take the lead. China, Japan and Korea play a key role in both oceans. Russia through effective roles in Syria, is back on the block. What the IOR requires is a liberal view of security with an ***inclusive structure.*** Arming fragile states with submarine sales in the region or its deployments does not contribute to that concept of security or the benign façade of a peaceful rise.

Three key players to achieve that desired stability in the IOR are India, China and the USA. A deeper accommodation and understanding of each other's concerns in that triangle, and in turn their accommodation of the other nation's interests, is the key to peace in the region.

NOTES

1. This chapter relies on an article by the author "Indian Ocean Regional Security: Mechanisms Problems and Prospects", *Journal of Indian Ocean*, Vol. 24, No.3, Dec 2016. The author is grateful to the editor of Indian Ocean Journal for permissions.
2. The *Periplus Maris Erythraei* or the Circumnavigation of the Red Sea, is a guide made by unknown Greek Mariner(s) in first century AD, regarding the journey from Red Sea to East Africa, Arabia, and India, by sea. This is the oldest 'sailing directions' or 'pilot'. Its modern avatars are also called 'pilots' and are essential for the mariners for navigation.
3. "Which Are the World's Fastest-Growing Economies?," *World Economic Forum*, accessed June 15, 2017, https://www.weforum.org/agenda/2016/04/worlds-fastest-growing-economies/.
4. Word Bank Data.
5. Kevin Cullinane, *International Handbook of Maritime Economics* (Edward Elgar Publishing, 2011).
6. Review of Maritime Trade- 2016 UNCTAD.
7. Ibid.
8. Ibid.
9. Ibid.
10. "How China Rules the Waves," accessed April 24, 2017, https://ig.ft.com/sites/china-ports.
11. Ibid.
12. Prepared by author from multiple sources as cited.
13. "Hutchison Ports," accessed June 27, 2017, /en/.
14. Others include China Merchants, COSCO, China Overseas Port Holding (Pakistan), CCCC etc.
15. State Political Reporter Liz Foschia, "World's Biggest Coal Port Sold by NSW Government for $1.75 Billion," Text, *ABC News*, (April 30, 2014), http://www.abc.net.au/news/2014-04-30/nsw-government-sells-port-of-newcastle-for-1.75-billion/5421800.
16. "Australian Port Sold for $7.3 Billion to Consortium; China Fund among Backers," *Reuters*, accessed June 27, 2017, http://www.reuters.com/article/us-australia-privatisation-ports-idUSKCN11P04O.
17. "As Part of Asia Pivot, Netanyahu Pushes Israeli Hi-Tech in China," *Reuters*, March 20, 2017, http://www.reuters.com/article/us-israel-china-business-idUSKBN16R1AV.
18. "How China Rules the Waves."
19. Mercy A. Kuo, "The Power of Ports: China's Maritime March," *The Diplomat*, accessed May 26, 2017, http://thediplomat.com/2017/03/the-power-of-ports-chinas-maritime-march/.

20. "Why China Wants Malaysia on the Major-Port Radar," *South China Morning Post*, accessed May 26, 2017, http://www.scmp.com/week-asia/politics/article/2087402/can-china-really-deliver-malaysias-singapore-slayer.
21. "How China Rules the Waves."
22. Ibid.
23. RMT 2016.
24. http://www.hellenicshippingnews.com/giant-ore-carriers-set-to-play-a-bigger-role-in-the-global-shipping-fleet-china-embraces-valemaxes/
25. http://www.hellenicshippingnews.com/giant-ore-carriers-set-to-play-a-bigger-role-in-the-global-shipping-fleet-china-embraces-valemaxes/
26. Ibid.
27. "The World Factbook—Central Intelligence Agency," accessed June 15, 2017, https://www.cia.gov/library/publications/the-world-factbook/geos/xo.html.
28. Ibid.
29. British Petroleum, "BP Energy Outlook 2017 Edition," n.d., https://www.bp.com/content/dam/bp/pdf/energy-economics/energy-outlook-2017/bp-energy-outlook-2017.pdf.
30. Ibid.
31. Blasko Dennis, Chinas Merchant Marine.
32. British Petroleum, "BP Energy Outlook 2017 Edition."
33. Author's calculations.
34. "Statistical Review of World Energy," *Energy Economics, BP*, accessed August 28, 2017, http://www.bp.com/en/global/corporate/energy-economics/statistical-review-of-world-energy.html. (2016 edition)
35. http://www.stats.gov.cn/tjsj/ndsj/2016/indexeh.htm
36. The comparison as a grouping has been made to highlight the IOR's significance in China's calculus.
37. "The Indo-Pacific: What's in a Name?," *Lowy Institute for International Policy*, accessed November 12, 2015, http://www.lowyinstitute.org/publications/indo-pacific-whats-name.
38. Barry Buzan and Ole Wæver, *Regions and Powers: The Structure of International Security* (Cambridge University Press, 2003).
39. "Global Trends 2030," accessed November 12, 2015, http://www.dni.gov/index.php/about/organization/global-trends-2030.
40. "Interview – Barry Buzan," accessed November 12, 2015, http://www.e-ir.info/2013/03/27/interview-barry-buzan-2/.
41. "Global Trends 2030."
42. Ibid.
43. Ibid.
44. "GDP (current US$), Data Table," accessed November 12, 2015, http://data.worldbank.org/indicator/NY.GDP.MKTP.CD.
45. "Indian Ocean Rim Association for Regional Co-Operation (IOR-ARC)," accessed November 10, 2015, http://mea.gov.in/in-focus-article.htm?20707/Indian+Ocean+Rim+Association+for+ Regional+Cooperation+IORARC.
46. "The Indo-Pacific: What's in a Name?," Lowy Institute for International Policy.
47. "Japan Unveils $110 Billion Plan to Fund Asia Infrastructure, Eye on AIIB," *Reuters*, May 21, 2015, http://www.reuters.com/article/2015/05/21/us-japan-asia-investment-idUSKBN0O617G20150521.
48. "Japan Open to Joining Belt and Road Push, East Asia News & Top Stories," *The Straits*

Times, accessed June 13, 2017, http://www.straitstimes.com/asia/east-asia/japan-open-to-joining-belt-and-road-push.

49. "Johann Hari: You Are Being Lied to about Pirates," *The Independent*, accessed November 3, 2015, http://www.independent.co.uk/voices/commentators/johann-hari/johann-hari-you-are-being-lied-to-about-pirates-1225817.html.
50. "Global Trends 2030."
51. "Snapshot," accessed November 3, 2015, http://thediplomat.com/2012/08/plenty-of-fish-in-the-sea-food-security-in-the-indian-ocean/.
52. "Notre Dame University -GAIN Index," accessed November 8, 2015, http://index.gain.org/
53. "China Offers Humanitarian Aid for Sri Lanka Flood Relief," *Xinhua, English.news.cn*, accessed June 15, 2017, http://news.xinhuanet.com/english/2017-05/29/c_136323571.htm.
54. "Chinese Government Continues to Provide Emergency Assistance to the Maldives," accessed June 15, 2017, http://www.fmprc.gov.cn/mfa_eng/zxxx_662805/t1217941.shtml.
55. "China Blocks Bid for U.N. Action on Pak. over Lakhvi," *The Hindu*, June 24, 2015, http://www.thehindu.com/news/national/china-blocks-bid-for-un-action-on-pak-over-lakhvi/article7347637.ece.
56. "The 1267 Committee, China's Hold and Masood Azhar: A Short History," *The Hindu*, accessed June 15, 2017, http://www.thehindu.com/news/international/the-1267-committee-chinas-hold-and-masood-azhar-a-short-history/article17353817.ece.
57 "Drug Trafficking and the Financing of Terrorism," accessed November 8, 2015, https://www.unodc.org/unodc/en/frontpage/drug-trafficking-and-the-financing-of-terrorism.html.
58. "Myanmar's Strongest Ethnic Armed Group Says Drug Label 'Not Fair,'" *Reuters*, October 7, 2016, http://www.reuters.com/article/us-myanmar-wa-idUSKCN1270R3.
59. "African Standby Force Starts First Military Exercises," *BBC News*, accessed November 12, 2015, http://www.bbc.com/news/world-africa-34570755.
60. MANAMA, "GCC Troops Dispatched to Bahrain to Maintain Order," accessed November 12, 2015, https://www.alarabiya.net/articles/2011/03/14/141445.html.
61. "Snapshot," accessed November 12, 2015, http://www.al-monitor.com/pulse/politics/2013/01/saudi-arabia-gcc-announcement.html#.
62. Covered in detail in Chapter Nine.
63. "NDRRM-South Asian Disaster Knowledge Network," accessed November 12, 2015, http://saarc-sadkn.org/ndrrm.aspx.
64. "NSA Level Meeting on Trilateral Maritime Security Cooperation between India, Sri Lanka and Maldives," accessed November 12, 2015, http://mea.gov.in/in-focus-article.htm?23037/NSA+level+meeting+on+trilateral+Maritime+Security+Cooperation+between+India+Sri+Lanka+and+Maldives.
65. "China and India Hold First Round of Dialogue on Maritime Cooperation," accessed August 28, 2017, http://www.fmprc.gov.cn/mfa_eng/wjbxw/t1339176.shtml.
66. "BIMSTEC Convention on Cooperation in Combating International Terrorism, Transnational Organised Crime And Illicit Drug Trafficking," accessed November 12, 2015, http://mea.gov.in/bilateral-documents.htm?dtl/5070/BIMSTEC+Convention+on+ Cooperation+in+Combating+International+Terrorism+Transnational+Organised+Crime+And+Illicit+Drug+Trafficking.
67. "ADMM-Plus - ASEAN Defence Minister's Meeting (ADMM)," accessed November 12, 2015, https://admm.asean.org/index.php/about-admm/about-admm-plus.html.
68. "ADMM, ASEAN Defence Ministers Meeting," accessed November 12, 2015, https://admm.asean.org/.
69. "The Indo-Pacific: What's in a Name?," Lowy Institute for International Policy.

70. Laura Zhou, South China Morning Post, "China and Asean Agree to Draft Code of Conduct in South China Sea," May 18, 2017, http://www.cnbc.com/2017/05/18/china-and-asean-agree-to-draft-code-of-conduct-in-south-china-sea.html.
71. "Background - IORA - Indian Ocean Rim Association," accessed November 12, 2015, http://www.iora.net/about-us/background.aspx.
72. "Member's Country, Indian Ocean Naval Symposium," accessed November 12, 2015, http://ions.gov.in/member_country.
73. "Julie Bishop MP Speeches - IORA - Indian Ocean Rim Association," accessed November 10, 2015, http://www.iora.net/documents/speeches.aspx.
74. "Communiqué - IORA - Indian Ocean Rim Association," accessed November 12, 2015, http://www.iora.net/documents/communique.aspx.
75. "Communiqué - IORA - Indian Ocean Rim Association," accessed November 4, 2015, http://www.iora.net/documents/communique.aspx.
76. "OBP Reports and Analysis," *OBP*, accessed November 3, 2015, http://oceansbeyondpiracy.org/obp-reports.
77. Compiled from various sources.
78. MH370 was a passenger flight that disappeared over the oceans on 8 March 2014 while flying from Kuala Lumpur to Beijing.
79. *"NDRRM-South Asian Disaster Knowledge Network."*
80. Martin Stopford, *Maritime Economics 3e*, 3 edition (London/ ; New York: Routledge, 2008).

Chapter 6

The Strategy of Nexus to Alliance: The China Pakistan Economic Corridor

Introduction

On November 13, 2016, Pakistan's Prime Minister along with the Army Chief flagged off the first ship from Gwadar port that was carrying a consignment which had arrived from China.[1] It comprised 120 truckloads of goods which took the western route through Balochistan to arrive at Gwadar, and thereafter was despatched to Africa on a Chinese ship. This symbolic event furthered two carefully nurtured myths regarding the China Pakistan Economic Corridor (CPEC): the first that the CPEC is about a western route through Balochistan and the second is that this is indeed a land bridge to the Indian Ocean, reducing China's Malacca vulnerability and transit time. This event was followed by some more fund infusion from China into the project, taking the total Chinese investment in the CPEC to USD 51 billion.[2] The perspectives and myths associated with the CPEC have been manifold; some significant facets of the project have got masked in the spiel. This chapter tries to provide some clarity from the copious information available on the CPEC, as available from open sources.

The case of the China Pakistan Economic Corridor (CPEC)—the rubric under which the BRI has unfolded in that country—is slightly different from the other projects of the BRI for two reasons. One, Pakistan is China's only noteworthy ally. This alliance is majorly borne of Pakistan's own insecurity as a nation, as well as China's desire to use Pakistan as a tool against India. This adds to the concerns that India has about the project. The second reason is that this segment of the BRI passes through the illegally occupied territory of Kashmir and is the root cause of India's position on the entire Chinese project.

The details of the Sino-Pak relationship have been covered extremely well by Andrew Small in the book *The China Pakistan Axis: Asia's New Geopolitics*. This chapter will not dwell on those aspects. It will instead attempt to provide an overview of how a whole new layer of economy has been added to that relationship through the BRI-CPEC. This could perhaps alter the strategic nexus between China and Pakistan, making it an alliance that complicates the security balance in South Asia.

The BRI as discussed in the previous chapters of this book, deploys the idle capital and infrastructure capacities of China commencing with its neighbourhood in a Sino-centric fashion. It rebrands the Chinese economic and foreign policy under one umbrella, giving it a recall value and synergy. This is as a strategy for China's further growth, which has become tenuous, having reached the upper levels of middle income. Even from the BRI perspective, the CPEC has a special status as the flagship project of that grand plan. The basic rationale that applies to the BRI discussed in Chapter Two is applicable to the CPEC also. As one of the earliest initiatives under its ambit, announced in 2013, with a large budgetary outlay of USD 40–50 billion,[3] the CPEC lays an economic warp over the existing strategic weft of the China–Pakistan relationship.

An 'Economic Corridor' is a bundle of 'focused' infrastructure projects beneficial to a geographic space, woven around a transportation axis. It connects economic hubs and nodes in order to target a diversified, synergised growth.[4] The CPEC definitely fits the definition as it is indeed a bouquet of projects along a spine. The projects under the CPEC include mines, power generation and transmission lines in the energy sector, fibre optic links and as sea and land ports spread across Pakistan. It has a prominent transportation spine, albeit not a continuous one, with road, rail and seaport projects in separate segments.

At the seaward end, it originates from Gwadar in Balochistan, winds through a yet undecided trajectory, enhances certain sections of the existing roads that lead up to the Karakoram Highway, which thence leads to Kashgar in Xinjiang, China. It aspires to integrate Pakistan's economy with China and in turn, by some accounts, attempts to connect China to the Indian Ocean bypassing the Malacca. President Xi Jinping sums it up as, "*China and Pakistan … need to form a "1+4" cooperation structure with the Economic Corridor at the centre and the Gwadar Port, energy, infrastructure and industrial cooperation being the four key areas to drive development across Pakistan and deliver tangible benefits to its people*".[5]

This chapter uses the data available on the Pakistani government websites to examine the CPEC, addressing the spatial distribution of projects and budgetary outlays and focuses on the energy sector. Energy, being the dominant factor in the CPEC, was chosen to be the central theme of this Chapter.

Types of CPEC Projects

For the purpose of this study, only those projects which have been budgeted for, as per the Pakistani government websites at the time of writing this book, have been considered. Unbudgeted projects have been listed but not used for calculations. It has been observed that the list of projects and costs have varied over time due to political pressures. The investment in July 2017 amounts to about USD 39.4 billion only (refer to **Annexure 1**). The comparative, sector-wise share of budgetary allocation is depicted in Figure 6.1.

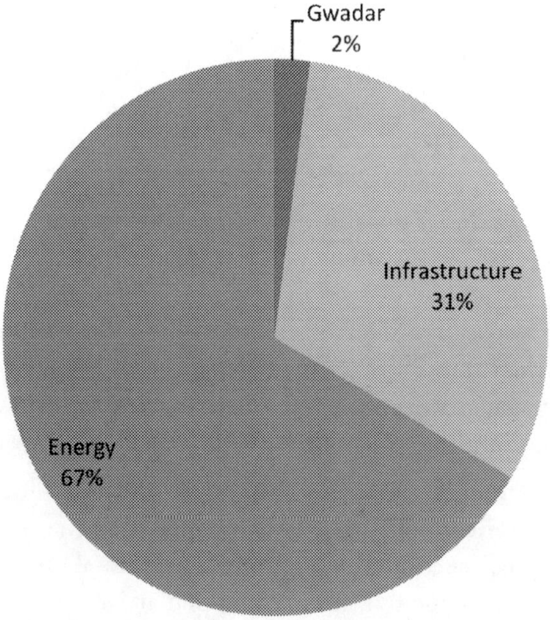

Figure 6.1. Sector-wise Investments in the CPEC (Road, Rail, Dry Port and Fibre Optics have been depicted under the sector of infrastructure)

The Transportation Network

The central spine of the corridor involves the following:

Roads. Presently, the CPEC has only budgeted for two specific road segments.

- **Havelian to Thakot-Karakoram Highway.** A section between Havelian, the northern most railhead and Thakot on the Karakoram Highway (KKH), at an approximate budget of USD 1.3 billion, is being built through the CPEC. The crucial link between China and Pakistan is the Karakoram Highway (KKH/N35). The KKH, also called as the China Pakistan Friendship Highway, runs for 800 km within Pakistan. In 2010, the KKH suffered extensive damage during floods, when a landslide blocked the Hunza River, formed a lake at Attabad and sunk approximately 20 km of the highway.[6] It took five years for an alternate route to become operational. This alternate route, inaugurated in September 2015, circumvented the Attabad Lake through five tunnels and bridges. The CPEC, in this tranche of investment, has addressed a section well south of this alternate section, calling it Phase II of the KKH work. This route is not open round the year as the Khunjerab Pass gets closed in winter due to snowfall for around four months, from the end of November to early April.[7] Roughly 8 per cent of the Sino-Pak trade used to take place through the Karakoram Highway.[8] This low volume of traffic can be attributed to the fact that most of Pakistan's trade with China is with the Guangdong and Zhejiang provinces, which are along the Chinese coast, and not with Xinjiang.[9]
- **Multan to Sukkur.** A section between Sukkur and Multan is being built at a cost of USD 2.8 billion, in the industrial heartland. This follows the Indus River along the Motorway 4. When conjoined with existing roads, it forms a part of the network from Khunjerab to Gwadar along the existing industrial belt.

Other Road Investments. Apart from the KKH, the only allocation of funds is for the eastern network of roads. This is contrary to the reports regarding separate alignments, especially highlighting a western alignment, which was alluded to during the inaugural run of cargo that arrived from China, flagged off from Gwadar by the Pakistani political leadership.[10] However, there is now a plan of a network of roads in the western regions, with unbudgeted road work from Khuzdar to Basima and Dera Ismail Khan to Zhob. The Thakot to Raikot section, along the KKH within Pakistan-Occupied Kashmir

(PoK), has also recently emerged as an unbudgeted CPEC project. These projects have been included after the 6th Joint Coordination Committee (JCC) on the CPEC, which met in December 2016 at Beijing, and were made public in early 2017.[11] As of June 2017, it emerges that the CPEC road investments are in pockets and does not cover the entire stretch between Khunjerab and Gwadar. Hence the investment in road projects alone is insufficient to arrive at any discernible alignment for the connectivity between Khunjareb and Gwadar. However, when viewed in conjunction with energy projects, patterns of a regional bias become evident. An overwhelmingly large number of CPEC energy projects are in the eastern parts of the country, whereas it is the western portions, in Balochistan and Khyber Pakhtunkhwa (KPK), that need real development. This is contrary to what the Pakistani political establishment claims that the CPEC is about the development of a western alignment through Balochistan.

Rail. Pakistan has three major railway lines which connect the various cities and industrial centres. Main Line 1 (ML1) runs from Karachi to Peshawar. ML2 runs parallel to the Indus River unlike ML1 which is biased eastward towards Lahore. ML3 branches off from ML1 at Rohri as a north–south line and heads westwards, just short of Quetta, parallel to the Afghan border onwards to Iran. The focus, insofar as rail connectivity is concerned, has been on the main railway line (ML1) which carries 70 per cent of the domestic traffic. This line will be improved for achieving higher speeds. The original investment of USD 3,650 million has been enhanced with a second tranche after the 6th JCC meeting. This has raised the overall investment in ML1 to USD 8,172 million. This is one of the largest Chinese financed infrastructure plans in Pakistan so far, and certainly the largest in the CPEC for any single project. In connection with the rail investment, the CPEC also envisages a dry port at the northern most rail head at Havelian, for onward routing via the Karakoram Highway.

Port. The main and only budgeted investment is in Gwadar Port presently. Though less than two per cent of the total CPEC investment, it is technically the geographic spot in the BRI where the land and maritime networks converge. There is a gamut of investments here including port works, airport, projects to deal with water shortage, etc. These projects are listed in Figure 6.2 and **Annexure 1**. Gwadar's commercial viability as a transhipment port is suspect, considering its distance from the circum-equatorial navigation route. Surprisingly, Gwadar also lacks rail connectivity with the hinterland, a basic prerequisite for a port. The plans for investments on rail projects under the

CPEC also do not include connectivity to Gwadar, though a map on the Pakistan Railway website shows a prospective line that would cost USD 4.5 billion![12]

The firm that constructed and is operating the Gwadar port, the China Overseas Port Holding (Pakistan), is a Chinese state-owned company and has very thin commercial presence elsewhere unlike other Chinese firms like China Merchants Port Holdings, Landbridge, Hutchison or COSCO. In fact, China Overseas Holding Ltd, a 'real' company, put out a media message saying it has nothing to do with Gwadar.[13] The COPH had in turn outsourced the construction in Gwadar to another Chinese company named Zhuhai Port.[14] The Gwadar port is on a 40-year lease to this firm commencing in 2013. The company has three separate entities at Gwadar: the Gwadar International Terminals Ltd (GITL) for Container Operations, the Gwadar Marine Services Ltd (GMSL) for port services and the Gwadar Free Zone Ltd (GFZL) operating the SEZ.

Gwadar was originally an Omani enclave which was purchased by Pakistan. Attempts were made to hand over the port in the 1970s to the United States, which did not materialise. In 2006, after several years, the first phase of construction of the port was completed with Chinese assistance. The port was leased to the Port of Singapore Authority (PSA)[15] for operations. The port is connected to Karachi via the Makaran coastal highway which was completed in 2004. The development of the port needed acquisition of naval land, which was not given up by the Pakistan Navy. Since the port started operations in 2007, it has been operating at 15 per cent of its capacity,[16] with only 92 ships docking there in the first three years.[17]

Gwadar has three multipurpose berths. The depth alongside is 14.5 m, permitting vessels with 12.5 m draft to use the harbour. This is sufficient for all warships, which are low draft vessels, are lighter and have greater maneuverability as they generally have a twin-shaft configuration. This is unlike merchant ships which normally have a single shaft, larger and with deeper draft. For example, *Liaoning*, the largest ship of the PLA Navy, draws 8.9 m of water, whereas a merchant vessel usually draws more, with fully laden ULCCs drawing up to 24 m. Presently, the dimensions of Gwadar port precludes ships larger than 70,000 DWT from using the port.[18]

In 2011, the tables turned as China took over the port. The Singaporean firm withdrew from the contract and some of the naval land requisitioned for development was handed over to the Chinese firm. Since then, there have been strong indications that this port is headed to be a naval harbour.

Considering these aspects, this port, in all likelihood, is planned to be a strategic port for military use and could end up being a military base. This is in line with the latest US DoD report to the Congress which states "China most likely will seek to establish additional military bases in countries with which it has a longstanding friendly relationship and similar strategic interests, such as Pakistan, and in which there is a precedent for hosting foreign militaries".[19] The planned infrastructure development, along with the budget allocated for the Gwadar Port, is placed in Figure 6.2.

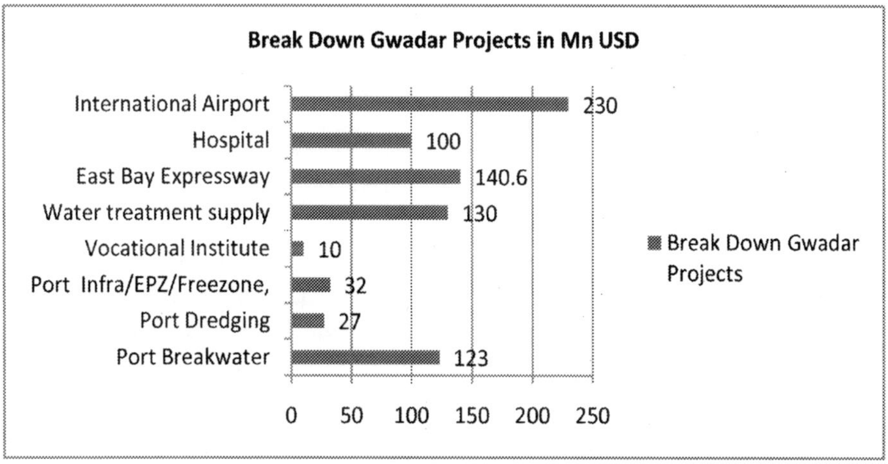

Figure 6.2. CPEC Projects at Gwadar[20]

The Gwadar port, along with the base at Djibouti, offers China the advantages of having a base at a short distance from the energy choke points of Hormuz and Bab Al Mandeb. Gwadar sits just 120 miles from the Straits of Hormuz through which 30 per cent of global oil flows and it leads to the Persian Gulf. Asian markets consume 85 per cent of that oil. Both China and India have a high level of dependence on oil that passes through that strait. 70 per cent of India's oil passes via the Hormuz. Therefore Gwadar's proximity to Hormuz makes it a significant cog in chokepoint politics. Incidentally, the US Fifth Fleet is based at Bahrain in the Persian Gulf. That makes any Chinese presence at Gwadar, a matter of concern not only for India, but also for the US with a rising Chinese influence in the Middle East.

Ever since navies made the transition from coal to oil and underway fuelling, whereby you can pump fuel from a tanker while moving, it has kept fleets away from ports. Ships no more need to touch harbours merely to refuel; specialised tankers quench their need for fuel at sea. The Chinese have operated away from their home ports for months, during the Anti-Piracy Expeditionary

Force patrols in the Gulf of Aden, to prove the point. However, these ships still have to head to harbour for repairs or replenishment of weapons like missiles or torpedoes, which cannot be done underway. Gwadar, along with Djibouti, and many other prospective ports can come handy in such circumstances.

Despite the capability to carry out underway replenishment, warships, like merchant ships, need ports, when tankers are not available. Such a requirement can be met by a port like Gwadar. Fuel and other consumables can easily be transported and prepositioned via sea or road at Gwadar, catering to this need quite easily. In certain cases, warships also need repairs of a unique nature. For example, high pressure air and hydraulic systems on board require quality welding. This will require special tools, infrastructure and trained manpower. First-level repairs can be arranged by locally stationed manpower and equipment. However, complicated repairs present larger infrastructure and manpower needs, often by Original Equipment Manufacturers (OEMs) or skilled yardsmen. Establishing such facilities on a permanent basis at Gwadar will take some time. Hull repairs need a dry dock, which is presently not available at Gwadar, and would take time to build. High technology vessels like nuclear submarines may require even more support when ashore, considering the nature of the safeties involved.

Naval logistics also involve replenishment of weapons. Weapons require timely turnaround and maintenance. In times of conflict, weapons are also utilised and require to be replenished. Weapons require specialised transportation due to their safety requirement, preferably by rail, which Gwadar lacks. However they can be transported by road and ship with some penalties on their service life. Transportation by air is another possibility.

Gwadar is short on drinking water supply. However, desalination plants can deal with small requirements. Desalination is not economical, but strategic needs can always be met through such initiatives. The maintenance of a township, which will be required, if Gwadar finally achieves its potential, will require far more water than it presently consumes, making desalination a costly affair.

Gwadar can aid the Chinese surveillance capability in the IOR. China can have a deeper stake of the Pakistan AIS or radar chain to closely monitor all traffic that passes nearby and correlate with the existing white shipping data. High promontories near coasts assist the creation of a surveillance chain with greater ranges. Smaller ships from Gwadar can quickly be deployed for investigation of contacts and for augmenting the surveillance chain. This surveillance capability would be utilised for the interdiction of contacts, either by air or sea. The possibility of Chinese DF 21D Anti-Ship Ballistic Missile (ASBM) batteries being located at Gwadar at a future date cannot be ruled out.

The International airport at Gwadar, that is being planned as a part of the CPEC, would be an asset for naval operations. It can increase the surveillance swathe by basing MR aircraft, transport personnel, weapons and spares. Ship-borne aircraft can be based at this airport for maintenance. Similarly, shore-based strike aircraft could be relocated or staged through for interdiction of ships at sea. The airport can thus act in tandem with the port, as is the case with most naval ports belonging to other navies. Another possibility is the deployment of the PLA Navy aircraft at Gwadar or cross-deployment of such aircraft from Djibouti.

Once developed as a naval port, Gwadar can serve as an alternate port for the Pakistan Navy, which presently operates from the Jinnah Naval Base at Ormara and the Karachi Harbour. Gwadar serves as an alternate port further away from Karachi and the Indian subcontinent. Ships sailing out from Gwadar can get into international sea lane from Hormuz more quickly and merge with the traffic and then operate in the IOR. Together with Djibouti, Gwadar opens multiple options to China in the northern Indian Ocean.

There are also plans to include the development of the Keti Bandar port near the Indian border, in the CPEC projects.

Fibre Optic Link. A key project is the Pakistan-China Fibre Optic Project, at a cost of USD 44 million. This will enhance telecommunication through the Gilgit Baltistan Region and is to be handled by the Strategic Communication Organisation. The Fibre Optic link will connect Rawalpindi with Kashgar.

Focus on Energy: Pakistan's Power Sector

The primary focus of the CPEC is energy which constitutes 67 per cent of the total investments. In fact, the dismal energy situation in Pakistan is the reason for this. Given that energy is central to any economy, issues with energy affect industries, with cascading effects on the investment climate, growth, employment, etc. Estimates by the Asian Development Bank reveal that power shortage results in a loss of 2–3 per cent of Pakistan's annual GDP.[21] Pakistan's power sector presently faces multiple problems as enumerated below:

(a) **Shortage.** Pakistan's installed energy capacity is 25 GW.[22] While the demand for energy is 21 GW, production hovers around

16 GW. Not all installed capacity can be utilised since some plants would be under maintenance. Thus, Pakistan has a power shortage of about 5 GW.[23] This figure varies depending on the time of the day and season. There is also a shortage in transmission capacity, which was around 16,300 MW in 2015[24] whereby, even if all the shortages in generation were made good, the transmission capacity would limit its distribution. The CPEC therefore, includes generation and transmission projects.

(b) **Cost of Electricity.** Pakistan has a very high cost of electricity production. Pakistan charges the consumer an average of PKR 16.95 for a unit of electricity, which is the highest in the SAARC region, whereas the equivalent cost of electricity in India is PKR 7.36, PKR 5.47 in Bangladesh and PKR 8.59 in the US.[25] This high cost also results in the non-payment of bills.

(c) **Use of Costly Fuel.** The primary cause of this high production cost of electricity is the present mix of fuel that is used for the generation of electricity. Pakistan produces electricity using oil (35 per cent), natural gas (29 per cent), hydroelectricity (30 per cent), nuclear and wind energy (5 per cent) and imports from Iran (1 per cent).[26] This mix avoids coal. Though coal is considered a polluting fuel, it is a cheap source of energy. Developing nations can hardly ignore the use of coal in case they want to keep electricity costs within reasonable limits. India uses 60 per cent coal and China uses 70 per cent coal in the production of electricity. However, the Pakistan energy sector has evolved differently, avoiding the use of coal. This contrasts with the usual pattern of developing nations and has been a major reason for the present high cost of electricity.

(d) **Subsidy and Circular Debt.** High costs lead to subsidies from the government, which in turn affects economy. Despite the subsidy, the cost to the consumer is high, incentivising non-payment and power theft, which triggers a 'circular debt'. This term describes the vicious cycle where the consumer doesn't pay the distribution company, affecting payments to transmission, generation and fuel companies. The results are debts, stoppage of production and power cuts. Currently, the overall debt in the power sector is around USD 5 billion.[27]

(e) **High Import Bill.** Pakistan imports far more goods than it exports, resulting in an unfavourable balance of payment situation.

> The oil and gas used for electricity generation in Pakistan is imported and constitutes 35 per cent of the import bill. The GDP of Pakistan is USD 269.9 billion with a growth rate of 4.1 per cent in 2016.[28] It has foreign exchange reserves of only USD 20 billion,[29] whereas the present external debt is USD 79 billion, or 30 per cent of the GDP, which is large when compared to similar economies.[30] Its economy is under an extended fund facility by the IMF which has already issued a warning pertaining to the energy sector, as well as CPEC payments. The extended fund facility by the IMF is a programme to assist countries facing a balance of payment crisis.[31] If the fuel import bill and low exports grow unchecked, the balance of payment and debt situation will only worsen.

Hence the present dismal energy situation in Pakistan is due to interlinked problems such as the under capacity of the energy sector in production and transmission, high costs caused by an inefficient energy mix and a subsidy burden which creates an unfavourable balance of payment situation. It, therefore, creates a negative spiral in the economy in multiple ways.

CPEC Solutions in the Energy Sector: Problems and Prospects

In case the Chinese want to undertake any investment or industrial cooperation in Pakistan, as President Xi Jinping has indicated, the power situation in Pakistan must improve in a comprehensive manner. It is with this aim of preparing the ground for further investments, that energy appears to be a core focus area in the CPEC.

The CPEC promises several solutions in the energy sector. First, it adds three times the current shortfall as new power projects. The total capacity of the power generation plants being launched under the CPEC is 14.8 GW of which 10.4 GW would be executed as priority 'early harvest' projects. Therefore, presently the planned investment is roughly three times the shortfall. This indicates that some legacy oil-based plants may be shut down in the future.

Secondly, it infuses coal, hydro and renewable power sources into the current energy mix reducing the overall cost, since coal is cheaper than oil and gas. Of these new projects that will add 14.8 GW of the power generation capacity, 10.8 GW would be from coal-based projects. The rest of the projects are based on renewable energy sources. Notably, oil is totally avoided in the CPEC projects.

It is expected that this will reduce the foreign exchange requirements to some degree, though not completely. Pakistan's oil import bill was USD 14.77 billion in 2014 and was down to USD 7 billion in 2016. This reduction was primarily due to low oil prices.[32] A cheaper fuel like coal will indeed decrease the cost of imports further and provide alternatives to Pakistan, making its electricity generation less vulnerable to the price shocks driven by a single commodity in a volatile market.

This high infusion of coal- based projects will change the energy mix of Pakistan. From a near-zero use of coal, with the CPEC, Pakistan's 27 per cent energy will be produced from coal. Renewables will go up from 1–4% in the energy mix for power production. Figures 6.3, 6.4 and 6.5 illustrate the transition infused by the CPEC. This is one attribute of the CPEC which gets missed in the myth-making about being the land bridge to the Indian Ocean and the Western Alignment through Balochistan.

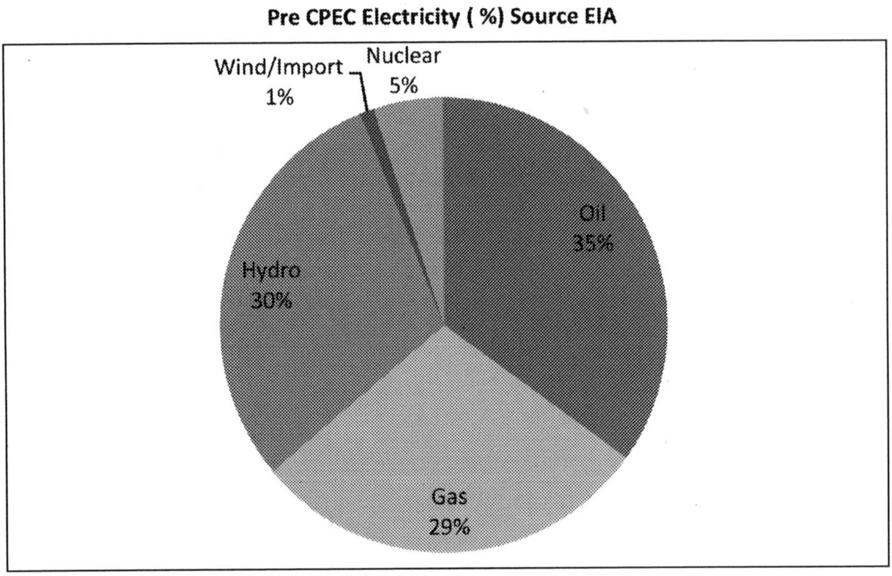

Figure 6.3. Type of Fuel presently used in Pakistan

Will Coal Solve the Problem?

At a time when the world is moving away from coal, Pakistan, through the CPEC, is commencing the generation of power with coal. This therefore requires some more analysis. A vast majority of the coal-based power plants coming up as a part of CPEC are supercritical steam-based coal power plants that are capable of working at higher temperatures. They will also use imported

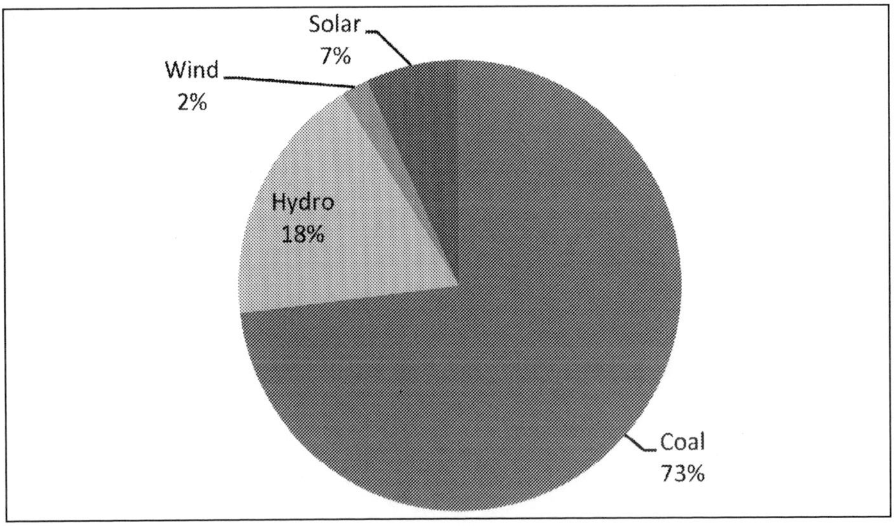

Figure 6.4. Type of Fuel Mix in the CPEC

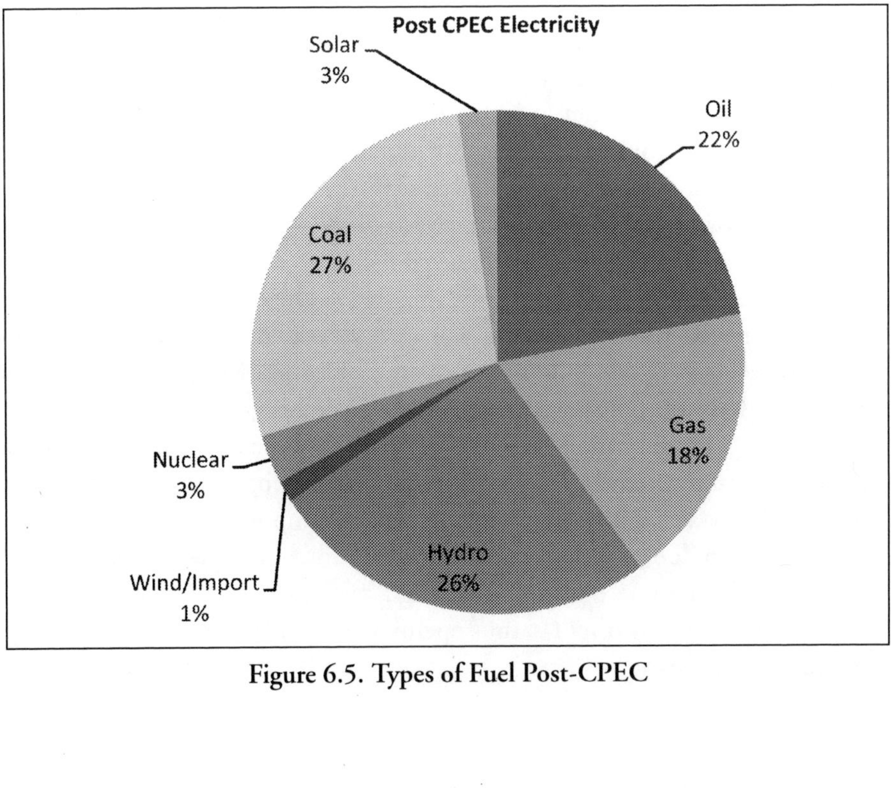

Figure 6.5. Types of Fuel Post-CPEC

bituminous coal with a high calorific value as Pakistan doesn't have large reserves of this variety of coal. Its reserves are mostly lignite, or low calorific coal (Refer **Table 6.1**). Hence barring power plants like Thar and Engro which are co-located with coal mines, high grade coal will be imported from abroad and, therefore, will not solve the external dependency or balance of trade and payment problems which the legacy energy sources have imposed. Coal-based power will also add to climate change. Pakistan, which has borne extreme weather calamities in recent years, has to be concerned about such an initiative, though climate change, unlike pollution, is not a localised event.[33]

Table 6.1. Pakistan's Coal Production versus Import (in kilotonnes)

Type of Coal	Bitumen	Lignite	Coke Gas	Coking Coal	Blast Furnace
Production	2383	1168	81	-	733
Import	2645	-	-	115	-

Source: International Energy Agency.[34]

Specifics of Thermal Plants and Coal

As far as new coal power plants being built under the CPEC are concerned, they will mostly be supercritical steam-based coal power plants. In a supercritical steam power plant, the steam needs to be heated to a higher temperature and to do that, it is maintained at a high pressure. Since there is a requirement of more heat, high calorific value coal is used. So, you get more heat from a less volume of coal. These plants need superior metallurgy. The new set of power plants, barring the Sino Sindh (SSRL) mine mouth water plant and Thar Engro, use imported coal. Pakistan doesn't have high calorific coal reserves, hence, coal needs to be imported. The coal reserves of Pakistan are concentrated in Thar and the Salt Range area where only lignite, a low calorific coal is available. Lignite is not an economical fuel when transported to a distant location. The lower the quality of coal, the higher the transportation cost as a percentage of the overall coal cost. Both these mines have subcritical plants integral to them in the CPEC plans considering the advantages of co-location. Since a majority of coal plants will use imported, high calorific coal which Pakistan does not possess, they will continue to impact the import bill, albeit to a lesser value than oil. This high calorific value coal will be, in all likelihood, sourced by imports, thus opening new sea-lanes of communications and resource politics.

Financial Aspects of the CPEC. Considering the vast number of Sino-Pak projects, there is an ambiguity regarding projects that constitute the CPEC. For purposes of this paper, only those projects which have been budgeted as a CPEC project, as per the Pakistani government websites, have been considered. This amounts to about only USD 39.48 billion worth of projects as of July 2017 (a tabular status of the CPEC Projects is attached as Annexure 1). This is a figure that has varied over time, as projects have been added or cancelled. This is a substantial amount when compared to the United States' cumulative assistance to Pakistan of USD67 billion (corrected to 2011 USD) for 60 years between 1951 and 2011.[35] An analysis of Chinese investment in Pakistan reveals that from 2005 to 2016, China invested around USD 44.4 billion in Pakistan including the CPEC investment.[36]

The CPEC also does not include major projects like the Lahore Metro[37] involving USD 1.55 billion[38] and nuclear power financing worth USD 6.5 billion, which are projects with substantial Chinese assistance.[39] Arms transfers like the Yuan-class submarine deal is a high value Sino-Pak transaction worth over USD 5 billion which has taken place outside CPEC structures.[40] There is also a USD 2.5 billion, 711-kilometre-long natural gas pipeline from Gwadar to Nawabshah,[41] contracted to a Chinese firm which is not part of the CPEC. Hence, though CPEC is the main rubric for Chinese assistance to Pakistan, there are significant and strategic Sino-Pak projects progressing concurrently, outside the CPEC umbrella.

The infrastructure projects of the CPEC are funded at an interest rate of about around 1.6 per cent. Unlike the infrastructure segment, where the government would normally be involved, the energy projects of the CPEC mostly involve Sino-Pak private partnership. Chinese banks like the EXIM bank and China Development Bank would be financing these private investments at an interest rate of 5–6 per cent. The energy sector is 67 per cent of the present investment. However, the projects at Gwadar will be interest-free, indicating the importance of the projects at Gwadar and the other concessions that may be offered or claimed by the Chinese in lieu of interest. The Government of Pakistan will also be contractually obliged to purchase electricity from those firms at pre-negotiated rates and provide a sovereign guarantee. The pre-negotiated rate is reported to be PKR 18 per unit, which is higher than the current cost of a unit of electricity in Pakistan, which in 2016–17 was PKR 16.95. This high rate of electricity that would be drawn from the CPEC projects, according to an analyst "*...is a classical colony-making exercise by China, which the Pakistan establishment and the Army is quite excited* *with*".[42] The Chinese firms seek a 'revolving fund' backed by sovereign guarantee, amounting to 22 per cent of the power tariffs,[43] which could amount to USD 700 million annually for all projects if the local firms default.[44] This could be unfavourable to Pakistan in the long-term. However, Pakistan's energy and economic scenario being where it is today, it has little choice but to take this bitter pill. The debt equity ratio of energy projects are to the order of 25 per cent equity: 75 per cent debt. The loan in addition to interest carries an insurance fee of 7 per cent with Sinosure, the Chinese insurance arm. The returns on equity for these projects are at a very high rate of up to 34 per cent, which will ultimately be borne by the consumer.[45] The CPEC loan repayments will amount to USD 3.5 billion per annum for which Pakistan has to find a source.[46] The International Monetary Fund (IMF) in its October 2016 review of the Pakistani economy had several observations about the impact of the CPEC.[47] Though it conceded that if implemented as envisaged, the CPEC would impact the Pakistan economy positively; it predicts a substantial impact on the balance of payment and outflows. It warns that outflows could reach about 0.4 per cent of the GDP per year in the longer run.

The FDI flow into Pakistan, which has been portrayed in a graph below, indicates that in the past 5 years, the annual FDI inflow has been less than USD 2 billion. At such a rate it can take more than 23 years for the infusion of USD 45 billion into the economy, thus stretching the timelines of the CPEC. (Refer Fig. 6.6).

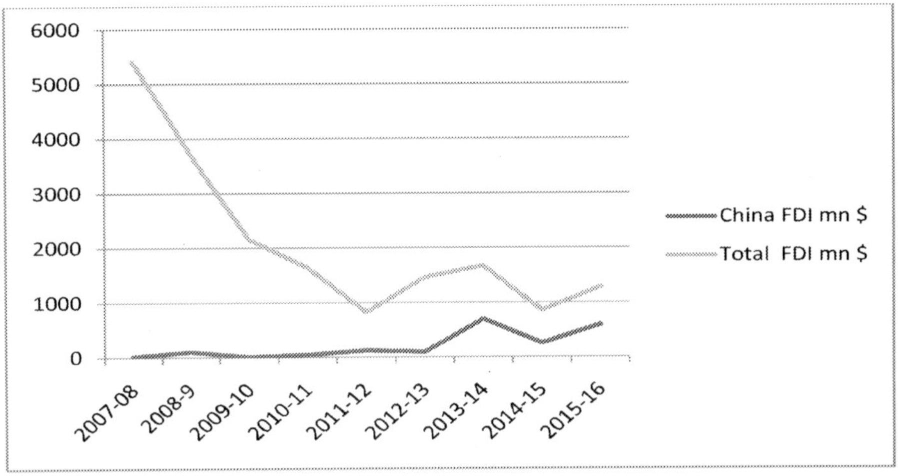

Figure 6.6. FDI Flow into Pakistan[48]
(*Source:* Board of Investment Pakistan, http://boi.gov.pk/foreigninvestmentinpakistan.aspx)

Cost of Installation

The CPEC-linked projects will eventually add 14.8 GW of power generation capacity at a cost of USD 26.2 billion, which works out to a rate of USD 1.7 billion per GW, when all projects are considered. The cost estimates for installation of power plants in the CPEC varies from USD 2.5 billion/GW for wind-powered plants, USD 1.215 billion/GW for solar-powered plants, USD 2.08 billion/GW for hydroelectric power plants and USD 1.45 billion/GW for coal-powered plants.[49] On the other hand, the cost of building thermal power plants in India is less than USD 1 billion/GW.[50] This will benefit the investors both in Pakistan and China. China also benefit with the Chinese firms getting contracts, besides the sovereign guarantee and power purchase commitments.

Other Issues

The Pakistani energy sector also suffers from the problems of load management, inefficient transmission, obsolete technology, theft, subsidies, obligation to provide free power, overstaffing, etc.[51] Barring Punjab, all other provinces, especially Khyber Pakhtunkhwa and Balochistan, have a suboptimal power distribution system and lack the capacity to distribute additional load to the consumers.[52]

Regional Spread of Projects

A study of the regional spread of the planned power projects reveals that they are focussed towards Sindh and Punjab. Balochistan has projects in Hub (on the border of Sindh) and Gwadar. The Kohala hydroelectric project is being planned in Pakistan-Occupied Kashmir. Of these power projects, the Karot project in Punjab is funded by the Silk Road Fund, a vehicle created exclusively for the BRI. Major projects of Balochistan like Gaddani have been cancelled as per the information available from the Pakistani government websites, leaving vast swathes of Balochistan devoid of any energy projects. Less than 10 per cent of the money being spent on the CPEC projects will be invested in Balochistan. As per a report, the committee to acquire land for the western route has not met till date.[53] Figure 6.7 provides a region-wise distribution of the investments planned to be made as a part of the CPEC. Road and rail projects that do not limit themselves to a province have been distributed proportionally between provinces in this graph.

If one were to connect the dots representing energy projects, the notional eastern alignment becomes far more prominent, indicating that CPEC-driven

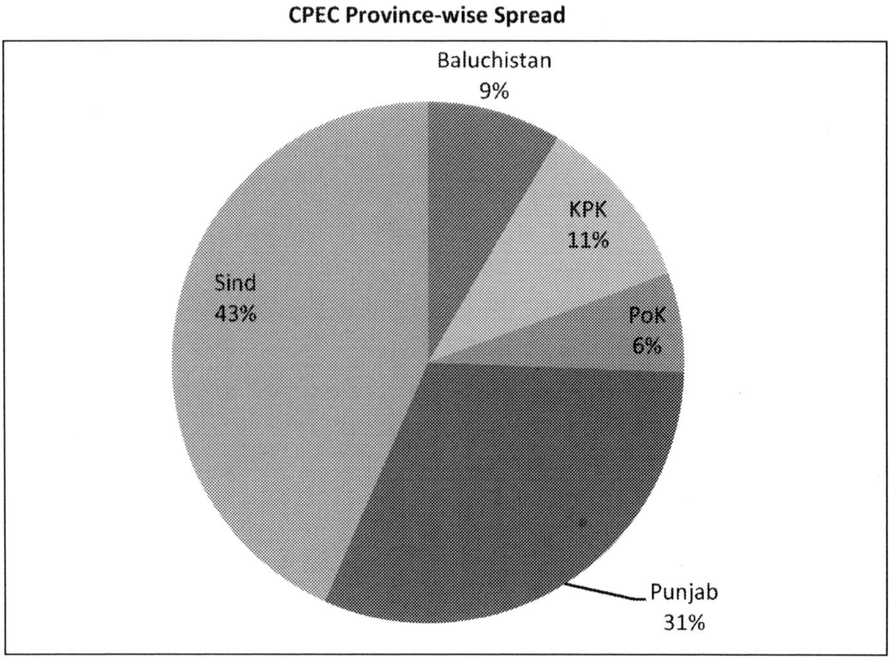

Figure 6.7. CPEC projects based on Provinces (Except Rail)
(*Source*: Calculated by the author from cpec.gov.pk)

development is presently evading most of Balochistan. The road between Multan and Sukkur, the budgeted road project other than the KKH, is also on the eastern alignment. Hence, one must conclude that the western alignment remains aspirational with projects being mostly along the eastern regions of Pakistan (Refer Fig. 6.8; stars indicate projects that have been budgeted). This is the reason why the much touted western alignment through Balochistan, with its inaugural run, appears to be a part of poorly executed myth-making.

CPEC Management.[55] There is a three-tier management system in place for the CPEC which involves a Sino-Pak joint management structure for respective domains, a parliamentary oversight committee and a high-power committee with provincial representation within Pakistan. It is expected that the Pakistani military, at some stage, will be involved in the management, though as of early 2017 the military is only involved in providing security to CPEC projects.[56] The 'inaugural run' in November 2017 saw the presence of the Army Chief in Gwadar, just prior to his retirement. This was well before the 'corridor' was ready. This indicates some eagerness by the military leadership

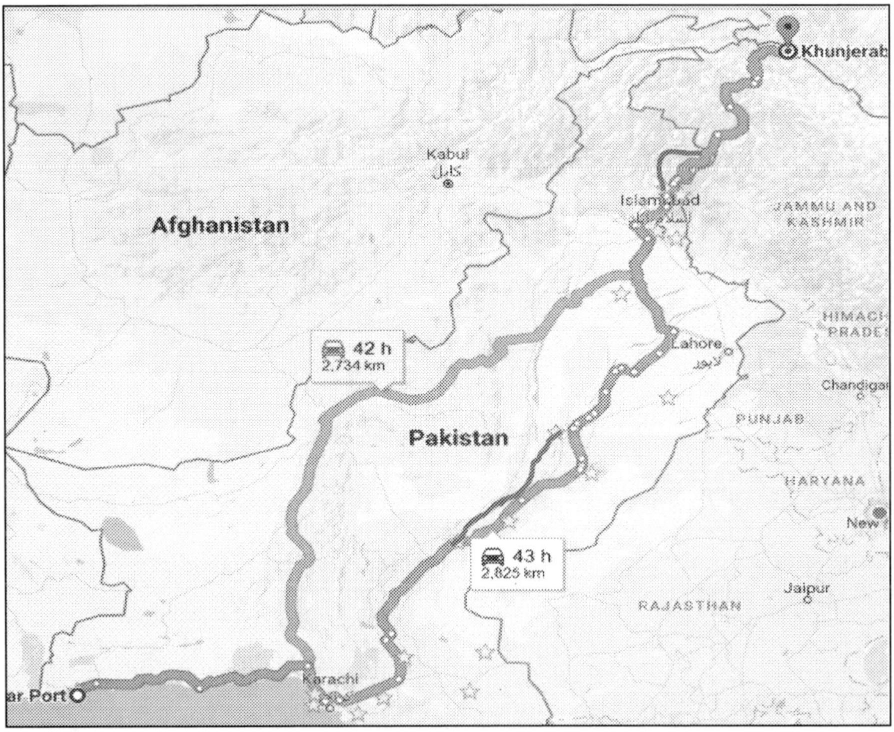

Figure 6.8. Power projects of the CPEC (denoted by stars) and approximate road segments in red showing an eastern bias. The grey line shows the notional western route.[54]

to showcase its support for CPEC especially, Gwadar and the Western Alignment segment, as a national project with strategic importance.

Conclusion

So far, the Pakistan–China Relations had been confined to military and strategic transactions. The CPEC has broken that trend to let this relationship spill over into the economic domain. What commenced as a symbiotic relation after the 1962 Sino-Indian conflict, mainly to deal with India, bloomed through the Cold War where Pakistan played an important role. Today, Pakistan is the only major ally of China on all political issues. The waning US interest and Trump administration's policy for the region has only brought them closer. The additional economic overlay through the CPEC makes the relations deeper, complicating the Asian and Indian Ocean Region politics. It is also a challenging relation to China as well as Pakistan as they are entering uncharted waters.

The CPEC reflects the economic rationale of the BRI. Through the CPEC, China is using its capital and idle capacity to create critical infrastructure in neighbourhood. It also grants it greater strategic purchase in the IOR littoral, while aiming to absorb the Pakistani economy into a Sino-centric value chain.

Flushed with a few trillions in reserves, USD 40–45 billion is a very small share which has been planned for deployment in Pakistan under the BRI-CPEC rubric. There too, it has been invested quite astutely, where a large percentage of the investments would fetch high returns, with sovereign guarantees and strategic collaterals safeguarding China's investments. There is an offset derivative of this investment where most of the investments will flow back to China, as the Chinese firms will get the contracts for the infrastructure projects, bringing employment and profits back to China. Yet, considering Pakistan's tenuous economic situation, the only country that has come forward to assist Pakistan, is China. It has not only brought in the money but also a plan for the development of power generation, industry and infrastructure for Pakistan. China expects that such a strengthening of an ally can assist its overall global position.

The CPEC is presently more about energy projects and less about the corridor. The blueprint addresses certain core concerns of the economy, while the corridor remains a metaphor. There is no 'one' continuous road or even a clear alignment in the CPEC as some imagine. If at all there is one, it is biased towards the prosperous eastern regions accentuating the existing domestic fissures of Pakistan. The CPEC investments are in those pockets where returns are high, like in Sindh and Punjab, ignoring Balochistan, earning it a sobriquet of the ***China Punjab Energy Corridor***.

Sensing the root cause of the dismal state of the Pakistani economy, China seems to have reckoned that it will be only by easing the deep energy crisis and by improving transportation within the country that Pakistan can be of any use to the BRI plans.

The current phase of the CPEC deals with improving this critical infrastructure. There is indeed an industrial phase of the CPEC which has not yet been publicised. Around the time of the Belt and Road Forum (BRF) summit in Many 2017, a masterplan which highlighted various industrial and agricultural centres was leaked by the Pakistani newspaper *Dawn*, giving a glimpse of these intentions. That industrial phase of the CPEC can only follow after the basic infrastructure is in place. In the energy domain the CPEC is also a bitter pill of infusing coal into the energy basket of Pakistan. This step is expected to make energy cheaper and adequate. However, only deep reforms can turn Pakistan's energy and economic situation around. Though climate has never been on Pakistan's priority list, the CPEC shepherds it into an age of coal when the rest of the world, ironically led by China, is weaning away from coal. There is hardly a qualm about pollution and climate issues amidst the euphoria over the CPEC. Just as it embraced the oil and gas route for the power sector earlier, ignoring coal to its own economic peril, it is now embracing coal at a time when renewables offer attractive alternatives.

Strategy and economy cannot be treated in silos. They influence one another. Strategic reasons continue to lie at the core of the Sino-Pak relationship. Pakistan has been the largest customer of Chinese arms till date. This Chinese policy has yielded for it high returns, considering the unsettled border with India. It expects that a well-armed Pakistan would keep India occupied, assuaging China's insecurities in the Indian Ocean. The impending sale of eight Yuan-class submarines gives a fillip to this strategy. Half of these will be built in Pakistan, which has ramifications—providing Pakistan with the ability to tweak its design to meet the requirements of 'full spectrum nuclear deterrence'. In the nuclear field, historically, both nations have cooperated and proliferated with impunity, bartering technologies.[57] Notably, both these major investments are outside the CPEC rubric. The availability of Chinese capital gives greater latitude to Pakistan, freeing up its meagre revenues for deployment in its military. Gwadar and Karakoram together use only ten percentage of the overall CPEC budget, but they have a disproportionate strategic effect. When the Karakoram Highway fuses these entities to present a double front from a continental perspective, Gwadar could extend this to a maritime domain with a base in the Indian Ocean.

Pakistan's ability to absorb the infusion of capital, as well as its ability to pay back the CPEC loans, is suspect. This can lead to China claiming strategic equity, reinforcing its grip over crucial assets in Pakistan. Gwadar turning into a Chinese staging post or a proper naval base could be a natural consequence of this. Gwadar has limited commercial utility with low connectivity indices to the global maritime network and has a politically volatile, barren hinterland it hopes to serve. Pipelines or rail to connect Gwadar with the rest of the country or China are neither there nor currently planned under the CPEC. Even the roads which the CPEC touts to develop through Balochistan appear as an unbudgeted afterthought to deflect the criticism of ignoring Balochistan. Port operations in Gwadar are being carried out by a Chinese firm with limited public presence. This is much unlike Colombo, Karachi, Hambantota or Tilawa which are carried out by well-heeled reputed

Chinese firms. The land for Gwadar Port was held up during the PSA's control over Gwadar and was released by the Pakistan Navy only after China took over the project. Hence, the matter of Gwadar becoming a Chinese staging post or a Chinese naval base is only a question of time. This will not only be beneficial for China, but will offer Pakistan an alternate base, should the naval bases at Karachi and Ormara become defunct during a crisis. The CPEC with its new found requirement for imported coal will give rise to new resource politics for coal. Australia, South Africa and Indonesia could be the source for this coal. There are also a few foreign institutions involved in the CPEC as per the Pakistani government website including France for airport design and the UAE, Malaysia and Qatar, though on a minimal scale.

In a carefully cultivated myth, Pakistan capitalises on China's dependence on Malacca and trade in the Indian Ocean. This is examined in Chapter Eight on access, since multiple options like Myanmar, Thailand and Malaysia need to be compared to get a comprehensive picture of access. The CPEC in its present form does not run the full distance in Pakistan by road, rail or pipeline to evacuate the high volumes that the ships can discharge. The transport spine of that corridor is only being reinforced in profitable segments. Even if it gets completed at some point in time, the basic economics of transportation, seasonal closures of the Khunjerab pass and Chinese provincial trade patterns with Pakistan, where the coastal provinces trade more than Xinjiang, will logically limit the volume of trade. Only 7–8 per cent of trade between China and Pakistan used to be carried out through the Karakoram Highway before it got flooded in 2010. Xinjiang, where the CPEC enters China, is not only energy-rich but also receives Central Asian oil and gas through pipelines. Hence the argument that the CPEC would be an alternate conduit for trade through the Malacca Straits doesn't cut ice when one compares it with the Chinese land bridges being planned through Myanmar, Malaysia and Thailand which are not only shorter, but also serve Chinese regions which have an energy deficit, like Yunnan and the coastal provinces. However, in a crisis situation involving sea lanes, the Karakoram highway may become handy, in a small, albeit critical measure—a lesson that the Stilwell Road taught China during World War II.[58] Even though the better surveillance and interdiction capabilities available today, may foreclose such options during a crisis, it is possibly this thought, among other strategic advantages, of pleasing an ally that lay at the Chinese calculus when it risked Indian outrage by planning the CPEC through the disputed Indian territory illegally occupied by Pakistan. This has led to a very strong response from India, since it lies at the core of Indian indifference and protests over the BRI.

There is an alternate narrative with regard to the CPEC which propounds that, as the energy situation improves with the CPEC, the industries can grow and generate employment resulting in societal change in Pakistan. It may then need markets for its products, or be a part of the value chain. Both need connectivity. However, Pakistan has a hardened self-inflicted policy of political and geographic isolation from India which is its natural, adjacent market. Such a scenario limits its trading options affecting economic progress. Therefore, in a curious twist of fate, China's BRI connectivity plan for growth has played into Pakistan's paranoia and has become an extension of Pakistan's India policy. This in effect has distanced India from the BRI project itself, including the BCIM plan in the eastern flank of India which China really needs.

The consequences of Chinese investment, for example in the power sector to meet the aspirations of the common people, are yet to be seen. So far, the military and nuclear elite used to deal with China in a slew of strategic projects like weapons and reactors, for which there was very little competition at that price point. Chinese commercial products definitely worked as a social interface between these nations. Now it is the turn of critical infrastructure, especially the power sector, that affects society. Not all of the projects are going to live up to the present euphoria in an era of high expectations fuelled by the information age. The dismal power sector also demands reforms in Pakistan which are politically sensitive. This is where China will prefer the Pakistan military, with little pressures of constituency, just as the military finds China as its self-serving option against India. This quid-pro-quo relationship can affect democracy in Pakistan. The man in the driver's seat on the flagging-off of empty containers from Gwadar was the Army Chief—something that China will prefer in Islamabad too, with serious implications for Pakistan and South Asia.

The China–Pakistan trade is also tilted in China's favour, like most other nations. Pakistan has not been able to take advantage of the Free Trade Agreement between them. If the China– Pakistan trade increases as a result of the CPEC, the Chinese products could further flood Pakistani markets with negative impacts on the Pakistan domestic industry.

As far as India is concerned, the CPEC has added a layer of complexity, with projects in Pakistan-Occupied Kashmir being drawn into its ambit, without taking the Indian concerns on board. That makes projects in the disputed areas politically vulnerable. If the CPEC and the BRI are actually about regional economic growth, China as the lending nation has perhaps erred in making the investments in Pakistan-Occupied Kashmir. Currently, it appears that the CPEC narrative is only being driven by Pakistan, with very few Chinese statements about the projects and issue of the sovereignty of the disputed territories. After all, it is not easy for a region to grow economically, ignoring the security concerns of India and the economic prospects it offers. This is especially relevant at a time of weak cues from global economy and Western fatigue about globalisation. A stable and peaceful South Asia is crucial for an Asia-led growth. Investments in contested areas do not augur well for that purpose. It will only distance India further from any China-led initiatives like the BRI.

NOTES

1. "PM Inaugurates Gwadar Port as Trade Activities Open", www.nation.com.pk, November 13, 2016, http://nation.com.pk/national/13-Nov-2016/pm-inaugurates-gwadar-port-as-trade-activities-open
2. "With a New Chinese Loan, CPEC Is Now Worth $51.5bn," *DAWN.COM*, September 30, 2016, http://www.dawn.com/news/1287040.
3. Trishia P. Octaviano and Researcher, "Popular Economics: Economic Corridors Boost Markets, Living Conditions," *BusinessWorld Research*, accessed December 19, 2016, http://research.bworldonline.com/popular-economics/story.php?id=350&title=Economic-corridors-boost-markets,-living-conditions.
4. "Important Documents," accessed June 29, 2016, http://pk.chineseembassy.org/eng/zbgx/importantdocuments/.
5. Andrew Small, *The China-Pakistan Axis: Asia's New Geopolitics* (Oxford University Press, 2015).
6. "Khunjerab Pass Reopens after Winter Closure," *ePaper, Dawn.com*, accessed June 20, 2017, http://epaper.dawn.com/DetailImage.php?StoryImage=06_04_2017_007_006.
7. Small, *The China-Pakistan Axis.*
8. Ibid.
9. "PM Inaugurates Gwadar Port as Trade Activities Open", www.nation.com.pk, November 13, 2016, http://nation.com.pk/national/13-Nov-2016/pm-inaugurates-gwadar-port-as-trade-activities-open.
10. "Dialogue with Prof. Ahsan Iqbal On CPEC," *YouTube*, accessed January 5, 2017, https://www.youtube.com/watch?v=9dkQxmycuu8&t=1045s.
11. "Railway-Network-of-CPAC_newjpg.jpg (962×722)," accessed August 30, 2016, http://www.pc.gov.pk/wp-content/uploads/2016/01/Railway-Network-of-CPAC_newjpg.jpg.
12. http://www.cohl.com/en/News/show/1997.html
13. "Zhuhai Port Scores Big with Deal in Pakistan," *Business, chinadaily.com.cn*, accessed June 19, 2017, http://usa.chinadaily.com.cn/epaper/2015-10/30/content_22326165.htm.
14. PSA has expanded to be a global company named PSA international with several terminals across the globe
15. Small, *The China-Pakistan Axis.*
16. "China's Interest in Pakistan's Gwadar Port," *Stratfor*, accessed September 26, 2016, https://www.stratfor.com/analysis/chinas-interest-pakistans-gwadar-port.
17. "COPHC Pakistan," accessed June 22, 2017, http://cophcgwadar.com.192-185-11-

8.pss19.hgwin.temp.domains/about.aspx.

18. Annual Report to Congress: Military and Security Developments Involving the People's Republic of China 2017. A Report to Congress Pursuant to the National Defense Authorization Act for Fiscal Year 2000, https://www.defense.gov/Portals/1/Documents/pubs/2017_China_Military_Power_Report.PDF
19. "Gwadar Port City, China-Pakistan Economic Corridor (CPEC)," accessed August 5, 2016, http://www.cpecinfo.com/gwadar-port-city.php.
20. "Pakistan - International - Analysis - U.S. Energy Information Administration (EIA)," accessed October 4, 2016, https://www.eia.gov/beta/international/analysis.cfm?iso=PAK.
21. Ibid.
22. Khaleeq Kiani, "Power Shortfall Nears 5,000MW," *Dawn.com*, June 9, 2016, http://www.dawn.com/news/1263672.
23. "Power Transmission Capacity Surges to 16,300MW - Pakistan," *Dawn.com*, accessed June 22, 2017, https://www.dawn.com/news/1192470.
24. Ibid.
25. "Pakistan - International - Analysis - U.S. Energy Information Administration (EIA)."
26. Nasir Jamal, "Industry Profile: Circular Debt Cycle," *Dawn.com*, March 6, 2017, https://www.dawn.com/news/1318680.
27. "Pakistan, Data," accessed October 3, 2016, http://data.worldbank.org/country/pakistan.
28. To compare major economic indicators of regional nations refer table 7.2
29. "Moody's Says Pakistan's External Debt Will Increase to $79 Billion - The Express Tribune," accessed June 20, 2017, https://tribune.com.pk/story/1404569/moodys-says-pakistans-external-debt-will-increase-79-billion-june-end/.
30. "The IMF's Extended Fund Facility (EFF)," accessed October 3, 2016, https://www.imf.org/en/About/Factsheets/Sheets/2016/08/01/20/56/Extended-Fund-Facility.
31. "Pakistan Saved $4.5bn on Oil Imports in FY16," *Dawn.com*, July 24, 2016, http://www.dawn.com/news/1272751.
32. Maha Qasim, "The Dangers of Pakistan's Coal Revival," February 27, 2016, //www.dawn.com/news/1242279.
33. Ibid.
34. "Aid to Pakistan by the Numbers," *Center For Global Development*, accessed January 8, 2017, http://www.cgdev.org/page/aid-pakistan-numbers.
35. "China Global Investment Tracker," *AEI*, accessed January 15, 2017, https://www.aei.org/china-global-investment-tracker/.
36. The calculations in this Chapter do not include the Lahore Metro, though it finds a mention in the CPEC official website
37. Kevin Smith, "China Signs Funding Agreement for Lahore Metro," accessed January 12, 2017, http://www.railjournal.com/index.php/asia/funding-agreed-for-lahore-metro-line.html.
38. "Exclusive: China Commits $6.5 Billion for Pakistani Nuclear Project," *Reuters*, accessed June 20, 2017, http://www.reuters.com/article/us-pakistan-china-nuclear-idUSBRE9BN06220131224.
39. "China Confirms Mega-Deal for 8 Attack Submarines with Pakistan," *World News, India Today*," accessed June 20, 2017, http://indiatoday.intoday.in/story/china-confirms-mega-deal-for-8-attack-submarines-with-pakistan/1/791786.html.
40. "Pakistan, China Agree to Build Gwadar-Nawabshah Gas Pipeline," accessed September 15, 2016, https://www.thenews.com.pk/print/119897-Pakistan-China-agree-to-build-Gwadar-Nawabshah-gas-pipeline.
41. "China-Pak Economic Corridor: Why Gwadar Is An Overrated Port," accessed September

26, 2016, http://swarajyamag.com/world/china-pak-economic-corridor-why-gwadar-is-an-overrated-port.

42. "ECC Approves Plan to Set up Special Funds for CPEC Projects," *Dawn.com*, February 19, 2016, http://www.dawn.com/news/1240546.
43. Satyabrata Pal, "The China-Pakistan Corridor Is All About Power. Not Electricity, but the Real Thing," *The Wire*, June 3, 2016, http://thewire.in/39874/the-china-pakistan-corridor-is-all-about-power-not-electricity-but-the-real-thing/.
44. "Windfall for Chinese on Coal Fired Projects," *The Express Tribune*, February 15, 2017, https://tribune.com.pk/story/1327172/windfall-chinese-coal-fired-projects/.
45. Ishrat Husain, "Financing Burden of CPEC," *Dawn.com*, February 11, 2017, http://www.dawn.com/news/1313992.
46. Twelfth And Final Review Under The Extended Arrangement, Request For Waivers Of Nonobservance Of Performance Criteria, And Proposal For Post-Program Monitoring— Press Release; Staff Report; And Statement By The Executive Director For Pakistan, http://www.imf.org/external/pubs/cat/longres.aspx?sk=44327, accessed October 19, 2016
47. "Welcome to the Board of Investment," accessed October 5, 2016, http://boi.gov.pk/foreigninvestmentinpakistan.aspx.
48. As per calculations by the author based on the costing available from official Pakistani websites, divide by the power generation capability of those plants.
49. "China-Pak Economic Corridor." https://swarajyamag.com/world/china-pak-economic-corridor-why-gwadar-is-an-overrated-port
50. James M. Roberts and Huma Sattar, "Pakistan's Economic Disarray and How to Fix It," *The Heritage Foundation*, accessed October 4, 2016, http://www.heritage.org/research/reports/2015/06/pakistans-economic-disarray-and-how-to-fix-it.
51. Syed Irfan Raza, "Government Fails to Satisfy Opposition over CPEC Issues," *Dawn.com*, October 27, 2016, http://www.dawn.com/news/1292529.
52. Salman Rafi, "CPEC the Game Changer Might Change Nothing," accessed August 29, 2017, http://www.atimes.com/cpec-game-changer-might-change-nothing/.
53. Prepared by author using Google Map, road sections in red are approximate. Non-budgeted projects not shown
54. "High-Powered Committee on China-Pakistan Economic Corridor (CPEC)," accessed August 30, 2016, http://www.cpecinfo.com/high-powered-committee.php.
55. "Army Seeks Role in CPEC Administration," *The Express Tribune*, April 16, 2016, http://tribune.com.pk/story/1085784/for-timely-completion-army-seeks-role-in-cpec-administration/.
56. Small, *The China-Pakistan Axis*. For details read Chapter 2, Nuclear Fusion.
57. With Japanese advances in Indian Ocean during world war, the supply chain to China from West had taken the overland route and air route from Assam in India, via the Stillwell Road into China vis Burma.
58. "China-Pakistan Economic Corridor (CPEC) Official Website," accessed June 17, 2017, http://cpec.gov.pk/#.

ANNEXURE 1

Details of Projects under the CPEC

Overall Status of the CPEC Projects[59]	Total Power	Cost (USDmn)	Technology	Location	Province
Energy Coal (Priority 2017-19)					
Port Qasim Electric Company 2 x 660 MW Coal Fired Power Plant	1320	1,980	Supercritical	Port Qasim	Sindh
Sahiwal 2 x 660 MW Coal-fired Power Plant	1320	1,600	Supercritical	Sahiwal	Punjab
Engro Thar 4 x 330 MW Coal Fired Power Plant	1320	2,000	Sub Critical	Thar-Block-II	Sindh
Surface Mine in Block II of Thar Coal Field, 6.5 metric ton per annum (mtpa)		1,470	Open Pit	Thar-Block-II	Sindh
Gwadar Coal /LNG/Oil Power Project	300	600	Not Decided	Gwadar	Balochistan
Rahimyar Khan 2 x 660 MW Coal Fired Power Project	1320	1,600	Supercritical	Rahimyar Khan	Punjab
Thar Mine Mouth Oracle Power Plant (1320 MW) and Surface Mine	1320	1,300	Subcritical?		Sindh
SSRL 2 × 660 MW Mine Mouth Coal Fired Power Plant	1320	2,000	Subcritical	Thar-Block-I	Sindh
Energy Coal (Actively Promoted 2023-)					
HUBCO 2 x 660 MW Coal Fired Power Plant	1320	1940	Supercritical	Hub	Balochistan
Thar mine mouth oracle, Thar Sindh	1320	1,300		Thar	Sindh
Total (Coal related projects)	10860	15,790			
Energy Renewables (Priority)					
Quaid-e-Azam 1000 MW Solar Park	1000	1,215	PV	Bahawalpur	Punjab
Dawood 50 MW wind Farm	50	125	Wind Turbine	Bhambore, Sindh	Bhambore, Sindh
UEP 100 MW wind Farm	100	250	Wind Turbine	Jhimpir, Sindh	Jhimpir, Sindh
Sachal 50 MW Wind Farm	50	134	Wind Turbine	Jhimpir, Sindh	Jhimpir, Sindh
Suki Kinari Hydropower Station, KPK	870	1,802	Hydroelectric	Suki Kinari	KPK
Karot Hydropower Station	720	1,420	Hydroelectric	Karot	PoK & Punjab
Energy Renewables (Actively Promoted)					
Kohala Hydel Project	1100	2,397	Hydroelectric	Kohala	PoK
Pakistan Wind Farm II 2 x 50 MW	100	150	Wind Turbine	Jhimpir	Sindh
Total (Renewable energy projects)	3990	7,493			

Overall Status of the CPEC Projects	Total Power	Cost (USDmn)	Technology	Location	Province
Energy Transmission Infrastructure (Priority)					
Matiari to Lahore Transmission line	-	1,500	-	-	Sindh and Punjab
Matiari to Faisalabad Transmission line	-	1,500	-	-	Sindh and Punjab
Total (Energy transmission)		3,000			
Road	Length	Cost		-	Province
KKH Phase II (Thakot -Havelian Section)	118	1,305	-	-	KPK
Peshawar-Karachi Motorway (Multan-Sukkur Section)	392	2,846	-	-	Punjab Sind
Khuzdar-Basima Road N-30	110	NA	-	-	Balochistan
Upgradation of DI Khan-Zhob, N-50 Phase-I	210	NA	-	-	KPK Balochistan
KKH Thakot-Raikot N35 remaining portion	136	NA	-	-	KPK, PoK
Total (Road)	966	4,151			
Rail	Length	Cost			Province
Expansion and reconstruction of existing Line ML1	1736	8,172	-	-	
Havelian Dry port (450 m Twenty-Foot Equivalent Units)	-	40	-	-	KPK
Capacity Development of Pakistan Railways	-	NA	-	-	-
Total (Rail)	1736	8,212			
Gwadar			-	-	
Gwadar East-Bay Expressway	-	140.6	-	Gwadar	Balochistan
New Gwadar International Airport	-	230	-	Gwadar	Balochistan
Construction of Breakwaters	-	123	-	Gwadar	Balochistan
Dredging of berthing areas & channels	-	27	-	Gwadar	Balochistan
Development of Free Zone	-	32	-	Gwadar	Balochistan
Necessary facilities of fresh water treatment, water supply and distribution	-	130	-	Gwadar	Balochistan
Pak China Friendship Hospital	-	100	-	Gwadar	Balochistan
Technical and Vocational Institute at Gwadar	-	10	-	Gwadar	Balochistan
Gwadar Smart Port City Master Plan	-	NA	-	Gwadar	Balochistan
Bao Steel Park, petrochemicals, stainless steel and other industries in Gwadar	-	NA	-	Gwadar	Balochistan
Development of Gwadar University (Social Sector Development)	-	NA	-	Gwadar	Balochistan

Overall Status of the CPEC Projects	Total Power	Cost (USDmn)	Technology	Location	Province
Upgradation and development of fishing, boat making and maintenance services to protect and promote livelihoods of local population	-	NA	-	Gwadar	Balochistan
Total (Gwadar)		792.6			
Digital Connectivity			-		
Cross Border Optical Fiber Cable	-	44	-	-	
Pilot Project of Digital Terrestrial Multimedia Broadcast (DTMB)	-	NA	-	-	
Total (Digital connectivity)		44			
Urban Transit					
Karachi Circular Railway	-	NA	-	Karachi	Sind
Greater Peshawar Region Mass Transit	-	NA	-	Peshawar	KPK
Quetta Mass Transit	-	NA	-	Quetta	Balochistan
Orange Line - Lahore	-	NA	-	Lahore	Punjab
Provincial Projects			-		
Keti Bunder Sea Port Development Project	-	NA	-	KetiBunder	Sindh
Naukundi-Mashkhel-Panjgur Road Project connecting with M-8 & N-85	-	NA	-	-	Balochistan
Chitral CPEC link road from Gilgit, Shandor, Chitral to Chakdara	-	NA	-	-	Gilgit KPK
Mirpur-Muzaffarabad-Mansehra Road Construction for connectivity with CPEC route	-	NA	-	-	PoK KPK Punjab
Quetta Water Supply Scheme from Pat feeder Canal, Balochistan	-	NA	-	Quetta	Balochistan
Iron Ore Mining, Processing & Steel Mills complex at Chiniot, Punjab	-	NA	-	Chiniot	Punjab
Economic Zones			-		
Rashakai Economic Zone on M-1	-	NA	-	Rashakai	KPK
Special Economic Zone Dhabeji	-	NA	-	Dhabeji	Sindh
Bostan Industrial Zone	-	NA	-	Bostan	Balochistan
Punjab-China Economic Zone, M-2 District Sheikhupura	-	NA	-	Sheikhupura	Punjab
ICT Model Industrial Zone, Islamabad	-	NA	-	Islamabad	-
Development of Industrial Park on Pakistan Steel Mills Land at Port Qasim near Karachi	-	NA	-	Port Qasim	Sind
Bhimber Industrial Zone	-	NA	-	Bhimber	PoK
Mohmand Marble City	-	NA	-	Mohmand	KPK
Moqpondass SEZ Gilgit-Baltistan	-	NA	-	Moqpondass	GB, PoK

CHAPTER 7

THE STRATEGY OF MARITIME NODES AND NETWORKS: SRI LANKA, MALDIVES AND BANGLADESH AND CHINA'S COMMERCIAL MARITIME NETWORK

Ever since oceans emerged as the medium for trade, the maritime powers of the day strived to control maritime focal points across trade routes. Initially these were the ports along the patterns of wind; later they were coaling stations suitable for ships to refuel. The emergence of canals like Panama and Suez altered these 'pit stops' according to new patterns of shipping. Port Said, Aden, Colombo, Singapore, Seychelles and Mauritius were examples of these shipping nodes. The development in shipping technology like use of an internal combustion engine using oil, reduced the relevance of these coaling stations since refuelling oil, the new fuel, was not as complex as coaling. Many old nodes remained geographically significant and metamorphosed into entrepots and transhipment hubs staying relevant in days of containerisation serving as foci in the new centres of regional growth.

This chapter is about some of these nodes like Sri Lanka, Maldives and Bangladesh in South Asia. None of these nations have a physical connection to China unlike Myanmar or Pakistan. They neither offer an 'access' to the Indian Ocean unlike Myanmar, Pakistan, Malaysia and Thailand, nor are resource-rich like the Middle East and Africa. Another aspect related to oceans is the commercial maritime network that China is building across the globe. The chapter also examines that extensive maritime global network that China is creating. The chapter is arranged as four separate parts covering the three countries and China's maritime commercial network.

Part 1: Sri Lanka

Geographic Significance of Sri Lanka. Sri Lanka sits astride the important shipping lane that crosses the Indian Ocean right on the circumequatorial maritime superhighway. It was a port which was familiar to the colonialist, the trader and transoceanic religious ventures like the Buddhists heading east from India and the Haj pilgrimages heading west from the Far East. Be it the coastal maritime routes along India or a straight route from the West Coast of Africa, Sri Lanka, also known as Swarnadwipa, lay right on the path of monsoon winds which powered maritime exchanges in the pre-industrial period. From the earliest days of trade in the Indian Ocean, Sri Lanka was a natural stopover on the East–West transit. An example of such a stopover was by the Chinese Admiral Zheng He in his journeys to the Indian Ocean during the Ming period. He erected a stele in Galle commemorating his visit. His visits were not entirely peaceful, and on one occasion resulted in a regime change with a reigning Sri Lankan king being abducted back to Nanjing only to be released later.

Colonial Legacy. The earliest maritime adventurers such as the Portuguese and Dutch had maintained their presence in Sri Lanka considering the vantage spot it occupied in the Indian Ocean. The British who followed, established their colony here based on maritime factors. Ceylon, as it was then called, was also the spot from where the British watched over the Indian Ocean sea lanes. In the age of steam, stopovers continued for coaling, making it strategically important. The growth of modern shipping industry around these coaling hubs made them transhipment hubs and centres of thriving maritime service centres like insurance, bunkering, crew changes, chartering, repair centres, etc. Considering the strategic relevance of Sri Lanka and the Maldives, the British retained the Trincomalee and Gan airbase long after the colonial curtains came down. The US, which inherited the British legacy in the Indian Ocean, sensed the region's significance and maintained a station in the adjacent Diego Garcia.

Maritime Relevance. Sri Lanka continues to remain relevant today as a maritime hub due to Colombo being a short haul away from the main line of shipping, be it as a 'hub' in hub and spoke shipping pattern or as a 'relay point' or an 'intersection' of shipping routes. Transportation including aviation and shipping is a major contributor of revenues from the service industry in Sri Lanka amounting up to 35 per cent.[1] This mostly constitutes the traffic from India which occupies 75 per cent share in that transhipment. Sri Lanka also ranks high in the Liner Shipping Connectivity Index (LSCI) which is a measure of connectivity to the shipping networks.[2] In 2016, Sri Lanka had a score of 63.21 which is the highest LSCI in South Asia. It is this key attribute of Sri Lanka that China finds attractive. Aware of the strategic relevance of shipping, there is a foreign ownership cap of 49 per cent in Lankan Shipping Industry, which is seen by many as a hindrance to growth.[3] A list of the LSCI of the South Asian nations is given below:

Table 7.1. Liner Shipping Indices of Select Nations

Nation	LSCI	Nation	LSCI
India	46.24	Myanmar	6.37
Thailand	44.32	Madagascar	10.73
Pakistan	36.58	Mauritius	28.64
Bangladesh	12.62	Djibouti	
Seychelles	7.92	China	
Maldives	7.59		

Source: UNCTAD.

SHIPPING LANES NEAR SRI LANKA

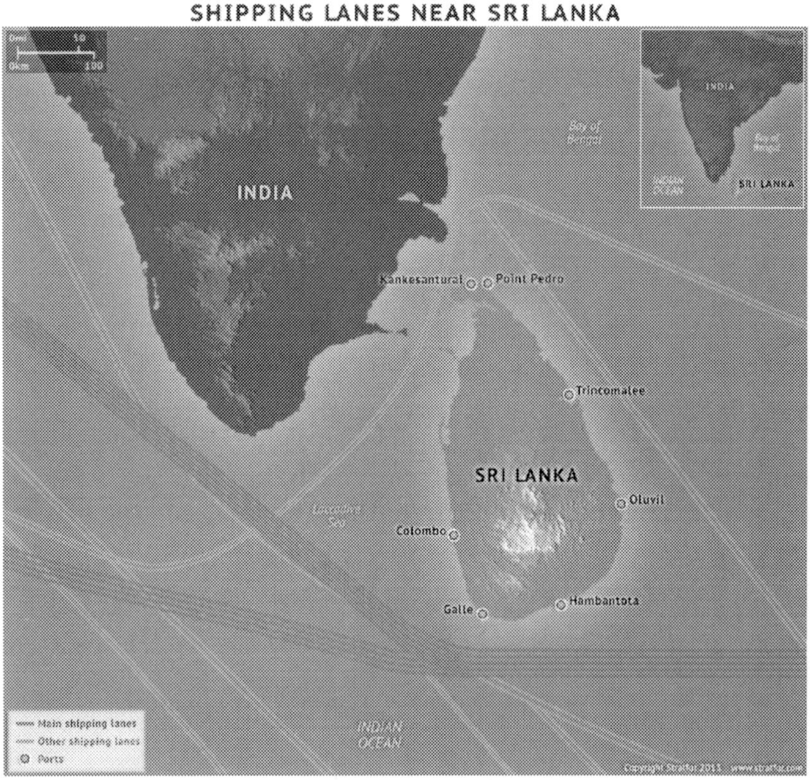

Figure 7.1. Sri Lanka and Shipping Lanes
(*Source:* Stratfor)

Domestic Politics: Civil War. Sri Lanka is an ethnically diverse nation. The population constitutes of 74.9 per cent Sinhalese, 11.2 per cent Sri Lankan Tamils, 9.2 per cent Sri Lankan Moors[6] and 4.2 per cent Indian Tamils.[7] The call for a separate homeland or 'Eelam' for Tamils commenced soon after Sri Lanka became independent from the British in 1948. It was in a large measure a result of the colonial administrative policies. This triggered an ethnic strife which evolved through various phases. A series of discriminatory actions over citizenship, education and language by the Sinhalese majority stoked the divide. The phase of strife till 1972 was largely nonviolent. With the emergence of leaders like Velupillai Prabhakaran of the LTTE, the situation changed. Both sides upped the ante with violence which became a full-blown civil war by 1983. The Tamils have strong ethnic relations with India and naturally had a bearing on Indian domestic politics. After a period of empathy and hope for a solution, India became involved militarily on the island with the Indian Peace Keeping Force from 1987, upon signing of the Indo-Sri Lanka Peace Accord. An associated development was the 13th Amendment to the constitution which mandated the formation of the North Eastern Province and granting the Tamil language a constitutional status. This is something that has not yet been fully implemented 30 years down the line.

The role of the IPKF was to ensure a ceasefire and accept the surrender of arms by the Tamil militants. By 1990, the ground had shifted with a change of government in Sri Lanka and the IPKF had to withdraw. The assassination of ex-PM Rajiv Gandhi in 1991 was a crucial turning point when the movement lost sympathy in India. The civil war in Sri Lanka too had worsened. A West-led mediation led by Norway briefly held hopes of a resolution till 2003. The Rajapaksa government came to power in 2004 in this background. After many years of impasse, it was the hard-line Rajapaksa government which finally resorted to iron-fisted options to put an end to the civil war. The final phase of the civil war was from 2004–2009 ending the decades-long strife on the Sri Lankan government's terms. There were serious violations of human rights during this period. This was also the period that saw Sri Lanka turn to China in a far more decisive manner than before. Details of that relationship are elucidated subsequently.

Domestic Politics: Dynamics of a Multiparty System. The foreign policy being an extension of domestic politics, it is important to look at the domestic politics of Sri Lanka. There are two major parties that lead two principal coalitions in that democracy. They are the United National Party (UNP) and the Sri Lanka Freedom Party (SLFP). These two parties, now leading coalitions, have roughly shared rule for half the post-independence period. The coalitions are listed below:

- **Right-Leaning Coalition.** The United National Front for Good Governance (UNFGG), a right-leaning new coalition in Sri Lanka, was formed in 2015 to fight the elections. The United National Party (UNP), led by PM Ranil Wickremesinghe, is presently the major party in this coalition. The UNP historically fielded leaders like Senanayake, Jayawardene and Premadasa.
- **Left-Leaning Coalition.** The United People's Freedom Alliance, a left-leaning old coalition, was founded in 2004. This is led by SLFP. The well-known SLFP leaders have been Bandaranaike, Kumaratunga, Rajapaksa and Sirisena.

Civil War Victory and Impacts on Domestic Politics. The civil war in Sri Lanka was won by Rajapaksa's UNP government. Expecting an electoral victory on that momentum, President Rajapaksa called for elections early in 2010 and defeated his own military leader, Gen Sarath Fonseka, who was the opposition leader. His second term was to end in 2016, after which he could not have become president again as per a two-term limit laid down by the constitution. In order to retain power, he carried out the eighteenth amendment removing the two-term limit so that he could contest for a third term. He had also taken the judiciary on his side by impeaching the chief justice and putting an ally in place to remove judicial obstacles. In 2015, he called for early elections and stood for a third time as candidate of the SLFP party under the coalition. However, history had surprises in store for him. In a surprise move just prior to the elections, Rajapaksa's health minister Maithripala Sirisena, sensing the widespread discontent about the autocratic tendencies of Rajapaksa, moved over to the opposition and became its consensus candidate, winning the 2015 elections. One of the first steps taken by the Sirisena government was a repeal of the 18th amendment through the 19th amendment.

China Factor in Domestic Politics. An important factor in the entire incident culminating in the 2015 election was 'China'. Particular issues were a slew of investments done by China in Sri Lanka during Rajapaksa's tenure and interestingly, a submarine's port call. Rajapaksa's overt support to China, large business deals and an authoritarian style of governance had become his undoing, and come to be resented by the domestic and international constituencies. The pragmatic Rajapaksa had also maintained very close relations with India. A year earlier, in mid-September 2014, Sri Lanka had allowed a Chinese submarine to dock in Colombo, which according to the

Chinese was on its way to the Gulf of Aden for an anti-piracy patrol. India conveyed its protests to the Defence Minister, who was also the brother of the President. Notwithstanding that protest, the Submarine docked again in November on its return leg disregarding the Indian protests.[8] To add to it, this happened a week before Japanese Prime Minister Abe's visit. The sealanes adjacent to Sri Lanka are important to Japan also, which was a big donor of aid to Sri Lanka before China took over that mantle.

This event during the tenure of Rajapaksa was a point of inflection in the Indian Ocean politics. Till then, the Chinese Navy had sent only surface ships to the Indian Ocean. The deployment of a submarine indicated a clear intent to up the ante and take the deployments to a greater level altogether. Submarines have no less than war roles and they have very limited role in 'presence missions' such as anti-piracy which require a visible fast moving force with firepower on the surface to deter and speed to chase the fast skiffs launched by pirate vessels. The choice of a conventional submarine also indicated that these were assured of a local port support which in this case was Sri Lanka. Conventional submarines have limited space and water facilities on board and need support often either from a ship or harbour. The Chinese also sent a nuclear submarine thereafter to Pakistan, which docked at Karachi. The submarine deployments continued through 2016 intermittently and in end-2016, a submarine transited back from the Indian Ocean and was sighted at Kota Kinabalu in Malaysia.[9] This was reported to be the sixth deployment since 2013.[10]

However, the submarine in Sri Lanka was seen as an affront by India which had in fact gone out on a limb, taking serious domestic and regional political risks in supporting Sri Lanka in the final phase of the war. The submarine also breached some other understandings with India. The 1987 Indo-Lanka Accord has an exchange of letters between the heads of state which says that Trincomalee or any other ports in Sri Lanka will not be made available for military use by any country in a manner prejudicial to India's interests. The docking of the submarine clearly violated that understanding.

Such a strategic bonhomie with China ties was not without a political price for the Rajapaksa government. The present Prime Minister, although from the same party, had played up the China card calling the process 'colonisation' during the election campaign. The relations with China were one of Sirisena's core campaign areas during the elections. This eventually played up during the elections, changing the government.

The political effects of China's initiatives continued well into the Sirisena regime. In a strange twist to events, Sirisena himself could not wean away from Chinese investment. This led to an acerbic acrimony over China's demand for strategic equities in lieu of unpaid loans. The relations also reached a nadir when there was a serious diplomatic back-and-forth between Sri Lanka and China over the repayment of loans in 2016. The debt to equity swap of the Matala airport and Hambantota port that was offered was not deemed appropriate by China in mid-2016. The Chinese ambassador was summoned officially over the matter in end-2016. The domestic point of inflection happened in mid-2016 when a big parcel of 15000 acres of land was demanded by China for an SEZ. There was a large scale uprising against this move.[11] The terms included a 99-year lease and 80 per cent Chinese ownership.[12] The proposal was for Chinese firms to set up units in the SEZ at Hambantota. Rajapaksa, in yet another twist of events, had reversed roles with Sirisena in this issue, wherein he criticised the government for giving away more than required to China. Such are the shifts of Sri Lankan domestic politics over the China policy.

Sri Lankan Economy.[13] A major reason behind Sri Lanka gradually slipping into the Chinese grip is perhaps economics. Some key economic factors of Sri Lanka need a mention. The country has a GDP of around USD82.24 billion. Its volume of public debt is USD81billion. This has amounted to 77.1 per cent of the GDP. Its external debt is USD47.65 billion. The debt to China is approximately USD8 billion. It exports around USD10.12 billion and imports USD18.64 billion (all as per 2016 figures). Hence there is a balance of payment deficit from trade. Debt servicing will add another layer to it. The government debt remains among the highest in emerging markets. It has the highest external debt in South Asia at almost three times the norm. Sri Lanka also has high per capita income, at almost twice the normal in South Asia. Sri Lanka has been on an IMF loan of USD1.5 billion since May 2016.[14] The IMF has recommended measures such as the control of reduction of debt, fiscal deficit, increase in forex reserves, and improving tax to GDP ratio[15] if Sri Lanka has to come out of this vortex. This indicates that Sri Lanka has some serious restructuring to do in times to come or swap some equity for debt, which is presently the exact Chinese demand.

Economic Relations with China. The Chinese economic initiatives in Sri Lanka have FDI, ODA and Private investments which have increased drastically since 2005. China emerged as Sri Lanka's number one investor and donor by 2015. The relations in the contemporary period between China and Sri Lanka began with the Rice for Rubber pact in 1952, at a time when China was a pariah in the international system.[16] Natural rubber from Sri Lanka was

Table 7.2. Regional Economic Indicators

	India	Bangladesh	Pakistan	Sri Lanka	Myanmar	Maldives
GDP (bn USD)	2200	226	271	82.24	68.28	5.4
Growth (%)	7.6	6.9	4.7	5	8.10	3
Public Debt (%)	52.3	25.9	58.50	77	NA	72
External Debt (bn USD)	507	37.2	64.04	47.65	9.04	0.741
Ext Debt (%)	23	16	23	58.10	13	14
Import (bn USD)	402	39	38.25	10.12	13.49	1.9
Export (bn USD)	271	33	20.96	18.64	10.49	0.3
Revenue (bn USD)	200	23	41.77	10.98	8.9	0.96
Expenses (bn USD)	283	35	54.63	15.54	10.9	1.1
Deficit (%)	-3.7	-5.1	-4.7	-5.5	-3	-6
FOREX (bn USD)	359	29.7	20.53	7.6	8.9	0.627
FDI Stock (bn USD)	351	13.24	33.82	NA	NA	NA
China Investment (bn USD)	NA	24	46	8	15	NA
Savings (%)	30	28	14.3	26	16.13	8.1
Per Capita USD	6700	3900	5100D	11200	6000	15300
Domestic Credit (bn USD)	1.5	128	142	44.73	21.22	1.5

Source: CIA World Fact Book, accessed Jul 2017.

exchanged for the much-needed rice from China. This continued for 30 years till 1982 at terms highly favourable to Sri Lanka. This trade link sowed the seeds of a strong political and economic relation. Diplomatic relations were established in 1957. An economic and technical cooperation agreement followed in 1962. An important development came when Sri Lanka signed a maritime agreement with China in 1963 granting rights for ships from either nation to use each other's ports. Politically, Sri Lanka also co-sponsored the draft resolution making the PRC represent China in the United Nations. What started as a simple barter of rice with rubber, slowly expanded in scope and quantity. Trade is increasing with a Free Trade Agreement in the making which will be signed very soon. However, the trade deficit is widening much like other nations. Sri Lanka exports agriculture products and imports machinery, cotton and fabrics from China.[17]

As China gained financial heft, it also started disbursing aid to Sri Lanka. Therefore, a crucial factor to consider in this bilateral relation is the aid from China which crossed USD 1 billion in 2008.[18] The Indian Ocean tsunami and the civil war, provided the necessary opportunity for China to expand the aid flow. The Chinese aid to Sri Lanka saw a quantum leap during the final period of the civil war when most other countries were not forthcoming with aid, given the human right records of government forces.

The third factor in economic relations are the investments from China. As the Chinese investors and industries ventured out, Sri Lanka was a natural destination. It needed infrastructure, especially for post-war reconstruction. The Chinese investments have mostly been in telecom, and critical infrastructure fields of energy, roads, ports, rail and airports. The relations have also transitioned to oil exploration by CNPC in the Gulf of Mannar and even space cooperation where China is assisting Sri Lanka to launch a satellite. The late Saman Kelegama, one of Sri Lanka's leading economists, reported that in quick time, 25 per cent of foreign commitments to Sri Lanka became Chinese by 2010. The Chinese investments are also not without their share of woes, where high interest rates, lack of transparency, reluctance in technology transfers and use of Chinese labour have been widely resented within Sri Lanka. Of late, the plan involves separate SEZs as well as long leases to Chinese investors. Especially tricky amongst them is the handing over of parts of crucial ports like Colombo and Hambantota to the Chinese. This leads to the extraction of a strategic equity by China in lieu of unpayable loans. The conduit for investments from China is mainly through the Exim Bank of China, the China Development Bank and the Industrial Commercial Bank of China which is along the same pattern as in Pakistan and other nations.

China and the Sri Lankan Civil War. The circumstances that the civil war presented in this relation need a closer look. China is devoid of any ethnic connection with Sri Lanka, unlike Sri Lanka's closest neighbour India. Therefore it enjoyed a greater latitude of action during the civil war. China increased military and economic relations with Sri Lanka during this period to cement its links. One tipping point that gave China a firmer foothold in Sri Lanka is the denial of military aid by the US and West in the course of the civil war due to human rights violations. China not only filled that void, but politically assisted Sri Lanka by vetoing an inquiry by the UN into excesses by the Sri Lankan army during the final stages of the civil war. This Sri Lankan requirement coincided with a period when China commenced its naval forays into the Indian Ocean. China also stepped up initiatives for people-to-people contact gaining traction with Confucius institutes, sister-city relations, scholarships for students and setting up of rehabilitation villages during calamities and the civil war. There is also a Buddhist diplomacy at work, where Kandy is being developed through a grant of USD100 million. The FTA with China being negotiated presently will increase its footprints in Sri Lanka.

Prominent Chinese Funded Projects in Sri Lanka[19,20]

Maritime Infrastructure Investment. Since this book is about the Indian Ocean, the maritime infrastructure being built by China in Sri Lanka needs a closer look.

Table 7.3. Chinese Funded Projects in Sri Lanka

Project	Cost USDmn	Remarks
Colombo South Port Container Terminal	500	35-year lease China Merchants Port Holdings, built by Colombo International Container Terminals Ltd. (CICT), a joint venture Company between China Merchants Holdings (International) Co. Ltd. (CMHI) and the Sri Lanka Ports Authority (SLPA)
Colombo International Financial City[21]	1400	Commenced as Port City but revived as International Financial City. Expects USD13 billion investments from 2018
Hambantota Port[22]	1393.93	CHEC has operating rights to four of the seven container berths at Hambantota port on a 35-year lease. Original plan was the first phase loan; second and third phase SOT basis only for terminals, not the entire port. Terminals had to pay for land.
Matthala Hambantota International Airport	209	Presently underutilised with only one flight. USD18 million per year as losses.
Supply of Two Nos. MA - 60 Aircraft Project	106	This will be used for passenger transportation between domestic & regional destinations
Lakwijaya Power Plant Norochcholoi Coal Power Plant[23] Phase 1	450	Loan of 300mn@2% interest rate and 150mn@6% interest rate. Total 900mw, Ph1-300mw, Ph2 -600mw China Machinery Engineering Corporation
Puttalam Coal Power I, II & III	1346	The project aims at the national importance given to the growing electricity demand in the country at a minimum cost to the economy by reducing the high reliance thermal power generation.
Norochcholoi Coal Power Plant[24] Phase 2	891	Same as above
MoragahakandaKalu Ganga Development Project- Hydel Power[25]	370	Multi-purpose Development Project. A dam, for irrigation and small power project of 25MW. SMEC Holdings Australia and Sino-hydro are involved. Kalu Ganga 167mnUSD and Moragahakanda 180mn USD
Extension of Southern Railway- Matara- Kataragama	272	Aims at improving the southern regions' connectivity. China Machinery Corporation (CMC)
Supply of 13 Nos. Diesel Multiple Units to Sri Lanka Railways Project	102	The main objective is to strengthen the passenger service of the Sri Lankan Railway by adding 13 DMUs to its present fleet of rolling stock.
Northern Roads Rehabilitation Project Kandy Jaffna[26]	424	Loan by China Exim Bank

Project	Cost USDmn	Remarks
Colombo Katunayake expressway	292	USD248 million, 26km four-lane highway to the Bandaranaike International Airport. Chinese Contract
Extension of Southern Expressway (ESEP) Hambantota - Matara Highway	180	This connects the Southern Expressway that terminates at Matara to Hambantota in three stages: Matara-Beliatta, Beliatta-Wetiya, Mattala-Hambantota Mattala Airport Loans from EXIM Bank, ADB and JICA
Extension of Southern Expressway	804	Matara and Beliaththe by 26km
Extension of Southern Expressway	429.8	Matara and Watiya by 30km
Construction of Selected Roads in Hambantota International Hub Development	252.5	250 km of roads selected and will connect Airport, Seaport, Cricket Stadium, Safari Park, BOI site, Convention Centre, Administrative Complex and tourism-related development and residential areas.
Emergency Purchase of Container Handling Equipment Jaya Terminal	35	6 ship to shore container cranes and transfer cranes (rubber tyred gantry cranes 30).
Construction of Expressway from Hambantota Seaport to Mattala Airport	412	25-km long expressway will connect Hambantota port and Mattala airport to provide access to economic activities.
AVIC Housing Complex[27]	250	Housing Project
Broadlands Water Projects	69	This is a Run of the River Hydel Power Project of 35 MW
Lotus Tower	100	A landmark tower funded by the China EXIM Bank
Greater Karunegala Water Supply and Sewerage	77.3	The objective of the project is to meet the present & future demand of drinking water in the Greater Kurunegala area by increasing water supply capacity from 6500m3/d to 13000m3/d and establish a proper waste water disposal system with a capacity 0f 4500m^3/d.
Gampaha, Attanagalla, Minuwangoda Integrated Water Supply Scheme	229	Water supply to 80,000 households through construction of 54,000 m^3/day treatment plant 600km distribution line.
Waste Water Infrastructure for Greater Hambantota	75	Provide 9,000 sewerage connections. 12,000m^3/day capacity treatment plant and 142 km collection network will be constructed
Shangrila Hotel	450	
Muthurajawela Oil Tank Storage Project	72	2001 project EXIM Bank of China 14 km to the north of Colombo. The offshore section of the project will have a one-point mooring system and a 5.6 km submarine oil transmission pipeline. The onshore section of the project will have 29 diesel and kerosene storage tanks and all the matching facilities. It was declared open on 27 May 2004.
Kattankudy Division	92.9	Provide sewerage connections for The Batticaloa municipal

Sewerage Disposal Project		council area and Kattankudy DS division area will be covered. 50km collection network and 10,500m^3/day wastewater treatment plant will be constructed.
Loan Facility USD 300 Million from China Development Bank	300	15 roads traverse through several districts such as Kandy, Galle, NuwareEliya, Ratnapura, Puttalam, Kurunegala, Kegalle, Gampaha, Monaragala, Hambantota and Kalutara
Outer Circular Highway from Kadawatha to Kerawalapitiya	520	9.32km long highway will provide connectivity between Colombo Katunayake Expressway and Southern expressway through Kottawa - Kadawatta Outer Circular Highway
Construction of Outer Circular Road in Trincomalee	272	47km long road will make access to proposed Sampur coal plant and Trincomalee Harbour
Pinnaduwa to Kodagoda to Godagama and balance work in Galle Port Access Roads	292	The objective of the project is to assist development of the economic activities of the Southern Province by encouraging growth in industries ,tourism, fisheries & agriculture sectors.
Rehabilitation & improvement of Priority Road Projects - 1 and 2	495	The project would provide an efficient national roads system that will contribute to lower transportation costs & improve the integration of all parts of the country.
Relocation and Development of Institute of Technology, University of Moratuwa	76	This will help to increase present student intake from 1,050 to 3,000 students annually; will help the middle level skilled technicians. The IET will be shifted to new location at Diyagama, Homagama Northern
Province Power Sector Development Programme Project (UthuruWasanthaya)	37.25	This will be used to procure material for construction of medium & low voltage network in the Northern Province to achieve 100% electricity coverage.
Lighting Sri Lanka Uva Province (Uva Udanaya) Project	29.32	This will be used to procure material required for construction of 250 new substations , 625km new MV lines & 2250km new low voltage line
Lighting Sri Lanka Eastern Province Project (Negenahira Nawodaya)	33.33	Objective is to electrify 268 villages in Trincomalee & Batticaloa Districts

- **Colombo Port.** The Colombo International Container Terminals Ltd (CICT) is a joint venture company between the Sri Lanka Ports Authority (SLPA) and the China Merchants Port Holdings Company Limited (CMPH). This Chinese firm is also known as the China Merchants Holdings International (CMHI) and CM Port. The CICT is under a 35-year Build Operate and Transfer (BoT) Agreement with the SLPA. This venture created Colombo's third container terminal with a 2.4 million TEU capacity under the Colombo South Harbour expansion project. The CMPH holds 85 per cent of the partnership whilst the balance 15 per cent is being held by the SLPA. This port commenced operation in 2013 and by April 2014, had completed 1200m of the terminal. It has a container yard of 58Ha, which is critical for transhipment hubs. It has a basin with a two-lane access channel with a 20 metre depth and 18m water depth alongside the berths. For Container terminals, quay cranes with a large outreach are critical. It has quay cranes with a 70 metre outreach, with a capability to handle the largest vessels with an 18,000 TEU capacity. These are the largest of container vessels in the industry, which run the main maritime lines. The harbour routinely feeds traffic to Tuticorin, Chennai, Chittagong, Vishakhapatnam, Cochin, Krishnapatnam, and Haldia in India. It also serves most mainline networks. The CMPH's parent company is the China Merchants Group. It was established in 1872 and its core businesses include transportation, finance and property. Shipping and Ports are a key area of this company. CMPH, its port division, is the largest public port operator in China accounting for 29 per cent of China's total container traffic at 83.66 million TEUs. Its other overseas projects include 47.5 per cent stake of the Tin-Can Island Container Terminal Ltd in Nigeria under the China–Africa Development Fund. The Sri Lanka Ports Authority (SLPA) administers all commercial ports in Sri Lanka, including Colombo, Galle, Trincomalee, Kankesanturai and Point Pedru and a new Port at Hambantota.

- **Hambantota.** The construction of the Hambantota Port is one of the major development projects that have been undertaken by the Sri Lanka Ports Authority using Chinese assistance. There is no other project that has caused greater flutter than the Magampura Mahinda Rajapaksa Port at Hambantota. This greenfield harbour project located on the south-eastern tip of Sri Lanka is closer to the international shipping lanes than the existing harbours of Sri Lanka. The project, which commenced in 2008, has two phases. The first phase was completed in 2010. The second phase is presently in progress. The project cost USD361 million in phase I and USD810 million in phase 2. The harbour area is protected by two breakwaters 312m and 988m long. A 210 m wide access channel with a 17m depth is provided with a turning circle of 600m diameter to facilitate vessels up to 100,000 DWT. A land parcel of 1115 Ha has been acquired for Phase I and 700 Ha have been acquired for phase II. The construction of the port is carried out by China Harbour Engineering Company and Sinohydro Corporation. The port intends services like supply of fuel, water, and crew change in addition to the usual port operations. As per the present status of this port, there are following facilities:
  - Completed Projects in Phase I.

    * Ro-Ro Terminal 600m
    * Oil Terminal-1- 300m
    * Oil Terminal-2 300m (Dolphins)
- Under Construction for Phase II.
    * Multipurpose Terminal
    * Container Terminal
- Future Plans
    * Dry Dock

Since the port was making heavy losses, CMPH, the same Chinese conglomerate that is a partner of the CICT at Colombo, has taken an 80 per cent stake in the port. It will infuse the necessary capital to revive the project. However, more clauses have followed. A very large Special Economic Zone of 15,000 acres was soon demanded. This is in addition to the two tranches of 1815 Ha for the harbour. This turned the tables, reversing the roles in politics vs Chinese investment. The SEZ agreement was initiated during Sirisena's time and opposed by Rajapaksa who hails from the same area. The other important development is that Hambantota has emerged as the hub of car and truck exports from India, especially Chennai, which has the presence of automobile production centres like Hyundai. In fact, the major transhipments from Hambantota are the automobiles from India.

Colombo South City/Financial City. This was a reclamation project in Colombo inaugurated by Chinese President Xi Jinping in September 2014. This project aims to reclaim 233 hectares of land adjacent to the existing port. Conditions of this lease are to be on a 20 per cent freehold and 80 per cent on a 99-year lease to the China Harbour Engineering Company (CHEC), which is literally ownership. A public sector firm, the China Communication Construction Company and the CHEC are to carry out the work. From being a 'port city' prior to the elections, it was converted into the Colombo International Financial and Business District or The Colombo International Financial Centre to act as a destination for businessmen in the region. The 'city' is to have its own jurisdiction with separate economic commercial laws, courts, arbitration centres which in effect are separate from that of Colombo. The current President also carried out a volte-face over this project. His election campaign said that he will scrap the project. However, the project has been revived as an international financial city. It is expected to cost USD1.4 billion and expects to draw USD13 billion investments from 2018. The vision is to make this project a financial hub between Dubai and Singapore.[28] This reflects how the economic shifts within China itself from manufacturing to the services industry can also affect projects in the Indian Ocean.

Arms Sales[29]

China has been the top supplier of arms to Sri Lanka with around USD686 million worth of arms transfers thus far.[30] Regionally, Chinese arms transfers to Sri Lanka are way below its arms transfers to Myanmar and Bangladesh at USD3 billion each and Pakistan which is in a different league at USD14 billion. The China–Sri Lanka arms relations commenced in 1972 when Sri Lanka obtained the Shanghai-class Type-062 patrol craft. After a gap, as the LTTE insurgency peaked, Y12 light transport aircraft were supplied in late 1980s. In 1990s, arms transfers graduated to the acquisition of fighter aircraft F-7A/J-7 and FT-5/JJ-5 trainers. The Air Force also acquired the Y-8 transport aircraft in this period. The Navy has over time acquired four different types of patrol craft and one landing craft. Around the same period, twenty-five Type-59 tanks were provided to the Army. Other army weapons were Type-59-1 (122mm) and Type-83 (130mm) towed guns, APCs and IFVs. The sales post-2000 included the BT F-7MG fighter aircraft-6/PT-6 trainer aircraft and K-8 Karakorum-8 trainer/combat aircraft. The Army received a fairly large share of arms with 70 WZ-551/Type-92 IFV, 40 Type-89/ZSD-89APCs. These were obviously the transfers at the end of civil war. When the Chinese supply waned during the Olympics period, Pakistan stepped in to fill the void. The arms transfers peaked during the time of the civil war when Western sources had dried up due to the human rights records in Sri Lanka. Rajapaksa had upgraded ties with China to a "strategic cooperative partnership".[31] Both these nations closed their gaps during the civil war when India or the Western nations could not be active due to political sensitivities and human rights issues.

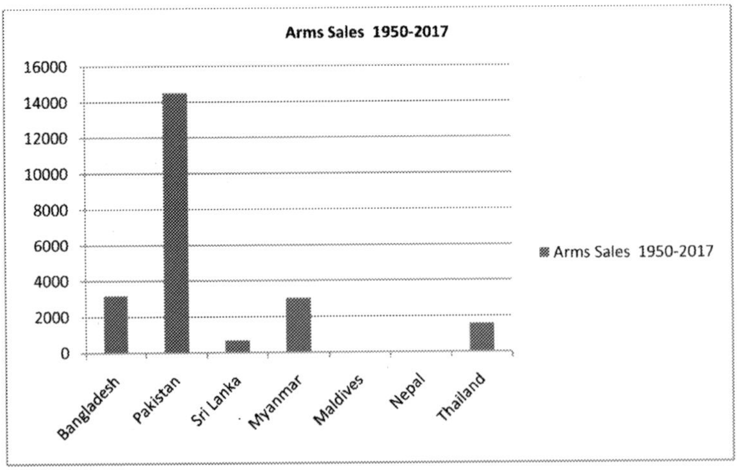

Figure 7.2. Cumulative Arms Sales from China – Select Nations

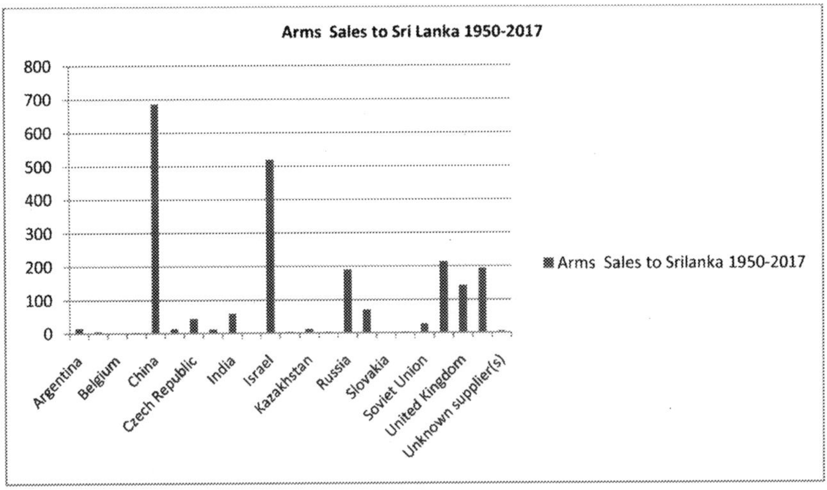

Figure 7.3. Country-wise Arms Sales to Sri Lanka
(*Source:* SIPRI Database)

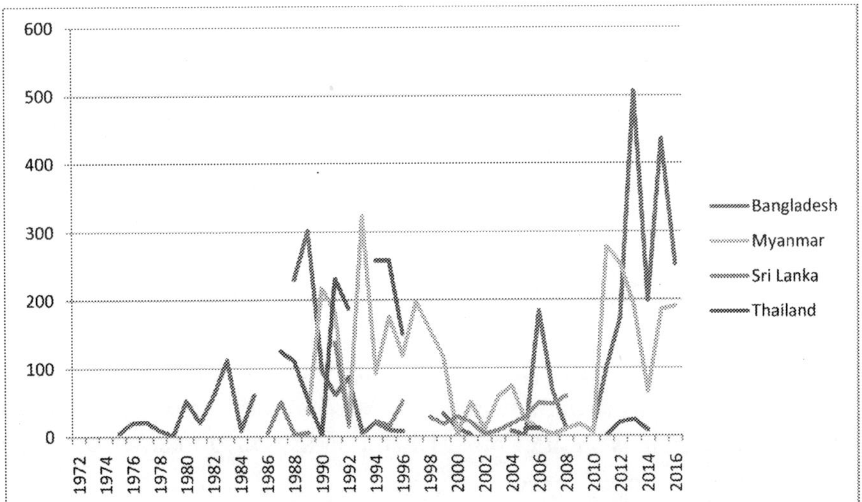

Figure 7.4. Trend of Arms Transfers from China to Select Nations
(*Source*: SIPRI database)

Sri Lanka and Other Crucial Relations Connected to China. The China-Sri Lanka-India triangle can never be complete without discussions of other neighbours who affect this relationship. For e.g., Pakistan shares a very good relationship with Sri Lanka and so does the Maldives. The Chinese influence over these three nations has a bearing on their relationships with India.

- **Pakistan.** Sri Lanka shares a very cordial relationship with Pakistan. The origins of this lay in the fact that prior to 1971, the transportation links between East and West Pakistan invariably crossed Sri Lanka. Just as China became important in the peak of the civil war, Pakistan also became important during that phase since it doled out weapons during that period of isolation of Sri Lanka. Both China and Pakistan invariably found common cause jockeying for Sri Lanka with an eye on India. China and Pakistan have territorial disputes with India and Sri Lanka has the 'big neighbour small island' sense with the ethnic Tamil issues which makes common ground there. This is despite the tremendous political risks taken by India in not interfering in the final stages of the civil war despite domestic and international pressures. Sri Lanka is the first country with which Pakistan entered into a Free Trade Agreement and expects to raise the bilateral trade from USD350 million with this FTA. The strategic question was summed up well by Prime Minister Nawaz Sharif's statement when he said '*Pakistan still remembers the strong support extended by the Government and people of Sri Lanka in 1971, despite external pressure. It gives me great satisfaction to recall that Pakistan too was able to extend its modest support to the people and the Government of Sri Lanka, when this great nation faced threats of terrorism and secession*".[32]
- The high commissioners from Sri Lanka to Pakistan are usually retired military officers as if it is a strategic signal to India. There are a large number of basic to senior level training of Sri Lankan officers in Pakistan. Training in the field of intelligence has also provided by Pakistan. The military elite of Sri Lanka continue connections through alumni links with Pakistan like the Quetta and National Defence University Associations in Sri Lanka. Amongst the military hardware links, there is an offer of Al Khalid tanks, C130 maintenance, small arms, and even nuclear cooperation on the cards between Pakistan and Sri Lanka.[33] Sri Lanka has been supplied KRL-122mm self-propelled MRL and Red Arrow-8 anti-tank missiles from Pakistan.
- The Sri Lanka and Pakistan relations are majorly driven by Sri Lanka's desire to have leverage against India despite it having a cordial, but complex relation with India. Sri Lanka also has a very large Muslim population. Overall, the Muslims include the Tamil Muslims, South-East Asian Muslims and Muslims from other parts of India. The Tamil Muslims—also called as Sri Lankan Moors—are the third largest ethnic group in the country. They are concentrated in the East Coast

and West Coast in the northern half of the island. The LTTE forced the Muslims out of Jaffna and did not share good relations despite Prabhakaran's subsequent reconciliation with them. Religion, therefore, has been a factor in the domestic ethnic issues. This in turn does have an influence over Sri Lanka's relations with Pakistan, or for that matter with other Islamic nations.

- **Maldives.** Sri Lanka also shares very good relations with the Maldives. The simple reason is proximity. This dates back to the days of colonialism when the British protectorate of Maldives had very close links with the British Colony of Ceylon. The Maldivian capital is around 370 miles from the southern tip of India and 500 miles from Colombo. However, Colombo was the main stopover for onward journeys, education and health. The coup in Maldives in 1987 was executed by Sri Lankan Tamil mercenaries with connivance of the Maldivian political and business elite. Even as this section is being written in the middle of 2017, the rapprochement between the erstwhile president Nasheed and his arch-rival Gayoom is being orchestrated in neighbouring Colombo. The new coalition is working against the current president Yameen's increasing bonding with Saudi Arabia and Wahhabism.
- **US Relations.** Sri Lanka is just 1000 nm from Diego Garcia, the US base in the region. The US had largely left the Sri Lankan ethnic problem to India. However, the US along with the West had reservations about the human rights violations during the end-phase of the civil war. Despite this, sharing of intelligence and supply of arms including that of a ship SLNS *Samudura* from the US occurred during the period. The Rajapaksa government's relations with the US were not as cordial and as soon as the government changed in 2015, the US described this event as one that 'ushered in a new political era and opportunity for renewed U.S. diplomatic and development engagement'. Secretary Kerry quickly made a visit in May 2015 and announced a USD 40 million assistance to Sri Lanka.

Conclusion: Sri Lanka

Considering the stakes in the maritime networks, China much like other powers that ventured into the Indian Ocean before it, considers Sri Lanka extremely important. The current Chinese overtures in Sri Lanka have this as one key factor, though it is not the only factor. It has the highest liner shipping connectivity index in South Asia and from the ancient times has been a coveted spot by all trading nations.

The main driver in the Sri Lanka–India bilateral relations has been the ethnic Tamils. This has had profound effects on the domestic politics of both nations. Apart from the natural worries about having a large neighbour nearby, the Tamil issue and its ethnic connection to India adds a unique dimension to the relation. In order to balance India, Sri Lanka has been cultivating warm relations with nations with strained relations with India, such as Pakistan and China. In turn, both these nations utilise opportunities to enhance their clout with Sri Lanka. It is this balancing and an increasing maritime need by China which makes the state of play what it is today.

At a tactical level, China fulfils Sri Lanka's needs for arms, finances, critical infrastructure and necessary vetoes at the UN. At the strategic level, it balances India. In that tactical manoeuvring, China did also prop up authoritarian governments which had scant regard for human rights and ethics. Presently, the island is redrafting its constitution to address some of the very lacunae which had caused the civil war. This is a crucial opportunity in the nation's vibrant democracy to arrive at the constitutional tenets that ensure enduring peace domestically and regionally.

This has even affected investments which have a geographical bias, Chinese investments have been in the south and Indian investments have been in the north. Recently India has also started reaching out to the Malayaha (Hill) Tamils, who are the immigrant plantation workers in the central provinces who deserved an engagement.

China is not having its way unopposed in Sri Lanka. The Port City was first cancelled and then came up as a new avatar—the loans have become a sour point in that relation with unpleasant exchanges—there is widespread opposition to the SEZ in Hambantota, and the port and airport which China built for itself are lacking business. The major business there is from the export of automobiles from India. The Indian Prime Minister visited Sri Lanka after a gap of 28 years and has offered a series of projects to assist Sri Lanka which have not been listed or discussed here. The Trincomalee harbour and oil storage project are two major projects. This is besides cooperation on the maritime security front. India, Sri Lanka and Maldives could build on their current trilateral maritime agreement in this regard. India also has as a separate maritime agreement with China where there can be a sharing of information over this important tri-junction crucial to the globe.

In May 2017—two and half years after the first Chinese submarine docked in the Container terminal in Colombo both on its way in as well as its way out of Indian Ocean—a request was made again for the berthing of a submarine by China. If it was timed around Prime Minister Abe's visit to Sri Lanka then, this time it was around Prime Minister Modi's visit during a Buddhist festival. This time the submarine was refused permission, and it possibly snorted its way up to Pakistan for a port call. Grounds have shifted in Sri Lanka and the government itself has changed. So have some other related events in the Indian Ocean, for this was the seventh such deployment of Chinese submarines in the Indian Ocean.

Part II: Maldives

The Maldives is an island nation that is geographically close to India and occupies a crucial position in the busy sea lanes of the Indian Ocean. Male, the Maldivian capital, is 500 miles from Colombo and around 370 miles from the southern tip of India. The northern most island of Maldives—the Ihavandippolu—where a China-led investment is taking shape, is just 90 miles from the Indian island of Minicoy. Maldives is a mere 350 miles from the US base of Diego Garcia. Locational advantages make it an important cog in the regional maritime security. Nature has not endowedit with special natural resources in the form of oil or other strategic materials. Its status as a low-lying coral island makes it vulnerable in an era of climate change. However, geography has bestowed on it a prime location in the navigational charts on the major east-west trade route.

Therefore, from time immemorial, it has seized significance far above its physical, demographic or economic size. This was known to the Arab seafarers, colonial powers like the UK, the USA and now increasingly, China and Japan. It also shares a special relation with Saudi Arabia due to religion and Sri Lanka due to geography. The Maldives has therefore been serenaded by all major powers ever since trans-oceanic trade became a prominent factor in the global economy. The nation has also evolved politically, graduating from a monarchy to republic to autocracy to the present form of presidential multiparty democracy and an Islamic republic. This section traces that journey in the light of the latest political developments in Maldives where the two erstwhile political arch-rivals, and ex-Presidents, Gayoom and Nasheed, have joined hands against the present President Yameen. Along that way, it examines the role China plays in that country and region.

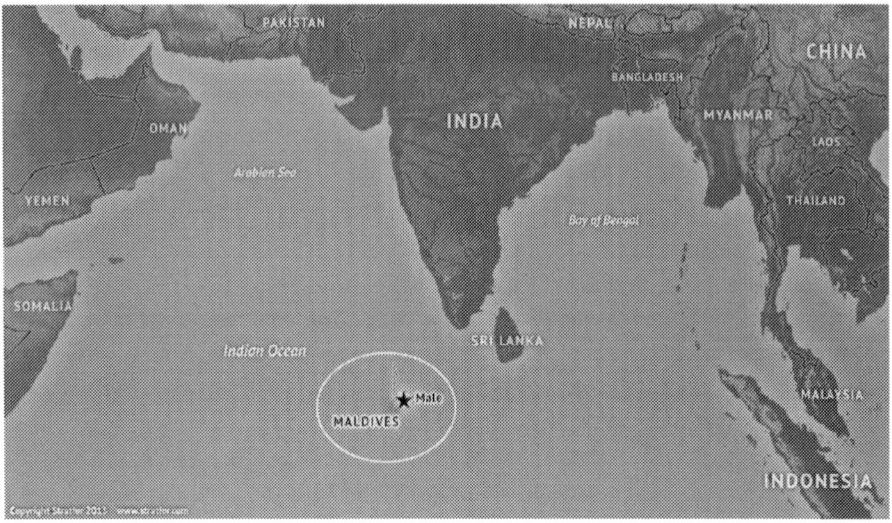

Figure 7.5. Maldives in the Indian Ocean
(*Source*: Stratfor)

Of Republics and Constitutions. Maldives has meandered through a series of changes in its forms of government. In 1887, the British made the Maldives a protectorate through an agreement with the then Maldivian Sultan.[34] In 1932, Sultan Iskandar paved the way for the first written constitution of the Maldives. As a result, a unicameral legislature, the People's Majlis, came into being. The second avatar of the constitution came into being in 1942 directed by the then Sultan. Under the British protectorate system, monarchy was briefly abolished in 1953. This led to a brief republican period—termed the 'first' republican period. This period heralded the third constitution that mandated a presidential form of governance. The polity reversed course when the Maldives returned to be a monarchy in 1954 in just one year, this time with a fourth constitution. In the ensuing period, the British continued to retain rights over the Gan Airfield and Addu atoll which soon became a rallying point for independence. Maldives became independent in 1965 from British Rule, establishing a republic for the second time. The fifth constitution was thereafter prepared in 1968. President Nasir who was the first President ended his two terms in 1978 when, Maumoon Abdul Gayoom entered the scene, leading to a prolonged regime that lasted 30 years.

There was no multiparty democracy yet in Maldives. In 2004, a constitutional assembly was established to sow seeds of multiparty democracy after a period of political unrest. This led to the preparation of a sixth constitution in 2008. Cardinal features of it were devolution of powers between the directly elected President, Legislature and Judiciary. The legislature was to be a unicameral Parliament called the People's Majlis with 85 seats where members were directly elected by constituencies by simple majority in a multiparty democratic setup for a 5-year term. The judiciary remained Sharia-based as an Islamic Republic of Sunni strain.

The two major political parties that have emerged out of the new system are the Maldivian Democratic Party (MDP) led by Mohammed Nasheed and the Progressive Party of Maldives (PPM) led by Gayoom, which is currently in power. There are also the Jumhooree Party (JP), and the Maldives Development Alliance (MDA), as well as Islamist Parties like Adhaalath Party (AP) and the Islamic Democratic Party. There are other parties such as the Dhivehi Rayyithunge Party (DRP).

In the first multiparty elections held in 2008, President Nasheed, contesting on the Maldives Democratic Party ticket, became the President of the island state ending the 30 years rule of Gayoom. Nasheed was an activist long known for his political activism and for having served several jail terms under Gayoom. He grabbed global spotlight in October 2009, when he conducted his first Cabinet meeting in an underwater chamber highlighting to the world the threat of submergence faced by the country's islands due to global warming. Climate change therefore is an important driver in the islands. However, the Nasheed presidency was curtailed in 2012 when he had to step down amidst protests that primarily emanated from the police and Armed Forces. The trigger for these protests was Nasheed's internment of a judge, as well as other contentious issues. His vice president Mohammed Waheed Hassan was sworn in on February 2012.

Post-stepping down, high drama ensued when Nasheed took asylum in the Indian embassy on February 13, 2012. The situation diffused after his arrest and subsequent release. A significant fallout of the 2012 crisis was the cancellation of a major contract with India's GMR Group over management of the airport in Male. For a nation which has tourism as its main source of revenue, the airport is a strategic asset. The cancellation was significant, considering that GMR is an Indian company and the contract was signed during Nasheed's presidency. In the typical way of balancing India and China depending on domestic politics, the contract for expanding the airport was subsequently handed out to a Chinese firm during President Xi Jinping's visit to Maldives in 2014.[35]

In spite of being the favourite in the 2013 presidential election, Nasheed lost in the second stage of voting by a small margin to Abdulla Yaameen, the half-brother of the former Maldivian President Maumoon Abdul Gayoom. In 2015, another crisis broke out. The former President and now opposition leader, Nasheed was arrested in February, shocking international observers. It was a setback to the country's political system. The arrest appeared to be one of a series of controversial actions taken by the government. The immediate event preceding this was that President Abdulla Yameen had removed defense minister Mohammed Nazim and some of his supporters allegedly over fears of them staging a coup. Nasheed's arrest on charges of terrorism worsened the situation even further. This charge is a vestige of the 2012 crisis, when President Nasheed had ordered the arrest of a judge—a charge which was withdrawn by the prosecutor general himself earlier in 2015. President Nasheed subsequently received asylum in the UK in 2016 where he went for the treatment of spinal injuries, and later shifted his base closer home to Sri Lanka when this chapter was written.

In the interim, paranoia has been at full play in Male. The half-brother Yameen, now in power, till date, has fired two of his vice presidents and a defence minister. By the end of 2016, matters had reached a stage where he had fallen out with his protégé, the senior Gayoom—the party head of PPM. His Foreign Minister, Dunia Maumoon, who is also Gayoom's daughter, resigned in a related event. The rift was over the lease of islands for development without proper procedures.[36] In 2015, a constitutional amendment was cleared by the government that allowed foreigners to lease and own land on a freehold basis in the Maldives provided they invest at least USD 1 billion and reclaimed at least 70 percent of the land. This is a serious matter of concern to India, since it opened the scope for a free hand for foreign powers in India's neighbourhood. This was also to facilitate a land transfer to the Saudi King who wanted an island to himself. This closeness to the source of Wahhabism is of discomfort to Gayoom who is deemed a moderate. The closer link to Wahhabi ideology also unnerves the Maldivian leadership since a large number of Maldivians are reported to be ISIS fighters[37] and would be a source of trouble when they return.

The political drama in the Maldives has had some paranoid crests. Maldives' former vice president Ahmed Adheeb Abdul Ghafoor was sentenced to 15 years in prison after he was found guilty of an assassination attempt on the President.[38] The September 16 cancellation of passport of notable persons also, interestingly, had Abdulla Luthufi, the leader of the 1988 coup attempt.[39] Luthufi was reportedly backed in 1988 by factions that oppose Gayoom. Historic twists, family concerns, business and politics comingle in a curious way in the Maldives.

Maldives is now going into another election in 2018 and the fallout between the Gayoom brothers becomes significant as the elder Gayoom as party patriarch has refused to endorse the current president as the next candidate. In an even more significant turn of events, the arch-rival Nasheed, now in Colombo, joined hands with the elder Gayoom against the President. They have cobbled a coalition including the Jumhooree party as well as the Adaalath party[40] in Mar 2017. This is not a small move considering the share of votes and seats they scored in the previous election. The Gayoom faction of the PPM can be also be a significant factor when the country goes to the hustings in 2018.

In the long view, the major internal political drivers are democracy, religion, economy and climate change. External powers calibrate its policies, catering to these driving factors as they engage the Maldives. The nation does a tightrope walk balancing extreme forms of religion and the obvious economic and political benefits of the religious card, both within and outside the country. Being a Sunni Muslim nation, it has warm relations with Pakistan and Bangladesh. Though the Maldives is moderately religious, the religious card often acts as a strong catalyst in both international and national political processes.

Critical pieces of the Maldivian jigsaw are the role played by Saudi Arabia and China. Both exercise strong economic clout over Maldives whose GDP is USD3 billion. Both attach no strings about democracy on their doles unlike other sources of assistance. The former also infuses hard-line Wahhabi religious strains into the polity. In a recent event the Fafu Atoll was to be given on lease to the Saudi Royals for USD10 billion, and a visit was due by King Salman which however got cancelled due to 'flu'.

Historically, the Indian Ocean traders used the cowries from Maldives as a medium of exchange when they traded across the oceans. The cowries of these islands were the 'dollar' of those days. Today, as new players emerge in global trade, the Maldives continue to remain an important node in the IOR — a fact not lost on China, which has serious interests and investment in the island state. China has therefore been a key player in the Maldives. China and the Maldives established diplomatic relations in October 1972. By 1985, Chinese firms started getting a foothold in Maldivian business. In 2001 Chinese Premier Zhu Rongji visited Maldives. There are several projects where China is involved. The major ones are construction of the Foreign Ministry, the National Museum and Housing Projects. Defence exchanges are a regular feature of this relation. The tourism sector contributes heavily to the Maldivian economy accounting for nearly 50 per cent of GDP. China has been a major source of tourists visiting the Maldives. The airport expansion project, pulled away from an Indian Company—GMR—was subsequently awarded to a Chinese company, which will plough in USD800 million.[41] The Chinese EXIM bank had granted a USD373 million loan for developing the Male airport in 2015.[42] As an aside, the GMR, incidentally, has won arbitration against the Maldives[43] for terminating its contract.

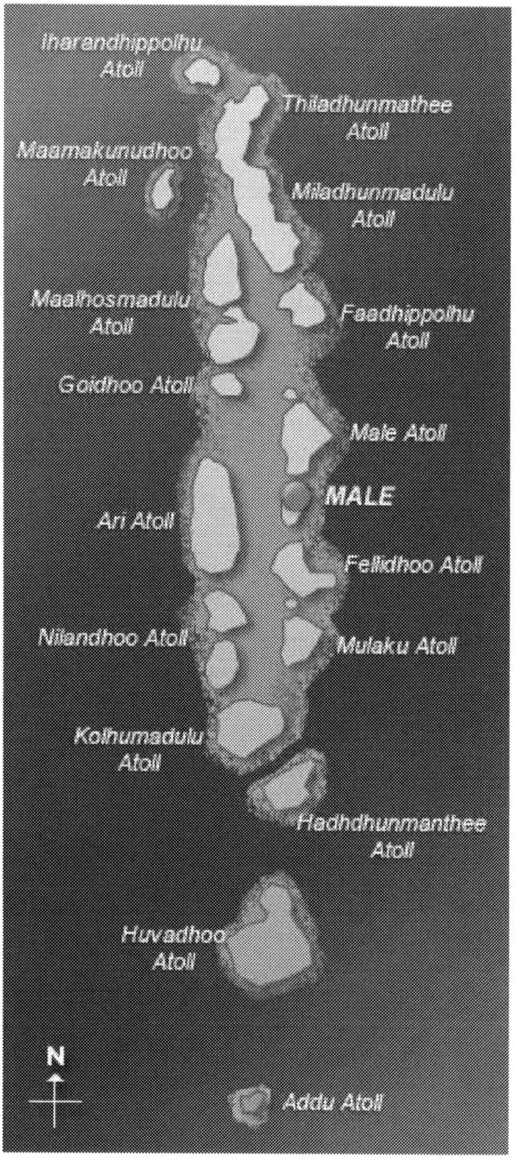

Figure 7.6. The Maldives with Different Atolls

Chinese President Xi Jinping visited the archipelago nation in September 2014 becoming the first Chinese President to do so. This has been a sign of its growing importance, which in turn reflects vigour in the IOR policy of China. China has invested in a bridge between Male and the Hulhule airport symbolically named the 'Bridge of Friendship'. It has assisted in capacity expansion of the airport, created housing projects and is involved in power and agriculture sectors—all which can be called critical infrastructure. In December 2014 when Maldives was hit by a severe water shortage, China sent 1,000 tonnes of fresh water to the Maldives by air[44] and dispatched a military vessel with water. There are also reports that the Chinese may build a port at the Gaadhoo Island in the southern atoll.[45] The Ihavan project[46] at

Ihavandipolu next to India has invited closer attention due to Chinese interests. The Maldives has transferred on lease Feydhoo Finolhu, the island in the Kaafu atoll previously used for Maldives Police Service activities, to a China firm for USD4 million.[47] The Maldives has also endorsed the Maritime Silk Route.[48]

Sri Lanka continues to play a crucial role in Maldivian politics. The Dhivehis, or the Maldivian people, have ethnic linkages with Sri Lanka which makes that relation unique. Both nations were under British rule and the atolls were watched over through its offices in Sri Lanka with no serious and continuous presence in the Atoll as it was a protectorate and not a colony. Due to proximity and shipping lanes, Colombo was the stopover from the West before an onward journey to Male. Hence, most western missions operate through missions in Sri Lanka. Therefore Colombo and Male remain hyphenated through transport and diplomatic network and with impacts on the islands' affairs. The relations with the UK continued through the Commonwealth. However, in a recent turn of events the Maldives decided to leave the Commonwealth, when it faced criticism over its records over human rights and democracy.[49]

Maldives has carefully balanced major powers to maximise its benefits and retain its autonomy. It juggles China, India, Japan, UK and USA carefully, weighing what each relationship brings to the table. The advocates of liberal democratic movements derive strengths from democracies, especially India, and yet they balance it with China. The conservative regime draws its strength from China and Saudi Arabia and uses that card astutely to draw maximum benefits from India and other democracies. The internal political dynamics in turn gets affected making the matrix a highly complex web. Any assessment of the Maldives hinges on the state of play of that matrix at a given point of time.

From an Indian perspective, Maldives is its key neighbour in the Indian Ocean with whom relations have been cordial. People-to-people contacts have been high, for medical tourism, education, etc. India has also been active in the training of the Maldivian government personnel. India is also the closest neighbour and first country that Maldives turns to in times of crisis. A good example in this regard was the crisis of 1988 when the Sri Lankan Tamil mercenaries staged a coup d'état. The problem was resolved by virtue of a quick intervention from India on the request of President Gayoom. The country returned to normalcy thereafter. The recent political uncertainties led to the cancellation of Indian Prime Minister Narendra Modi's scheduled visit to the islands in March 2015. However, bilateral relations between India and Maldives have been on track with the Foreign Minister and Foreign Secretary visiting Maldives and the Maldives President visiting India in 2016.

To the world, it is one amongst the *many* maritime traffic convergence points. However, to India, it is far more critical, being a close neighbour, and having a direct bearing on its security. It is only a just a few miles away from the Lakshadweep group of islands. Therefore, events inside the Maldives attain prominence for India since they have a potential to affect the Indian Ocean and the trading world. It is in such a backdrop of the larger geopolitical construct of the Indian Ocean that the events in Maldives, including domestic politics, need to be seen.

As far as China is concerned, the Chinese investments are to be seen as an engagement aimed at wooing a vital nation that sits on its crucial sea lanes relevant to its Maritime Silk Road. China has carefully chosen the fields of investments/loans, which are in critical infrastructure segments. Though high level visits have taken place in the defence field, no arms transfer has taken place yet. In mid-2017, the focus of the Maldivian politics seems to be dealing with a President who is cosying up to hard-line Wahhabist religious ideology. China in the interim plays a key economic role in the islands with 70 per cent[50] of Male's external debt emerging out of Beijing just as sparring factions in the Maldivian domestic politics are cobbling a coalition for liberal democracy and against Wahhabism.

Part III: Bangladesh

Introduction. Bangladesh broke away from Pakistan when the idea of Pakistan failed to meet the aspirations of the Bengali Muslims in its eastern landmass. The turning point was the 1970 elections, where the Awami League got the majority and was not allowed to form the government. Sheikh Mujib Ur Rahman spearheaded a political movement based on Bengali nationalism which was dealt with brutally by West Pakistan. The result was a genocide and mass migration to India. Faced with a severe refugee crisis, India had to intervene and assist the Bengali population militarily to bring stability in the periphery. The result was a brilliant victory by India over Pakistan in 1971 which made Bangladesh a reality.

Geography. Geographically, Bangladesh has India on three sides and Myanmar's Rakhine region on its south-eastern Border. Bangladesh, unlike Myanmar or Pakistan, doesn't offer connectivity directly from the Chinese

Figure 7.7. Political Map of Bangladesh
(*Source*: http://www.mofa.gov.bd/sites/default/files/bangladesh-political-map_0.jpg)

mainland to the Indian Ocean Region. However, through Myanmar and India, it has the potential to become an access route. At present, it serves as a foothold as the title of the chapter indicates.

It is a riverine deltaic country with major rivers being the Padma, Jamuna and Meghna. They form the deltaic entwinements, one swallowing another before finally reaching the Bay of Bengal. The Ganga transforms into the Hooghly in India and its distributary Padma heads to Bangladesh. The Brahmaputra becomes the Jamuna in Bangladesh which later joins the Padma. Meghna, another major river known as Barak in India, also joins the Padma before draining into the Bay of Bengal. Such confluence of several rivers, their tributaries and distributaries, disconnects landmasses and demands several bridges in Bangladesh. This is a key investment being carried out by China through a series of ***friendship bridges***. The ninth such bridge has just been declared in May 2017.

Bangladesh is also crucial to subcontinental connectivity. The partition of India in 1947 was unfair to that connectivity. To the west it cut off Central Asia and to the east it cut traditional connectivity networks to India's North Eastern Region (NER) with the creation of Bangladesh. For 67 years since independence, the supply lines to the North Eastern Region wound their way tediously and slowly through the Siliguri corridor. The effect was very serious on the Southern Areas in NER in India like Tripura at the end of that network. For instance, the distance from Kolkata to Agartala, the capital of Tripura, which was 450km before partition, increased to 1687km, nearly fourfold, at the stroke of that midnight. If one shifts the starting point to the Chittagong harbour, the natural entry point from the sea to the North East of India, the comparison will only get starker. The Indo-Pak war of 1965 worsened the transit problem cutting the minimal rail lines that existed.

What lay between the littoral subcontinent and NER was East Pakistan, what is now Bangladesh. Despite being instrumental in liberating Bangladesh in 1971, India could not convert that landslide geopolitical victory to resolve a connectivity problem with NER. Relations with the new-found nation took its own trajectory and legacies of partition stopped us from realising the access issue to NER through Bangladesh. For hauling heavy loads, an essential for economic development and even for basic necessities such as rice, India had to be dependent on Bangladesh on a case-to-case basis. Part of the reason was the land and maritime boundary disputes between India and Bangladesh. India and Bangladesh during the tenure of the present Awami League government resolved both land and maritime boundary issues. The first was the maritime boundary which got settled in The Hague, in favour of Bangladesh and then there was the exchange of enclaves within each other's land borders. The exchange of conclaves was a significant step and the result of the settlement have impacted connectivity with a far multiplier effect to the North East of India, besides offering options in regional geopolitical transportation initiatives. The opening of a direct shipping route between India and Bangladesh in lieu of indirect ones was another gain with positive effects on the economy on either sides of border.

Domestic Politics. The domestic politics of Bangladesh has a bearing on its relation with China, just as foreign policy is an extension of domestic politics of all nations. The new nation formed in 1971 soon fell into domestic political and economic turmoil. The popular leader Mujib, the chief protagonist of the liberation struggle, and his family, except his daughter Sheikh Hasina, got assassinated in 1975. Events spiralled down further with coup attempts and Maj Gen Zia Ur Rahman emerged as the military leader. By 1976 he became the Chief Martial Law Administrator and became President in 1978. In a pattern one repeatedly witnesses in South Asia right up to Musharraf in Pakistan, Gen Zia formed a new party named the Bangladesh Nationalist Party (BNP) after becoming President. Zia removed the principle of secularism from the constitution, which was subsequently restored in 2010 by the judiciary. Gen Zia too was assassinated in 1981. Power returned to the BNP for a year, and then in 1982, Army Chief Gen Hussain Mohammed Ershad took over, declaring martial law. In 1986, he too, following trends, founded a party named the Jatiya Party with leanings towards the Awami League. He made necessary amendments to the constitution to legitimise his own martial law and made Bangladesh an Islamic State, much like his Pakistan counterpart Gen Zia Ul Haq. He ruled till 1991 when elections were held and Khalida Zia, wife of Gen Zia, by then the head of BNP, became the Prime Minister. Bangladesh today therefore has three major parties; The Bangladesh Awami League, which is a left-leaning nationalist party, the Bangladesh Nationalist Party (BNP) which is a centre-right party having the support of religious parties like the Jamaat-e-Islami Bangladesh and the third party named the Jatiya Party.

Subsequent elections have thrown up alternate governments between the BNP led by Khalida Zia (1991–96, 2001–06) and the Awami League led by Sheikh Hasina (1996–2001, 2009–14, 2014 onwards). Therefore, the BNP and the Awami League are today the major poles in Bangladeshi politics. Presently, the Awami League under Sheikh Hasina is in power. The relations with India have been on an upward trajectory during the Awami League's rule. Many important treaties were signed with India after Sheikh Hasina won the 1996 elections. The Chittagong hill tract treaty and the Ganga water-sharing treaty were the cardinal ones. In the 2008 elections, when Hasina returned to power, after prolonged negotiations, the land boundary and transportation agreements were signed in 2015 with India. Her domestic dreams included a 10-year poverty alleviation strategy to make Bangladesh a middle-income country by 2021 and a developed nation by 2041. A problem that besieges Bangladesh today is the rise of radical Islam. There are gruesome murders of bloggers, and a more severe grade of violence with blasts targeted at spaces frequented by foreigners and a local hard-line Islamic movement that supports the Islamic State. Any external relations with Bangladesh have to deal with the above domestic realities getting shaped and shaping them in the process of politics.

To weave China in to this narrative, when Bangladesh was formed in 1971, certain cardinal events were occurring in modern Chinese history. It was the year when the PRC had become a member of the UN and replaced Taiwan in the Security Council. This was also a period of the Sino-US rapprochement where Pakistan played a major role. China was also the bête noire of the former USSR due to differences in ideology. India, with whose help Bangladesh had become independent, was also an ally of the former USSR. China had by then begun to value Pakistan deeply and saw the dismemberment of its ally as an unwelcome event. Therefore, China's relations were not so cordial when the new nation was formed in 1971. Bangladesh could join the UN only in 1974 due to China's vetoes. When the Awami League and its leader Mujib Ur Rahman had very close relationship with India, Gen Zia Ur Rahman initiated the China–Bangladesh relationship. Modern China–Bangladesh relations thus began in 1976. This was also the period when China was opening up to the world after the Mao era. Traditionally, therefore the BNP has had very cordial relations with China and the Awami League has deftly managed excellent relations with India as well as cordial relations with China. The Sino-Bangla relations have to be viewed in this context.

Presently, Bangladesh has a GDP of USD226 billion. It has the lowest public debt in South Asia of only 25.9 per cent and very low external debt of a mere 16 per cent of the GDP. It is a fast growing economy at 6.9 per cent[51] which has a dire need for critical infrastructure in power, road, rail, port and energy sources. Therefore, economically, China is an important factor in Bangladesh with its appetite for critical infrastructure investment under the BRI umbrella. Bilateral trade has increased to USD14.7 billion in 2015, with a growth rate of 20 per cent since 2000. In a recent visit to Bangladesh, President Xi announced a slew of investments that amount to USD24 billion,[52] next only to Pakistan in the region.

Arms Deals with China. Bangladesh ranks only after Pakistan, North Korea, Iran and Iraq as a recipient of Chinese arms. If one discounts the latter three in the list, it ranks quite high in arms transfers from China. So far it has received USD3.1 billion worth of armaments from China. It has resolved its maritime boundary with India in a case which can be an exemplar of the use of international law in the resolution of maritime disputes despite power differentials between the affected parties. Bangladesh is yet to resolve its maritime boundary issue with Myanmar. The relations with Myanmar are also sensitive due to the ethnic Rohingyas of the Rakhine province whom Myanmar does not consider as citizens. In its desire to build a powerful navy Bangladesh has acquired vessels from the UK, the USA and China including a recent acquisition of submarines from China. The Bangladesh–China Defence Cooperation Agreement was signed in 2002 under the Khalida Zia government. As articulated by analysts.[53] this was a move by China to keep India engaged in the eastern flank also and came just after President Musharraf's cursory apology over genocides by Pakistan army in Bangladesh. The purchase of such complex weaponry like submarines provides extraordinary long-term inroads to China. India has resolved most of its bilateral issues except perhaps water-sharing on the Teesta River. Despite an excellent situation in bilateral relations with India, China has played on its insecurities and fans the fear through the arms sales quite successfully.

China's arms relations with Bangladesh started with second-hand MiG-15 UTI trainer aircraft in 1974, the very year it accepted Bangladesh as a state in the UN.[54] In 1981, land weapons started getting included in the package with Type-53 120mm mortar and Type-59 tanks. Advanced and modern Type-90-2/MBT-2000 tanks were transferred in 2011. The major chunk of weapons supplied from China is naval weapons. In 1980, naval vessels started arriving with the Shanghai FAC with the Bangladeshi designation of 'Shaheed'. Type-037/Hainan patrol craft were received between 1982 and 1985. They have the Bangladeshi designation of 'Durjoy'. In 1982, Bangladesh acquired its first missile, the HY-2/SY-1A/CSS-N-2 anti-ship missile. The naval inventory transfer that year also includes the Type-021/ Huangfen FAC. The first large vessel from China was a frigate in 1989 – the Type-053/Jianghu-1 Version-4 Frigate with the Bangladeshi designation 'Osman'. In 1993, a new type of vessel, the Project-254/T-43 minesweeper named Sagar, was added to the inventory. The missile transfers include SAMs, portable SAMs and the Crotale SAM system C-802/CSS-N-8 anti-ship missile. The cooperation expanded with the Type-053H2/Jianghu-3Frigate in 2012. They were second-hand and have the Bangladeshi designation Abu Bakar. The transfer reached a new level in 2013 when the Type-035G/Song-class submarine was transferred. These second-hand modernised submarines were ordered for a USD203 million deal, which is extremely cheap by global standards. It has the Bangladeshi designation 'Nabajatra'. In a separate deal the Yu-4 533mm anti-ship torpedo was signed in 2013 for a probable use from submarine. In 2015, Bangladesh acquired Type-056 Shadhinata frigates equipped with the C-802/CSS-N-8 anti-ship missile. These are the corvette-class vessels being made by China in very large numbers described in Chapter 3 as the cheaper smaller platforms used for augmenting the territorial claims of China.

Some cardinal observations come to the fore when we look at Bangladesh's arms transfers. Firstly, it has second highest inventory after Pakistan in the region. It is also the first country after Egypt in the 1980s and North Korea to get Chinese submarines. This appears as a clever ploy by China to populate the region with weapons that can unsettle India, and earn an ally. Refer to Figures 7.2 and 7.3 for the cumulative sale of weapons and trends respectively.

Chinese Investments

In 1983, China and Bangladesh established a Joint Economic Commission (JEC). Till 2016, a USD1.5 billion worth business has been carried out through this conduit. A series of investment in the Bridges of Friendship has been a major facet of development diplomacy in riverine Bangladesh of which the ninth bridge is in progress now. The other projects have been listed to get a perspective and trends in investment.

In early 2000s, China funded the development of 210 MW Khulna Thermal Power Plant, the Pagla Water Treatment Plant, North Dhaka (East) Sewerage Treatment Plant and Associated Sewerage System. In 2005 China also assisted in the installation of communication infrastructure and grass-roots development issues like funding the creation of District Headquarters and Upazila Growth Centres. As part energy initiatives the Barapukuria Coal Mine has been a part of the funding plan. The 2005 agreement between China and Bangladesh for Cooperation in the Peaceful Uses of Nuclear Energy is indicative of the quality and trend in this relation. Water being a major issue in the subcontinent, China and Bangladesh signed an Implementation Plan on Provision of Hydrological Information of the Brahmaputra River in Flood Season in 2008. The Brahmaputra originates in Tibet as the Yarlung Tsangpo and becomes the Jamuna in Bangladesh.

The 2016 visit by President Xi elevated the relation from 'comprehensive partnership of cooperation' to a 'strategic partnership of cooperation'.

Institutionalised cooperation in maritime affairs and efforts towards counter-terrorism are part of the Sino-Bangla cooperation. Twenty-seven deals worth USD24 billion have been signed which will now be a major component of this relationship. Forty instruments include fifteen agreements and G2G MoUs, 12 loan agreements and 13 agreements that are between State Owned Enterprises and private industries. A brief list of these agreements is placed in this chapter.

The Chinese investment in Bangladesh declared during President Xi's visit had two components: government-to-government critical infrastructure projects and business-to-business joint ventures in the private sector. The former involved 27 agreements with roughly USD24 billion investments and the latter involves 13 agreements with roughly USD13 billion worth of projects. The infrastructure projects involve power projects, bridge projects, road and rail projects, maritime infrastructure projects and information technology investments. There are loans for disaster management infrastructure also woven into the scheme of affairs. The time line of completion targets fifty years of Bangladesh in 2021.

Power and connectivity dominate the areas of investment. There are power projects worth USD6 billion including the coal-based Ultra Super Critical Power Plant at Kalapara and Banshkhali. The power investment also includes transmission lines worth USD2 billion including for Dhaka and the National Grid. Around USD8 billion worth of railway projects include the Padma River Railbridge, Akhaura-Sylhet, Dhaka-Ishwardi and Dhaka–Chittagong projects. For road connectivity, USD6 billion worth projects have been rolled out including the Dhaka–Sylhet and Dhaka Ashulia elevated corridor. A tunnel is planned under the Karnaphuliriver to connect the upcoming Anwara SEZ. The Airstrip at Anwara SEZ will be upgraded. Coastal expressways from Sitakunda to Coxs Bazaar Marine Drive include coastal protection plans.

A major maritime component has been USD583 million in financial assistance for maritime programmes. The Mongla Port is being modernised where the China National Complete Engineering Corporation is to carry out work for an estimated cost of USD550 million of which USD249 million is from Chinese funds. For shipping, there is Chinese assistance to buy six ships from China with a loan of USD184 million. This includes three bulk carriers and three oil tankers. The designated use of these ships is for coal for the Rampal Thermal Power Plant and oil tankers to carry imported oil for the Bangladesh Petroleum Corporation (BPC). In addition, the Bangladesh Shipping Corporation (BSC) can purchase two tanker vessels with capacity of 1,00,000–1,25,000 tonnes and 16 vessels from China including two liquefied natural gas (LNG) carrier vessels. An LNG import terminal is being set up by Petrobangla at Moheshkhali in Chittagong.

The other projects include USD280 million credit agreement for the Dasherkandi Sewerage Treatment Plant project, USD83 million in grants for "The Project of Disaster Emergency Operation Centre and Information Platform" and USD500 million from 2016 to 2020 for special assistance projects aimed at disaster prevention and reduction. Cultural exchanges include setting up of a Confucius Institute at the Dhaka University. China has also funded information technology initiatives with the National Data Centre in Gazipur's Kaliakoir and the National ICT Infra-Network for Bangladesh Government Phase III at around USD1 billion. A major private investment project has been the Shahjalal Fertiliser Company Limited in Fenchuganj.

Table 7.4. Chinese Funded Bangladesh Projects (Preliminary information tabulated from various reports. May change as work/negotiation progresses).

Project Name	Type	Cost
Kalapara (Payra)[55]	1320 MW Coal Based Ultra Super Critical Power Plant at Kalapara Upazilla, Patuakhali. This is being carried out by China National Machinery Import & Export Corporation and North-west Power Generation Company Limited	1.9
Banshkhali[56]	1320 MW coal-fired power plant in Chittagong's Banshkhali. The investment also includes transmission lines worth USD2bn.	1.75
Dhaka Power Grid[57]	The plan is to upgrade the capital's power grid. The work is being done by China's state-owned Tebian Electricity Apparatus, Dhaka Power and Jiangsu Etern	1.6
Bangladesh Grid[58]	Aims at improvement of the National Power Grid	1.1
Railways		
Akhaura-Sylhet[59]	Railway line from Akhaura to the northern city of Sylhet	1.76
Joydevpur-Ishwardi[60]	A 173km dual-gauge double-line rail track from Joydevpur to Ishwardi. Cost of the project is USD941 million, of which China will provide USD753 million China Civil Engineering Construction Cooperation	0.753
Dhaka-Chittagong[61]	Dhaka-Chittagong railway project	3.03
Padma Railbridge[62]	Padma Bridge rail link	3.3
Dhaka-Sylhet [63]	Four-lane highway between Dhaka and Sylhet	1.6
Dhaka Ashulia[64]	Elevated highway from Dhaka Ashulia	1.39
Karnaphuli[65]	Tunnel under the Karnaphuli River between SEZ Anwara and Chittagong Harbour	0.7
Chittagong	Marine drive expressway in the Chittagong Division- This is from	2.85

Project Name	Type	Cost
Sitakunda Cox[66] Bazar Marine Drive Expressway Coastal Protection	Sitakunda-Cox's Bazar. Termed the Coastal Protection Project.	
Loans	The funding is through soft loan from the China Exim Bank at 2% interest. The commitment charge is 0.2% and management fees 0.2%. The loan repayment period is 20 years including five years of grace period. China has offered two loans. Anwara Airstrip project is through this loan.	0. 583
Mongla Port[67]	Modernisation of Mongla Port where China National Complete Engineering Corporation is to carry out work for an estimated cost of USD 550 million of which USD249 million is from Chinese funds.	0.249
Purchase of Ships[68]	Assistance to buy six ships from China with a loan.This includes three bulk carriers and three oil tankers. The designated use of these ships is for coal for the Rampal thermal power plant and oil tankers to carry imported oil for the Bangladesh Petroleum Corporation (BPC) (In addition, Bangladesh Shipping Corporation (BSC) can purchase two tanker vessels with capacity of 1,00,000-1,25,000 tonnes and 16 vessels from China including two liquefied natural gas (LNG) carrier vessels. An LNG import terminal has been set up by Petrobangla at Moheshkhali in Chittagong)	0.184
Dasherkandi[69]	Credit agreement for Dasherkandi Sewerage Treatment Plant project	0.28
Disater Relief[70]	Grants for "The Project of Disaster Emergency Operation Centre and Information Platform	0.083
Disaster Relief[71]	from 2016 to 2020 for special assistance projects aimed at disaster prevention and reduction	0.5
Digital Infrastructure[72]	China has also invested in tnformation technology with Tier-4 National Data Centre in Gazipur'sKaliakoir and National ICT Infra-Network for Bangladesh Government Phase III (Info Sarkar)	1

Conclusion

China has invested deeply in Bangladesh across the spectrum from developmental projects to highly potent weapons like submarines. As far as infrastructure is concerned, China has focussed on critical infrastructure such as bridges, energy projects, rail, road, ports and shipping. A stark feature is the high maritime content in arms sales to Bangladesh including the sale of submarines. Submarines are purely offensive weapons, with very limited less-than-war role. China has so far sold submarines only to Egypt, North Korea and now to Bangladesh. Pakistan and Thailand have signed for Chinese submarines, albeit a more modern class. It is felt that these transfers are primarily India-centric. They are also a part of the Indian Ocean Strategy of China. Submarines are tech-intensive and require training and support for a long time. They assist China to have a deep military relationship with that country. This draws Bangladesh naturally into the Chinese orbit and the infrastructure built for them can serve as plug and play docking and repair facilities for future Chinese submarine forays into the Indian Ocean in the Bay of Bengal and the Arabian Sea. Further up in the north-western Indian Ocean, Djibouti offers another base for them. The impending sale to Thailand and warm relations with Malaysia, which is covered in next chapter, will offer support on either end of the Malacca Straits.

As far as China's investment in Bangladesh goes, it will double Bangladesh's foreign debt which is presently moderate and sustainable.[73] By June of 2017, differences of opinion on how much constitutes a soft loan and how much is commercial had surfaced between China and Bangladesh regarding the promised USD24 billion.[74] This large access to Chinese finance is a clear shift away by Bangladesh from low interest rate loans, which can give China leverage over critical assets. In combination with arms sales, this new development of large scale financing has potential for affecting the stability of the region.

As far as Bangladeshi domestic politics is concerned, the anti-incumbency alternate rules of the Awami League and the BNP are likely to continue. The 2002 Defence Agreement with China has been a major step which has worsened the India–Bangladesh relationship. This was signed during the BNP rule. This deal was around the time Pakistan re-imagined this relation with President Musharaf's overtures and an expression of 'regret' over the East Pakistan genocides. Even though the present regime has received submarines as fait accompli, the damage has been done by the Sino-Pak nexus at work. Unlike Sri Lanka or Maldives which give China the excuse of protection of maritime sealanes or even Myanmar which offers it a conduit to the IOR, Bangladesh offers nothing but an offensive capability against India and an opportunity to distract India. Therefore, Bangladesh perplexes the analyst with its contradictory policies. The present disposition offers friendship at one end and acquires deeply potent weapons at the other playing to the Sino-Pak scripts. Therefore, India must re-imagine this relationship. The vulnerability of this relationship is that any further push on the Awami League will set the stage for a possible takeover by the hard-line religious right. Hence, Bangladesh offers difficult choices for India.

Part IV: The Commercial Maritime Network of China

Thus far the chapter has dealt with footholds China is creating in the Indian Ocean Region. There is also a wider network of ports and shipping that China is creating across the globe. The Indian Ocean is just a part of that wider foray in the maritime world. A look at the maritime top seeds tells that story. From shipbuilding, shipping operations, port building, port operations, including container operations, China has been gradually progressing ahead.

Shipping Operations. Overall, the China-owned merchant shipping by tonnage is third after Greece and Japan.[75] Today, it is 11 per cent of global shipping. In a ten-year period, Chinese shipping tripled from 44 million gross tonnage in 2005 to 130 million gross tonnage in 2015.[76] One discernible aim is to increase the carrying of crude by own ships to 85 per cent, states Dennis Blasko in his article on China's Merchant Marine.[77] Blasko also states that by the number of ships, China plus Hong Kong is already the top ship-operating nation in the globe. This trend of being the top-ship operator is likely to continue with China overtaking Greece by 2030 eventually carrying 19–20 per cent of the global trade. 71 per cent gross tonnage of Chinese shipping is held by the COSCO, China Shipping Group and Sino-Trans CSC, forming the big three shipping firms of China. Of these, the China Shipping Group and COSCO have merged several operations.

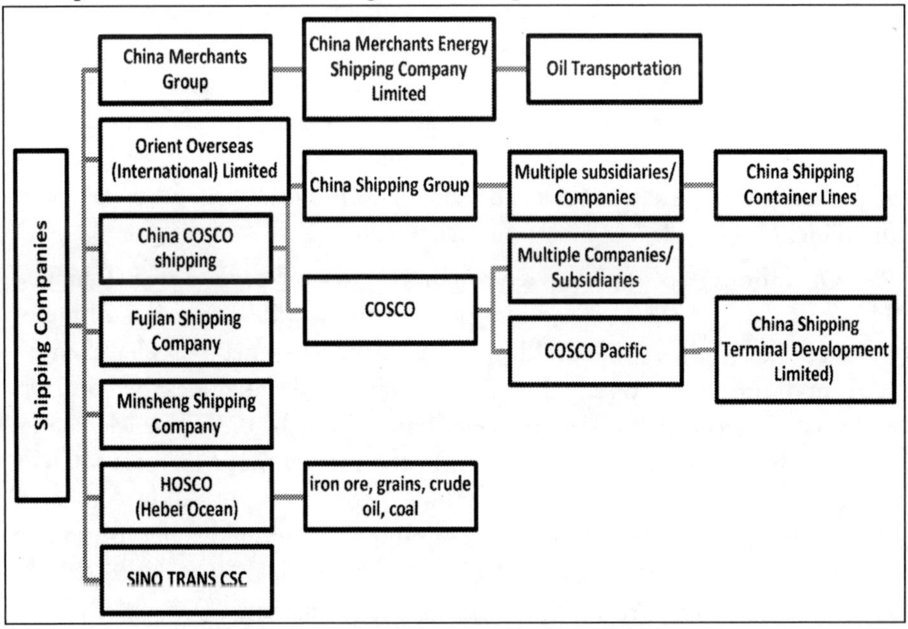

Figure 7.8. China Shipping Industry Overview

(*Source*: Dennis Blasko, "China's Merchant Marine", updated status by the author)

The Chinese merchant ships have a role in Civil Military Integration. Blasko informs that the Chinese merchant marine was an essential part of the Libya evacuation. It is also noteworthy that it was the CICT in Colombo, built using China's funds, that allowed the PLAN submarine to dock on its way out and in from the Indian Ocean in 2014.[78] There is also a long-standing Chinese system of ship reporting named CHISREP which allows the PLA to know the exact location of merchantships across the globe at any given time. In order to better explain the various Chinese maritime initiatives, three figures are placed below addressing three main sectors of shipping, shipbuilding and port building, and operations. They only address prominent companies and institutions that are involved in the industry and include Hong Kong operations. Some shipping companies have also invested in ports like COSCO in the Piraeus project in Greece. The COPH Pakistan which handles the Gwadar port stands out as a company which is not one of the mainstream companies, and appears as a special purpose vehicle.[79]

Shipbuilding. China is also the largest shipbuilder in the world. China overtook South Korea in 2010 and has maintained that position ever since, producing 35 per cent of the global output.[80] China is presently consolidating the shipbuilding industry, separating it geographically into two major conglomerates—the CSSC and the CSIC. The details of the various yards under them have been covered in Chapter 3. The yards are also scaling the value chain, producing more complex vessels like LNG carriers. Most yards produce both military and civil ships. In a significant move in 2015, the shipbuilding standards of China have been upgraded to make civil ships suitable for military roles.[81] The major shipbuilding conglomerates of China with their geographic focus, within China and important institutions under them including yards, are placed in Figure 7.9.

Port Operations. Six of the top ten container ports in the world are in China.[82] Thirty-two out of top 50 container ports in the world were either Chinese-owned or had Chinese shareholding. These Chinese owned posts handled 67 per cent of the global container volumes.[83] The list also includes the Houston and Miami ports which had 49 per cent shareholding by the China Merchants Port Holding limited which bought into the French maritime group CMA CMG's firm named Terminal Link. Chinese container ships didn't do badly either and carried 18 per cent of container shipping.[84] The volume of investment in the ports involved was USD45.6 billion in 40 ports since 2010.[85] A brief overview of port building, an operations segment of China, is placed in Figure 7.9.

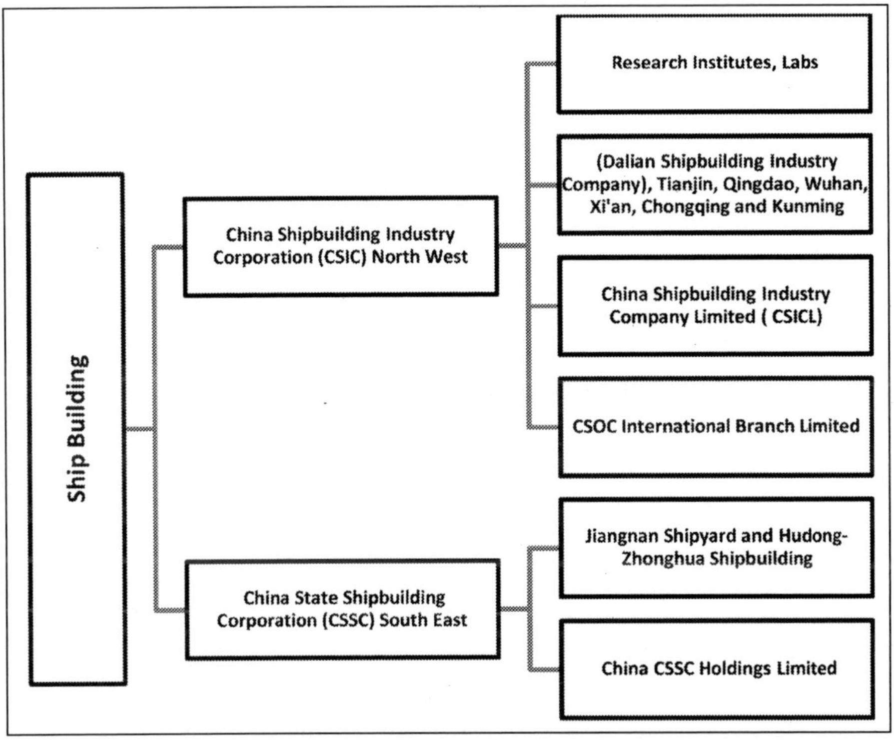

Figure 7.9. Overview: Select Ship Building Industry China

An ocean-wise list of ports which have partial or full Chinese/Hong Kong ownership is placed below to give a perspective on China's investments in this sector. Ports in China are not mentioned. The two major port management firm's ports are listed separately ocean-wise. They are from Hutchison Marine and Terminal Link. As one can see in the table, China has invested in Sao Tome and Principe, which is a critical entrance to the oil-rich Gulf of Guinea to Florida in USA, to Sri Lanka and Myanmar.

Table 7.5. Ocean-wise Investments by Chinese Companies

Ocean	Firms	Port
Indian Ocean	Hutchison Port (HP)[86]	HP Westports, Kuala Lumpur, Malaysia, HP MITT, Yangon (Tilawa), Myanmar, HP KICT, HP Pakistan, Karachi, Pakistan, HP Sohar, Oman, HP Dammam Saudi Arabia, HP Dar-Es-Salaam, Tanzania, HP Ajman, United Arab Emirates
	Others	Colombo(CICT), Hambantota, Maday Island (Kyuakphyu), Gwadar, Darwin (Landbridge Group), New Castle,[87] Melbourne (China

Ocean	Firms	Port
		Investment Fund),[88] Ashdod,[89] Singapore[90] (3 berths, COSCO-PSA 49 per cent), Port Said East, Suez Canal Container Terminal (COSCO 20 per cent)
	Others[91]	Bagamoyo,[92] Port Klang,[93] Meleka,[94] Carey Island,[95] Djibouti Doraleh Port including reserved berthing for PLAN Ships.
Mediterranean	Hutchison Port (HP)	HP Alexandria, HP El Dekheila Alexandria, Egypt, HP Best Barcelona, Spain
	Terminal Link[96] Others	Tangier Morocco (TL) Piraeus[97] (Greece), Ambarli (Turkey),[98] Kumport 26 per cent stake Haifa[99],
Atlantic Ocean	Hutchison Port (HP)[100]	HP Willebroek, Belgium, HP Duisburg, Germany, HP Gdynia, Poland, HP Stockholm, Sweden, HP Amsterdam, Ect Delta Rotterdam, The Netherlands, HP EctEuromax Rotterdam, Moerdijk Container Terminals The Netherlands, HP Venlo, The Netherlands, HP Harwich International Essex, HP Harwich International (Cruise Terminal) Essex, HP London Thamesport Kent, HP Felixstowe Suffolk, HP TNG, Veracruz, Mexico, HP PPC, Cristobal (Cruise Terminal), HP PPC – Cristobal, Colon, Panama, HP BACTSSA, Ciudad De Buenos Aires, HP FCP, HP FHC (Cruise Terminal), and HP GBAC, Grand Bahama Island, Bahamas
	Terminal Link (TL)[101]	Marsaxlokk (Malta) (TL) Houston (TL), Florida (TL), Le Havre, Montoir, Fos, Dunkirk – France (TL) Zeebrugge Antwerp Belgium (TL) Casablanca – Morocco (TL) Abidjan – Ivory Coast (TL)
	Others	Antwerp Terminal (COSCO 20 per cent), Zeebrugge Terminal (COSCO 24 per cent) Lamu Kenya[102] (CCCC-480MN), Kribi Cameroon[103] (1bn), Cabinda Angola[104] (600mn), Walvis Bay-Namibia,[105] Sao Tome and Principe[106] (800mn), Archangelsk (Russia),[107] TIL Togo,[108] Tin-Can Island Container Terminal Ltd Nigeria (47.5 per cent stake CMPH)
Pacific Ocean	Hutchison Port (HP)[109]	HP Jakarta International Container Terminal, Tanjung Priok, HP Koja Terminal, Jakarta Utara, Indonesia, HP Busan, HP Gwangyang Korea, HP – HLT, Chonburi, HP – TLT, Chonburi, Thailand, HP SITV, Ho Chi Minh City, Vietnam, HP Brisbane Queensland, Australia, HP Sydney New South Wales, Australia, HP ECV, HP EIT, Baja

	California, Mexico HP ICAVE, HP LCT, HP TILH, HP TIMSA, Veracruz, Mexico HP PPC – Balboa, Ancon, Panama
Terminal Link[110]	Busan (TL)
Others	Kuantan (Malaysia),[111,112] Busan[113] COSCO KBCT (19.99 per cent), Seattle[114] (COSCO-13.33 per cent), Singapore (COSCO)[115]

Source: COSCO, Terminal Link, Hutchison Ports Websites.

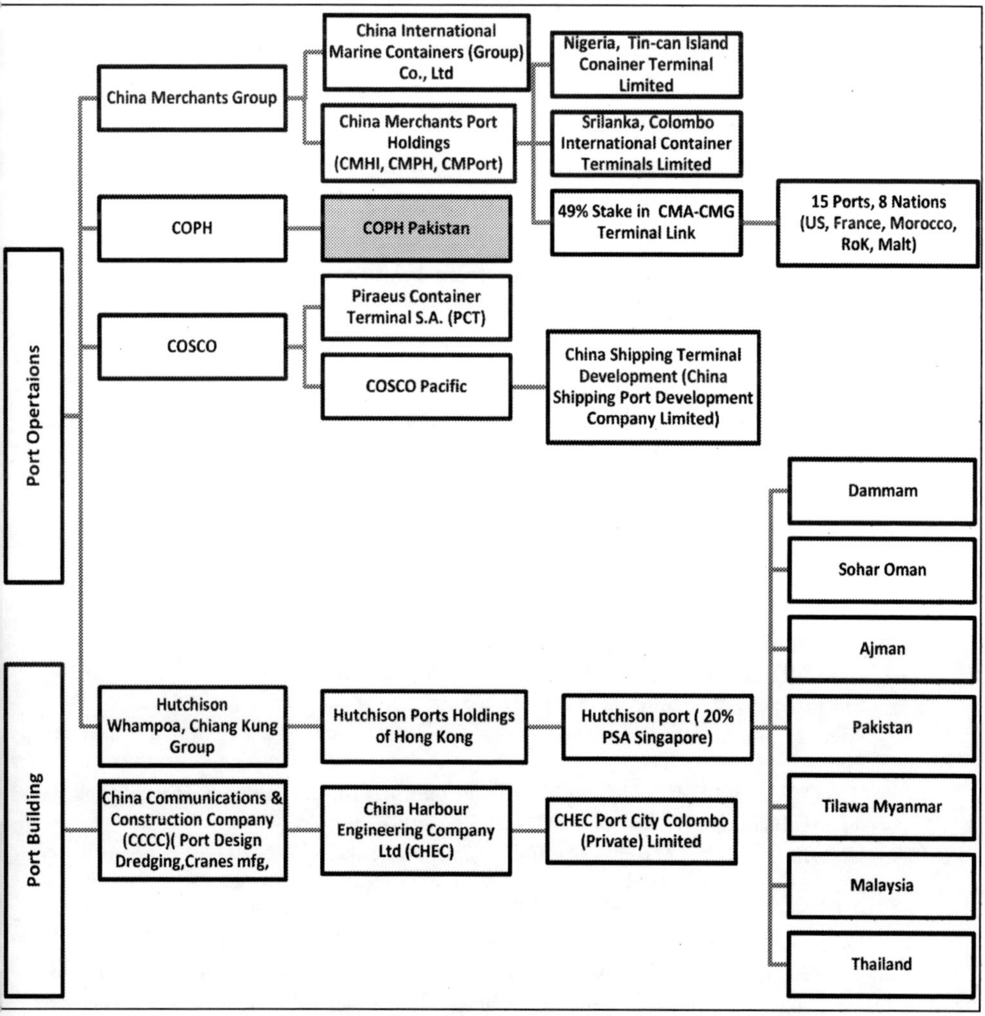

Figure 7.10. China's Port Operations and Industry Overview
(Select Companies, select ports)

Conclusion

This chapter dealt with maritime footholds being created in the three specific nations in the Indian Ocean Region as well as the commercial network being created by China across the spectrum of the maritime industry. The China factor in these three nations has a regional impact in this part of the Indian Ocean. Shipping by nature is a global industry transnational in character; even by those standards, the Chinese maritime industry has spread its network far and wide. Its indigenous shipbuilding has maintained top position. China has also been in the forefront of building as well as operations of ports across the globe, from Panama, Miami, Piraeus to Tilawa and Colombo in the Indian neighbourhood. The quest for access has also made the Chinese plan investment in Archangelsk in Russia, which is crucial for the Arctic routes; at the other end, it has invested in the Namibian Walvis Bay from where China ships uranium from the local mines. In some of the ports, China only has a minority stake, but most have been built by Chinese companies using Chinese loans. As time progresses, many of these loans will get defaulted, yielding higher stakes or concessions like in Sri Lanka or Malaysia where the submarines had come visiting. That has the potential to alter the politics of the region. The data on global ports with Chinese connection indicates that it is a well-established network which probably preceded the MSR itself through various corporate mergers and acquisitions. The MSR will give it a new direction with newer, non-corporate, strategic investments as an overlay to the existing network.

NOTES

1. Anushka Wijesinha Diplomat The, "Can Sri Lanka Leverage Its Location as Indian Ocean Hub?," *The Diplomat*, accessed March 10, 2017, http://thediplomat.com/2016/06/can-sri-lanka-leverage-its-location-as-indian-ocean-hub/.
2. Ibid.
3. Ibid.
4. "UNCTADstat," accessed March 26, 2017, http://unctadstat.unctad.org/wds/ReportFolders/reportFolders.aspx?IF_ActivePath=P,11&sCS_ChosenLang=en.
5. UNCTAD, "UNCTADstat - Maritime Profile: Sri Lanka," *UNCTADstat*, accessed March 26, 2017, http://unctadstat.unctad.org/CountryProfile/MaritimeProfile/en-GB/144/index.html.
6. Descendants of Arab Traders
7. They are Tamils who were brought by the British for employment in the tea gardens.
8. "Sri Lanka Snubs India, Opens Port to Chinese Submarine Again," *Times of India*, *The Times of India*, accessed February 25, 2017, http://timesofindia.indiatimes.com/india/Sri-Lanka-snubs-India-opens-port-to-Chinese-submarine-again/articleshow/45008757.cms.
9. "Chinese Submarine, 'Fighting Pirates' in Indian Ocean, Shows Up in Malaysia," *NDTV.com*,

accessed February 25, 2017, http://www.ndtv.com/world-news/chinese-submarine-fighting-pirates-in-indian-ocean-shows-up-in-malaysia-1646247.

10. "India Navy Keeping Its Powder Dry, Confident of Prevailing over China - Times of India," *The Times of India*, accessed February 25, 2017, http://timesofindia.indiatimes.com/india/Indian-Navy-keeping-a-close-eye-on-Chinese-ships-in-Indian-Ocean-region-says-Navy-chief-Sunil-Lanba/articleshow/55753696.cms.
11. Wade Shepard, "China Requests 15,000 Acres of Land in Sri Lanka to Create a Million Jobs," *Forbes*, accessed February 25, 2017, http://www.forbes.com/sites/wadeshepard/2016/07/27/china-just-asked-for-15000-acres-of-land-in-sri-lanka-for-a-million-worker-sez/.
12. "Sri Lanka Protest over Chinese Investment Turns Ugly," *BBC News*, January 7, 2017, sec. Asia, http://www.bbc.com/news/world-asia-38541673.
13. "The World Factbook — Central Intelligence Agency," accessed August 23, 2017, https://www.cia.gov/library/publications/the-world-factbook/docs/history.html.
14. *Reuters*, "Sri Lanka PM Blames Hidden Debt for Financial Crisis," *The Wire*, August 11, 2016, https://thewire.in/58160/sri-lankan-pm-wickremesinghe-blames-hidden-debt-for-financial-crisis/.
15. "IMF Survey/ : Sri Lanka to Reboot Economic Policies," accessed February 26, 2017, http://www.imf.org/external/pubs/ft/survey/so/2016/car061416a.htm.
16. Saman Kelegama, "China–Sri Lanka Economic Relations: An Overview," *China Report* 50, no. 2 (May 1, 2014): 131–49, doi:10.1177/0009445514523646.
17. Ibid.
18. Ibid.
19. "Chinese Investments in Sri Lanka," *Gateway House*, December 1, 2016, http://www.gatewayhouse.in/chinese-investments-sri-lanka/.
20. http://www.erd.gov.lk/files/Parliament%20Question%20-%20Export%20Credit%2022.052014.pdf
21. "Colombo's Seafront Makes Way for China-Backed Financial City - The Hindu," accessed April 13, 2017, http://www.thehindu.com/news/international/colombos-seafront-makes-way-for-china-backed-financial-city/article17957779.ece.
22. "Exclusive: Sri Lankan Government Selling the Country, Says Ex-President Mahinda Rajapaksa," *WION*, April 17, 2017, /south-asia/exclusive-sri-lankan-government-selling-the-country-says-ex-president-mahinda-rajapaksa-14601.
23. "Norochchole Coal Power Project (3X300MW)," *Ministry of Power and Energy*, accessed February 25, 2017, http://powermin.gov.lk/english/?page_id=1517.
24. Ibid.
25. "My Dissent with MR Began with Moragahakanda Project," accessed June 25, 2017, http://www.dailymirror.lk/article/My-dissent-with-MR-began-with-Moragahakanda-project-113032.html?fbrefresh=refresh.
26. https://www.adb.org/sites/default/files/linked-documents/42254-014-sri-dc.pdf
27. "AVIC to Invest in Housing, Leisure Projects," *Daily News*, accessed April 15, 2017, http://dailynews.lk/2015/12/17/business/avic-invest-housing-leisure-projects.
28. http://www.mnpea.gov.lk/web/index.php?option=com_content&view=article&id=150&catid=9&Itemid=112&lang=en
29. "SIPRI Arms Transfers Database — Www.sipri.org," Page, accessed November 13, 2015, http://www.sipri.org/databases/armstransfers.
30. SIPRI database
31. Jeff M. Smith, "China and Sri Lanka: Between a Dream and a Nightmare," *The Diplomat*, accessed February 25, 2017, http://thediplomat.com/2016/11/china-and-sri-lanka-between-

a-dream-and-a-nightmare/.

32. "Pakistan-Sri Lanka Relations," *The Lakshman Kadirgamar Institute*, accessed April 16, 2017, http://www.lki.lk/publication/speech-prime-minister-nawaz-sharif/.
33. "Pakistans Help to Sri Lanka for Nuclear Plant Alarms India," accessed April 16, 2017, http://indiatoday.intoday.in/story/pak-help-to-lanka-for-n—plant-alarms-india/1/209895.html.
34. For a detailed account read "Multi-Party Democracy in the Maldives and the Emerging Security Environment in the Indian Ocean Region," Institute for Defence Studies and Analyses, accessed March 31, 2017, http://www.idsa.in/book/multi-party-democracy-in-the-maldives-and-the-emerging-security-environment.
35. Agence France-Presse, "Maldives Airport to Be Expanded with Controversial $800m China Contract," *The Guardian*, April 8, 2016, sec. World news, https://www.theguardian.com/world/2016/apr/08/maldives-airport-expanded-800m-china-contract.
36. "Sibling Rivalry," *The Economist*, accessed March 31, 2017, http://www.economist.com/news/asia/21709335-president-falls-out-his-brother-sibling-rivalry.
37. "Islamic State: The Maldives - a Recruiting Paradise for Jihadists," *The Independent*, accessed September 1, 2017, http://www.independent.co.uk/news/world/asia/islamic-state-the-maldives-a-recruiting-paradise-for-jihadists-9731574.html.
38. "Maldives Ex-VP Sentenced to 15 Years over Pres Boat Blast – Mihaaru," accessed March 31, 2017, http://en.mihaaru.com/maldives-ex-vp-sentenced-to-15-years-over-pres-boat-blast/
39. "Maldives Revokes Former President Nasheed and Former VP Jameel Ahmed's Passports," *WION*, September 7, 2016, /south-asia/maldives-revokes-former-president-nasheed-and-former-vp-jameel-ahmeds-passports-6065.
40. "Maldivian Arch-Rivals Mohammad Nasheed and Maumoon Abdul Gayoom Join Forces," *The Hindu*, accessed March 31, 2017, http://www.thehindu.com/news/international/maldivian-arch-rivals-join-forces/article17665223.ece.
41. Agence France-Presse, "Maldives Airport to Be Expanded with Controversial USD800m China Contract," *The Guardian*, April 8, 2016, sec. World news, https://www.theguardian.com/world/2016/apr/08/maldives-airport-expanded-800m-china-contract.
42. South Asia Monitor, "Indian Concerns Over Maldives Island-Lease: Not About China, But About Sovereignty Talk – Analysis," *Eurasia Review*, February 4, 2017, http://www.eurasiareview.com/04022017-indian-concerns-over-maldives-island-lease-not-about-china-but-about-sovereignty-talk-analysis/.
43. "India Maldives Relations at a Glance," *The Hindu*, accessed March 31, 2017, http://www.thehindu.com/specials/india-maldives-relations-at-a-glance/article14247670.ece.
44. "Maldives Water Crisis," *The Indian Express*, accessed September 1, 2017, http://indianexpress.com/article/world/asia/china-ships-1000-tonnes-of-fresh-water-to-maldives-to-overcome-its-acute-water-crisis/.
45. Sachin Parashar, "China May Build Port in Southern Maldives," *The Economic Times*, April 11, 2016, http://economictimes.indiatimes.com/news/politics-and-nation/China-may-build-port-in-southern-Maldives/articleshow/51775294.cms.
46. "Ihavanddhippolhu Integrated Development Project (iHavan)," Invest Maldives, accessed September 1, 2017, http://investmaldives.org/investmaldives/strategic-investment-guide/strategic-investment-projects/ihavanddhippolhu-integrated-development-project-ihavan/.
47. "Feydhoo Finolhu Island Sold to China Firm for USD4 Million," Mihaaru, accessed March 31, 2017, http://en.mihaaru.com/feydhoo-finolhu-island-sold-to-china-firm-for-usd4-million/
48. "Maldives Signs up for China's Maritime Silk Road," *The Economic Times*, December 18, 2014, http://economictimes.indiatimes.com/news/international/world-news/maldives-signs-up-for-chinas-maritime-silk-road/articleshow/45564985.cms.
49. Michael Safi, "Maldives Quits Commonwealth over Alleged Rights Abuses," *The Guardian*,

October 13, 2016, sec. World news, http://www.theguardian.com/world/2016/oct/13/maldives-quits-commonwealth-over-alleged-rights-abuses.
50. Parashar, "China May Build Port in Southern Maldives."
51. Refer Table 7.2
52. "China to Sign $24 Billion in Loans to Bangladesh, Overtakes PM Modi's $2 Billion Credit Line, *The Indian Express*, accessed May 31, 2017, http://indianexpress.com/article/india/india-news-india/china-to-sign-24-billion-in-loans-to-bangladesh-overtakes-pm-modis-2-billion-credit-line-3081974/.
53. "Bangladesh-china Defence Co-operation Agreement' Strategic Implications: An Analysis," accessed May 21, 2017, /paper582.
54. Details of Arms transfer from SIPRI database.
55. "BD, China to Build 1,320MW Coal Power Plant at $ 2b," accessed September 1, 2017, http://www.thefinancialexpress-bd.com/2017/07/01/75574/BD,-China-to-build-1,320MW-coal-power-plant-at-$-2b.
56. "Beximco, Meghna Tie up with Chinese Investors for Power," *The Daily Star*, October 18, 2016, http://www.thedailystar.net/business/beximco-meghna-tie-chinese-investors-power-1300171.
57. "Bangladesh Asks Chinese Bank to Fund $1bn-Worth of Development Projects," *Dhaka Tribune*, August 3, 2017, http://www.dhakatribune.com/bangladesh/development/2017/08/03/aiib-development-projects-bangladesh/.
58. Ibid.
59. "$2.76b Chinese Fund: Quick Move to Execute 3 Projects," *The Daily Star*, October 20, 2016, http://www.thedailystar.net/frontpage/quick-move-execute-3-projects-1301407.
60. Ibid., 76.
61. "AidData," accessed April 16, 2017, http://china.aiddata.org/projects/33184.
62. "Foundation Stone for Padma Rail Bridge in April, Says Railways Minister," *bdnews24.com*, accessed September 1, 2017, http://bdnews24.com/economy/2017/02/20/foundation-stone-for-padma-rail-bridge-in-april-says-railways-minister.
63. "Govt Signs Deal with Chinese Firm to Upgrade Dhaka-Sylhet Highway to Four Lanes," *bdnews24.com*, accessed September 1, 2017, http://bdnews24.com/economy/2016/10/09/govt-signs-deal-with-chinese-firm-to-upgrade-dhaka-sylhet-highway-to-four-lanes.
64. "China Firm to Construct Dhaka-Ashulia Elevated Expressway," *The Bangladesh Post*, accessed September 1, 2017, http://www.thebangladeshpost.com./supplement/3480.
65. "Karnaphuli Tunnel Deal with China Tuesday - National," *News Bangladesh*, accessed September 1, 2017, http://www.newsbangladesh.com/english/details/4407.
66. "Sitakunda-Cox's Bazar Marine Drive to Be Linked with Asian Highway," *Dhaka Tribune*, September 22, 2016, http://www.dhakatribune.com/business/2016/09/22/sitakunda-coxs-bazar-marine-drive-linked-asian-highway/.
67. "China to Fund Mongla Port Modernisation," *Hellenic Shipping News Worldwide*, accessed September 1, 2017, http://www.hellenicshippingnews.com/china-to-fund-mongla-port-modernisation/.
68. "Shipping Ministry Signs MoU with China," *Shipping Ministry Signs MoU with China, Theindependentbd.com*, accessed September 1, 2017, http://www.theindependentbd.com/arcprint/details/80862/2017-02-15.
69. "AidData."
70. "Joint Statement of the People's Republic of China and the People's Republic of Bangladesh on Establishing Strategic Partnership of Cooperation 14 October 2016," Dhaka, Welcome to MOFA Website, accessed September 1, 2017, http://www.mofa.gov.bd/media/joint-

statement-people%E2%80%99s-republic-china-and-people%E2%80%99s-republic-bangladesh-establishing.
71. Ibid.
72. "Bangladesh Signs US$13.6bn Investment Package with China," 6, accessed June 26, 2017, http://country.eiu.com/article.aspx?articleid=1544727338&Country= Bangladesh&topic=Economy.
73. "Bangladesh Signs USD13.6bn Investment Package with China," accessed June 26, 2017, http://country.eiu.com/article.aspx?articleid=1544727338&Country=Bangladesh&topic=Economy.
74. Dipanjan Roy Chaudhury, "Chinese Loans May Put Bangladesh in Debt Trap," *The Economic Times*, June 17, 2017, http://economictimes.indiatimes.com/news/politics-and-nation/chinese-loans-may-put-bangladesh-in-debt-trap/articleshow/59185012.cms.
75. "China-Owned Ships: Fleet Expansion Accelerates," Hellenic Shipping News Worldwide, accessed June 26, 2017, http://www.hellenicshippingnews.com/china-owned-ships-fleet-expansion-accelerates/.
76. Ibid.
77. "China's Merchant Marine" A paper for the China as "Maritime Power" Conference July 28-29, 2015
78. CNA Conference Facility Arlington, Virginia by Dennis J. Blasko.
79. Refer Chapter 6 on CPEC with a section on Gwadar
80. China's Shipbuilding, Michael McDevitt, Chapter Six, Becoming a Great "Maritime Power": A Chinese Dream Rear Admiral Michael McDevitt, USN (retired)
81. "China Prepares Its 172,000 Civilian Ships for War," *The Diplomat*, accessed July 3, 2015, http://thediplomat.com/2015/06/china-prepares-its-172000-civilian-ships-for-war/.
82. "How China Rules the Waves," accessed April 24, 2017, https://ig.ft.com/sites/china-ports.
83. Ibid.
84. Ibid.
85. Ibid.
86. "Hutchison Ports," accessed June 27, 2017, /en/.
87. State political reporter Liz Foschia, "World's Biggest Coal Port Sold by NSW Government for USD1.75 Billion," *ABC News*, (April 30, 2014), http://www.abc.net.au/news/2014-04-30/nsw-government-sells-port-of-newcastle-for-1.75-billion/5421800.
88. "Australian Port Sold for USD7.3 Billion to Consortium; China Fund among Backers," *Reuters*, accessed June 27, 2017, http://www.reuters.com/article/us-australia-privatisation-ports-idUSKCN11P04O.
89. "As Part of Asia Pivot, Netanyahu Pushes Israeli Hi-Tech in China," *Reuters*, March 20, 2017, http://www.reuters.com/article/us-israel-china-business-idUSKBN16R1AV.
90. "How China Rules the Waves."
91. Others include China Merchants, COSCO, China Overseas Port Holding (Pakistan), CCCC etc.
92. Mercy A. Kuo, "The Power of Ports: China's Maritime March," *The Diplomat*, accessed May 26, 2017, http://thediplomat.com/2017/03/the-power-of-ports-chinas-maritime-march/.
93. "Why China Wants Malaysia on the Major-Port Radar," *South China Morning Post*, accessed May 26, 2017, http://www.scmp.com/week-asia/politics/article/2087402/can-china-really-deliver-malaysias-singapore-slayer.
94. Ibid.
95. "How China Rules the Waves."

96. "Terminals, CMA CGM Group Activities," accessed June 27, 2017, https://www.cma-cgm.com/the-group/activities/shipping/terminals.
97. "COSCO SHIPPING Ports Limited," accessed June 27, 2017, http://www.coscopac.com.hk/en/about_us.php?class_id=5.
98. "How China Rules the Waves."
99. *Diplomat,* "The Power of Ports."
100. "Hutchison Ports."
101. "Terminals, CMA CGM Group Activities."
102. "Kenya's China-Built Seaport to Open for Business by 2020," IHS Fairplay, accessed June 27, 2017, http://fairplay.ihs.com/ports/article/4278646/kenya%E2%80%99s-china-built-seaport-to-open-for-business-by-2020.
103. "Cameroon: China's Eximbank to Fund Second Phase of Kribi Port," Apanews.net, accessed June 27, 2017, http://apanews.net/en/news/cameroon-chinas-eximbank-to-fund-second-phase-of-kribi-port.
104. "Angolan Fund Says China Exim Will Lend USD600 Million for New Port - Bloomberg," accessed June 27, 2017, https://www.bloomberg.com/news/articles/2017-01-24/angola-s-sovereign-wealth-fund-plans-to-finance-deep-sea-port.
105. Brook Larmer, "Is China the World's New Colonial Power?," *The New York Times,* May 2, 2017, sec. Magazine, https://www.nytimes.com/2017/05/02/magazine/is-china-the-worlds-new-colonial-power.html.
106. "Sao Tome Signs Memorandum with China on Deep-Sea Port," *Reuters,* accessed June 27, 2017, http://uk.reuters.com/article/uk-saotome-port-china-idUKKCN0S607920151012.
107. "New Mega-Port in Arkhangelsk with Chinese Investments," *The Independent Barents Observer,* accessed June 27, 2017, https://thebarentsobserver.com/en/industry-and-energy/2016/10/new-mega-port-arkhangelsk-chinese-investments.
108. "Tiny Togo Thinks Big in Pursuit of Pan-African Dream," *Reuters,* June 11, 2015, http://www.reuters.com/article/us-africa-economy-togo-insight-idUSKBN0OR0HY20150611.
109. "Hutchison Ports."
110. "Terminals, CMA CGM Group Activities."
111. admin, "Malaysia to Build S$64 Billion Port with Support from China," *States Times Review,* January 11, 2017, http://statestimesreview.com/2017/01/11/malaysia-to-build-s64-billion-port-with-support-from-china/.
112. "Chinese Investors Launch Oman Industrial Project," *Channel NewsAsia,* accessed June 27, 2017, http://www.channelnewsasia.com/news/business/chinese-investors-launch-oman-industrial-project-8754576.
113. COSCO Shipping Ports Limited," accessed June 27, 2017, http://www.coscopac.com.hk/en/about_us.php?class_id=5.
114. Ibid.
115. Ibid.

CHAPTER 8

MYANMAR, THAILAND, MALAYSIA AND INDONESIA: THE STRATEGY OF ACCESS

An ocean is of little use, if one cannot access it easily. The geography of the Chinese mainland provides it a convex coastline in the Western Pacific. The island chains relatively restrict its open access, and have, therefore, been a cardinal factor in China's maritime consciousness. This maritime consciousness finds articulation in its time-based control plans of the first and second island chains discussed in Chapter 3. As the Indian Ocean to its west has emerged critical to China's economy, access to the Indian Ocean becomes an important factor.

This chapter deals with the options that China has to access the Indian Ocean. The option with respect to Pakistan has already been covered in Chapter 6 and issues related to the South China Sea, which are vital to that access, have been discussed in Chapter 4. The nations that can assist China's access to the Indian Ocean are Myanmar and Thailand, the former offering access from Yunnan to the Indian Ocean, and Thailand possessing the potential to provide an alternative to the Straits of Malacca through the proposed Kra Canal or through land bridge options across the isthmus. The three nations that can influence the choke point at the Malacca Straits are Malaysia, Singapore and Indonesia. This chapter discusses China's strategy of access which involves these five nations.

Part 1: Myanmar

Geography. The geographic location of Myanmar adjacent to India and China —as a link from the Yunnan province in China to the Indian Ocean—makes it unique in strategic value to China. In addition to China, Myanmar has land borders with India, Bangladesh, Laos and Thailand. The rivers of Myanmar with untapped potential for hydropower are an important factor along with natural resources, ethnicity and democracy in its relation with China.

Most of the rivers in Myanmar flow from the north to the south and into the Indian Ocean, except for the Mekong, which flows along the border with Laos and drains into the Pacific. The three major rivers from a hydropower perspective are the Irrawaddy or Ayeyarwady, which is the longest river with several tributaries on which hydro projects have been planned, the Chindwin, which eventually joins the Ayeyarwady and the Thanlwin (also called Salween)—a river that originates in Tibet and flows south-east along the Thai border. There are also shorter rivers such as the Paunglaung, Tarpein, Dapein, Shweli and Myitnge on which hydro projects are planned.

Geographically, Myanmar can be divided into deltaic plains in the centre and a mountainous terrain around it, with distinct ethnic and political features. The Ayeyarwady delta and the Bay of Bengal littoral form a prosperous, fertile zone. The mountainous Arakan regions in the west, the Shan and Tenasserim Hills in the east and the Hengduan mountains in the north sandwich the central deltaic plain. The high mountains in the east offer passes through which historical routes such as the Stilwell Road passed and which are still being used by the latest gas and oil pipelines that run into China. Myanmar has a 2,000 km long coastline with ports such as Yangon, Tilawa, Kyuakphyu, Sittwe, Dawei and Moulmein.

Broad Introduction to Myanmar's Ethnic Mosaic

The population of Myanmar has several ethnic divisions. The majority are Bamars who inhabit the central plains and are Buddhists. Other ethnic minorities surround the central plain, in the hilly as well as coastal terrains. Some sections of these ethnic minorities follow Christianity whereas the Rohingyas from the Rakhine[1] state follow Islam. The ethnic distribution of population is 68 per cent Bamar or Burmese, 9 per cent Shan, 7 per cent Karen, 4 per cent Rakhine, 3 per cent Chinese, 2 per cent Indian, 2 per cent Mon and 5 per cent other ethnicities.[2]

One of the ways to understand the ethnic complexities of Myanmar is to look at the manner in which the administrative units of Myanmar are organised. The country is divided into a union territory, seven regions and seven states (Refer Figures 8.1 for Map and 8.2 for an organogram). In the

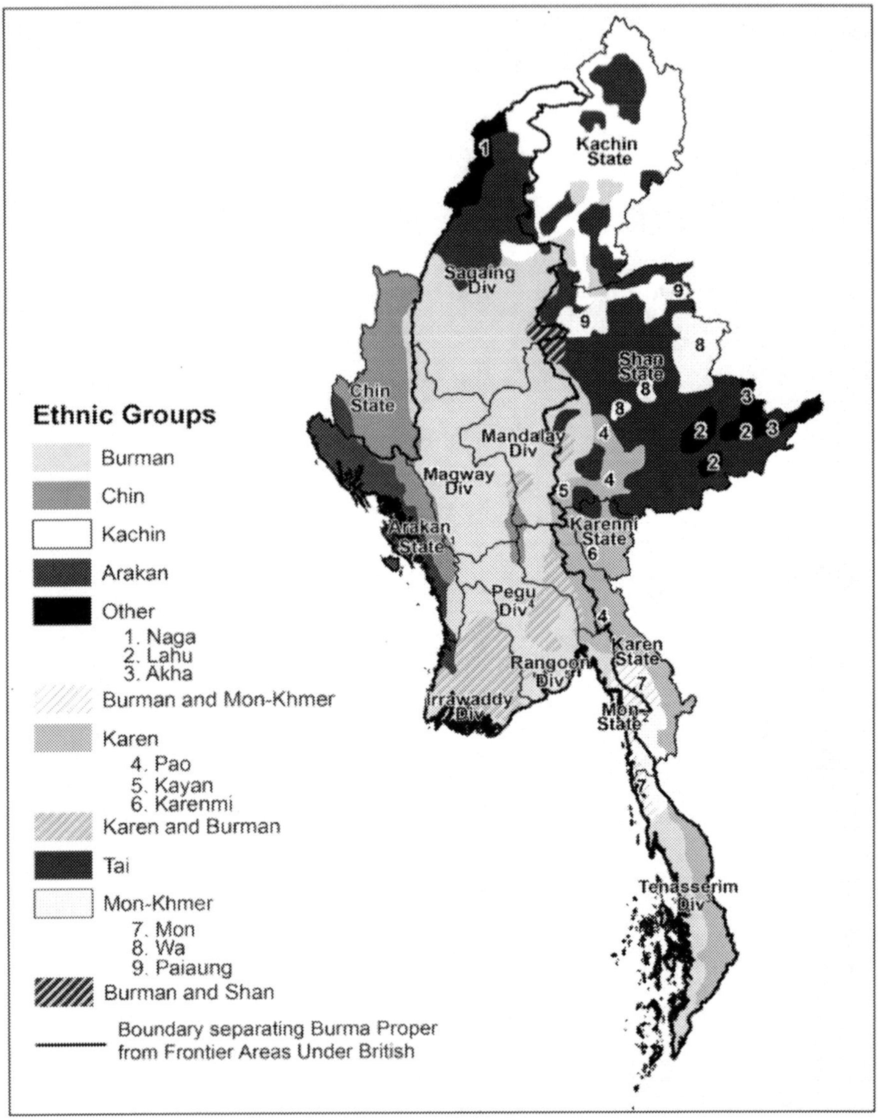

Figure 8.1. Ethnic Groups of Myanmar[4]

Shan State and Saigang region there are self-administered zones and divisions where the ethnic divisions are further complex. The Burman (Bamar) majority central plain is divided into regions[3], while the states, the zones and the single division of Wa are to cater to ethnic complexities. The western states of Chin and Rakhine (Arakan) are towards India and Bangladesh, where the Nagas and Chins extend across into India and the ethnic Muslim minority, the Rohingyas, shares linkages with Bangladesh. The Kayah, Kayin and Mon States are towards the east, where ethnicities like the Karen and Karenni extend over to Laos and Thailand. The Shan and Kachin States in the north-east towards China, with ethnicities like Kokang which is closely related to the Han Chinese, spread into Yunnan. Therefore, the ethnic issues of Myanmar are often trans-border in nature involving other regional nations. The union territory of Naypyidaw is the new capital. The complex ethnic relations have also resulted in several rebel militant groups and armies known as Ethnic Armed Organisations (EAOs) which are at loggerheads with the Myanmar state. The rebel groups which operate in the states, regions, zones and divisions are placed in the organogram inFigure 8.2.

Due to the ethnic divisions, debates over a unitary or federal structure of the statehave been a core political issue since Myanmar's independence. The Citizenship Law enacted in 1982 has deepened the crisis. The law created three categories of citizenship:

- Full Citizenship
  - From indigenous race
  - Lived before 1823 or the Anglo Burmese war which triggered immigration
  - Born to citizens
- Associate Citizenship
  - Cannot prove that their ancestors settled in Myanmar before 1823
  - Acquired citizenship in 1948
- Naturalised Citizenship
  - One parent Burmese citizen by the above two laws
  - Parents settled before 1948

One fallout of this has been that the Rohingyas, from the Rakhine State are not treated as one of the ethnic groups of Myanmar, making them stateless. They are considered migrants and are a source of tension with Bangladesh. Around one lakh twenty thousand Rohingyas are currently closeted in camps with restricted movements, in a futile exercise towards establishing their citizenship. The Kofi Annan Panel is currently looking into the case of these internally displaced people. Around 15,000 of them are in India presently. The Rohingya crisis has also led to the formation of a militant group named the Arakan Rohingya Salvation Army.

On the eastern border is the militant group of the Kokangs, the Myanmar National Democratic Alliance Army (MNDAA), a breakaway faction of the

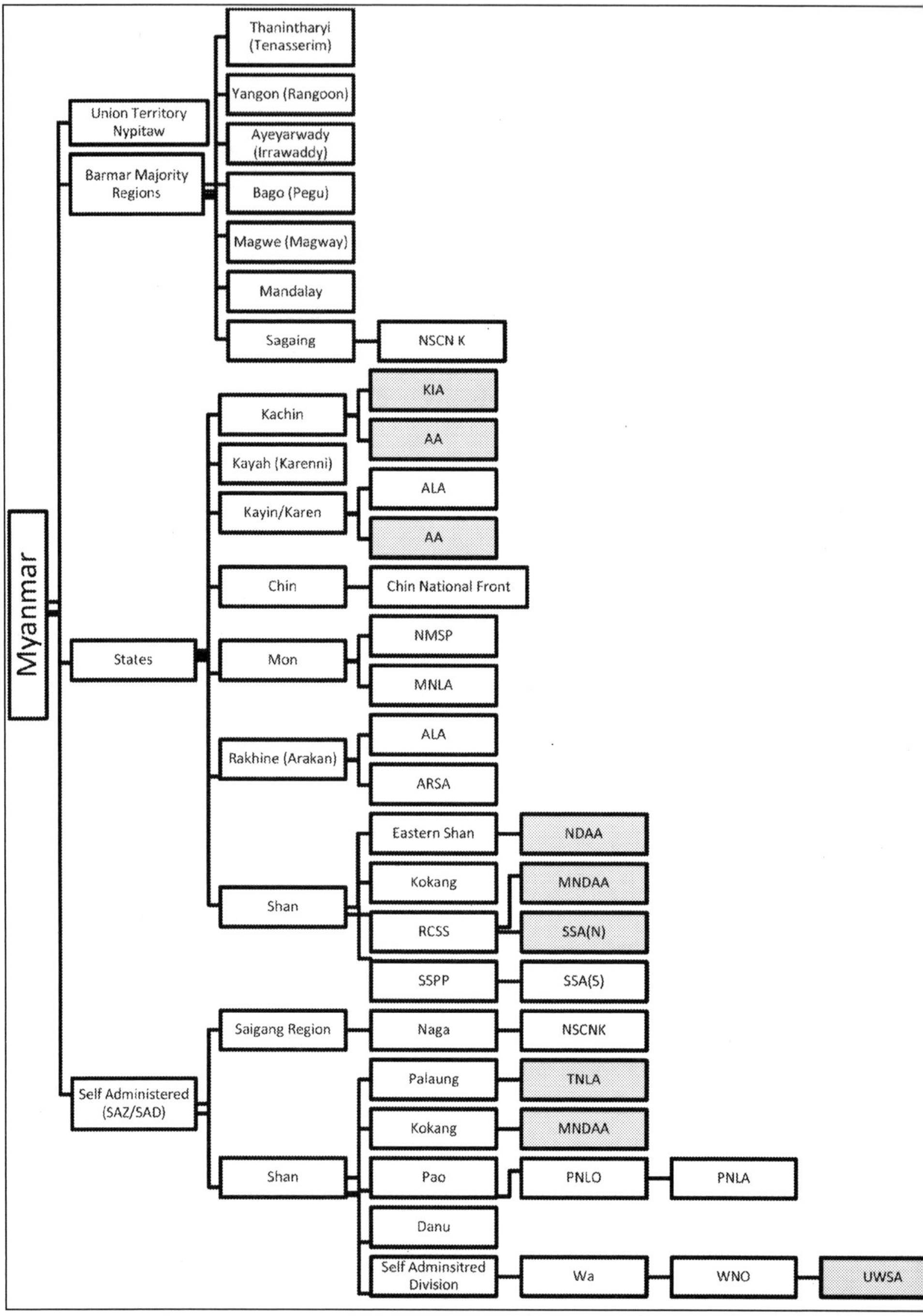

Figure 8.2. States, Regions and Divisions of the Myanmar Ethnic and Armed Organisations (Shaded areas indicate Groups influenced by China through the Wa Army which is 80 per cent of the EAOs)[5]

Communist Party of Burma as it collapsed in 1989. The Wa is the biggest of the Ethnic Armed Groups. Both have close links with China. The eastern region of Myanmar is also one of the largest drug producing regions of the world and a part of the Golden Triangle. Most militant groups use illegal opium cultivation and arms deals as their source of income and launder the money obtained from it through front organisations and businesses, including mining and infrastructure businesses. These lands are also buffer zones between the Bamar core and the Thai and Chinese core areas.

Political Evolution

Myanmar—also called Burma—was part of British India as a province till 1937. Thereafter, it was hived off as a separate British Colony. It became independent in 1948 and follows a parliamentary democracy system. The freedom struggle of Myanmar was driven by the majority race of Buddhist Bamars, whereas tribal minorities supported the British rule. As a result, the Japanese were supported by the Bamar whereas British won over the ethnic groups, during World War II. This resulted in the pre-independence Burmese army being manned by Indian or ethnic tribes and not by the majority Bamars, whereas Bamars led by Aung San, father of the present State Counsellor Aung San Su Kyi, formed the Burmese Independence Army or BIA,[6] which fought for the Japanese. The Myanmar military, known as the Tatmadaw, owes its lineage to these two armies which merged towards the end of World War II and is dominated by the Bamars.[7]

A popular leader and a Bamar, Aung San would have been the prominent leader of independent Myanmar, had he not been assassinated in 1947 at the age of 32. The honour of being the first President therefore fell on Sao ShweThaik, who was of Shan ethnicity. The first constitution was approved in 1948, the second one in 1974 and the third, which is presently in force, was adopted in 2008. Presently, Myanmar has a bicameral parliamentary system. The current constitution, the third in Myanmar, was drafted by the junta in 2008. The major political parties in Myanmar are the National League for Democracy and the Union Solidarity and Development Party.

The Tatmadaw had a role on the governance of Myanmar, with General Ne Win's prolonged rule from 1962 till 1988. General Win dissolved the parliament when ethnic struggles had weakened the government and abolished the constitution which had granted some degree of autonomy to the ethnic tribes. This gave rise to an uprising by the Kachins. Gen Win was a socialist in ideology and economically isolated Myanmar from most of the globe. The country joined the Non Aligned Movement during his period. General Win had friendly relations with China.

The China factor has remained important in Myanmar's history. China, which is geographically adjacent to Myanmar, was at war with Japan, where both the Nationalists and Communists initially fought Japan together and then engaged each other in a civil war. This civil war spilt over to the Myanmarese state of Shan, which often saw opposing groups, especially the Kuomintang, come to Myanmar. Though it was never in power, the formation and growth of the Communist Party of Burma (CPB), was an important factor since it enjoyed close relations with its Chinese counterparts. The events in China such as the Cultural Revolution and Sino-Soviet split also influenced Myanmar, as well as the CPB. There were severe anti-China riots in 1967 resulting in a withdrawal of ambassadors by both nations. BertilLintner, a noted Myanmar watcher, states that the relations picked up only in 1976 during the Khmer Rouge crisis, when Myanmar stepped in at China's behest to end Phnom Penh's diplomatic isolation.[8] Chinese leader Deng Xiaoping also visited Myanmar during this period.

When China opened up during the Deng period, it again had its ideological effects on the CPB. By 1989, the CPB collapsed after its tribal cadre split from its leadership. The Chinese had invited the CPB leadership to retire in China. This offer was refused by the CPB leadership and it reacted saying that "We have no desire to become revisionists".[9] Many of the CPB cadres joined Ethnic Armed Organisations (EAO) such as the MNDAA and the Wa army.

In 1988 there were massive protests in Myanmar, termed as the 8888 uprising. This led to some cosmetic overhaul in administration. The military rule was renamed the State Law and Order Restoration Council (SLORC) after this. This was also a period where ties with China improved. China soon witnessed the Tiananmen Square incident, and it found a partner in the internationally isolated regime in its neighbourhood.

In the post-Win period, by 1990, multiparty democracy took roots, and the election brought forth the National League for Democracy (NLD) which won 81 per cent seats in elections, led by Aung San's daughter, Aung San Su Kyi, popularly called 'Daw'.

The military junta refused to hand over power and put Daw Aung Sang under house arrest from that time for varying durations till 2010. In 1991, Daw during this phase won the Nobel Peace Prize, bringing a global focus to the Myanmar situation. This was a phase when Myanmar became a pariah to the Western world, which offered opportunity for China to gain a foothold-much like what would happen in Sri Lanka later, during the final phase of the civil war. Just as it did in Sri Lanka, arms transfers were used as the prime driver to cement that relationship during isolation.

In the early 1990s, Than Shwe was heading the SLORC, which changed its nomenclature to the State Peace and Development Council (SPDC). Myanmar joined the ASEAN in 1997. Relations with China peaked in 2003 under Prime Minister General KhinNyunt who was considered close to China. The relations started deteriorating when he was removed a year later in 2004. The seven-step road map to democracy was prepared during this phase. This period also coincided with large-scale Chinese investments in oil, gas, pipelines, mines, hydropower, etc. By 2009, relations with USA too improved. Elections were due in 2010 and the NLD did not take part then, yielding space to the Union Solidarity and Development Party which had strong support of the military. This brought Prime Minister Thein Sein to power. His government displaced the State Peace and Development Council- the Military Government. He commenced reforms which were pro-democratic and more importantly, took steps towards ***federalism***, accommodating ethnic and religious factors. He also opened up the economy, ushering in foreign investments. The relation with China was also upgraded, making it the largest trading partner and a strategic partner during this period.

Despite these, Thein Sein cancelled several projects from China during his tenure, including the high profile Myitsone Dam, Kyuakphyu–Kunming Rail and Letpadaung copper mine—all due to environmental concerns and displacement of the ethnic population. He visited China during his tenure several times, without reciprocal visits from China.

Daw Aung San, who had missed the earlier opportunity to form the government, got personally elected in a by-election in 2012 and became an MP in the Thein Sein Government. The general elections in 2015 saw the NLD win a landslide victory, with 85 per cent seats. However, due to a previous, crafty constitutional amendment, Daw Aung San could not become Prime Minister and HtinKyaw was appointed PM. Aung San remained the State Counsellor, the defacto power centre in the government.

Ceasefires and Peace Process: The Myanmar Groups and China

As Myanmar opened up, President Thein Sein also initiated a ceasefire and reconciliation process with various ethnic groups and armies. He followed it up with political dialogue towards greater federalism. The ethnic groups were represented by organisations such as the United Nationalities Federal Council (UNFC), an umbrella organisation with the support of the maximum number of ethnic groups. Out of the many EAOs, eight have signed a ceasefire with the centre, termed the National Ceasefire Agreement, while some other groups have a de facto ceasefire with the state.

The eight groups which have signed the Nationwide Ceasefire Agreement (NCA) are the Karen National Liberation Army, the Chin National Front, the Arakan Liberation Party, the Pa-Oh National Liberation Organisation, the Karen National Liberation Army-Peace Council, the Democratic Karen Benevolent Army, the All Burma Students' Democratic Front and the Restoration Council of Shan State.[10]

The groups that have not been included in the negotiations with government are: Myanmar National Democratic Alliance Army, Arakan Liberation Army and Ta'ang National Liberation Army. They are part of the seven groups operating outside the present peace process. The government's position is that they had taken to arms after the peace process started.[11]

There are four other groups who have refused to sign: the Shan State Progressive Party, New Mon State Party, Karenni National Progressive Party and the Kachin Independence Organisation. They have demanded the inclusion of the groups which are outside the peace process. The United Wa State Army (UWSA) is the largest of the groups that have not signed the NCA, but have a ceasefire arrangement with the state since 1989.

The National Socialist Council of Nagaland (NSCN-K) which is a key group in India, has a ceasefire with the Myanmarese government since 2012.

The primary opposition, therefore, now stems from the Northern Alliance, a cobbled alliance formed in 2016, with support of the largest rebel group—the United Wa State Army (UWSA)—which consists of 30,000 rebels. The USWA has a ceasefire agreement with Myanmar. Through the UWSA, China exerts control over the Northern Alliance whose members are:[12]

- Kachin Independence Army
- Arakan Army
- Myanmar National Democratic Alliance Army
- Ta'ang National Liberation Army
- National Democratic Alliance Army

This makes the NCA tenuous and makes China a significant player in Myanmar affairs, with the ability to influence 80 per cent of the rebel armies.[13] This influence helps China control the events in Myanmar, where it has high stakes in the port and pipelines projects, which is all about access to the Indian Ocean. Myanmar not only needs China to support its internal politics, but also for international support, especially in UN vetos, where its policy regarding the Rohingyas is under severe criticism.

Ceasefires and Peace Process: Linkages with Indian Groups

The ethnic linkages of Myanmar towards the west cross the border into India. The Nagas, Kukis, and Mizos—the last two being ethnically linked to the Chins of Myanmar—live in the states of Arunachal Pradesh, Nagaland, Mizoram and Manipur that share a border with Myanmar. The border between India and Myanmar has a free movement regime for 16 km on either side for the movement of tribals.

An overwhelming majority of Nagas live in the Indian states mentioned above, with only around 10 per cent of them living in Myanmar. The Nagas have several sub-tribes and so do the Chins, with subgroups like the Zomis, Mizos and Kukis. The Nagas have had a historical demand for a separate Naga State called Nagalim. A major group fighting for the liberation of Nagalim is the NSCN which was formed in 1980 by S.S. Khaplang, a Myanmarese Naga, IsakSwu and Muivah. It split into two groups in 1988, the Khaplang Group (NSCN-K) and the IsakSwu, Muivah Group (NSCN-IM). In August 1997, the IM group signed a ceasefire agreement with India. Khaplang followed with a separate ceasefire operationalised by 2001. In March 2015, the NSCN-K unilaterally withdrew from the ceasefire it had signed with the Indian government.

Myanmar had in the interim secured a ceasefire in 2012 with the NSCN-K. Khaplang also kept himself away from alliances with Myanmar's groups, though he had several economic activities in that country. He stayed in Taga, in the Saigang Region. Subsequently, Khaplang formed the United Liberation Front of West South Asia (ULFWSA) as an umbrella organisation of various groups. This unit carried out an attack on an Indian Army unit in June 2015 killing 20 soldiers. This was in retaliation to an Indian Army operation against militant strongholds in Myanmar which had preceded it.

In August 2016 the NSCN-IM signed a framework agreement with the Indian government. In a significant twist, the two prominent Naga leaders IsakSwu and the patriarch Khaplang passed away in 2016–17. The NSCN-K is now led by an Indian Naga, KhangoKonyak. The Naga movement was moving towards a solution with India when the two deaths occurred.

China has supported the Naga, Mizo and ULFA groups since 1967. Though their support has waxed and waned, it is highly possible that it can wax again considering the enormous Chinese influence and stakes in Myanmar. A new umbrella group, the United Liberation Front of Western South East Asia (UNLFW), has emerged, representing the ethnic factions on the Indian side. The UNLFW[14] constitutes the United Liberation Front of Assam (Independent), the Nationalist Socialist Council of Nagaland (Khaplang), the Kamatapur Liberation Organisation (KLO), the National Democratic Front of Bodoland (Songbijit) and Manipur's CorCom.[15] The cobbled ULFWSA group will also now seek a leader. One among the several contenders is Paresh Barua of the ULFA, from Assam, who is believed to be harboured in Ruili in the Yunnan Province.[16] The ULFA which began as a 'son of soil' issue has lost its relevance today due to its close ties to Bangladesh. The manner in which China could play a role to influence the region needs close monitoring. Equally significant is the future of the groups in Manipur under Cor Com. The non-tribal majority of Meiteis from Manipur's plains have formed several groups, as they face increasing pressure from the Naga and Chin uprisings.

Ceasefires and Peace Process: The 21st Century Panglong Conference

Coming back to the Myanmar peace process which is underway, to accommodate a larger degree of federalism, there is also a process which is presently underway called the 21st Century Panglong Conference. This is fashioned after the (first) Panglong Conference with similar aim, which got aborted after its architect General Aung San was assassinated. He had succeeded in signing an agreement with the Shan, Kachin and Chin representatives in 1947.

The Second 21st Century Panglong Union Peace Conference was held on May 24, 2017. Those who signed the 2015 NCA attended the conference. Considering the large concentration of the rebel groups on its border with Myanmar, China has invariably been a part of the process. The UWSA in fact has demanded that China must take lead in the peace process.[17] Overall, the situation provides China with leverage over the Bamars. Interestingly, during the Conference in May 2017, it was China that brought all the leaders of the seven northern groups of ethnic militants from Kunming to the conference. Bertil Lintner writes that China pressurised Myanmar to include these seven groups in the talks. He also concludes that the talks were inconclusive.[18]

What would be critical to watch is the trajectory that federalism and democracy take in Myanmar, in an age when they are taking roots in that country. Equally crucial to watch is China's role as it seeks a stake in a geographically crucial nation that guarantees it an access to the Indian Ocean Region bypassing Malacca.

China-Myanmar Relations: Economy and China's Projects

Myanmar with a GDP of USD 68.28 billion has the highest growth rate in South Asia at 8.10 per cent. It has an external debt of USD 9 billion and FOREX reserves of around USD 8.9 billion. The slew of Chinese investment comes in such a background. China is the biggest foreign investor with USD 15.42 billion in 115 projects.[19] However, it is a share that has steeply dropped toto 80 per cent from the Junta period and to 50 per cent of the FDI in 2016.[20] Its trade with China was USD10 billion in the fiscal year 2014–15.[21] Roughly 40 per cent of this trade takes place through the border post at Muse.[22]

Table 8.1. Regional Economic Indicators

	India	Bangladesh	Pakistan	Sri Lanka	Myanmar	Maldives
GDP (bn US$)	2200	226	271	82.24	68.28	5.4
Growth (%)	7.6	6.9	4.7	5	8.10	3
Public Debt (%)	52.3	25.9	58.50	77	NA	72
External Debt (bn US$)	507	37.2	64.04	47.65	9.04	0.741
Ext Debt (%)	23	16	23	58.10	13	14
Import (bn US$)	402	39	38.25	10.12	13.49	1.9
Export (bn US$)	271	33	20.96	18.64	10.49	0.3
Revenue (bn US$)	200	23	41.77	10.98	8.9	0.96
Expenses (bn US$)	283	35	54.63	15.54	10.9	1.1
Deficit (%)	-3.7	-5.1	-4.7	-5.5	-3	-6
FOREX (bn US$)	359	29.7	20.53	7.6	8.9	0.627
FDI Stock (bn US$)	351	13.24	33.82	NA	NA	NA
China Investment (bn US$)	NA	24	46	8	15	NA
Savings (%)	30	28	14.3	26	16.13	8.1
Per Capita US$	6700	3900	5100$	11200	6000	15300
Domestic Credit (bn US$)	1.5	128	142	44.73	21.22	1.5

Source: CIA World Fact Book, accessed July 2017.

There are several China-led projects in Myanmar. Predictably, a majority of them are in critical infrastructure segments like connectivity, power, mining, oil and gas.

Ports

The ports of Myanmar are Mawlamyine,[23] Kyuakphyu, Sittwe, Dawei, Tilawa and Yangon. Yangon is a riverine port and Tilawa is adjacent to Yangon. There are several ongoing port-linked connectivity and energy projects. The details of various projects in Myanmar are placed in the subsequent paragraphs:

- **Sittwe-Kaladan Project.** The port of Sittwe is being developed by India as a part of improving connectivity to its North East as the seaward node of the Kaladan Multi-modal Transit Transport Project.

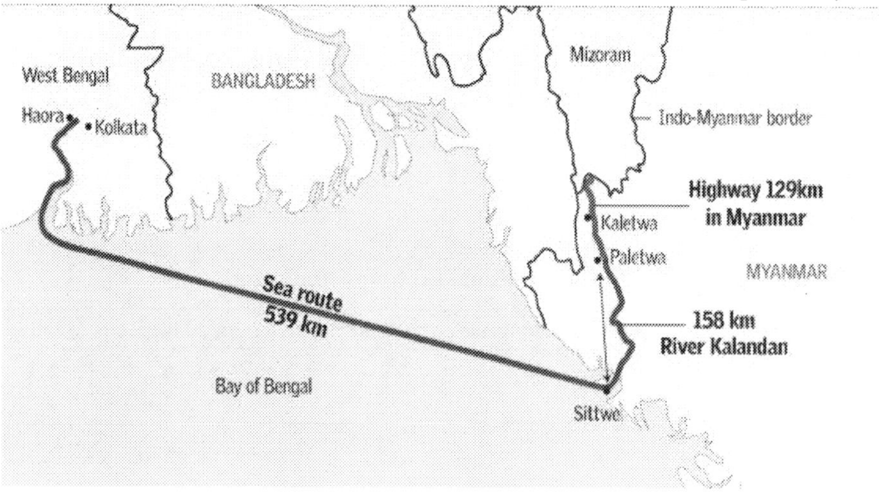

Figure 8.3. The Kaladan Project
(*Source*: *Hindu Business Line*)

- **Dawei.** Dawei port is being developed by the Thai–Italian Company, Italthai Industrial Company Limited, at a cost of around USD 8.6 billion. There are also plans for an SEZ. However the project is now looking at Japan as a partner. Though China is not involved directly in the port project, it is planning a refinery here. A USD 3 billion, 100,000 bpd refinery is being built by a Chinese firm Guangdong Zhenrong which holds 70 per cent of the stakes. The remaining 30 per cent stakes are held by three Myanmar firms—Union of Myanmar Economic Holdings Limited (with links to Tatmadaw), Myanmar Petrochemical Corporation and Yangon Engineering Group.[24]
- **Yangon.** Yangon which is a riverine port handles 90 per cent of Myanmar's cargo. There is a network of ports on the Yangon River such as:
  - Myanmar Port Authority, Yangon.

  - Asia World Port Terminal, located in the Ahlone Township of Yangon owned by a Kokang Magnate.
  - Myanmar International Terminal Thilawa (MITT), 25 km from Yangon, being developed by Hutchison Port Holdings, a Hong Kong-based company.
  - Myanmar Integrated Port Limited (MIPL), Yangon.
- **Kyaukpyu Port Project.** This port project is at Kyaukpyu in the south-western Rakhine Province of Myanmar. There is a three-pronged plan for the port. The port, SEZ and Industrial park together will cost nearly USD 10 billion. This is an important port since China's oil and gas pipelines from the coast start from the Maday Island in Kyaukpyu. The project involves the following:
  - Port project with two separate ports at USD 7.3 billion investment.
  - Maday Island port on 148 hectares.
  - Yan Byal Island[25] port on 95 hectares.
  - A USD 2.3 billion industrial park on 978-hectares.[26]
  - High-end housing project on 494 hectares.[27]
  - An SEZ on 1,735 hectares, at the cost of USD 280 million.

Initially, it was planned that there will be a 50 per cent stake for both China and Myanmar in the project. In the interim, the Myitsone Dam project went into a period of uncertainty and there was the likelihood of its cancelation with the compensation clauses kicking in. China has now demanded greater stakes in the port of up to 85 per cent for preferential access.[28] This is being planned through the China International Trust Investment Corporation (CITIC) group of China which had built these ports. Other than the CITIC, the other Chinese companies involved are the China Harbor Engineering Company Ltd., China Merchants Holdings, TEDA Investment Holding and Yunnan Construction Engineering Group. The project also includes Thailand's Charoen Pokphand Group run by ethnic Chinese, which has deep interests in China, including shareholding in the State Owned Enterprise (SOE), CITIC. It was one of the first foreign groups to operate in China when China opened up in the Deng Period. The port is predicted to add USD 10 billion to Myanmar's annual GDP by 2025.

Rail

There are several rail projects underway in Myanmar where China is involved. China gifted locomotives and coaches to Myanmar Railways in 2006. Thirty locomotive engines were again gifted by China in 2010. In 2011, the China Railway Engineering Corporation (CREC) and Ministry of Rail Transportation Myanmar signed an MoU for the Muse–Kyaukpyu rail link, to connect the Rakhine coast with Kunming in China at a cost of USD 20 billion on BOT basis with a tenure of 50 years. This rail was to originate in Ruili on the Chinese border, and pass through Muse, Lashio, Mandalay, Magwe, Minbu and Ann in Myanmar, traversing a length of 4 km in China and 808 km in Myanmar covering a total to 812 km.[29] After a survey, a feasibility Study Report was submitted in 2012. Due to rising public protests in Myanmar, the project currently stands suspended.[30] The suggestion of a Kunming–Yangon railway line by Xinhua has also been denied by Myanmar.[31] At the moment, the Yangon port remains connected to Mytikina in the north from where road connectivity exists to China. Further, the Kunming–Singapore leg of the pan-Asian Rail network has no branch through Myanmar. From the Chinese side the rail line from Kunming exists till Xiaguan also known as Dali. A rail line is being planned from Dali to Ruili a distance of approximately 400km.

Road Projects

Bridges. An early instance of Sino-Myanmar cooperation in road infrastructure sector was the construction of the Rangoon–Syriam Bridge in 1979. A project under consideration is the Kunlong Bridge[32] project over the Salween river with Chinese assistance. This bridge is a strategic project connecting the Wa region. Being a riverine nation, there are several bridge projects being built by China such as the Ayeyarwady bridge (Yadanabon), the Myitkyina bridge, the Pakokku Ayeyarwady bridge, the Magwe–Minbu bridge, the Dedaya bridge, the Nyaungdon (Bo MyatTun) bridge, etc.

Myitkyina-Tanai-PangsauPass Road. This is a strategically important road that connects the Pangsaupass on the Indian border at Arunachal Pradesh with Myitkyina. This project is being carried out by Yunnan Construction and Engineering Group (YCEG), Yunnan Construction Corporation and Myanmar's Yuzana Group Company with assistance from the Asian Development Bank. This is a potentially important road that is a part of the old Stillwell road or the Ledo Road that connected British India to China during World War II. The contemporary connectivity initiative of the Bangladesh-China-India-Myanmar corridor follows a different alignment from the Myitkyina-Tanai-Pangsau road, entering India from Manipur.

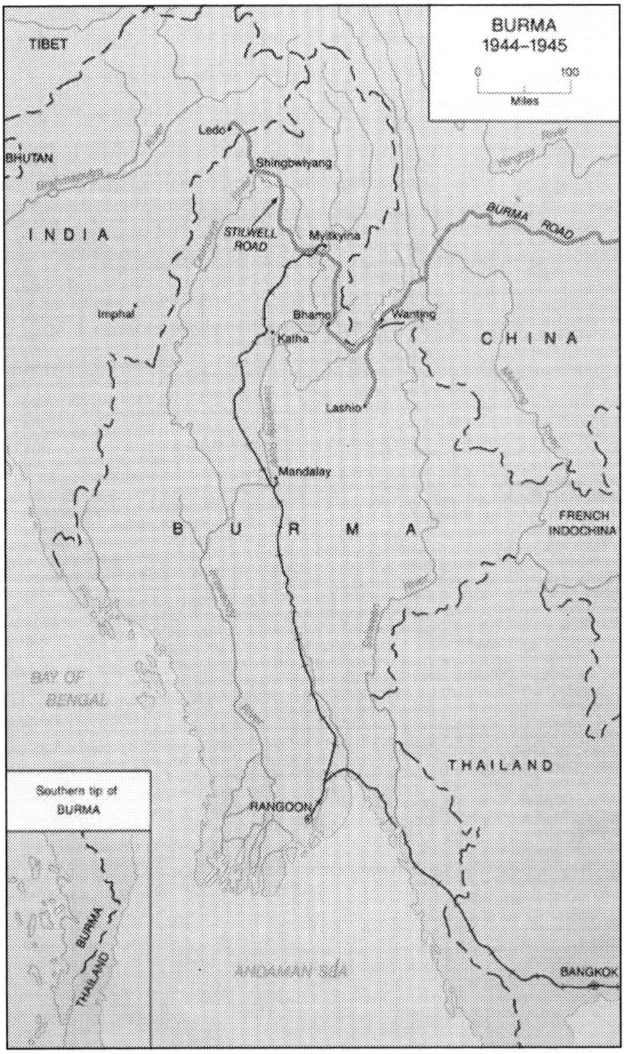

Figure 8.4. The Ledo or the Stillwell Road and Burma Road[33]

(*Source*: By the U.S. Army Center of Military History—India-Burma 2 April 1942-28 January 1945, U.S. Army Center of Military History, Public Domain, https://commons.wikimedia.org/w/index.php?curid=1836415)

BCIM Corridor. It is appropriate to discuss the corridor project involving Bangladesh, China, India, Myanmar, or the BCIM here in this chapter about access as it is a project involving India and China's access to the Indian Ocean bypassing Malacca. This is a project proposed to connect Kunming in the Yunnan province of China to the Indian port of Kolkata, through Myanmar and Bangladesh. This proposal was termed as the 'Kunming Initiative' in the

1990s and subsequently came to be known as the BCIM Forum for Regional Cooperation. It was planned to be a multimodal economic corridor aimed at improving connectivity. However, this remained a Track II initiative. This idea gained traction during the meeting between Premiers Li Keqiang and Manmohan Singh in 2013 and was included in their joint statement. The second and third meetings were held in Bangladesh and Kolkata in 2014 and April 2017, respectively. The route has been broadly defined as touching Kolkata, Silchar, Imphal in India, Dhaka Jessore and Sylhet in Bangladesh, Mandalay in Myanmar crossing over to China at Muse and Ruili and terminating at Kunming in China. Unlike the Stillwell Road, the BCIM corridor takes a southern route and passes via Manipur to Bangladesh to reach Kolkata. The Indian concerns over the Belt and Road Initiative, especially its CPEC branch, have cast a shadow over the future of the BCIM.

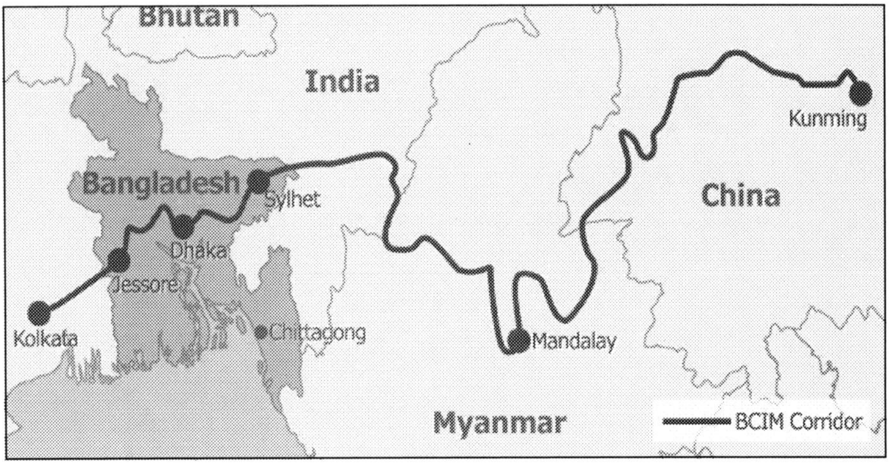

Figure 8.5. BCIM Corridor
(*Source:* HKTDC)

Power Projects

A vast majority of China-sponsored projects are hydropower projects. They can be linked to China's West-East Electricity Transfer Project which is a part of the PRC's 10th Five Year Plan. The logic of that project is to utilise the potential of power projects in the west of China with that of need for power in the East and to create a grid that assists both these regions. It has three corridors planned, which are the Northern, Central and Southern Corridors. The southern and central corridors affect Yunnan, and Myanmar is crucial to this project being adjacent to Yunnan.[34] Equally important to consider alongside this is the South to North Water Transfer Project of China which transfers water from rich southern regions to northern regions, which requires a serious study by the lower riparian states. The recent Indus cascade project in Pakistan at USD 50 billion needs to be seen in this light, which is a mammoth 40,000MW project, including the USD 15 billion Daimar Basha Dam[35] project.

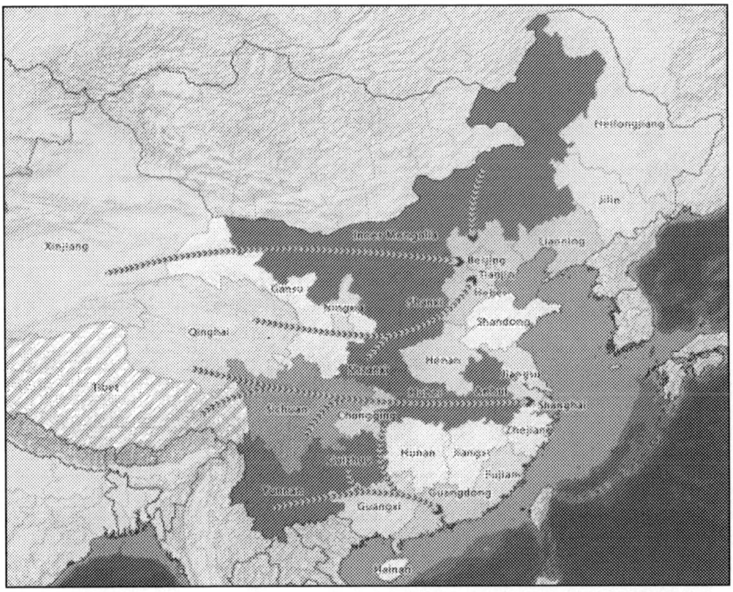

Figure 8.6. West to East Transfer Plan of Electricity in China
(*Source*: Wilson Centre)

- **Myanmar's Power Situation.** It has an underdeveloped hydropower and hydrocarbon sector. Due to international sanctions and the domestic political situation, investments were seldom made in the power sector. Most of the potential is therefore untapped.
- **Details of Select Power Projects.** The details of the power projects are enumerated below:
- **Gas Projects.** Myanmar's U Energy Thaketa Power Co. Ltd. and China's Union Resources and Engineering Company are developing a gas-fired plant, of 106 MW capacity.[36] This is scheduled for completion in early 2018 and is the first phase of a 500-MW capacity project. The project will supply power to Yangon.
- **Coal Projects.** Coal projects by China, unlike in Pakistan, are fewer in number. The Tigyit coal-fired power station was built by the China National Heavy Machinery Corporation (CHMC). This is the first coal-fired power station in Myanmar and was completed in 2001. It is a small power plant with a capacity of 2 × 60MW.

Hydro Projects in Myanmar[37,38,39]

According to the International Hydropower Association, Myanmar, particularly the states of Kayin, Shan and Kayah, with the Salween river running through them, has a potential of over 100 GW of hydropower, of which only 3 GW has been developed so far.[40] This power is produced by 25 operational projects and represents 62 per cent of Myanmar's energy mix. The national electrification plan reflects this reality, planning more hydropower projects. Plans for hydropower projects dominate the power sector as far as the Chinese projects in Myanmar are concerned. The pattern reflects the increase in hydropower consumption in China as indicated in the graph in the figure. China has a whopping 319 GW of installed hydropower capacity, which is seven times the capacity of the second-ranked nation in hydropower—Japan. Myanmar presently ranks 14th in hydropower globally. It aims to make electricity available for 100 per cent of its population by 2030. This demands tripling of its hydropower installed capacity to 9 GW by 2030. Projects worth 46 GW have been identified so far.

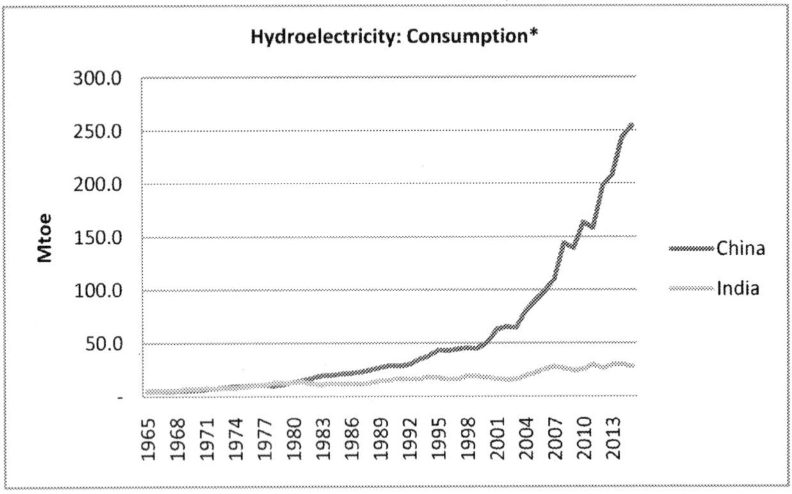

Figure 8.7. China's Consumption of Hydropower: Trends[41]
(*Source*: BP Statistical Review of World Energy 2016)

Major Chinese Projects: Completed

One of the early projects by China in Myanmar is the Pyinmana Hydro Project. In 1998, Myanmar and China agreed to construct a 280 MW hydroelectric power plant near Pyinmana. This was a USD 250 million deal under which Beijing provided the funds.[42] The Yeywa Dam on the Myitngeriver is a USD

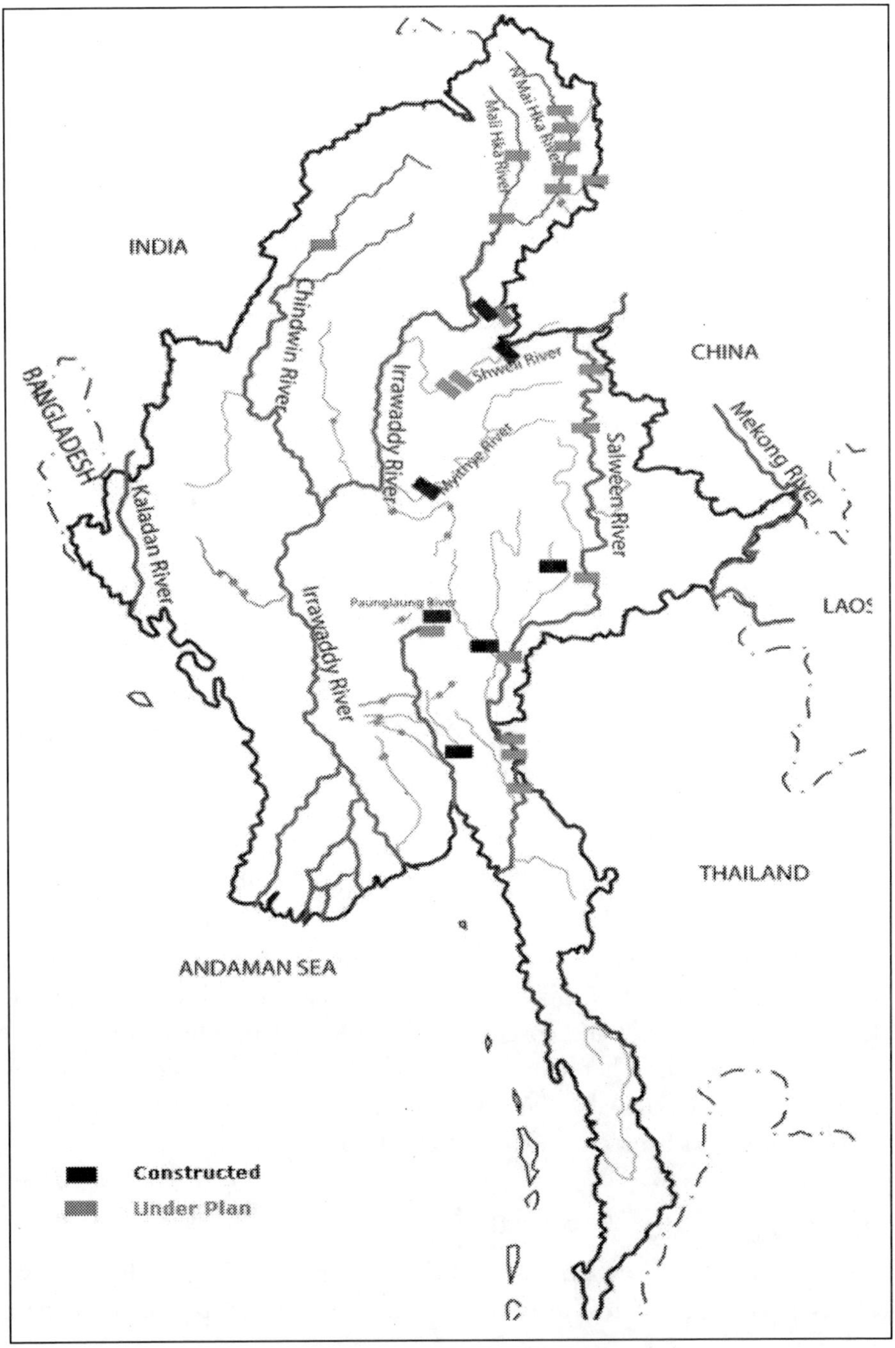

Figure 8.8. Dams on Myanmar Rivers
(*Source*: International Rivers.org)

700 million project completed in 2010, generating 790 MW. Multiple Chinese firms including CITIC were involved in the project.

Three dams have been planned on the Shweli River, which is a tributary of the Ayeyarwady. Phase I has been completed generating 600 MW, whereas Phase II and III are pending commission. This project is in the Shan State bordering China. The Myanmar Electric Power Enterprise (MEPE) and the Yunnan Joint Power Development Company are involved in the project. The three dams will have a total installed capacity of 1,440 MW and the total investment could reach USD 1.4 billion when completed. The electricity generated from this project will be exported to China and will also power government-run mining operations in Myanmar. The Yunnan Huaneng Lancang River Hydropower Company Ltd., which is one of the three partners with the Yunnan Joint Power Development Company has signed a Build-Operate-Transfer (BOT) deal with the Myanmarese government for the Shweli Phase 1 hydropower project.

The Dapein River has two dam projects run by the Myanmar Electric Power Enterprise. The two dams will have an installed capacity of 408 MW. The total cost is reportedly USD 10 million. 90 per cent of the electricity will be sold to China. Phase 1 has been completed in 2011 and Phase 2 is in progress.

The Paunglaung river projects can be divided into two groups. The Lower Paunglaung project has a dam 131 metres in height, with a capacity of 280 MW. This project is being executed by several Chinese firms. The Upper Paunglaung has a dam project with a 103 metre high dam, with an installed capacity of 140 MW. This has been commissioned in December 2015 as per the International Hydro Power Associations Annual Report 2016. The Shwegyin river has the Kengtawng Dam, built in 2011. This is a small project that generates 75 MW and cost USD 161 million. The Mu tributary of the Ayeyarwady has the Thaphanseik Dam which is a small project at 30 MW and was completed in May 2002. This project was executed with a loan from the China EXIM bank worth USD 20 million.

The Bigger Projects on Anvil

Dwarfing projects thus far, are the future plans for setting up hydropower plants in Myanmar with Chinese assistance. The river-wise plan is enumerated below.

Ayeyarwady Projects

A major hydropower project is being steered by the Ayeyarwady Confluence Basin Hydropower Co. Ltd. (ACHC), a Sino-Myanmar joint-venture company. This has CPI Yunnan International Power Investment Co. Ltd. as its Chinese partner, Ministry of Electric Power, and Asia World Company, with a shareholding structure of 80 per cent, 15 per cent and 5 per cent respectively.

There are seven large projects in the plan which promise 20,000 MW on the upstream Ayeyarwady river around Myitkyina, the capital city of the Kachin State. These are on BOT terms and will eventually get transferred to the Myanmarese government. The dams in this group include the following:

The Myitsone Dam which was commenced in December 2009 was halted in 2011 by President Thein Sein. This is a 6,000 MW major dam at the confluence of the Mali and N'Mai tributaries of the Ayeyarwady. The cost of the project is USD 3.6 billion. This is being steered by the Myanmar Ministry of Electric Power-1, China Power Investment Corporation, Asia World Company, Yunnan Machinery Equipment Import & Export Co. (YMEC) and China Southern Power Grid Co. This dam is located near Myitkyina, the capital of the Kachin State. There are serious concerns about the environment and livelihood of the Kachin people which has resulted in the stalling of the project, leading to several parleys between Myanmar and China. 90 per cent of the electricity of this project will go to China. 20 per cent of the revenue, or USD 500 million, will annually be given to Myanmar as per the plans.

The ambivalence regarding this project has made China demand USD 800 million in compensation if the project was scrapped and Myanmar would need to pay USD 50 million per year in interest before construction is resumed. As of May 2017, the future of the Myitsone Dam project is still undecided.[43] China has put forth several other demands including a higher stake in the Kyaukpyu port in lieu.

The Chibwe Dam is a 3,400 MW mega project on the Ayeyarwady cascade. It also has a minor Chibwe Creek Dam which is a smaller 99 MW (33 MW × 3) that commenced generation in 2011. The project suffered a setback due to conflicts. From 2013, it was repaired and supplies power to the Myitkyina area and the Chibwe town. The other major dams are Pasheat 1,600 MW, Laza on the Malikhariver at 1,560 MW, Kaunglanhpuatat 1,700 MW, Lakinat 1,400 MW and Hpizaw at 1,500 MW.

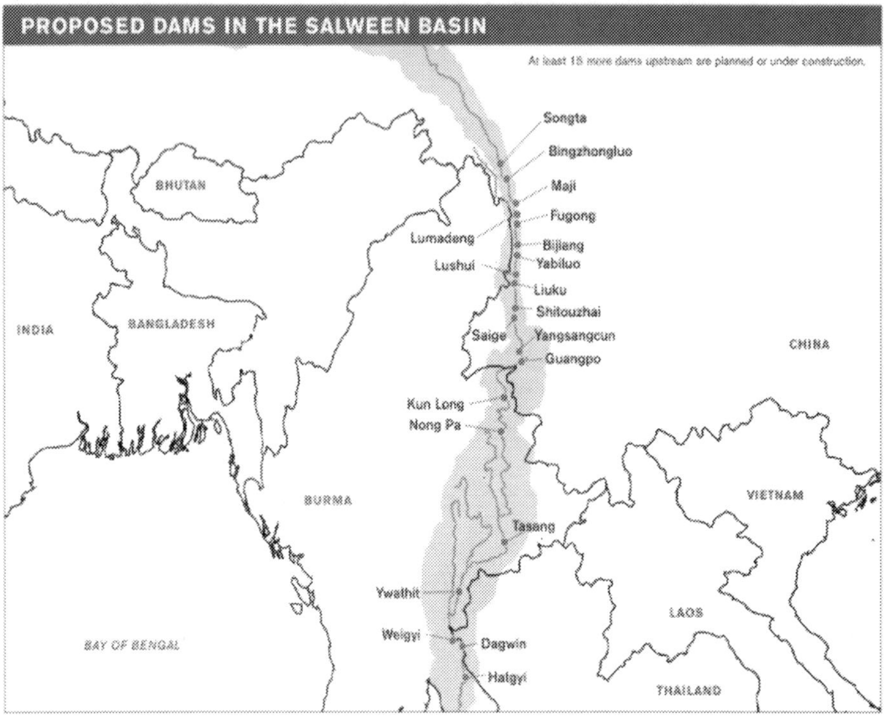

Figure 8.9. Proposed Dams in the Salween Basin including those in China
(*Source*: International Rivers.org)[44]

Salween/Thanlwin

The Salween or Thanlwin River is another major river in Myanmar. A series of dams are a part of China's plan, including what they are building on the Chinese side of the Salween.

- The largest dam on the river is the Tasang Dam (also called the Mai Tong Dam). Its capacity is very large at 7,100 MW and at 228 metres in height and taller than the Three Gorges Dam. This dam has been planned for the export of electricity to Thailand. This is now stalled due to ethnic and environmental issues in the Shan State. The work on the project is being carried out by the Union Resources and Engineering Company (UREC) and the China Gezhouba Group Co. (CGGC).
- The Kunlong Dam with plans to generate 1,400 MW in the Shan State is a project based on an MoU signed in 2010. This is on the Upper Salween River. The firms involved include Hydro China Zhong

Nan, Ministry of Electric Power and two Chinese companies Hanergy Holding Group Limited and Goldwater Resources Limited (GRL). It is also known as the Kunlong Hydropower Project.

- Manntaung. The Manntaung Dam is on a tributary of the Salween (200 MW) in Shan. This is being built by the China Three Gorges Corporation (CTGC) and the International Group of Entrepreneurs Company (IGOEC).
- Ywathit Dam (1,360 MW) in Kayah (Karenni). This is part of a three-dam cascade in the Kayah State. One is Ywathit, and two others are on its tributaries, the Pawn and Thabet rivers which are of 600 MW each at USD 600 million.
- Hatgyi Dam. This is a project involving the Ministry of Electric Power, the Thai-led Electricity Generating Authority of Thailand (EGAT), and China's Sinohydro based on an MoU signed in 2006. This is coming up in the Karen State. It is a 33 metre-high dam with an installed capacity of 1,200 MW at a cost of USD 1 billion. The majority of the electricity will be exported to Thailand. The firms involved are Zhejiang Fuchunjiang Hydropower Equipment, HydroChina, Zhong Nan, and China Hydropower Engineering Group Co. (CHECC).
- Weigyi Dam. This is again a Thai-led initiative, where EGAT signed an MOU with Myanmar in 2005. This dam is being development to provide electricity to Thailand. It will be a 168 metre high dam with an installed capacity of about 4,540 MW. The cost of the dam is USD 3 billion.
- Dagwin Dam. This is also called the Mae Sering-2 or Lower Thanlwin Dam. It will serve as a pumped storage facility for the upstream Weigyi Dam with an installed capacity of 792 MW. The cost of this project is USD 900 million and involves China, Myanmar and Thailand.
- Another large project on the Salween is the NongPha Dam (1,000 MW) in the Shan State.

Other Rivers. The Chindwin river has the Tamanthi Dam being developed by India's National Hydroelectric Power Corporation (NHPC) and the MoU for the project was signed in 2004. It will be 80 metres high and has a capacity of 1,200 MW. The project will export 80 per cent of its power to India.

On the Tarpein river[45] there is a 1,240MW project. The Tarpein 2 project of 168 MW has been stalled due to the 2008 trouble with KIO which is a group over which China has influence.

Table 8.2. Myanmar's Metal Resources

Mine and Mineral	Company	Location	Remarks
Tagaung Taung Nickel Mine	China Nonferrous Metal Mining (Group) Co. Ltd. (CNMC)	Thabeikkyin Mandalay Region	Operational Myanmar No. 3 Mining Enterprise (50% share in the project)
Letpadaung Copper Deposits	Myanmar Wanbao Mining Copper Limited	Sagaing Region	Under construction Myanmar No. 1 Mining Enterprise (51% share in the project)
Monywa Sabetaung and Kyisintaung Copper Deposits	Myanmar Yang Tse Copper Limited	Sagaing Region	Operational. MWMCL (30% and Myanmar Economic Holdings Limited 19% (Tatmadaw enterprise) Myanmar Ministry of Mines 51%.[46]
Mwetaung Nickel Mine	NORINCO	Tiddin Township, Chin State	Myanmar government (20% share in the project)
Tigyit coal mine	China National Heavy Machinery Corporation	Pinlaung Township, Southern Shan State	Operational Project owned by Shan Yoma Nagar Co. Ltd
MwayTaungPharTtaung copper mining project	China Minghua Group Ltd	Chin State	
Kalonta Tin mine	China Minghua Group Ltd	24 km NNE of Dawei, Tanintharyi region	
MwayTaung Phar Ttaung copper mining project	North Mining Investment Company	Chin State	

Source: Chinese Investments in Myanmar - A Scoping Study, Christopher Dunn, Lin Ji and Kui Peng, Global Environmental Institute, 2016.

Despite an overwhelmingly large number of hydropower projects with China, the 2016 Annual report of International Hydropower Association mentions that due to incomplete environmental and social impact measurements, several projects like the Shweli3, Yeywa, Middle Paunglaung, Bawgata will move to European and American companies.

Natural Resources

China's rush for minerals and metals is another driver of its Myanmar policy. China's interests in metals and minerals in Myanmar are related to copper in the Monywa mines (Sabetaung, Kyisintaung, Letpadaung), nickel mines at Tagaung Taung and Mwetaung, tin at Kalonta and coal at Tigyit, where there is also a power plant. Another important resource that drives the bilateral relation is oil and gas.

A detailed list of the mining projects is placed in Table 8.2. Of all the minerals projects, one that has attracted maximum attention is the Letpadaung copper mine project. The Wanbao Mining Limited, a company belonging to the China North Industries Corporation (NORINCO) group, which among other industries is also an arms firm, has a subsidiary in Myanmar which is the Myanmar Wanbao Mining Copper Limited (MWMCL). The main investment of this venture is the Letpadaung copper mine in the Sagaing Division, in which the Government of Myanmar holds a 51 per cent stake. The project hit a roadblock when the locals protested over compensation. However, it is proceeding ahead after a renewed focus on CSR including committing 2 per cent of the profits to the villages affected by the mine.[47]

Oil and Gas

Myanmar has one of region's oldest petroleum industries with exports dating back to the mid-19th Century. The Yenangyaung and Chauk fields were two of the oldest fields that began production for the London-based Burmah Oil Company in 1871. Soon the US followed with the Standard Oil Company in Burma. Petroleum has been Myanmar's primary source of income. However, it has now become a natural gas producer after the hiatus imposed by decades of junta rule, during which the country was isolated. The modern phase of Myanmar's energy initiatives commenced with the Apyauk gas field in 1991.

Myanmar has proven crude oil reserves of 50 million barrels as of January 2016 and it is the 79th largest country reserve and its crude oil production was 15,000 barrels/day in 2015 est. As far as natural gas is concerned, it has proven reserves of 283.2 billion cubic metres (as of January 2016 est.),

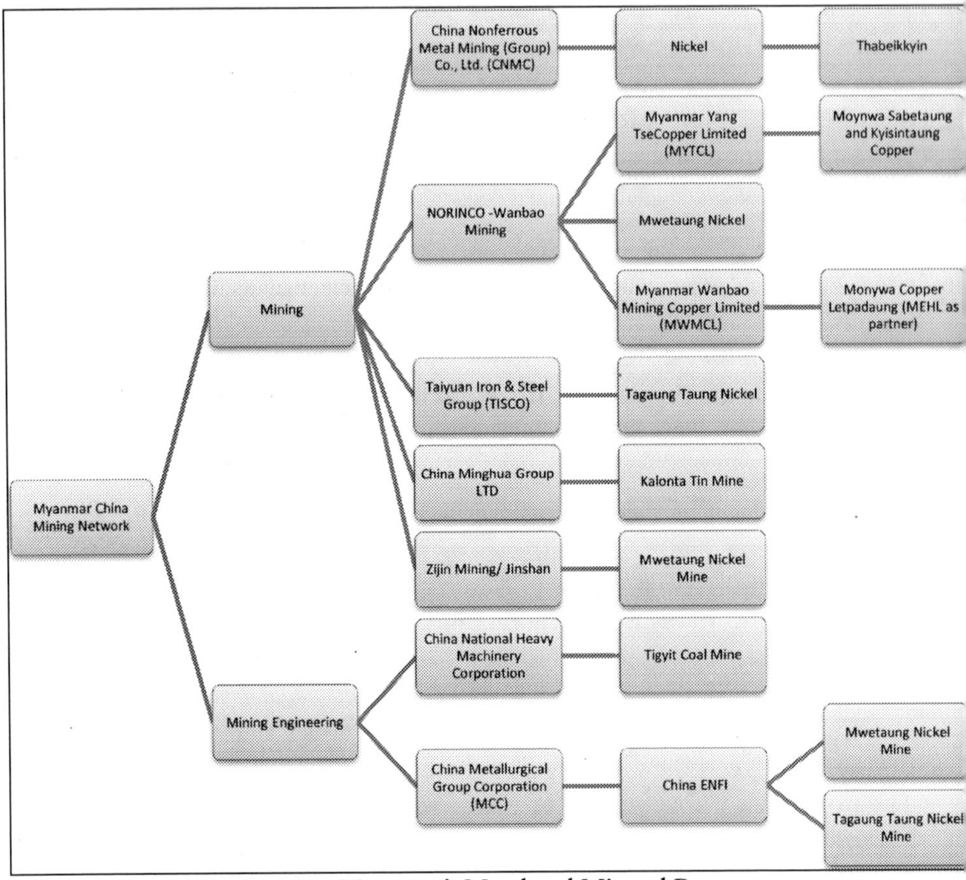

Figure 8.10. Myanmar's Metal and Mineral Resources
(*Source:* Chinese Investments in Myanmar - A Scoping Study, Christopher Dunn, Lin Ji and Kui Peng, Global Environmental Institute)

confirming possession of the 40th largest reserves in the world. Its natural gas production is 16.8 billion cubic metres per annum, as per 2014 estimates.[48] China has invested in exploration, refining, downstream industries, as well as pipelines in Myanmar.

Refining and Industries. China has also invested in refining and associated petro-chemical industries. The Dawei Refinery is being set up by Chinese firms in the southeastern coastal city of Dawei. Myanmar approved the construction of a 100,000 barrels/day refinery by China's Guangdong Zhenrong Energy Company in early 2016, one of the largest foreign investments costing USD 3 billion[49] in the country to date. The facility is designed to supply both domestic and export markets with oil products.[50] The Chinese firm, in its first foray into refining, will hold 70 per cent of the project, and the remaining 30 per cent will held by three Myanmar firms—Myanmar Economic Holdings Limited, a Tatmadaw-linked firm, Myanmar Petrochemical Corporation and the Yangon Engineering Group. In 2004, China National Petroleum Corporation (CNPC) signed a contract with the Myanmar Petrochemical Enterprise for the construction of the No 4A fertiliser plant, which included two 100-kilotonne synthetic ammonia units and two 150 kilotonne urea units.[51] The project went on stream in January 2011 becoming Myanmar's largest fertiliser plant. The project was designed to boost the development of agriculture in Myanmar.

Exploration

Natural Gas. Myanmar is today primarily a gas-producing nation which has four offshore fields. The Moattama basin has three fields named Yadana, Yetagun and Zawtika fields, which are in the south and feed Thailand. The Rakhine basin has the Shwe field, which is to the north, off the Rakhine coast and the gas is sent to China by pipelines. Due to the present state of industries, Myanmar has more gas than it can consume. Thailand and China have been, therefore, the markets for the gas. Petro China has developed the A1 Shwe fields off the Rakhine coast. A China Thailand offshore gas JV has invested about USD 367 million in the Zawtika Phase 1B.

CNPC Operations in Myanmar. The CNPC has been involved in oil and gas projects in Myanmar since 2001. These include deep-water exploration, oilfield services, construction of chemicals facilities and pipelines. Some of the projects that the CNPC has been involved in are tabulated at Table 3.

Table 8.3. CNPC Projects in Myanmar

Year	Project	Remarks
2001	Operation of two onshore oil and gas development and production projects	
2001	Acquisition of the Bagan field from TG World and a 25-year Production Sharing Contract (PSC)	Block IOR-3, TSF-2 and RSF-3
2001	20-year contract with Myanmar Oil and Gas Enterprise (MOGE) to improve oil recovery	Block IOR-4 in Southern Myanmar
2007	Exploration and exploitation of 3 deep water blocks	Block AD-1, AD-6 and AD-8 off-Rakhine coast covering 10,000 sq km
2008	30-year purchase, transportation and sale agreement with Daewoo International (South Korea) for import of natural gas from offshore blocks. Interestingly, ONGC Videsh and GAIL has 17.5 per cent and 8.5 per cent stakes in A1 and A3 fields along with Daewoo (51 per cent), MOGE (15 per cent) and Korea Gas (8.5per cent)[52]	Block A-1 and A-3

Oil and Gas Pipelines. The plans for a Myanmar–China gas and oil pipeline were originally proposed in 2004. The aforementioned CNPC Daewoo International offshore blocks A-1 and A-3 contract is what triggered the pipeline project. According to the agreement, the pipelines have been constructed to deliver natural gas from Myanmar to China. Myanmar will also be able to tap the pipeline running across its territory to meet local consumption. This oil and gas pipelines from Kyaukpyu to Kunming cost USD 2.5 billion.

The Southeast Asia Gas Pipeline Co. Ltd., a JV in which CNPC has 50.9 per cent stake, is responsible for designing, constructing, operating and maintaining the oil and gas pipelines. The Myanmar section of the Myanmar–China Oil Pipeline has been jointly invested in and built by the CNPC Southeast Asia Pipeline Company Ltd and the Myanmar Oil and Gas Enterprise (MOGE).

The main line of the Myanmar–China gas pipeline was constructed by October 2013. Of a total length of 2,520 kilometres, 793 kilometres of it runs in Myanmar and 1,727 kilometres in China. It has a designed capacity of 12 billion cubic metres/year. The CNPC has also built four gas distribution stations in Kyaukpyu, Yenangyaung, Mandalay and Taungtha to deliver 2 billion cubic metres of gas locally in Myanmar. At Kyaukpyu, it also supplies natural gas to a power plant. In January 2015, the gas pipeline was put into trial operations, and the Port of Maday Island in Kyaukpyu was officially opened. This port is in the Rakhine region slightly south of the deep water port at Sittwe that has been constructed by India which has linkages to the Kaladan Multimodal Project towards India's North Eastern Region.

The oil pipeline is designed to transport 22 million tonnes of oil per year. An oil terminal has been built in Kyaukpyu at the same time. The detailed plans for developing Kyaukpyu are in the maritime section in this chapter. The pipelines traverse through Mandalay, Lashio, and Muse entering China at Ruili in Yunnan. The oil pipeline was completed in 2014. However, the oil pipeline was entangled in transit fee issues and after prolonged negotiations, was inaugurated in April 2017. This pipeline feeds a refinery in Kunming and aims at increasing refining capacity in South West China breaking the coastal monopoly as envisaged by Zhou Yongkang, the ousted Politburo Standing Committee (PBSC) member and security head with a background in oil. According to the *Financial Times*, this line can feed 6 per cent of China's crude oil imports, bypassing Malacca.[53] This pipeline at its China end feeds a Petro China refinery in Anning. This is designed to take heavy, high sulphur

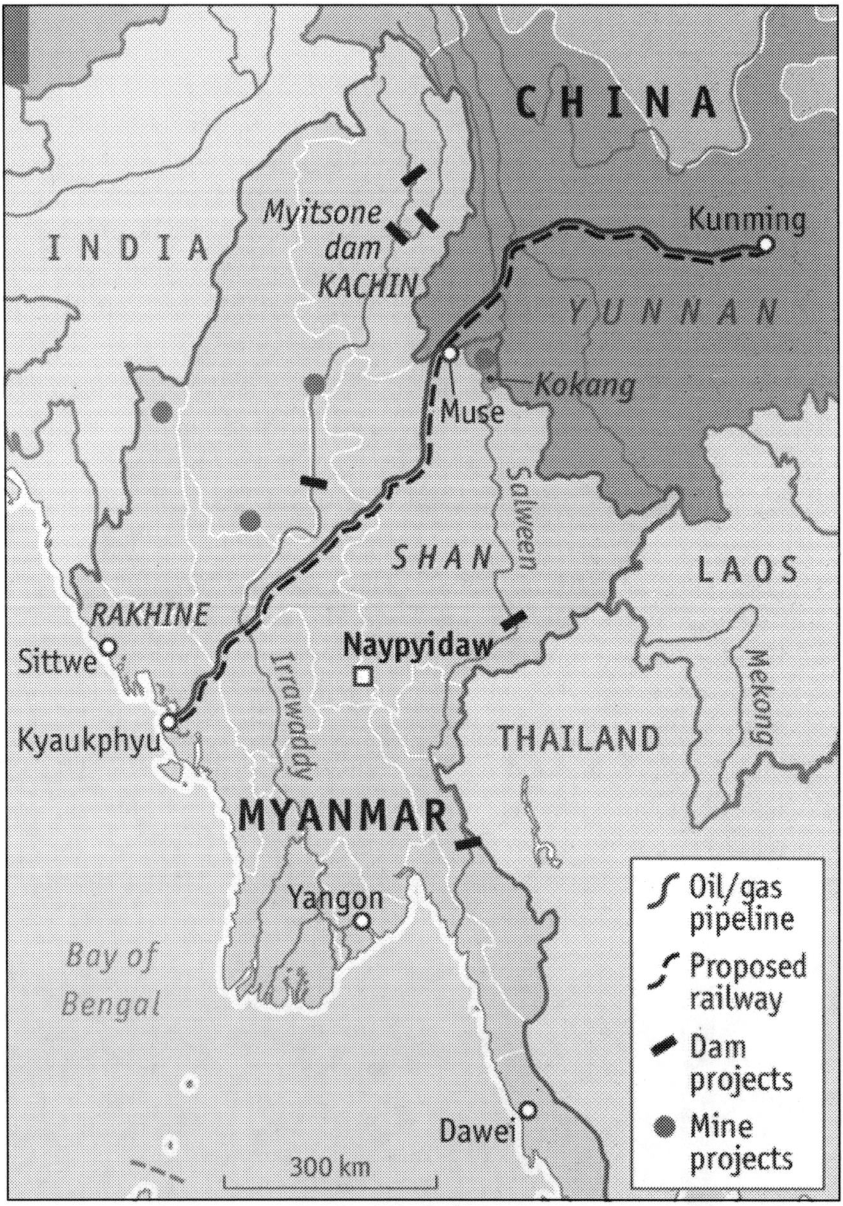

Figure 8.11. Oil and Gas Pipeline from IOR to China
(*Source*: Economist)

crudes with a capacity of 260000 barrels per day. Aramco has invested 1–1.5bn USD in the refinery. At least part of the crude oil will come from Kuwait[54] and Saudi Arabia.[55]

Arms Transfers[56]

Myanmar's arms relations with China commenced as late as in 1988 with the purchase of JLG-43 height-finding radars. The next Chinese weapon to enter the inventory was Type-63 light tank in 1989. This was quickly followed by the Type-69 tank and APCs in 1990. More modern Type-59D tanks were supplied in 2002. After a lull from 2000– 2010, the transfers of arms between China and Myanmar are on the rise again. Myanmar ranks third—very close to Bangladesh—at a very high USD 3 billion worth of arms transfers from China thus far.

The naval arms transfers began with the Type-037/Hainan patrol craft and guns in 1990. C-801 anti-ship missiles were included in the sales in 1994. They were augmented with the C-802/CSS-N-8 anti-ship missile in 2012 that came along with two second-hand Type-053H1 Jianghu-2 frigates.

The inventory transferred to the air force included F-6/J-6 fighter aircraft and HN-5A portable SAMs in 1990. Y-12 light transport aircraft were supplied in 1991. The aircraft stables expanded with the Y-8 transport aircraft, A-5C "Fantan" FGA aircraft and F-7M "Airguard" fighter aircraft in 1992. The K-8 Karakorum-8 trainer/combat aircraft joined the fleet in 2009 and 16 JF-17 Thunder/FC-1FGA aircraft were ordered in 2015, possibly from the Pakistani production line and its delivery is scheduled in 2017. This is an example of the China–Pakistan strategic value chain at work in South Asia. The Y-8F-200W transport aircraft too were ordered in 2016.

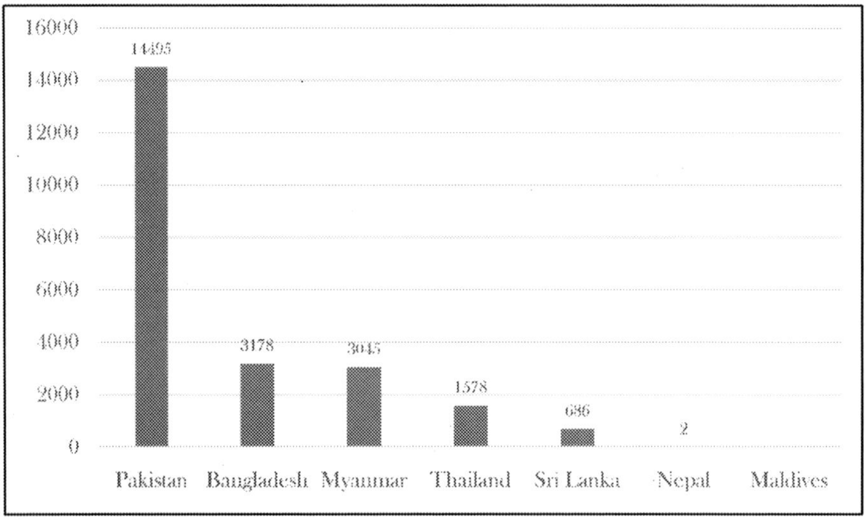

Figure 8.12. Chinese Arms Sales to Select Nations—1950 to 2016
(Data from SIPRI. Amount is Trend-Indicator Value.)

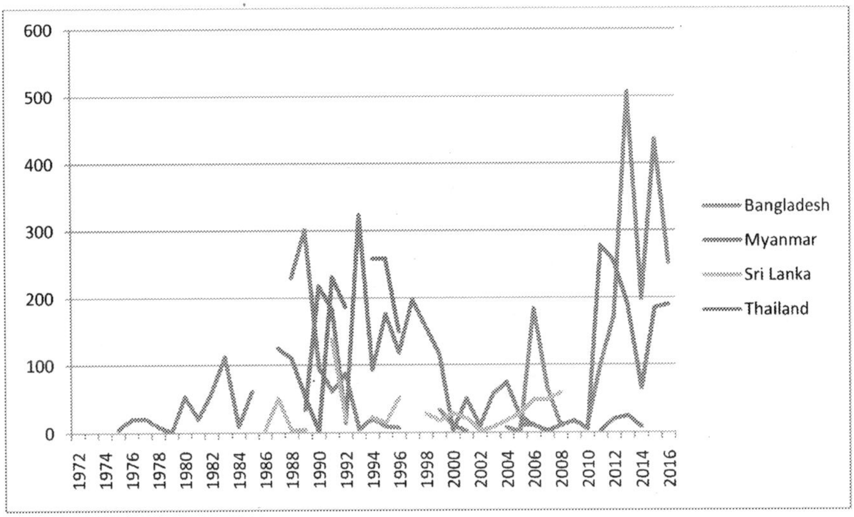

Figure 8.13. Trend of Arms Transfers from China to Select Nations
(*Source*: SIPRI database)

Conclusion

The Chinese strategy in Myanmar is driven by certain key factors like access, energy and investments. The ethnic divisions of Myanmar have a definitive role in its relations with China.

Aprimary motive for China's involvement in Myanmar, amongst all other drivers, is an access to the Indian Ocean Region (IOR). In this era where China is targeting its economic growth through resources and markets in the Indian Ocean, Myanmar provides China the shortest access to the IOR. This access also meets the requirements of its 'go west' policy which is about enhancing growth in its western provinces. Yunnan, which is adjacent to Myanmar, is one of the poorer provinces in China. The distance between Kyaukpyu, the sea port and Muse, the border town on the Sino-Myanmarese border, is a mere 900 km, over an all-weather terrain. This is one-third the distance between Gwadar and Khunjerab which is 2,700 km through inhospitable, seasonally open terrain. The Yunnan province which lies adjacent to Myanmar also has the need for energy since it is not energy-rich, unlike Xinjiang, where the CPEC and central Asian pipelines also terminate. Yunnan is also far poorer in ranking second-last in the GDP per capita with twice the population of Xinjiang which makes that region's growth critical to the overall growth of the Chinese economy and removal of provincial disparities. Besides, the choice of transportation of energy through Myanmar has been settled, at least temporarily, since China has already invested in refineries, port infrastructure, as well as in gas and oil pipelines in Myanmar, many of which involve external investors. This is a sharp contrast to Pakistan, where there are no investments for transportation of energy to China, even as a part of CPEC, thus far. As far as political turmoil goes, the CPEC has to deal with the Baloch issue, whereas the Myanmar route has to deal with the Rohingya problem on the Rakhine coast. It is pertinent to note that China was keen to mediate in the Rohingya issue which Myanmar has turned down.

Table 8.4. Comparison of Yunnan, Tibet and Xinjiang Provinces within China

	Tibet	Xinjiang	Yunnan
Ranking GDP	28	20	30
GDP per Capita (USD)	31,999	40,034	28,806
GDP Nominal (USD)	5,138	6,428	4,625
GDP PPP (International $)	9,073	11,351	8,168
Level of national GDP per capita (%)	64	81	58
GDP (in USD million)	1,02,639	9,32,480	13,71,788
Population (in 1000's)	3,208	23,292	47,279

China's Need for Energy. Energy is another key driver in the China–Myanmar relations. Myanmar is a major source of natural gas close to China, lying to its South West. Such availability is crucial to China in its development programme for the western regions, even though this gas reserve is not large. In the case of oil, Myanmar is not a major producer and China will have to import the oil from the Middle East for its refineries in Anning, near Kunming.

Myanmar is not only a source but also offers a conduit for transporting oil and gas. The oil pipeline is designed to transport 22 million tonnes of oil per year (0.44 million barrels/day). On an average, China imported 6.2 million barrels of crude oil per day in 2014. Thus, the Myanmar–China oil pipeline can only transport about 5 per cent of China's crude oil imports. The refinery in Dawei is expected to refine 100,000 barrels of crude per day sometime in the future. The gas pipeline is designed to transport 10 to 13 billion cubic metres of gas per year (420 BCF/year). China's total imports of natural gas by pipeline in 2014 were 1,133 billion cubic feet. Therefore, with a capacity of 420 BCF and total imports of 2,090 BCF of gas, the Myanmar pipeline can take care of 20 per cent gas imports to China. Hence, the pipelines have the capacity to carry 5.5 per cent of Chinese oil imports and 20 per cent of gas imports as on date. The utilisation of the full potential of the gas pipeline will depend on how much gas is available in the Myanmar fields. In case local production does not meet the capacity of the pipeline, import of LNG after regasification may be one option that may be considered in the future.

Equally important are the hydroprojects in Myanmar. They are important for Myanmar's domestic plans for electrification. They are also part of China's West to East Electricity Transfer Project. The development of hydro projects has environmental and social impacts with large scale submersions of land, affecting livelihood and displacements.

China's Influences: Ethnic Issues. China has certain strong levers to influence events in Myanmar. First is the ethnic division in Myanmar. Many of the rebel groups in Myanmar lean on China. In fact, it appears that both China and the ethnic groups balance the Bamars at the centre, using each other. The centre supports a unitary homogenous country and finds federalism a challenge. Myanmar's policy towards the Rohingyas is another case where the state has erred. They are stateless people, with close links to Bangladesh, and have the sympathy of many international organisations and nations, especially the Islamic states. The recent offer by China to mediate has been rejected by Myanmar. This also plays out geographically as the Bamars live in the central plain core and the ethnic regions are on the periphery through which trade and energy corridors traverse. The border is a modern affair whereas ethnicity and affiliations permeate across these modern lines!

Resource Economy. Myanmar is rich in minerals, oil, gas, metals, teak and hydropower. All of these are of value to China. Many of these projects also happen to be located in the states suffering from ethnic unrest. The extraction of these are environmentally sensitive processes and have the potential to displace the ethnic population. This has been a major reason for the cancellation of several projects, which has imposed political and economic costs on the centre. The control of rebel EAOs over resources also acts as a factor in China's relations with Myanmar and its rebels. The Chinese investments in Myanmar are predominantly through SOEs, though private companies also remain in business. Some Chinese companies like NORINCO have defence links and so do many Myanmar firms which have Tatmadaw connections. Today more investors find Myanmar, an attractive destination, offering greater options to the nation to choose from. Western nations and India are also interested in several projects in Myanmar. In fact, some of the hydro power projects are shifting to Western firms. Thailand too plays a major role in Myanmar's investment story.

Democracy. Democracy is another factor. Myanmar is in the middle of a transition to democracy. The military still plays a major role in the country and exerts influence over its transition to democracy.[57] The military still holds 25 per cent nominees in constitution. It was also the military and the military-supported Thein Sein government, which exercised hard options against the rebels. Even the cooling of relations between Myanmar and China resulting in the suspension of Chinese projects occurred during the Thein Sein period. The democratic successors of the Thein Sein government have appeared to be more pragmatic with respect to the rebels, callous about the Rohingyas and accommodative of China. Therefore, the China factor in the democratic process is another area to watch in the coming days. It is important that Daw Aug San is given adequate space by the international community to manoeuvre at this time, lest it limit her choice to China alone.

To China, Myanmar is one its crucial neighbours in the Indian Ocean Region. It ensures reliable access to the Indian Ocean but still does not solve the Malacca dilemma. Beyond access, it provides some alternative energy solutions for China. The oil pipeline that commence at the Rakhine port of Kyaukpyu brings in the needed oil to feed the refineries at Anning and Kunming, while the parallel natural gas pipeline transports the equity gas from the Shwe fields to China. Myanmar is also a source of untapped minerals and metals next door. Why travel far to Africa when Yunnan's neighbourhood has some of it in plenty?

The massive plans for dams across the rivers in Myanmar are expected to resolve the shortage of power not only for Myanmar, but also for the eastern regions of China. To Myanmar, China is a large neighbour with grand economic and energy plans, with the potential to trample over fragile ecological, social and ethnic fabric. Myanmar's capacity to pay back is another matter. It is also about ethnic play between the central Bamar core and the ethnic periphery, which hedges on China. Myanmar has the highest Chinese investment as a percentage of the GDP regionally in IOR littorals. That all this is occurring when Myanmar is transitioning to become a democracy, makes it a delicate situation. The relation between Myanmar and China is described as that of ***paukpaw*** or relations between brothers. Ironically some also describe it as one of hope in the west and fear about the east.

Part II: Thailand

Modern Thai–China relations started late in 1975. Historically, Thailand supported the Japanese during World War II and has guarded its independence

Figure 8.14. South East Asia with Relevant Ports

by aligning itself with the power of the day. It came under the US alliance thereafter, with the 1954 Manila Pact of the former Southeast Asia Treaty Organization (SEATO). Even today, the US is a close ally of Thailand, alongside China. When the US allies were unlocked by the Sino-US rapprochement, Thailand warmed up to China. Till then, Thailand was supportive of Taiwan and that included a state visit by the then King to Taiwan. The Taiwan link continues, primarily in the economic realm, without rocking the one-China policy.

The main turning point in the relations between Thailand and China was the spread of Maoism in neighbouring Cambodia and China's support in dealing with the crisis. Equally important was the 'Bamboo Network' or the network of the local Chinese diaspora. This includes entrepreneurs like the Charoen Pokphand Group, which is Thailand's largest private enterprise with deep links with China from the days of the warming of relations between the two countries. China used this network extensively in the opening up process, to learn and to attract investments. This is a major factor in the relationship with Thailand.

One of the reasons for China warming up more than ever, with the supply of arms and ammunition, especially submarines, has been the access to the IOR. The prospect of a Canal across the Isthmus of Kra, a narrow strip of land that separates the Indian Ocean from Pacific Ocean, holds promise to China. It can offer China alternative options to access the IOR. Such a canal across the Isthmus of Kra has been in the plans for over 200 years, offering an alternative to the Malacca Straits. The isthmus is 40 km at its narrowest and several options to construct the canal exist. However, the matter is sensitive for the Thais since it has the potential to cut the southern strip of Thailand into two. This southern portion of Thailand has an ethnic Muslim population, with Malaysia as a neighbour. However, even if the Kra does not materialise, the isthmus can serve as a land bridge connecting the IOR and Pacific trade networks.

The Thais have balanced their relation with China and the USA carefully, and reaped benefits of the same. An example is the recent purchase of the Yuan-class submarines from China at a very reasonable price, at cheaper than what was offered to Pakistan. Submarines are offensive, lethal weapons and can spearhead naval operations, with limited less-than-war roles. This will add more chaos to a region already populated with other submarine-operating nations like Vietnam, Indonesia, Singapore, Malaysia and Bangladesh. Curiously some arm against China and some are armed by China. The Thai submarines are to be based in Sattahip, the major Thai naval base in the Gulf of Thailand. The average depth of that Gulf is around 50 metres making it unviable for submarine operations. This may mean it will operate from the Thai bases in the deeper Andaman Sea in the IOR across Malacca Straits like Phuket or Phang Na. This was also stated by Deputy PM Prawit.[58] Such deployments add logistic hubs where Chinese-origin submarines can turn around and effect small scale repairs. As far as these Thai bases are concerned, they are geographically close to India's Andaman Islands. With a string of such bases in the Indian Ocean, from Djibouti and Gwadar on the western end of the Indian Ocean to the eastern end in the Thailand littorals, the Chinese vessels will have friendly bases with common military logistic chains.

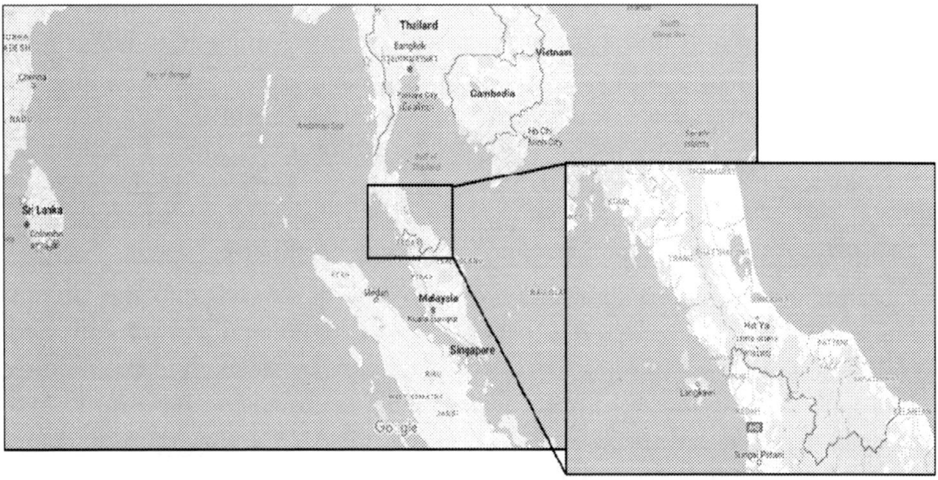

Figure 8.15. Kra Canal Location (*Source:* Google Maps)

Part III: Indonesia, Singapore and Malaysia

Indonesia, which will be the fourth largest economy in the world, also has a strategic location in the entrance to the IOR. Unlike Malaysia and Singapore which are connected to continental landmasses, Indonesia is an archipelagic landmass that forms part of the Malacca Straits. It is also an archipelagic nation not connected to continent-limiting connectivity options. Indonesia is large nation which has developed an identity of its own. Indonesia has had a tumultuous experience with Communism. The Peking-backed Partai Kommunist Indonesia was purged following a 1965 massacre of the Army Generals that eventually led to an Army rule of three decades under Suharto. The Communist Party of China (CCP)'s support of the PKI affected Indonesia–China ties, which strained to the point of severance of relations in 1967. This was followed by a period of anti-China sentiment. One reason behind the anti-China sentiment was the disproportionate economic clout enjoyed by the Chinese diaspora in Indonesia. To this day, China and an influx of Chinese citizens for infrastructure projects evoke worries in Indonesia. The relations improved only in the 1990s. Since then, the relations have been driven by economics and trade. Presently, China is the largest trading partner of Indonesia. In 2002, both nations signed an agreement for Strategic Partnership. Arms purchases from China have been another factor in the relationship. Interestingly, Malaysia, Thailand, Indonesia and Singapore which are being discussed as key to IOR access are also the top four ASEAN trading partners of China.

The most critical driver in this relation has been the need for construction of infrastructure in Indonesia. Its logistics cost is very high at 26 per cent of the GDP, whereas it is 14 per cent for adjacent Malaysia.[59] Indonesia supported the Asian Infrastructure Investment Bank (AIIB) considering its own infrastructure funding needs. It is also the nation from where President Xi announced the Maritime Silk Road during a speech to the Indonesian Parliament. This signals the relevance of Indonesia in China's IOR access plan. Indonesia has a dispute with China in the South China Sea near its Natuna Islands where the Indonesian Exclusive Economic Zone (EEZ) and China's nine-dashed line overlap. Yet, there has been careful handling by China and Indonesia despite standoffs over fishing rights between the two nations. Indonesia has also carefully managed China by balancing it with US and Japan. It supported the US presence in the ASEAN Regional Forum (ARF) to balance China. The 2016 Jakarta–Bandung high speed rail project is a major Chinese initiative in Indonesia. The recently concluded BRI summit was also attended by the Indonesian President Joko Widodo. For a country that controls the vital choke points of the Malacca, Sunda and Lombok Straits, China has not succeeded in making inroads into Indonesia on the scale that it has in most other countries, largely due to Indonesia's resistance and insecurity.

Singapore

Singapore is a physically small, island city state, at a strategic location in the busy Malacca Straits with two large neighbours of Indonesia and Malaysia in close proximity. With an area of 700 sq. km, it is just 50km long and 27 km wide. It was a part of Malaysia till 1965 when it achieved independence. This was also a period of racial and ethnic violence in South East Asia, including Singapore. There are continuing embers of nationalism in the region which makes a small nation like Singapore, with diverse ethnicities, highly insecure. As a result, Singapore has placed its bets on the USA, with which it shares a deep strategic relation. When the US had to vacate bases in the Philippines, Singapore offered bases, including creation of facilities for aircraft carriers at the Changi Naval Base before the turn of century.[60] This was much before China emerged as a power in the region. It has also invested in submarines, which are potent naval weapons. Singapore is today a key partner in the US rebalance to Asia. Four US Navy Littoral Combat Ships will be based at Singapore as a part of this strategy.

When China opened up, China's leader Deng Xiaoping saw Singapore as a good model of development and counted on the advice of Lee Kuan Yew. Yet, the official relations between Singapore and China commenced only as late as 1990. Singapore was second last[61] among the South East Asian nations to establish diplomatic ties with China. Till then Singapore officially recognised the ROC (Taiwan) and not the PRC. The Taiwan–Singapore relations also involve an annual military exercise named Starlight which has been conducted in Taiwan since 1975 for a various reasons including the shortage of area for exercises in Singapore. In 2016, Singapore Army APCs were seized by China en route from Taiwan, after the exercise. The vehicles were on a merchant ship contracted to transport them back to Singapore. Though the official Chinese explanation was that it had breached Hong Kong law, this was widely understood as a response to Singapore's position on the South China Sea disputes against China. The vehicles were detained at Hong Kong till January 2017, when they were returned. It is not that China has had issues with Singapore's proximity with Taiwan. The first-ever meeting between the Chinese President Xi Jinping and Taiwanese President Ma Ying-jeou took place at Singapore in November 2015.

China expects Singapore to support it since there is a strong and successful Chinese diaspora comprising 76 per cent of the country's population. On the other hand, Singapore does not want to lose its own identity as a cosmopolitan nation with Western values. It also values US support considering its strategic location, geography and neighbourhood. Therein lies the divergence.

The economic relations between Singapore and China are very robust. Both nations have invested in each other. Temasek,[62] the sovereign wealth fund of Singapore, holds assets in China and China has planned to invest in two container terminals in Singapore.[63] The major G2G Sino-Singapore initiatives in China are the Tianjin Eco-city, Suzhou Industrial Park and Chongqing Connectivity Initiative.[64] This is in addition to a bilateral trade of USD 66 billion.[65] The China–Singapore port imbroglio in Gwadar is relevant since it is a prominent factor in this book. The Gwadar port was originally contracted in 2007 to the Port of Singapore Authority (PSA)—a global leader in port management—on a 40-year lease. This was abruptly cancelled in 2010 and the port was handed over to China. In a sign of deteriorating relations, in a literal snub, the head of state of Singapore was not invited to Beijing for the inaugural Belt and Road Forum in May 2017.

Malaysia

Malaysia has a highly prosperous ethnic Chinese community constituting one-third of the population. Like other South East Asian counterparts, Malaysia too had anti-China riots in the late sixties. Malaysia is a stakeholder in the South China Sea imbroglio, but has not been as vocal, due to its increasing economic engagement with China[66] and has slowly drifted into the Chinese economic embrace. It has also periodically reduced its defence budget, presently cutting it by 12 per cent in 2017.[67]

China is developing a major deep-water port and associated investments named Melaka Gateway at a cost of USD 9.8 billion.[68] The deep-water port will cost USD 6.8 billion; out of this, $ 9.8 bn for the Melaka GW project.[69] This is just 200 km north of Singapore on the west coast of Malaysia. A further 100 km north, China is also involved in the Kuala Linggi International Port (KLIP) project, which is being developed as an oil hub[70] at a cost of USD 2.8 billion. 200 km away from Melaka, on the west coast, Port Klang is being developed at a cost of USD 46 billion[71,72] Some argue that the Melaka gateway can hardly be used since Kelang is being upgraded anyway.[73] The aim of such developments is not only to dislodge Singapore[74] from its position as key player in the region, but also to make the Malacca Straits less relevant. Another large infrastructure project that will connect the west and east coast of Malaysia is the East Coast Rail Line (ECRL), pegged at a cost of USD 13.1 billion.[75,76] This rail line will also act as a land bridge between Port Klang and Kuantan Port, enabling trade to bypass the Malacca Straits and Singapore, serving both China and other ASEAN nations. The ASEAN has revived a plan for a rail line connecting Kunming to Singapore through Laos, Thailand and Malaysia. The project is called Singapore Kunming Rail Link (SKRL). It also has plans to connect Cambodia, Myanmar and Vietnam.[77] Then there is a very large project plan at the Carey Island, just south of Kelang, which is touted as a $64 billion project.

Table 8.5. Summary of Infrastructure Projects in Malaysia

Project	Cost of Project (in billion USD)	Remarks
Melaka Gateway	9.8	Could be used as PLA (Navy) base
Port Kelang/Carey Island	46.0	Could be used as PLA (Navy) base
Kuala Linggi Port (KLIP)	2.8	
East Coast Rail Line (ECRL)	13.1	85% Finance
Port Kuantan	-	40% Stake
Total	71.7	

On the eastern coast of Malaysia, across the Malacca, Kota Kinabalu has already received PLAN submarines on short visits. This is an important port facing the South China Sea, along with other ports like Kuantanand Samalaju and can be used by China to exercise 'strategic dominance' over the South China Sea, as argued by an analyst.[78]

This is not all: there is over USD100 billion worth of real estate investment in Johor Baru that can tap the proximity to Singapore like Shenzhen did with the proximity to Hong Kong.[79]

Conclusion

In conclusion, the five South East Asian Nations discussed in the chapter play a crucial role in China's Indian Ocean access strategy. They are also the connecting links between Indian and Pacific Oceans and in that way crucial to the Indo-Pacific construct. Of the five, Myanmar offers China a direct and crucial land connection from the Yunnan province to the Indian Ocean Region. Myanmar is a far more a suitable transit route from the IOR when compared to Pakistan, which also offers a similar option from the Western parts of the Indian Ocean. China has invested in that option, with a focus on energy in the oil, gas and hydropower domains—both as a source and as a transit route from the Indian Ocean. The BCIM is to be seen very much as a part of that plan. Indonesia, Thailand, Malaysia and Singapore are equally crucial to China's Indian Ocean strategy, albeit without direct land borders with China. Of these, China has heavily invested in Malaysia, both from an economic perspective and an access perspective. It maintains good relations with Indonesia; however, unlike Malaysia, Myanmar or Thailand, it is an island nation and does not offer land connections from China. Yet, its geographic location makes it crucial to the sea lanes between the IOR and the Pacific. The Maritime Silk Road was announced for this reason in the Indonesian Parliament by President Xi. The Kra isthmus in southern Thailand is important to China's IOR access plan. China's relation with Thailand has reached a different strategic level with the recent sale of submarines. The strategy in Malaysia is to invest in an overland route efficient enough to bypass Malacca, with investments in ports on the Pacific and IOR coasts with a rail link between them. The investments are at a scale that can threaten Singapore's status as a major *entrepôt* and financial centre in the global maritime network. Singapore's assertion of its own identity and closeness to the US has been a major irritant to China's outlook towards securing its accesses to the IOR. This chapter has tried to state the current state of play for access to the IOR involving the nations that matter for that access. It will be interesting to see as to how China refines this strategy in the times to come, through geo-engineering, economic inducements and politics.

NOTES

1. Rakhine is the same as Arakan.
2. "The World Factbook—Central Intelligence Agency," accessed August 22, 2017, https://www.cia.gov/library/publications/the-world-factbook/geos/bm.html.
3. Depicted as Divisions in the map in Figure 8.1.
4. "Electoral Rules and Multiethnic Parties during Myanmar's Democratic Era (1948–1962) (Chapter 9) - Coalitions of the Well-Being," *Cambridge Core*, accessed June 29, 2017, /core/books/coalitions-of-the-well-being/electoral-rules-and-multiethnic-parties-during-myanmars-democratic-era-19481962/61402E36C1BC6FF47268090678100F89.
5. Bertil Lintner, "China Captures Myanmar's Peace Process," accessed June 4, 2017, http://www.atimes.com/article/china-captures-myanmars-peace-process/.
6. This later became the Burmese National Army.
7. Sithu Aung Myint, "The Challenge of Forging a New Tatmadaw," *Frontier Myanmar*, accessed September 2, 2017, https://frontiermyanmar.net/en/the-challenge-of-forging-a-new-tatmadaw.
8. "China and Myanmar: Not Only Pauk-Phaw," *The Irrawaddy*, June 5, 2017, https://www.irrawaddy.com/news/burma/china-and-burma-not-only-pauk-phaw.html. For full paper read 'The People's Republic of China and Burma Not Only Pauk-Phaw Bertil Lintner at http://www.project2049.net/documents/China_Burma_Lintner_Pauk_Phaw2049.pdf
9. "Timeline: Chinese-Burma Relations," *The Irrawaddy*, May 1, 2017, https://www.irrawaddy.com/news/burma/timeline-chinese-burma-relations.html.
10. Myanmar's Nationwide Ceasefire Agreement a BACKGROUNDER - October 2015 The Institute for Security and Development Policy – www.isdp.eu, accessible at http://isdp.eu/content/uploads/publications/2015-isdp-backgrounder-myanmar-nca.pdf
11. Lintner, "China Captures Myanmar's Peace Process."
12. "NAB Statement 1-17 – Northern Alliance (Burma)," accessed June 4, 2017, http://northernalliance.today/nab-statement-1-17/.
13. Lintner, "China Captures Myanmar's Peace Process."
14. "UNLFW: The New Name for Terror in NE - Times of India," *The Times of India*, accessed June 28, 2017, http://timesofindia.indiatimes.com/india/UNLFW-The-new-name-for-terror-in-NE/articleshow/47547899.cms.
15. CORCOM which includes the Kangleipak Communist Party (KCP), the Kanglei Yawol Kanna Lup (KYKL), the People's Revolutionary Party of Kangleipak (PREPAK), the PREPAK (Progressive), the Revolutionary People's Front, and the United National Liberation Front (UNLF).
16. "Chinese Agencies Helping North East Militants in Myanmar," *The Indian Express*, accessed September 2, 2017, http://indianexpress.com/article/india/chinese-agencies-helping-north-east-militants-in-myanmar-4468384/.
17. "UWSA Wants China in Peace Process," *The Myanmar Times*, accessed September 2, 2017, https://www.mmtimes.com/national-news/20059-uwsa-wants-china-in-peace-process.html.
18. Lintner, "China Captures Myanmar's Peace Process."
19. "Myanmar-China Bilateral Trade Hits over $9b in 10 Months of 2015-16 FY - Business - Chinadaily.com.cn," accessed May 18, 2017, http://www.chinadaily.com.cn/business/2016-02/16/content_23499905.htm.

20. "Why Does China Care so Much about Stalled Dam Project in Myanmar?," *South China Morning Post*, August 25, 2016, http://www.scmp.com/news/china/diplomacy-defence/article/2008816/why-does-beijing-care-so-much-about-stalled-dam-project.
21. "Myanmar-China Bilateral Trade Hits over $9b in 10 Months of 2015-16 FY - Business - Chinadaily.com.cn."
22. "Myanmar-China Border Trade Picks up in 5 Months of 2016-17 Fiscal Year - Business - Chinadaily.com.cn," accessed May 18, 2017, http://www.chinadaily.com.cn/business/2016-09/03/content_26688643.htm.(extrapolated by author)
23. Also spelt Moulmein.
24. "UPDATE 1-China Firm Wins Myanmar Approval for $3 Bln Refinery," *Reuters*, April 5, 2016, http://www.reuters.com/article/china-myanmar-refinery-idUSL3N1782MS.
25. Htoo Thant, "Govt Reserves Land for Rakhine State SEZ," *The Myanmar Times*, accessed May 9, 2017, http://www.mmtimes.com/index.php/business/17995-govt-reserves-land-for-rakhine-state-sez.html.
26. Ibid.
27. Ibid.
28. "Exclusive: China Seeks up to 85 Percent Stake in Strategic Port in Myanmar," *Reuters*, accessed May 31, 2017, http://www.reuters.com/article/us-china-silkroad-myanmar-port-exclusive-idUSKBN1811DF.
29. http://www.unescap.org/sites/default/files/Myanmar-TAR-WGM-4.pdf
30. "Populism Constitutes Risks to Belt & Road," *Global Times*, accessed May 9, 2017, http://www.globaltimes.cn/content/1040213.shtml.
31. "Kunming-Yangon Rail Project Rumors Denied," *Eleven Myanmar*, accessed May 9, 2017, http://elevenmyanmar.com/local/kunming-yangon-rail-project-rumors-denied.
32. "Myanmar's Suu Kyi to Ink Deals on Two Hospitals, Bridge during China Trip," *Reuters*, August 18, 2016, http://www.reuters.com/article/china-myanmar-idUSL3N1AZ24L.
33. By U.S. Army Center of Military History - India-Burma, 2 April 1942-28 January 1945, U.S. Army Center of Military History, Public Domain, https://commons.wikimedia.org/w/index.php?curid=1836415
34. "Map: China's West-East Electricity Transfer Project," *Wilson Center*, February 19, 2013, https://www.wilsoncenter.org/article/map-chinas-west-east-electricity-transfer-project.
35. Press Trust of India, "Pak-China to Invest $50 Bn on Indus Cascade to Generate 40,000 MW Power," *Business Standard India*, May 13, 2017, http://www.business-standard.com/article/international/pak-china-to-invest-50-bn-on-indus-cascade-to-generate-40-000-mw-power-117051300288_1.html.
36. "China-Myanmar Gas Power Plant to Supply Electricity to Yangon by Year-End," *Xinhua, English.news.cn*, accessed June 30, 2017, http://news.xinhuanet.com/english/2017-01/23/c_136007012.htm.
37. "Current Myanmar Hydro-Electric Power Projects List," accessed May 6, 2017, http://www.oilseedcrops.org/2012/11/30/current-myanmar-hydro-electric-power-projects/.
38. "Irrawaddy Myitsone Dam," *International Rivers*, accessed May 6, 2017, https://www.internationalrivers.org/campaigns/irrawaddy-myitsone-dam-0.
39. Connor Bebb, "A Dry and Anxious North Awaits China's Giant, Unproven Water Transport Scheme," *Circle of Blue*, March 1, 2011, http://www.circleofblue.org/2011/world/a-dry-and-anxious-north-awaits-china%e2%80%99s-giant-unproven-water-transport-scheme/.
40. "Myanmar: International Hydropower Association," accessed June 30, 2017, https://www.hydropower.org/country-profiles/myanmar.
41. BP statistical review of world energy 2016.

42. "Timeline."
43. Ye Mon and Htoo Thant, "'Wait and See' for Myitsone Dam's Future," *The Myanmar Times*, accessed May 16, 2017, http://www.mmtimes.com/index.php/national-news/25721-wait-and-see-for-myitsone-dam-s-future.html.
44. "Current Status of Dam Projects on Burma's Salween River," *International Rivers*, accessed September 2, 2017, https://www.internationalrivers.org/resources/current-status-of-dam-projects-on-burma%E2%80%99s-salween-river-7867.
45. "Chinese Dam Incurs KIO Wrath," Institute for Defence Studies and Analyses, accessed May 8, 2017, http://www.idsa.in/TWIR/9_5_2008_KIO.
46. https://myanmarbiodiversity.org/wp-content/uploads/2016/06/Myanmar-Scoping-Study-Draft-Report.pdf
47. "Myanmar Wanbao Mining Copper," *Myanmar Wanbao Copper Mining Limited*, accessed May 5, 2017, http://www.myanmarwanbao.com.mm/.
48. Oil with Crude oil - proved reserves of India 5.675 billion bbl (1 January 2016 es) Crude oil – production 761,000 bbl/day (2015 est.) Natural gas - proved reserves 1.489 trillion cu m (1 January 2016 es) 30.4 billion cu m (2014 est.)
49. "UPDATE 1-China Firm Wins Myanmar Approval for $3 Bln Refinery," *Reuters*, April 5, 2016, http://www.reuters.com/article/china-myanmar-refinery-idUSL3N1782MS.
50. "Burma (Myanmar) - International - Analysis - U.S. Energy Information Administration (EIA)," accessed May 7, 2017, https://www.eia.gov/beta/international/analysis.cfm?iso=MMR.
51. http://china.aiddata.org/projects/35600
52. "Two Indian Firms Help China Ship Myanmar Gas over Land," *The Indian Express*, September 18, 2014, http://indianexpress.com/article/india/india-others/two-indian-firms-help-china-ship-myanmar-gas-over-land/.
53. https://www.ft.com/content/21d5f650-1e6a-11e7-a454-ab04428977f9
54. "China - International - Analysis - U.S. Energy Information Administration (EIA)," accessed August 23, 2017, https://www.eia.gov/beta/international/analysis.cfm?iso=CHN.
55. "PetroChina to Start New Refinery in Oct, Boost China Crude Imports," accessed August 23, 2017, http://in.reuters.com/article/petrochina-refinery-idINL4N19F31A.
56. "SIPRI Arms Transfers Database - Www.sipri.org," Page, accessed November 13, 2015, http://www.sipri.org/databases/armstransfers.
57. The Pyidaungsu Hluttaw, Myanmar's parliament, consists of 664 members, of which 75% of MPs are directly elected by voters, while the remaining 25% are military personnel appointed by the Defence Services' Commander-in-Chief. http://news.bbc.co.uk/1/hi/world/asia-pacific/7338815.stm
58. "Submarine Deal Steams into Choppy Waters," accessed August 24, 2017, http://www.nationmultimedia.com/news/national/30314763.
59. Prashanth Parameswaran, "Indonesia and China's AIIB," *The Diplomat*, accessed July 1, 2017, http://thediplomat.com/2016/07/indonesia-and-chinas-aiib/.
60. The U.S.-Singapore Partnership: A Critical Element of U.S. Engagement and Stability in the Asia-Pacific Lynn Kuok
61. Brunei established ties after Singapore. Dates of establishing ties with China as follows:

East Timor	20 May 02,	Brunei	30 Sep 91,	Singapore	03 Oct 90,
Thailand	01 Jul 75,	Philippines	09 Jun 75,	Malaysia	31 May 74,
Laos	25 Apr 61,	Cambodia	19 Jul 58,	Myanmar	08 Jun 50,
Indonesia	13 Apr 50,	Vietnam	18 Jan 50; (E Timor gained independence much later).		

62. Temasek Holdings (Private) Limited is a sovereign wealth fund of the Government of Singapore

63. "How China Rules the Waves," accessed April 24, 2017, https://ig.ft.com/sites/china-ports.
64. "Singapore, China Reaffirm 'Good and Warm' Relations," *Channel NewsAsia*, accessed July 1, 2017, http://www.channelnewsasia.com/news/singapore/singapore-china-reaffirm-good-and-warm-relations-7617246.
65. "China, Singapore Vow Trade Cooperation in Sign of Thaw," *Bloomberg.com*, June 12, 2017, https://www.bloomberg.com/news/articles/2017-06-12/china-singapore-vow-trade-cooperation-in-sign-of-warmer-ties.
66. Ralph Jennings, "Why Malaysia Stays Quiet About Its Claims In The South China Sea," *Forbes*, accessed July 3, 2017, http://www.forbes.com/sites/ralphjennings/2016/06/02/why-malaysia-stays-quiet-about-its-claims-in-the-disputed-south-china-sea/.
67. "Malaysia Cuts Defence Budget by 12%," *Jane's 360*, accessed July 3, 2017, http://www.janes.com/article/64867/malaysia-cuts-defence-budget-by-12.
68. "Why China Wants Malaysia on the Major-Port Radar," *South China Morning Post*, accessed May 26, 2017, http://www.scmp.com/week-asia/politics/article/2087402/can-china-really-deliver-malaysias-singapore-slayer.
69. "One Belt One Road in Malaysia: China's Strategic Enabler?," The Strategist, April 20, 2017, https://www.aspistrategist.org.au/one-belt-one-road-malaysia-chinas-strategic-enabler/.
70. "China Projects to Hit Singapore," *Nation, The Star Online*, accessed May 26, 2017, http://www.thestar.com.my/news/nation/2017/01/15/china-projects-to-hit-singapore-the-giant-republics-aggressive-investments-in-ports-and-rail-links-i/.
71. "Why China Wants Malaysia on the Major-Port Radar."
72. admin, "Malaysia to Build S$64 Billion Port with Support from China," *States Times Review*, January 11, 2017, http://statestimesreview.com/2017/01/11/malaysia-to-build-s64-billion-port-with-support-from-china/.
73. "One Belt One Road in Malaysia."
74. "China Projects to Hit Singapore," *Nation, The Star Online.*
75. admin, "Malaysia to Build S$64 Billion Port with Support from China."
76. "China Projects to Hit Singapore," *Nation, The Star Online.*
77. POCS, "Singapore-Kunming Rail Link Project to Sync with Master Plan on ASEAN Connectivity, One Vision One Identity One Community," *ASEAN, One Vision One Identity One Community*, August 12, 2011, http://asean.org/singapore-kunming-rail-link-project-to-sync-with-master-plan-on-asean-connectivity/.
78. "One Belt One Road in Malaysia."
79. "This $100 Billion Chinese-Made City Near Singapore is 'Scaring Everybody,'" *Bloomberg.com*, November 21, 2016, https://www.bloomberg.com/news/features/2016-11-21/-100-billion-chinese-made-city-near-singapore-scares-the-hell-out-of-everybody.

CHAPTER 9

THE STRATEGY FOR RESOURCES (Middle East, Africa, Mauritius, Seychelles, Australia and the Seabed)

'As to your entreaty to send one of your nationals to be accredited to my Celestial Court and to be in control of your country's trade with China, this request is contrary to all usage of my dynasty and cannot possibly be entertained.'[1] Thus, wrote Qing Emperor Qianlong in reply to Lord McCartney's mission, which was sent by England in 1793 to open up trade with China. The reply revealed that the emperor believed that China had very little to gain from trading with the world. In a role reversal, by 2014, China had overtaken the US as the world's largest trading nation in the world.[2] Cut to March 23, 2015, to the White Paper on the Belt and Road Initiative released at the Boao Forum—the indifference of Qianlong has given way to an exhortation to open up more. The White Paper repeats the word "opening up" 18 times in a manner that is hard to miss. So much has changed with China in two centuries.

While the previous two chapters have looked at access and foothold, one motivation for China to come to the Indian Ocean is its quest for resources. These resources include oil, natural gas, metals and minerals such as iron ore, copper, bauxite, nickel, tin, etc. For the Chinese industrial juggernaut to continue chugging, an assured supply of these essentials is a must. The Indian Ocean littorals not only supply many of these, but the IOR's safe sea lanes of communication ensure that trade from the littorals of the Atlantic and Indian Ocean traverses the Indian Ocean to arrive in China. These sea lanes through the Indian Ocean sometimes commence as far as South America since ships that are too large to cross the Panama Canal have to traverse via the Atlantic and IOR to China. For e.g. a VLCC from Venezuela or Colombia from where 7 per cent of China's oil imports are sourced, may have to travel 18400nm rounding the Cape Horn into the Pacific, whereas it is 4000nm shorter via the Atlantic, IOR and Malacca. 90 per cent of China's imported oil from South America traversed the IOR in Very Large Crude Carriers in 2016 (70 per cent VLCC, 20 per cent ULCC and Rest 10 per cent to be precise!). Quite similar is the case with the Brazilian ore destined for China in very large ore carriers whose very name is Chinamax[3] carriers, which at 400000DWT are twice the size of their predecessor, the capsize bulk carrier.

'Natural Resources have been a flashpoint between emerging and established powers', states Elizabeth Economy and Michael Levi, authors of the book *By All Means Necessary: How China's Resource Quest is Changing the World.*[4] In iron ore, China is the largest mover, being the top importer and producer.[5] In 2015, 70 per cent of it headed to China, of which 54 per cent went from Australia, whereas 20 per cent went from Brazil.[6] Its demand for aluminium, nickel, copper and zinc[7] is roughly half the world's demand.

China accounted for 23 per cent of the global energy demand in 2014, increasing it to 25 per cent by 2035.[8] China burns roughly half the world's coal.[9] Its environmental concerns are driving up its demand for natural gas at 8–10 per cent per year. The natural gas share in China's domestic usage will double to 11 per cent by 2035.[10] It is the third largest importer of LNG[11] and has gas deals with pipelines in place from Myanmar, Central Asia and Russia. It will be the world's largest net importer of energy by 2035.[12] The import dependence of oil is projected to rise from 59 per cent in 2014 to 76 per cent by 2035 and gas from 30 per cent in 2014 to 42 per cent in 2035.[13] Nearly eighty percent of that oil and thirty percent of LNG has traversed the Indian Ocean. Both in the case of oil as well as LNG, China's dependence on the IOR is only going to increase and not decrease in the times to come.

That must partially explain what drives its foray across the globe for energy resources. The need for energy, trade and opportunity for investment takes China to the Middle East, Australia and Africa, for which Mauritius and Seychelles have an envisaged role. This chapter describe some salient features of that foray.

Middle East–China Relations

Energy is a major factor in China's outlook towards the Middle East. The Middle East possesses 47 per cent of the global oil reserves and produces 75 per cent of the OPEC's oil.[14] The nature of the Middle East fields makes production cheapest at around $10/barrel, which is half the cost of the next cheap source.[15] The Middle East has, therefore, been important ever since China became a net importer of oil in 1993. As much as 51 per cent of China's oil imports in 2014 were from the Middle East.

Middle East is a politically volatile space, and due to its strategic importance has always had substantial US presence. With the rise of the US domestic shale production and greater worries about China's rise in the Pacific, the Middle East is a space from where US is pivoting away gradually. Sensing the drift of that pivot, China and Japan have recently established bases in Djibouti. The UK too has come back into the IOR and is establishing a base in Mina Salman in Bahrain after a gap of 40 years, when it vacated its last outpost, Maldives's Gan Island Airbase in 1976. China has incrementally normalised its presence, having conducted its anti-piracy missions in the IOR since 2008, and carried out a non-combatant evacuation operation in Libya in 2011 employing its frigate *Xuzhou* in a debut operation of such kind.

In its engagement with the Middle East, China seems to neatly package the relations into three separate tracks along the traditional divisions in the Middle East—that of the Arab League, Iran and Israel. Therefore, these three tracks are examined separately in the chapter. This historical division in the Middle East has religious and ethnic reasons at the core. The Arab League is predominantly Sunni Arab, led by Saudi Arabia, which follows the orthodox Salafi-Wahhabi strain of Islam. Racially, Iran is Persian and from an Islamic perspective, is also predominantly Shiite. In this context, there is also a third Turkic Hanafi strain of Islam, though not on the littorals of the IOR but spreads along the hinterlands reaching as far as Xinjiang where the East Turkistan Islamic Movement or ETIM has been on the boil in China. Xinjiang is a major concern, described as a 'core' issue politically by China. Xinjiang is also important from the OBOR perspective, since it is literally the gateway to the SREB towards Central Asia. So China's engagement in the Middle East has a bearing not only on resources but also on its domestic Islamic population.

The Middle East as a market for China is estimated to be worth $135 billion by 2020. Chinese investment in the Middle East stands at $230 billion USD. China announced investments worth $60 billion, from 2010–16. Some of them are the Light Rail in Mecca, the UAE-IOR pipeline, Bahrain Housing, Duqm Port, Railways in Oman, etc. The AIIB gave a loan of $1.7 billion in loan to Oman's Duqm port and the Oman railways.[16]

Arab League. Though China has established strong economic relations with individual nations such as Saudi Arabia, there is a vibrant China–Arab League

Forum through which China engages the Arab nations. The Arab League includes nations in West Asia, North Africa, Horn of Africa and the Comoros Islands. If one examines the littorals of the Indian Ocean, in the Middle East Region, all except Iran, Israel and Eritrea are part of the Arab League. Out of the 22 nations in the Arab League, China has established relations with all, commencing in 1956 when China supported Nasser of Egypt in nationalising the Suez Canal and the Aswan Dam. China set up the China-Arab States Cooperation Forum in 2004.

The economic mainstay of this relation is oil, with the Arab League states providing the highest amount of oil as a group, besides being the seventh biggest trading partner[17] to China. Over and above the BRI plan, China is 'establishing a "1+2+3" cooperation pattern (to take energy cooperation as the core (1), infrastructure construction and trade and investment facilitation as the two wings (2), and three high tech fields of nuclear energy, space and renewable energy as the three breakthrough emerging areas, through industrial cooperation (3)' (Refer Fig. 9.1).

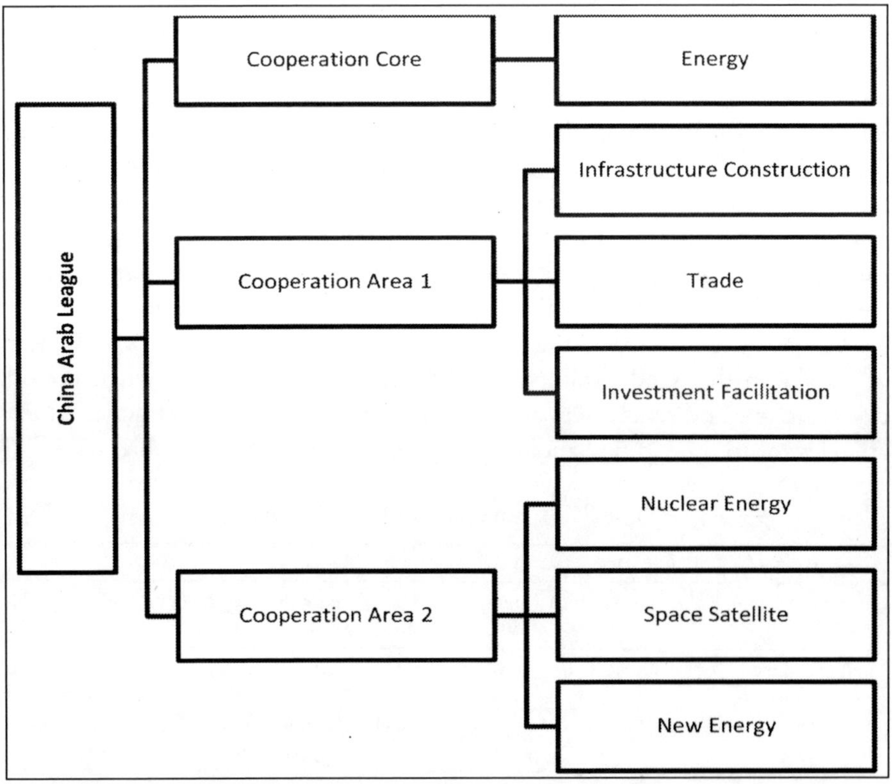

Figure 9.1. The Envisaged China-Arab League Structure of Relationship (China Arab Policy Paper)

China's Palestine policy supports a sovereign state with pre-1967 borders. The recent Chinese policy paper also states that the Middle East must remain a nuclear weapon-free zone.

In the field of financial cooperation, there is far more clarity in the envisaged relationship. China plans investments through 'equities and debts and mezzanine financing which is a hybrid of debt and equity, as well as direct investment and funds'.[18] Out of the Arab League, Saudi Arabia has been a special partner with whom it established military relations in the late 1980s with a supply of the nuclear-capable CSS2 IRBM missiles. This missile cooperation predated Saudi Arabia's recognition of the PRC over Taiwan and the establishment of diplomatic relations in the 1990s. This cooperation in missiles has to be seen in a wider canvas involving Pakistan, touted to own the 'Islamic' bomb, which is also a strong ally of China. Saudi Arabia also holds 21.19 per cent of the OPECs crude oil reserves.[19]

In 1999, Chinese President Jiang Zemin visited Riyadh. The visit was reciprocated by King Abdullah to Beijing in 2008. Cooperation in oil has progressed rapidly through CNPC investments in Saudi Arabia and Saudi Arabia's Aramco investments in China in the oil sector. Aramco investments were primarily focusing on making the refineries capable of taking the varieties of Saudi Oil. Some notable investments were in the Anning refinery, the Fujian refinery and the oil storage facility at Hainan. The former refines oil arriving by ship at the Kyaukphu port in the Rakhine Province of Myanmar, further transported to Yunnan by a pipeline. The investments also involved petroleum-related projects in China and metal industries, especially in aluminium. In early 2017 King Salman undertook a visit to Beijing where he signed a deal worth $65 billion.[20] The details of the deals are not yet fully known. Twenty MoUs have been signed in the oil sector including a discussion over the sale of a stake in the Saudi Aramco.[21] All of this comes at a time when the oil prices are low and renewables are getting popular. The list of refineries which are relevant to the China Saudi Oil Cooperation is placed in Table 9.1.

Table 9.1. China-Saudi Oil Investments

Refinery	Capacity	Firm	Status/Remarks
Caofeidian/Tianjin	240,000 bbl/d	Sinopec	Under construction and will be ready by 2020. Plans to process crude oil from Saudi Arabia
Anning/Yunnan	200,000 bbl/d	CNPC/ PetroChina	CNPC/PetroChina plans to process oil from Saudi Arabia and Kuwait via the crude oil pipeline from Myanmar; JV with Saudi Aramco (39 per cent) and Yuntianhua Group (10 per cent),
Yanbu refinery, Saudi Arabia	400,000 bbl/d	Sinopec	China purchased a 37.5 per cent stake and began processing heavy crude oils in 2015

China's engagement with the Middle East also has some regional political hues since it backs Bashar Al Assad in Syria and also backs Saudis against the Houthis who are backed by Iran.[22] One mega project outside Saudi Arabia is in the Omani port of Duqm, where $10.7 billion is likely to be invested in a power plant and a refinery. The refinery investment is estimated as $7 billion and will be a Kuwait–Oman joint project.[23] This port was built to compete with Port Jebel Ali in Dubai.[24] The firm Ninxia Arab Wanfang has been set up to implement the project, which in addition to the refinery will host steel, concrete, glass, aluminium, methanol and solar projects.[25] In China's overseas oil production, Iraq accounted for 26 per cent in 2013.

A study of Chinese interests in this area will be incomplete without touching its Belt and Road Initiative (BRI), which is the Chinese vision of its economic empire. The vision document for the Belt and Road Initiative cites the China-Arab States Cooperation Forum (CASCF) and the China-Gulf Cooperation Council Strategic Dialogue as formal avenues to push the BRI. In informal forums to push the BRI, the China Arab Expo has been cited. The latter is a Chinese initiative, with 57 Islamic and Arabian countries participating, primarily from the Arab League.[26]

Iran. China established diplomatic relations with Iran in 1971. The anti-Soviet outlook of both nations during that period helped the growth of this relation. However, the Shah of Iran was also wary of China due to his worries about the spread of communism. He was assuaged when China ceased its support to the Marxist movements in the Gulf region like the Popular Front for the Liberation of Oman.[27] The Islamic revolution in Iran which was recognised by China coincided with China's opening up phase post-Mao. Oil and gas now remains the core of the relationship. Iran has the fourth largest reserve of oil and the second largest reserve of natural gas.[28] As the largest net importer of oil and a rising importer of gas, this relation with an untapped energy giant is valuable to China. So far the US sanctions had stymied the exploration and production of these reserves. With the Iran deal and the P5+1 initiative of the Joint Comprehensive Plan of Action (JCPOA), China has become free to invest in developing these reserves in a symbiotic relationship. China's surplus capital infrastructure capacity and energy needs and the Iranian need for investments have been complementary. The SINOPEC and CNPC are therefore highly active in Iran.

China is Iran's biggest trading partner. Despite having the world's second-largest gas reserves, Iran doesn't have an LNG export facility and hence its natural gas markets are limited to the existing pipelines. Hence, unless pipelines that connect to China or LNG facilities are created, China may not be able to tap this resource. However, it may be able to use equity to sell the gas locally or swap it with the Central Asian states with whom it has existing ties in the energy sector. The CNPC partnered with Total to sign a preliminary agreement on Phase 11 of the South Pars gas field in May 17 which is the world's largest gas field.[29]

China has developed several new oil fields in Iran as listed in Table 9.2.

Table 9.2. Fields in Iran being Developed by China

Project	Developer	Plateau output (000 b/d)	Est. plateau year
Yadavaran phase 1	Sinopec	85	2016
Yadavaran phase 2	Sinopec	95	2019-20
Yadavaran phase 3	Sinopec	120	post 2020
North Azadegan phase 1	CNPC	75	2016-17
North Azadegan phase 2	CNPC	75	2019

The Yadavaran, South Azadegan, and Forouzan fields are currently producing crude oil, but below their plateau levels. CNPC is China National Petroleum Corporation. PEDCO is PetroIran Development Company. Sinopec is China Petroleum & C

China sees political scope in this relation as Iran is not an ally of the United States. China also has strong military relations with Iran. Around the time it delivered the CCS2 IRBMs to Saudi Arabia, it also supplied missiles to Iran in 1986. China has also allegedly assisted Iran with the technology to make missiles. There is a talk of sale of fighter jets to Iran by China. China and Iran also conducted a joint naval drill in the waters of the Persian Gulf. China has also helped Iran re-develop its nuclear facilities in accordance with the nuclear deal. Accordingly, the heavy water reactor in Arak will be reconfigured so as not to yield weapon-grade plutonium through Chinese help.

Though China joined the sanctions in 2010, it had been traditionally wary of sanctions and argued for negotiations in lieu. It also worked hard to see that the sanctions end and negotiations take place.[30] Overall, the deal legitimised the China–Iran relations giving a head start over the rest of the world.

The Chinese have played their cards carefully avoiding antagonising anyone in the strategically important Middle East, which, according to the *Economist*, is the "Great China (Oil) Well".[31.] It is observed that China has carefully avoided taking any sides in the Middle East quagmire. This had lead Obama to call the Chinese as "free riders" over the US security initiatives in the Middle East. China has increased its trade by 600 per cent in the last decade with the Middle East. Today, it stands at $230 billion.

Energy is a prime driver of the Sino-Iran relations with oil occupying 80 per cent of the Chinese imports from Iran. In the shadow of the deal, China has already ramped up buying from Iran according to the *Wall Street Journal.*[32] In 2011, the highest importer of Iranian oil was the EU. Post-sanctions, this top spot in 2014 was occupied by China, closely followed by India and Japan. Iran currently wants to ramp up its oil production from 3 billion barrels to 6 billion barrels per day by 2020, a figure higher than its pre-sanction days. This is estimated to require an investment of up to a 100bn USD,[33] a capital that only a few countries like China or Japan can infuse. Japan is also a country that relies heavily on Iranian oil. It is likely that these two Asian sources could be tapped by Iran to fund its expansion to meet its 2020 targets.

Iran is a partner in the Asian Infrastructure Investment Bank (AIIB) and may be brought into the Shanghai Cooperation Organization (SCO) at some point in the future.

The Iran–China cooperation, historically, has covered a wide gamut from chemical weapons to missiles to nuclear cooperation. The article '*Nuclear Pipeline*'[34] *in the journal Foreign Affairs* explains the nuclear angle to the cooperation.

From an Islamic perspective, the vast majority of Chinese Muslims are Sunnis. The remainder are spread across other strains of Islam with a very limited number of Shias, including in Xinjiang. Iran did play the religious card raising the Xinjiang issue when China joined the sanctions. Overall, post-P5+1 deal with Iran, the China–Iran Relations, which hitherto were retarded by sanctions, have gained a fillip. It gives it a head start over the rest of the world vis-à-vis Iran. All indications from both Iran and the USA are that the deal is just an exception to an otherwise difficult bilateral relationship which will maintain the status quo. President Donald Trump has tried to roll back that deal, yielding China a strategic space in Iran. With no baggage of contemporary history of Middle East politics, China has managed to balance the entire spectrum of conflict in the Middle East very well, antagonising none. The painfully crafted Iran deal is now on a tenuous ground, as a result of the Trump administration's approach to the deal. This has opened up the old rivalries of the Middle East. The recent episode where Qatar was isolated in the Gulf Cooperation Council is one ripple of the US policy. In the Indian Ocean this was felt as near as the Maldives which aligned itself with Saudi Arabia, giving the extent of that ripple. China, on the other hand, has managed its relations engaging everyone and avoiding taking positions under the US umbrella. While Qatar is its largest supplier of gas, Saudi Arabia is the largest supplier oil and Iran is a fast growing source of oil and destination of investments where China is in a pole position. It balances all three astutely.

Israel. The third track of the Middle East Policy is Israel. Israel–China official relations commenced in 1992. China had a deep reluctance in establishing relations with Israel—much like India—and continued a very subdued relationship. China has committed to an investment of $10 billion in the past three years in critical infrastructure like the Ashdod Port in the Med-Red Railway line, and a Metro in Tel Aviv, besides investments in Israel's high-tech sector. China has absorbed several defence technologies ex-Israel, like the Lavi Jet. The SIPRI has on record the transfer of the Harpy ARM. The US has been exerting pressure to cancel many of the transfers.[35] Chinese military leaders like Admiral Wu Shengli have visited Israel. A notable feature is that Israel's Ambassador to China since 2013 has been a veteran from the military[36] which shows a renewed thrust in this security relationship.

Energy Transportation: Options in the IOR. China by 2035 will consume 25 per cent of the global energy. China is already the top importer of oil and its import dependence will only increase over time. Eighty percent of its oil originates from the IOR or traverses the IOR. The sources of its crude oil imports are placed in Figure 9.2. According to an article from the Oxford Institute of Energy Studies,[37] the trends in China's share of oil imports from the Middle East, the Former Soviet Union (FSU), South America and Africa are increasing, whereas the share of Asia Pacific and North America is decreasing (refer Figure 9.3). The country-wise trend indicates that imports from Iran, Iraq and Russia have been on the rise (Refer Figure 9.4). This trend reiterates a higher dependence on the IOR in the future.

Its import of LNG is also increasing rapidly with over 30 per cent of it from, or traversing the IOR. The sources of LNG are shown in Figure 9.5. Since energy is a major factor in its dependence on the IOR, some details of its transportation including the options of pipelines, both for oil as well as for gas, by China, is discussed in this section.

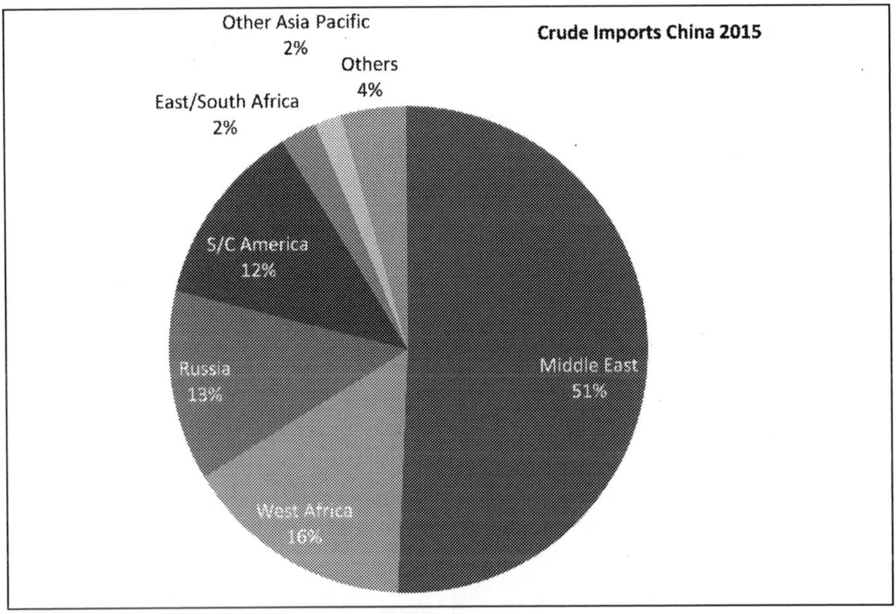

Figure 9.2. Crude oil imports into China 2015
(*Source*: BP Statistical Review of World Energy 2016)

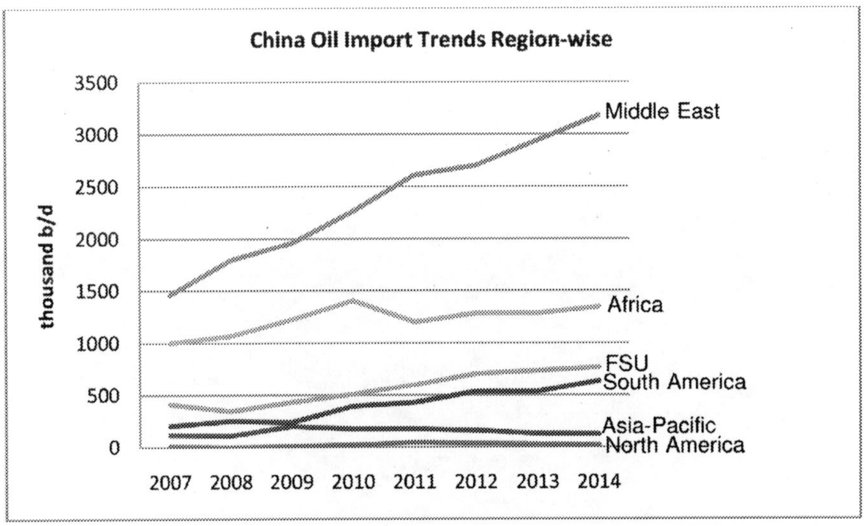

Figure 9.3. The Historical Trends in Oil Import to China-Region-wise
(*Source*: Oxford Institute for Energy Studies)

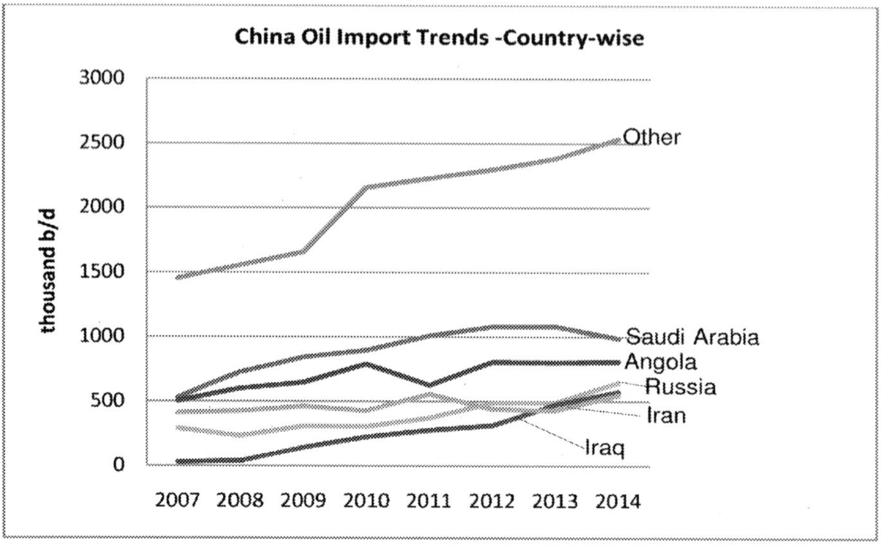

Figure 9.4. The Historical Trends in Oil Import to China from Select Countries
(*Source*: Oxford Institute for Energy Studies)

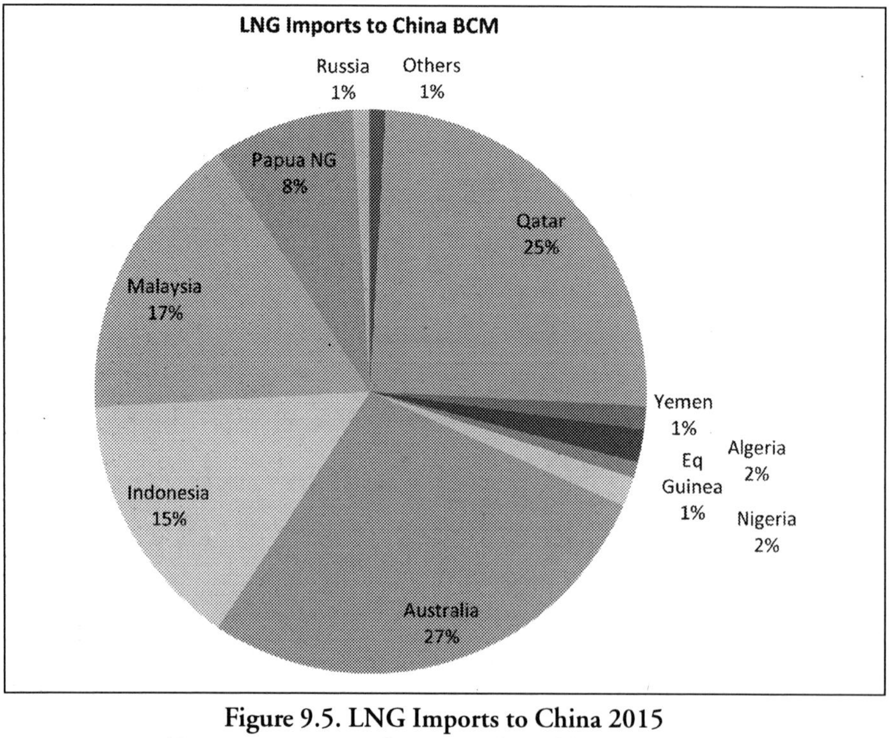

Figure 9.5. LNG Imports to China 2015
(*Source*: BP Statistical Review of World Energy 2016)

China's Pipeline Deals: Oil

Internally, China has a robust network of pipelines for oil and gas. It also has been incrementally building transnational pipelines for oil and gas.

- **The Kazakhstan Line**. In 2006, China and its neighbour Kazakhstan commenced transporting Kazakh oil to China through the Kazmunay Gas (KMG)–CNPC pipeline. This is the Atyrau-Alashankou pipeline which commences from the Caspian Sea. From Atasu in Central Kazakhstan, the pipeline doubles its capacity to 400,000bbl/d.[38] This capacity may increase further in the future. Russia has a swap deal with Kazakhstan to transfer gas from the Western Siberian fields to China through this pipeline.[39]
- **The Russian Oil Pipe Line.** The Eastern Siberia-Pacific Ocean (ESPO) was originally a Russian Pipeline from Taishet in Siberia to serve the Asian countries from its Pacific coast terminating at Kozmino. There is a 597km branch leading to China from the Skovorodino Refinery to the Daqing oil production centre in China.[40] This line has a capacity of 300000bbl/d in its branch to China.[41] The contract between Russia and China is for 20 years. It is reported that China gave a loan of $25 billion to Trasneft and Rosneft in return. There is a plan in place to increase the capacity of this line to 1.6mn bbl/d by 2020. From the Chinese side, the CNPC manages the pipeline.[42]
- **The Myanmar Line**. In its south-western region, there is a twin oil and gas pipeline through Myanmar. This is a transit line to bypass Malacca through which 80 per cent of the Chinese import traverses. This has a capacity of 440000 bbl/d.[43] The Middle Eastern crude imports, from Saudi Arabia and Kuwait, can be sent to the south-western regions of China using this line. China has also built a refinery in Anning which has a capacity of 200000bbl/d.[44] This refinery is a JV with Saudi Aramco. The pipeline commences at Maday Island, near Kyuakphyu, as described in the previous chapter. It crosses over to Yunnan at Ruili and terminates at Kunming, traversing 771km. This was built at a cost of $1.5 billion. This line has separate gas and oil pipelines.

Table 9.3. Piped Oil vs. Oil Import Trends of China

Year	Production	Consumption	Import	Pipeline	Shipborne
2013/4	4.6mn barrels per day[45]	10.7 mnbbl/d[46]	6.2mn bbl/d[47]	Kazakh -400000bbl/d Russian-300000bbl/d Myanmarese-440000bbl/d Total-1130000bbl/d (1.13mn bbl/d) 5.07million bbl/d[48]	
2035 (BP)	5.6mn barrels/day[49]	18.4mn bbl/d	Increases to 76% dependence import[50]	More than doubles to 2.43mn bbls/d by 2020, Russian line 1.6mnbbl/d[51]	Will continue to increase

Piped Oil Imports to China Versus Imports

The trend of oil import is projected to rise from 59 per cent in 2014 to 76 per cent in 2035. The gas import will rise from under 30 per cent to 42 per cent in 2035. As a result of this trend, the oil imports will continue to play a major role in the region and the piped capacity may not meet the requirements, thus increasing pressure on the sea lanes of communication.

Gas Status

China is in the process of replacing coal with gas for its power plants to reduce the coal intake. The production of gas in China is 4.4 tcf[52] and consumption was 5.7[53]tcf in 2013. There was an import of 1.8tcf that year.[54] Of this, 1133bcf/y was through pipelines.[55] The major production centres of gas are in western China. The consumers are in the east, along the coast. To meet this requirement there is an East West gas pipeline in China. The CNPC is the key operator of the gas pipelines in China. The following pipelines to China are significant:

- **The Central Asian Gas Pipeline (CAGP).** The CAGP lifts gas in three parallel lines from Turkmenistan, Uzbekistan and Kazakhstan before terminating at Khorgos in Xinjiang. Its capacity is 1.9tcf/y.[56] This links internally with the three East West lines. The China and Turkmenistan gas deal will touch 2.3tcf/y by 2020 from the current 1.4tcf/y. This is to cater to the emerging Galkynysh field, which incidentally is the likely source of the TAPI pipeline also.
- **Myanmar Gas.** The pipeline was a logical extension of the gas deal in 2005 between Petrochina and the Myanmarese government for a 30-year gas purchase deal. This also involves the CNPC deal in 2008 with Daewoo which was extracting gas from the Shwe offshore block

A1. This pipeline is longer than the oil line and extends further from Kunming to reach the neighbouring provinces of Guizhou and Guangxi, traversing 2806km. The investment in this pipeline is $1.04 billion. The management of the pipelines is done jointly by the CNPC and the Myanmar Oil and Gas Enterprise. The China Myanmar line is presently operational from Shwe gas fields. It has a total capacity of 420bcf/y. However, this line is underutilised now and will be ramped up, based on production in the Myanmar fields. This line also supplies gas to Myanmar.

- **The Russia-China Gas Deal.** China and Russia have also signed a 1.3tcf/y deal from the East Siberian gas fields for 30 years at a cost of $400 billion.[57] There is a separate smaller deal for 1.1bcf/y from the Western Siberian field which is in the planning stage.[58]

LNG Options. Gas can be transported via pipelines as well as LNG (liquefied natural gas). The LNG is seaborne trade and once filled in ships can be transported via sea. However, the liquefaction facility is required at the export end and regasification facilities are required at the import end. Therefore, it has lesser geographic restrictions yielding greater trading opportunities. Despite being a late entrant, coming in 2006 to the LNG field, China has 12 LNG terminals with 8 under construction. In 2014, China imported 957bcf[59] of LNG, which is half their import. China's regasification capacity in 2014 was 1.9tcf/y.[60] The source and destination being more rigidly knit, regasification terminals in China are to be matched with the liquefaction capacity at source such as Australia, Indonesia, Malaysia and Qatar. China is also building floating regasification and storage terminals. The CNOOC is the major player in this field. Private players are making inroads.

Gas Status: Imports versus Piped Capacity

Impact of Pipelines for Oil and Gas Transportation. Both in the case of oil as well as gas, there are pipelines in place or are being planned. Roughly 10 per cent of oil imports arrived China through pipelines in 2014. This will only marginally improve to around 13 per cent by 2035 with the available data on pipelines. Hence, reliance on seaborne transportation of oil will remain and increase in absolute terms. In the case of gas, roughly 50 per cent imports happened through pipelines in 2014. The rest 50 per cent was imported as LNG via ships. With the available data, as the imports rise by 2035, the pipeline share will drop to one-fourth and the LNG share will proportionally increase.

Table 9.4. Gas to China Imports vs. Pipeline (tcf-trillion cubic feet)

Year	*Production*	*Consumption*	*Import*	*Pipeline*	*LNG*	*Total Imp. Capacity (LNG+Pipelines)*
2013/4	4.4 tcf	5.7tcf	1.8tcf/y	CAGP: 1.9tcf/y Myanmar: 420bcf/y Total: 2.320tcf/y	RGCap: 1.9tcf/y Import: 957bcf/14	4.2tcf/y
2035[61]	NA	193% increase in demand predicted[62] 16.7tcf/y	Increases from 30% to 42% (7tcf)	Russian line: 2.4tcf/y, Total: 4.72tcf/y	RG Cap: 1.9 tcf/y New Capacity Not Available	Minimum 6.62 tcf/y In 2035 their piped capacity as a share of imports will decrease, increasing the share of LNG

Source: EIA Country Analysis, China and BP Energy Outlook, 2017.

An important factor as the source of energy is the routing options of oil and gas. The Pacific Ocean, where China is situated, is three times as large as the Atlantic and Indian Oceans at the equator. This implies that shipping from the Atlantic Coast of the Americas has the option of heading west to China through the Indian Ocean route, either taking the Suez Canal or rounding the Cape of Good Hope, depending on the size of the ship.

From a routing perspective, that opens up two major routes that run through the IOR. One is from the Atlantic littorals to China rounding the Cape from the south and another from the north—ex-Suez Canal/Middle East/East Africa to China. The latter converge at Dondra Head in Sri Lanka before proceeding east.

From the Indian Ocean to the Pacific, the routes are through the straits of Malacca, Sunda, Lombok or Ombai Wetar. A vessel that rounds the Cape of Good Hope, will find the Sunda Straits marginally shorter than Malacca while traversing to China. However, from the Dondra Head in Sri Lanka, Malacca is the shortest route to the Chinese coast followed by Sunda, Lombok and Ombai Wetar. The straits too differ in capabilities, with Ombei Wetar being most suitable for navigation including ULCCs and submarines, and the Lombok Straits too suitable for ULCCs.

Though the Malacca Straits offer the shortest route, they have a depth limitation because of which submarines cannot dive and ships of size beyond the Malacca Max—which is a VLCC with a displacement around 300000 dwt—cannot traverse.

Due to such factors of geography and distances involved, approximately around 80 per cent of Chinese oil traverses the Indian Ocean. This is one major factor that leads to its concerns about access through Malacca and the South China Sea. A very small part of this oil is now being taken through Myanmar. Yet, these terrestrial options are costlier than tankers. The cost of transportation of oil per barrel per 1000km is $0.163 by tanker, $0.793 by pipeline and $7.19 by train;[63] the land route being nearly 70 times the sea route. Economies of scale are highly in favour of sea transportation. A ULCC will need a whopping 20000 trucks or 200 trains to evacuate its cargo. This is true even in case of containerised commodities. An 18000 TEU Triple E container ship, which is becoming industry standard, may require a 100km convoy of trucks to evacuate that cargo.

The Kyaukpyu port which supplies refineries in Kunming, therefore, is indeed an expensive proposition when compared to the transportation cost through Malacca and subsequent haulage by pipelines or rail from the Chinese coast to arrive at the same destination. Yet it offers an alternative along with equity gas and oil investment in Myanmar by China which anyway requires a pipeline to Yunnan. The Gwadar–Kashgar line is not discussed since in the short term there are no plans for pipelines or rail there when considering factors discussed in the previous chapters. The pipeline option through Khunjerab is also a highly challenging one, since the track rises to the 4693m high Khunjerab Pass on the Sino-Pak border through treacherous terrain prone to landslides and harsh weather, whereas Muse-Ruili, a crossover point from Myanmar to China, is at a comfortable 777m. It is possibly due to these multiple reasons that a pipeline option is not planned in the CPEC.

Overall, the Chinese oil and gas pipeline deals may barely keep pace with the demand and import dependence due to a large increase in demand by 2035. In this matter, the oil pipelines lag behind gas pipelines in an effort to catch up with the imports. This leads to China's increased dependence on the sealanes of communication for both oil and LNG for the future.

The changes in the field of energy—characterised recently by a rise of shale and subsequently with the rise of renewables, have taken some sheen off oil. This has impacted the oil economies and affected the politics centred on oil. The Middle East oil economies have commenced recalibrating themselves to these changes. The sale of stakes in Aramco of Saudi Arabia and recent investments in East Asia are part of a change to look beyond oil. Renewables are still on a trickle, yet it is the fastest growing fuel source and by 2035, half the increase will be Nuclear, Hydro and Renewables in a process of decarbonising fuels.[64] From 85 per cent of the global share of primary energy, it will drop to

75 per cent by 2035.[65] The natural gas growth is higher than oil and coal and the LNG market may get integrated. As China is the largest consumer of energy, shifts in the domestic trends there have an impact on global energy trends. The BP 2017 Energy Outlook predicts the Chinese energy demand to slow to 2 per cent from a scorching 6 per cent clocked in the last 20 years.[66] The reasons behind this are a slower economic growth and the shift of economy from energy-intense manufacturing industries to services and lighter industries. China's energy intensity is expected to decline faster than expected, equalling US standards by 2035.[67] Natural gas, nuclear and non-fossil fuels are growing fast in the mix. This will mostly displace coal use, which will plateau and fall to 45 per cent by 2035 from the current two-third.[68]

Coal. China is self-sufficient in coal. However, it imports coal for its coastal power plants. China imports around 360 million short tonnes of coal, compared to its 4 billion consumption. This is imported from Australia and Indonesia and therefore does not route via IOR.

Metals and Minerals. Metals are critical commodities in the global economy and their consumption is a bell weather of an economy. They can be broadly divided into base metals and noble metals. In base metals, there are ferrous (iron) and non-ferrous metals like copper, nickel and zinc. Noble metals are gold, platinum, silver, rhodium, iridium and palladium. China is the top importer of metals consuming 46 per cent of the global production. China is also the top producer of a whopping 27 different elements or element groups of economic value when most nations lead the production of one or two elements, if at all they lead. The nearest to China in the domination of element production is Australia which is a top producer of 4 elements.[69] The discernible trend in the metal market is a shift of centre of consumption from the West to East, towards the Asia Pacific. Overall, the Chinese demand has been decreasing since the economy is shifting gears to services. Another global trend is that production centres are shifting from the developed North to the developing South. This will demand new lines of communications, critical infrastructure and connectivity.

Coming to rare earths which are important for modern industries, China controls 95 per cent of the rare earth market. It has the largest deposits and it is the largest producer of rare earths. In the case of top four metals, the top iron-ore-producing country is China, whose share is about half of the world's production. China is also the top consumer of that iron ore. The largest producer of aluminium is China. China consumes about half of the world's refined nickel and copper, but it is not a large producer of both these metals. China is also the top producer of gold, tin and bismuth.

China in Africa

To China, Africa is an important continent for resources and markets. Zheng He, the Chinese Admiral in his historic voyages had also visited Africa and had interestingly shipped a giraffe back to China as a gift to his emperor. He convinced the emperor that it was a mythical unicorn which was symbol of his greatness. To recall that connection, a statue of Zheng He has been inaugurated at the Mombassa Railway station which is the seaward terminal of the Chinese-built railway. In the modern period, China held a socialist appeal to the African nations as they emerged out of imperialism. The TAZARA rail line from Zambia is a vestige of that political relationship. There is a substantial Chinese diaspora in Africa. China has diplomatic relations with most African nations except Burkina Faso and Swaziland which recognise Taiwan.

China is Africa's largest trading partner. Oil, metals and minerals and trade are the major drivers of its relations with Africa. China imports over 14 per cent of its oil from Africa and it ranks after Middle East as the highest supplier of crude to China. Angola has been one of China's primary sources of crude oil. The two other significant suppliers of oil from Africa are South Sudan and Congo.

Relations between China and Africa are steered by the Forum on China-Africa Cooperation (FOCAC) which is a ministerial body formed by the nations. The China–Africa trade has been on the rise and in 2009 China surpassed the US as Africa's top trading partner. Africa mainly exports raw material to China and imports finished products from China in a typical colonial trade. However, in case of trade with China, this is ironically true of even a developed nation like Australia.

China has a special purpose fund named the China-Africa Development Fund, over and above the traditional banks facilitating Chinese business and investment in Africa such as the China EXIM bank, China Development Bank, Peoples Bank of China, ICBC, etc. The AIIB has Egypt and South Africa as its founding members and has plans to fund projects in Africa. In the period 2000–2014, the Chinese loans to Africa were of the order of $86 billion[70] and naturally it went to the countries from where it imports oil – Angola, Congo and South Sudan, besides Ethiopia and Kenya.

A major feature in China's projects in Africa is the connectivity of the landlocked states to the ports, the creation of new ports and upgrading of railway lines—particularly, the ones that eases connectivity from the ports to the hinterland.

One such port is the Lamu Port in Kenya, which is the seaward terminal of the Lamu Port-South Sudan-Ethiopia-Transport (LAPSSET) Corridor. LAPSSET is a regional project between the countries of Ethiopia, Kenya and South Sudan with an aim of linking them to each other and to their neighbours in eastern Africa. There are rail projects, port, airport, pipeline, etc., which are part of that project. Three berths will be completed by the China Communication Construction Company by the year 2020 at $480 million.[71] The funding of this project is a part of the LAPSSET corridor.

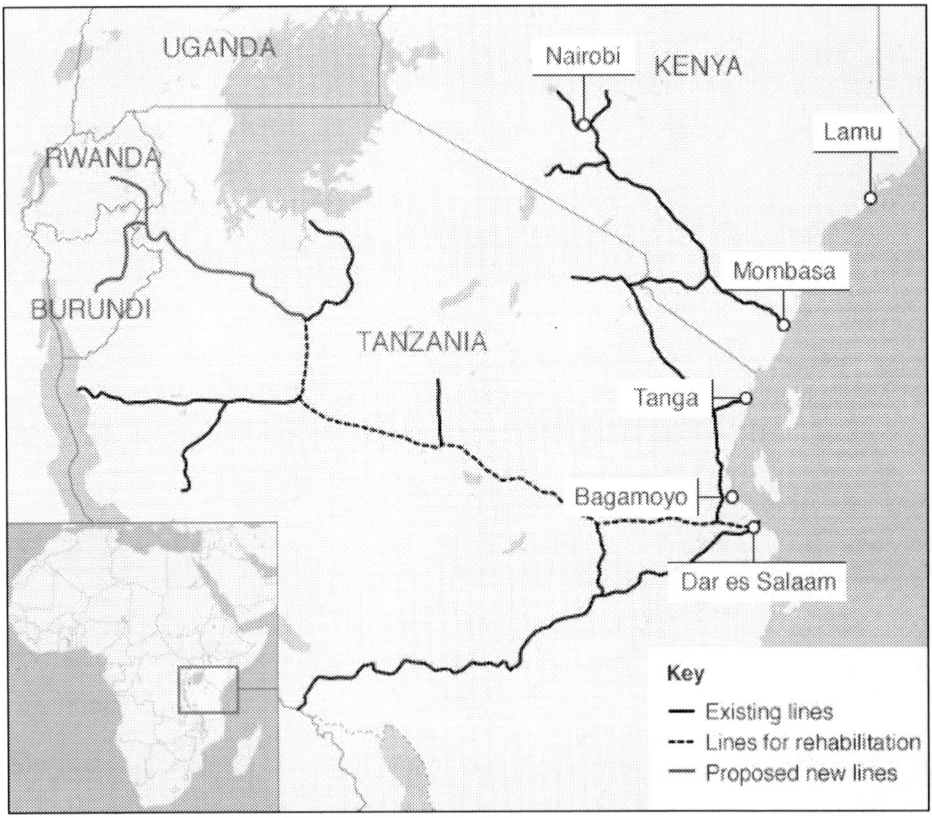

Figure 9.6. Select Port and Rail Projects in Africa
(*Source:* http://www.bbc.com/news/world-africa-27368877)

The Bagomayo Port in Tanzania at $10 billion[72] is probably the highest-ever investment by China in a single project. Its contours are therefore important to understand. It is designed to handle a cargo of 20 mnteu/year. Designed as Africa's largest port, its investors are the China Merchants Holdings International (CMHI) and Oman's State General Reserve Fund (SGRF). It will be a modern large port in 800 ha, supporting infrastructure such as rail and road, and will house a 1,700 ha industrial park. It has a one km-long quay with two container berths each approximately 300 m, a 220 m ro-ro berth, one 200m auxiliary berth. It is planned with depths alongside ranging from 14–15 m.

An important project in Africa from the security perspective is China's investment in Djibouti. China is not only building a port but also a base in Djibouti, adjacent to the Doraleh Multipurpose Port in the Gulf of Tadjoura. China Merchant Holding is a shareholder in this venture as well as in the adjacent Port de Djibouti S.A. The Doraleh Port has six 200m berths with 16–18 m depth alongside. Planned on 690 hectares of land, it has terminals for containers, general cargo, bulk terminal and vehicles. It is capable of handling Capesize vessels of (<100,000 DWT)[73]. One of the berths will be for the Chinese Navy. It was built by the China State Construction Engineering Corporation (CSCEC) in less than three years and inaugurated in May 2017. The port will connect landlocked Ethiopia to sea via Djibouti. Djibouti already handles 95 per cent[74] of the seaborne trade of Ethiopia and the investment in Ethiopia Djibouti Rail will complement this port investment.

Linked to the port projects are the railway projects being carried out by China. Africa did not have standard gauge railway lines till recently. From 2004 to 2014, the African nations borrowed $10 billion for railways.[75] One of the oldest projects in Africa was the Tanzania Zambia Rail[76] made with Chinese assistance in 1976. This 1860km rail line was planned to link Kapiri Mposhi in Zambia to Dar-es-Salaam in the Indian Ocean bypassing the apartheid states. The aim of the rail was economic—to carry resources like copper out of Zambia—but it also had political overtones regarding Third World cooperation, quite different from the debates of the day. This was a cape gauge rail unique to the region, marginally wider than the metre gauge popular in Africa.

China has presently funded and built the Standard Gauge Railway project in Kenya amounting to $ 3.8 billion. The first phase connects the Kenyan capital of Nairobi to Mombasa which is a port in the Indian Ocean. This is part of a seven-country network planned in Africa involving Uganda, Congo,

Rwanda, Burundi, South Sudan and Ethiopia.[77] This is the biggest infrastructure investment in Kenya after independence which cuts the travel time between the capital and the port city by half. The Mombasa railway station, as the *New York Times* reported, has a Zheng He statue to commemorate his visit to Africa.[78] The first train was inaugurated on this line in May 2017.

While the Naval Base in Djibouti has been a cynosure for analysts, there is a rail line that connects the landlocked Ethiopia to that port. The Ethiopia Djibouti Rail at $4 billion connects Addis Ababa, the capital of Ethiopia, to Djibouti. Like the SGR in Kenya, this line replaces an older Ethio-Djibouti metre gauge line. This is a 756km rail line, whereas the SGR in Kenya is a 485km line. A portion of this was Africa's first standard gauge rail line inaugurated in 2016.[79] There are 15 landlocked countries in Africa which need access to oceans, locking 400mn people[80]. Such a factor makes projects such as these connecting hinterlands to ports an attractive proposition in Africa.

There is a Khartoum Port Sudan rail line which is a $1.5 billion project covering 782km. There is also the shorter 187 km Abuja–Kaduna Railway in Nigeria which costs $874 million.

One of the most strategic investments by China in Africa is in Namibia. The China General Nuclear has invested in the Husab Uranium Mine worth $4.6 billion.[81] Here, China owns a 90 per cent stake against a 10 per cent Namibian stake.[82] China is also involved in building a port in the Walvis Bay[83] in Namibia. That will give it a foothold in the Atlantic, through which the South American trade, especially for oil and ore, is routed.

Investments in Africa are like those in most other regions in terms of critical infrastructure. China also invests in extractive industries from oil, copper to uranium. Not all of them have been successful. A notable setback was the Zambia Mines which faced hurdles from locals. Financing plans, labour, displacement and environment have been the major criticisms of Chinese investment in Africa. China is now being emboldened as it is in the Middle East to take a position on the region's political events. Its first base in Djibouti augurs in this direction. Off the strategic horn of Africa, the Djibouti base will assist China in its anti-piracy patrols, besides having a base and a port next to one of the world's crucial chokepoints.

Elizabeth Economy sums this up well when she says, 'It is an urgent synergetic act of the state and the private actors in a nationalist fashion that benefits China'.[84]

Seychelles and Mauritius

Seychelles is a thinly populated 115 island archipelago in the Indian Ocean between the African Coast and India, north-east of Madagascar. It was under British rule and became independent in 1976. In 1993, single-party rule led by President France-Albert Rene came to an end and a new constitution came into being and free elections held. It has a GDP PPP of $2.608 billion (2016 est.)[85] and its main source of income is tourism. It was nonaligned during the Cold War, yet used to allow warships to regularly dock in its ports. Seychelles simultaneously promises support to both China as well as India in an astute balancing act. In 2011, there were reports about a Chinese base in Seychelles which according to open-source Indian government assessments, does not exist.[86] In December 2016, the Seychelles President promised the Assumption Island to India for a base and a setting up of a radar chain.[87] Seychelles has acquired ships and aircraft from both India as well as China. This is a classic way in which smaller nations are hedging by developing relations with India and China simultaneously.

The China–Mauritius relations officially commenced in 1972 and have been on an upswing after Chinese President Hu Jintao visited Mauritius in 2009. There are people of Chinese descent in Mauritius called Sino-Mauritians who form 3 per cent of the population and are engaged in trade.

China provided a concessionary loan of $260 million for the Sir Seewoosagur Ramgoolam (SSR) International Airport from the China Exim Bank. It has also financed stadiums, bridges, housing and activity centres, developing soft power. China has invested in Mauritius for an amount of $750 million for the 521-acre Jinfei Special Economic Zone which is yet to take off even after 10 years of investment.[88] This was intended as a Chinese commercial staging post for Africa.

Apart from the investments per se, China is trying to use Mauritius as a financial staging post for its projects in Africa which are worth $60 billion of the Chinese investments. This is since Mauritius ranks very high in terms of ease of doing business. The Chinese high net worth individuals could use Mauritius to invest in the emerging economies easily from there. In 2016 the Bank of China obtained a license for banking operations in Mauritius.[89] That such a Chinese step comes at a time when India has decided to tighten the Mauritius financial route, due to entirely domestic reasons, can swing that nation into a Chinese orbit. The India-Mauritius Avoidance of Double Tax Treaty was amended in 2016 where the capital gains of the investors in India will be taxable from April 2017. This could have ramifications as it accounted for 30 per cent FDI to India and has been a major source of revenue for Mauritius at 12.3 per cent of the GDP.[90]

Tourism, textiles and fishing are a major area of China–Mauritius cooperation. In 2016, China signed an MoU[91] for writing off of debt, setting up an Overseas Cultural Centre in Mauritius, for tourism, setting up a multipurpose sports complex of Olympic standards at Saint Pierre, donation of a fleet of 30 semi-floor buses, a feasibility study on the Mauritius-China Free Trade Agreement and setting up of a fishing port at Bain des Dames. China also provides technical expertise in the agricultural sector to encourage bio-farming and in setting up projects for the desalination of seawater.

Chinese Foreign Minister Wang Yi's words sum up the policy.[92] He said, "China will advance connection in two fields, explore expansion in two sectors and deepen cooperation in two aspects with Mauritius".

- The two fields are a link to Africa and synergising bilaterally, plans for development.
- The two sectors are a Westwards Gateway to Africa and making Mauritius a financial hub, and to look eastwards to the Indian Ocean as a part of the Maritime Silk Road.
- The two aspects are about increasing bilateral exchanges as well as aligning together for international affairs and the UN.

Mauritius has claims to the Chagos archipelago which includes the Diego Garcia and a case is in progress at the international courts over the sovereignty and lease of the island from the UK to the USA. As this relation progresses, the Chinese position on this will be a key determinant as there is a sense of quid pro quo regarding Taiwan.[93] What is significant for India is that Mauritius is high on the Chinese radar for the economic surge in Africa where it plans to invest $64 billion. Only deft balancing can effectively protect the Indian interests there.

Australia

Australia–China relations have strong economic foundations. Its abundance of natural resources, proximity to China and China's voracious appetite for resources have been symbiotic drivers of that relationship. Just as Australia's resources flow into China, Chinese capital flows back for investments in Australia. The only two Indian Ocean nations that figured in the top ten import partner list of China in 2015 were Australia at 4.39 per cent and Malaysia at 3.7 per cent.[94] China is also the largest trading partner of Australia.

There has been a free-trade agreement in place since 2015. Bilateral trade is worth $107 billion.[95] The Australian economy depends on the export of commodities. Australia exports iron ore and concentrates, coal, gold, wool and other animal hair. It imports telecom equipment and parts, computers and household goods.[96] In the energy sector, 28 per cent of the LNG imports to China were supplied by Australia in 2014. Thermal coal is a large part of export from Australia at 13 per cent. Its low sulphur coal and haematite ores are of high quality as inputs to China's industry.[97] Iron ore and natural gas are other major exports to China. Over 54 per cent of the Chinese iron ore demand is met by Australia[98] and it also symbiotically constitutes more than 50 per cent of Australia's exports.[99] As much as 85 per cent bauxite and 20 per cent coal exports of Australia head to China.[100] Australia has a substantial number of Chinese population. Mandarin is the second most spoken language in Australia.[101]

Apart from trade, Australia also receives the largest Chinese investment in the Indian Ocean Region. After the US, Australia is China's second largest destination of investment. Cumulative investment has crossed $90 billion in the past 10 years.[102] Unlike its investment in other nations of the Indian Ocean rim, the focal areas of China have been real estate (45 per cent), renewable energy (20 per cent), healthcare (17 per cent), mining (9 per cent) and agribusiness infrastructure and energy at 3 per cent each.[103] The last two sectors are prime sectors in most other countries in the IOR, whereas in Australia, the trend is towards real estate, especially with a focus on New South Wales.

Traditionally, Australia has relied for security on the US. Australia being a liberal democracy, shares values with the US which has been its ally since it became independent. The Australian position on the SCS has reflected those positions. However, it is now economically deeply engaged with China. The strategic community in Australia has expressed its concerns over this engagement. The blocking of the sale of the electricity grid (Ausgrid) in New South Wales to the Hong Kong-based Cheung Kong Group in a $7 billion deal is one such step triggered by this caution. China has been quick to protest about it,[104] The US pullout from TPP and nativist tendencies have led Australia to come closer to China. Australia is now a member of the AIIB after long deliberations. The recent sale of Port Darwin, which is a part of the US Pivot plan with a US Marine Base there, to the Chinese Company Shandong Land Bridge Group along with defence ties[105] has underlined the drift of this relation.

There are other port investments of interest in Australia. China Merchant Holdings purchased a 50 per cent stake[106] in Port of New Castle from the

New South Wales Government. China's US$200 billion sovereign wealth fund, CIC Capital, has a 20 per cent stake worth 2bn USD for a 50 year lease on the Melbourne Port.[107] The Freemantle port is another disinvestment plan where the Australian resolve could soon be tested.

In mid-2017, the news of China funding several Australian politicians brought out the seamier side of the relationship.[108] The Foreign Investment Regulatory Board of Australia has raised concerns regarding Chinese investments. The Kidman cattle farm, which had its substantial share sold to China, was one such case. The cancellation of the Rio Tinto sale was also one such measure out of a concern over growing Chinese investments. If it needs to reduce such risks, Australia may need to diversify the destinations of its exports and investments into emerging growth centres like Indonesia, with whom it shares a shaky relationship, or India. It may also have to adapt and accommodate to the styles of business of these nations in case it is serious about diversification. Indian entrepreneur Adani's coal mine in Queensland has been stuck for two years over environmental concerns. Similarly, Australia's initially harsh stand over India's nuclear tests in 1998 has only strengthened inroads by China.

Ocean for Oceans' Sake

China has been a signatory of the UNCLOS and the International Seabed authority has given it 15-year rights from 2011 to mine a 10000 sq. miles area in the IOR south-west of Madagascar. The area is called the South West Indian Ridge. China has had an earlier contract in the Atlantic and i also mining areas in the Pacific. The latter was for polymetallic nodules. The IOR area is for polymetallic sulphides, which are abundant in the IOR. The exploration is being done by the Jialong deep sea submersible. This step could someday aid it get metals which are of value like copper, zinc and even gold. As the value of metals goes up, there will be a time when this deep sea mining becomes a viable option. It is of interest that China which is a signatory to the UNCLOS disregards the UNCLOS in the SCS and the US has not signed the UNCLOS since it feels that the Sea Bed treaty is too socialist. As a consumer of 46 per cent of metals, China will continue its mining efforts in the oceans. This is an ongoing initiative since 2002 for exploiting oceans for economic as well as nationalist reasons. Rare earth elements are another area of promise in the seabed. This is a field where China is a leader controlling 95 per cent of the global market.[109] It has used this near monopoly to put pressure on Japan. The organisation in China responsible for its seabed foraysis the Mineral

Resource Development Association under the State Oceanic Administration. So it is not merely the littorals and sealanes but the seabed itself as a source for mining that has increased the value of the Indian Ocean to China.

Conclusion

China's interest in resources in the Indian Ocean littorals is not a new phenomenon. Some initiatives predated its opening up in late 1970s like the TAZARA railway in Africa. However, the need for resources and energy grew manifold since the opening up of its markets. Though this chapter has focused on resources, trade and investment are equally important drivers in its IOR forays today. Safe sea lines of IOR are needed for the transportation of finished goods as well as resources. The guarantor of peaceful sea lines has so far been a system led by the United States through its own presence and regional arrangements. The rise of China has challenged that system, drawing some US attention away from the IOR to the Pacific. That void in IOR needs filling. Apart from the resident powers and the US, other nations that rely of IOR and global trade like China, Japan, and the UK have set up bases in the IOR partly to guarantee the resources and peaceful sea lines.

As an essential ingredient to the economy, the security of energy is important to China. Around eighty percent of oil and thirty percent of gas imports occur through the IOR. The Middle East, Africa and South America are suppliers of this energy and are key to the security of energy for China. Due to the distances involved, even the South American Crude goes via IOR. As far as Africa is concerned, it is not only a source for energy, metals and minerals; it is also a destination investment by China in critical infrastructure. Part of it serves the extractive economy involving resources. Australia, which is an IOR nation, is not only a substantial destination of China's investment, but its economy also relies heavily on China's demand for resources. However, its sea lines to China are through the Pacific and not the IOR.The stability of these regions in the IOR and peaceful shipping through it are vital for China and rest of the globe.

Over time, the BRI can have impacts on China's resource strategy. Right now, the overwhelming flow is towards China which is the major production centre. Part of the vision of the BRI is to shift the resource and energy-intensive production outside China. This will create new production centres in a Sino-centric value chain. From a resource perspective, this also implies the fragmentation of present networks with distributed production centres. Not all that ore and energy will move to China if it succeeds. Such a fragmented network can alter the regional resource and energy flows including that of sealanes in the region.

Irrespective of the fragmentation, China will remain interested in the source of metals, minerals and energy and sea lanes in the IOR. What is important to watch is that such interests in a long-term may not always align with the rest of the powers and can interfere with regional politics.

NOTES

1. "Qinglong's Letter to King George," accessed June 23, 2016, http://academics.wellesley.edu/Polisci/wj/China/208/READINGS/qianlong.html.
2. Angela Monaghan, "China Surpasses US as World's Largest Trading Nation," *The Guardian*, January 10, 2014, sec. Business, http://www.theguardian.com/business/2014/jan/10/china-surpasses-us-world-largest-trading-nation.
3. These are now called the Valemax carriers after the company Vale.
4. Elizabeth Economy and Michael Levi, *By All Means Necessary: How China's Resource Quest Is Changing the World* (OUP USA, 2014).
5. RMT 2016.
6. http://www.hellenicshippingnews.com/giant-ore-carriers-set-to-play-a-bigger-role-in-the-global-shipping-fleet-china-embraces-valemaxes/
7. Henry Sanderson, "Commodities Demand and China: An Explainer," *Financial Times*, January 19, 2016, https://www.ft.com/content/56a3dbce-bae6-11e5-bf7e-8a339b6f2164.
8. BP Energy Outlook Country and regional insights – China
9. "China, the King of Coal, Is Getting Gassy," *Bloomberg.com*, May 25, 2017, https://www.bloomberg.com/news/articles/2017-05-25/coal-king-s-shift-to-more-gas-wins-believers-as-china-use-surges.
10. BP Energy Outlook Country and regional insights – China
11. Jude Clemente, "China's Rising Natural Gas Demand, Pipelines, and LNG," *Forbes*, accessed July 3, 2017, http://www.forbes.com/sites/judeclemente/2016/04/24/chinas-rising-natural-gas-demand-pipelines-and-lng/.
12. BP Energy Outlook Country and regional insights – China
13. BP Energy Outlook Country and regional insights – China
14. "Middle Eastern Oil Producers Still Have Strong Hand," *Financial Times*, April 5, 2017, https://www.ft.com/content/a24df9ba-1a08-11e7-bcac-6d03d067f81f.
15. Ibid.
16. "Is China Pivoting towards the Middle East?," *World Economic Forum*, accessed May 20, 2017, https://www.weforum.org/agenda/2017/04/is-china-pivoting-towards-the-middle-east/
17. "China's Arab Policy Paper," accessed May 20, 2017, http://www.fmprc.gov.cn/mfa_eng/wjdt_665385/2649_665393/t1331683.shtml.
18. Ibid.
19. "OPEC: OPEC Share of World Crude Oil Reserves," accessed July 5, 2017, http://www.opec.org/opec_web/en/data_graphs/330.htm.
20. "Saudi Arabia, China Sign Deals Worth Up to $65 Billion," *Foreign Policy*, accessed May 20, 2017, https://foreignpolicy.com/2017/03/16/saudi-arabia-china-sign-deals-worth-65-billion-boost-trade-ties-oil-energy-one-belt-one-road-saudi-vision-2030/.
21. Ibid.

22. Ibid.
23. "Chinese Investors Launch Oman Industrial Project," *Channel NewsAsia*, accessed June 27, 2017, http://www.channelnewsasia.com/news/business/chinese-investors-launch-oman-industrial-project-8754576.
24. Ibid.
25. "Groundbreaking for $10.7bn Sino-Oman Industrial City Due next Week," *The National*, accessed June 27, 2017, http://www.thenational.ae/business/economy/groundbreaking-for-107bn-sino-oman-industrial-city-due-next-week.
26. "*Xinhua*, http://news.xinhuanet.com/english/special/2013-01/15/c_132200680.htm," n.d., http://news.xinhuanet.com/english/special/2013-01/15/c_132200680.htm.
27. "Lubricated With Oil: Iran-China Relations in a Changing World," Middle East Policy Council, accessed May 20, 2017, http://www.mepc.org/lubricated-oil-iran-china-relations-changing-world.
28. "Iran - International - Analysis - U.S. Energy Information Administration (EIA)," accessed May 20, 2017, https://www.eia.gov/beta/international/analysis.cfm?iso=IRN.
29. "China's Big Play for Middle East Oil," *Bloomberg.com*, May 10, 2017, https://www.bloomberg.com/view/articles/2017-05-10/china-s-big-play-for-middle-east-oil.
30. Reuters in Beijing, "China Calls for Iran-Style Nuclear Talks with North Korea instead of Sanctions," *The Guardian*, accessed July 18, 2015, http://www.theguardian.com/world/2015/jul/15/china-calls-for-iran-style-nuclear-talks-with-north-korea-instead-of-sanctions.
31. "The Great Well of China," The Economist, June 20, 2015, http://www.economist.com/news/middle-east-and-africa/21654655-oil-bringing-china-and-arab-world-closer-economically-politics-will.
32. Brian Spegele, "Oil-Thirsty China a Winner in Iran Deal," Wall Street Journal, July 14, 2015, sec. World, http://www.wsj.com/articles/oil-thirsty-china-a-winner-in-iran-deal-1436909582.
33. "Stratfor," Stratfor, accessed July 18, 2015, https://www.stratfor.com/.
34. "The China-Iran Nuclear Pipeline," Foreign Affairs, accessed July 18, 2015, https://www.foreignaffairs.com/articles/china/2015-07-13/china-iran-nuclear-pipeline.
35. "Israel-China Arms Trade and the US Factor," *International Strategic and Security Studies Programme, NIAS, India*, April 11, 2014, http://isssp.in/israel-china-arms-trade-and-the-us-factor/.
36. Ibid.
37. China the New Normal' , Oxford Institute of Energy Studies
38. "China - International - Analysis - U.S. Energy Information Administration (EIA)," accessed August 23, 2017, https://www.eia.gov/beta/international/analysis.cfm?iso=CHN.
39. Ibid.
40. Ibid.
41. Ibid.
42. Ibid.
43. Ibid.
44. Ibid.
45. Ibid.
46. Ibid.
47. Ibid.
48. Estimated as Import less pipeline capacity
49. "China - International - Analysis - U.S. Energy Information Administration (EIA)."
50. British Petroleum, "BP Energy Outlook 2017 Edition," n.d., https://www.bp.com/content/

dam/bp/pdf/energy-economics/energy-outlook-2017/bp-energy-outlook-2017.pdf.
51. "China - International - Analysis - U.S. Energy Information Administration (EIA)."
52. Ibid.
53. Ibid.
54. Ibid.
55. Ibid.
56. Ibid.
57. Ibid.
58. Ibid.
59. Ibid.
60. Ibid.
61. British Petroleum, "BP Energy Outlook 2017 Edition."
62. Ibid.
63. *Sea Lanes and Pipelines Energy Security in Asia* (Westport, Conn: Pentagon Energy Press, 2008).
64. British Petroleum, "BP Energy Outlook 2017 Edition," n.d., https://www.bp.com/content/dam/bp/pdf/energy-economics/energy-outlook-2017/bp-energy-outlook-2017.pdf.
65. Ibid.
66. Ibid.
67. Ibid.
68. BGS World Mineral Statistics
69. "China in Africa," *Council on Foreign Relations*, accessed May 20, 2017, https://www.cfr.org/backgrounder/china-africa.
70. "Chinese Firm Signs $478.9 Million Kenya Lamu Port Deal - Frontier Markets News - Emerging & Growth Markets - WSJ," accessed September 6, 2017, https://blogs.wsj.com/frontiers/2014/08/03/chinese-firm-signs-478-9-million-kenya-lamu-port-deal/.
71. "Bagamoyo Port Project Shelved," IHS Fairplay, accessed May 20, 2017, http://fairplay.ihs.com/dredging/article/4262731/bagamoyo-port-project-shelved.
72. "Doraleh Multi-Purpose Port," *Port De Djibouti*, accessed July 8, 2017, http://www.portdedjibouti.com/doraleh-multi-purpose-port/.
73. "Djibouti Opens New Port as Part of $7 Bln/Year Free-Trade Zone Plan," *Reuters*, accessed July 8, 2017, http://af.reuters.com/article/investingNews/idAFKBN18K2I2-OZABS.
74. "The 5 Largest Chinese-Funded Railways in Africa," *CNN*, accessed July 8, 2017, http://www.cnn.com/2016/11/21/africa/gallery/chinese-african-railways/index.html.
75. Brook Larmer, "Is China the World's New Colonial Power?," *The New York Times*, May 2, 2017, sec. Magazine, https://www.nytimes.com/2017/05/02/magazine/is-china-the-worlds-new-colonial-power.html.
76. Conor Gaffey On 5/31/17 at 11:54 AM, "What You Should Know about Kenya's Mega-Railway, Built with Chinese Money," *Newsweek*, May 31, 2017, http://www.newsweek.com/kenya-railway-china-madaraka-express-618357.
77. Kimiko de Freytas-Tamura, "Kenyans Fear Chinese-Backed Railway Is Another 'Lunatic Express,'" *The New York Times*, June 8, 2017, sec. Africa, https://www.nytimes.com/2017/06/08/world/africa/kenyans-fear-chinese-backed-railway-is-another-lunatic-express.html.
78. John Aglionby, "Djibouti-Ethiopia Railway Carries Hope for Pan-African Trade," *Financial Times*, January 16, 2017, https://www.ft.com/content/42d7af2e-d95a-11e6-944b-e7eb37a6aa8e.
79. Ibid.

80. Larmer, "Is China the World's New Colonial Power?"
81. Ibid.
82. Ibid.
83. Justin McDonnell Diplomat The, "Elizabeth C. Economy," *The Diplomat*, accessed May 20, 2017, http://thediplomat.com/2014/04/elizabeth-c-economy/.
84. "The World Factbook—Central Intelligence Agency," accessed May 20, 2017, https://www.cia.gov/library/publications/the-world-factbook/geos/se.html.
85. "Chinese Naval Base at Seychelles Island," accessed May 20, 2017, http://pib.nic.in/newsite/PrintRelease.aspx?relid=119836.
86. Kallol Bhattacherjee, "'Seychelles Committed to Indian Naval Base,'" *The Hindu*, December 23, 2015, http://www.thehindu.com/news/international/seychelles-committed-to-indian-naval-base/article8022404.ece.
87. "Rise and Stall: China's Stepping Stone to Nowhere," *African Business Magazine*, April 8, 2015, http://africanbusinessmagazine.com/zSuku.
88. "Mauritius Rides Wave of Asian Investment in Africa," *Financial Times*, accessed May 20, 2017, https://www.ft.com/content/929f41d0-75b3-11e6-bf48-b372cdb1043a.
89. "Contribution to GDP - Financial Services Commission - Mauritius," accessed May 20, 2017, https://www.fscmauritius.org/en/media-publications/contribution-to-gdp.
90. "Republic of Mauritius- China-Mauritius: China Writes off Debts Amounting to Rs 450 Million," accessed May 20, 2017, http://www.govmu.org/English/News/Pages/China-writes-off-debts-amounting-Rs-450-million-for-Mauritius.aspx.
91. "Wang Yi: China Will Advance Connection in Two Fields, Explore Expansion in Two Sectors and Deepen Cooperation in Two Aspects with Mauritius," accessed May 20, 2017, http://www.fmprc.gov.cn/mfa_eng/zxxx_662805/t1337829.shtml.
92. "FACTBOX-Relations between Mauritius and China," *Reuters*, May 26, 2008, http://www.reuters.com/article/us-mauritius-china-relations-idUSL1282817920080526.
93. "China: Import Trade & Tariff by Country 2015," *WITS Data*, accessed July 8, 2017, http://wits.worldbank.org/CountryProfile/en/Country/CHN/Year/2015/TradeFlow/Import/Partner/by-country/Show/Partner%20Name;MPRT-SHR-TTL-PRDCT;MPRT-TRD-VL;MPRT-PRTNR-SHR;AHS-WGHTD-AVRG;MFN-WGHTD-AVRG;TRF-NMBR-AGGRMNT;/Sort/MPRT-TRD-VL/Chart/top10.
94. Deutsche Welle (www.dw.com), "Australia Drifts toward China amid Wobbly US Ties," *Asia: DW*, 24 March 2017, *DW.COM*, accessed July 3, 2017, http://www.dw.com/en/australia-drifts-toward-china-amid-wobbly-us-ties/a-38103688.
95. https://dfat.gov.au/trade/resources/Documents/chin.pdf
96. Economy and Levi, *By All Means Necessary*.
97. "Rethinking Australia's Relationship with China," *East Asia Forum*, April 13, 2017, http://www.eastasiaforum.org/2017/04/13/rethinking-australias-relationship-with-china/.
98. https://dfat.gov.au/trade/resources/Documents/chin.pdf
99. Economy and Levi, *By All Means Necessary*.
100. "Rethinking Australia's Relationship with China."
101. Business reporter Sue Lannin, "Chinese Investment in Australia at Highest Point since GFC," Text, *ABC News*, (May 1, 2017), http://www.abc.net.au/news/2017-05-01/chinese-investment-in-australia-at-highest-point-since-gfc/8485828.
102. "5 Things to Know about China and Australia's Economic Ties," *World Economic Forum*, accessed July 3, 2017, https://www.weforum.org/agenda/2016/04/5-things-to-know-about-china-and-australia-s-economic-ties/.
103. "China Blasts Australian Blocking of Grid Sale; Door Open to Locals," *Reuters*, August 19, 2016, http://www.reuters.com/article/us-australia-privatisation-ausgrid-idUSKCN10U0LA.

104. Jane Perlez, "U.S. Casts Wary Eye on Australian Port Leased by Chinese," *The New York Times,* March 20, 2016, sec. World, https://www.nytimes.com/2016/03/21/world/australia/china-darwin-port-landbridge.html.
105. "Shareholders – Newcastle Port," accessed July 9, 2017, http://www.portofnewcastle.com.au/Company-Information/Shareholders.aspx.
106. "China Tips in $2bn for Port Stake," September 19, 2016, http://at.theaustralian.com.au/link/88d87a1affad98f8e824378af2666585?domain=theaustralian.com.au.
107. Damien Cave and Jacqueline Williams, "Australian Politics Is Open to Foreign Cash, and China Has Much to Gain," *The New York Times,* June 6, 2017, sec. Australia, https://www.nytimes.com/2017/06/06/world/australia/china-political-influence-campaign-finance.html.
108. "Resource-Hungry China Plumbs the Depths of the Indian Ocean as India Plays Catch-up in the Race to the Seabed: Neighbours," *India Today,* accessed June 11, 2015, http://indiatoday.intoday.in/story/china-indian-ocean-india-seabed-jiaolong-aquatic-dragon-beijing/1/442277.html.

CHAPTER 10

CONCLUSION: CHINA'S STRATEGY IN THE INDIAN OCEAN

The Indian Ocean is the cradle of human seafaring, where maritime interactions between its civilizations date back to five thousand years. However, in contemporary terms, it is yet to evolve as a separate geopolitical entity with its own security and economic structures such as that of the Atlantic or the Pacific. The major powers across history have forayed into the Indian Ocean for economic advancement just as China is doing today. This book has presented that Chinese foray broadly in two sections. The first, till Chapter Four, has described the set of generic events involving China which have a bearing on its IOR strategy, such as its economic plans, naval growth and perspectives from geopolitical events like the South China Sea imbroglio. The latter chapters in this book try to look at discernible patterns and drivers of China's strategy in the Indian Ocean, packaging them into manageable themes and regions. The entire structure of that strategy is influenced by the global trends, the domestic situation within China and other nations and regional and other dynamics. Some of those which didn't fit in the previous chapters have been listed here.

Global Issues

The world is constantly affected by power shifts. After over a quarter century of unipolarity, it is tending towards a multipolar order. A continued but waning eminence of the USA combined with the rise of China, India, Indonesia, Japan, South Korea, Germany and the re-emergence of Russia portends in this direction. The South China Sea episodes and the US rebalance to Asia are symptoms and responses to that shift. The BRI which entered the third year in 2017 since its inception, is another facet of that shift symbolising China's rise. This was marked by a summit in Beijing, attended by around 60 nations including the USA and Japan. This power shift will indeed have a bearing on several events in the IOR including China's strategy. China's increasing presence in the Indian Ocean is itself a sign of it.

A series of referendums across the globe, such as for 'Brexit', and elections in the recent past around the globe, have underlined the rise of extreme views, mandates for hard-line options and elections of decisive leaders. This has global impacts, including the Indian Ocean. The most significant change has been the result of an election in the United States—the current global hegemon. It played itself out in Asia where the future of the US rebalancing to Asia came under a cloud with its allies being asked to pay more for security. At the same time, there has been no respite in the security situation in the South China Sea and the situation in the Korean Peninsula has only worsened with the DPRK testing ballistic missiles and fusion devices with nonchalance. These have impacted the US allies' position regarding the US and China. The location of the THAAD radar in South Korea has taken those questions to China's doorsteps. The US relations with a rising China also became complicated by the US upping the ante with protectionist trade policies and demanding more from China on North Korea. Yet China, with trade surpluses and capital, is deeply invested in the USA, including the US treasury bonds, partially balancing the security deficit.

The liberal spirit that broke down walls in the late eighties appears to be weakening, affecting liberalism and globalisation. One is increasingly witnessing the hardening of identities on national, ethnic and religious lines. It has also led to nativism and protectionism in trade. The global trade growth rate plummeted below the GDP growth rate for the first time in 15 years in 2016. This is quite a large dip when we consider that from 1985 to 2007, the global trade had grown at twice the pace of the GDP.[1] China's growth was a major factor in that phenomenon. That has hit a 'new normal' and China itself is reordering its domestic economy after a scorching double digit growth for three decades.

Belt and Road as Strategy

A major reason behind this slowdown is the plateauing of the FDI-Manufacture-Export driven growth model which filled the sails of that growth. This is also the infamous middle income trap from where a mere thirteen nations have escaped historically.[2] That is something that the Communist Party of China, which barters prosperity for legitimacy, cannot risk. The present period is also marked by a strong crackdown on corruption in China, which is shaking up the political system. So, there are multiple actions at work in China to break out from this slowdown. The shift from manufacturing to services is one step. Priming domestic consumption over export income is another. Yet another measure is to shift manufacturing to countries with lower costs—to a model where China has to "go out and bring in". In simpler terms, it wants to repeat what the US and Asian tigers did in China 40 years ago. This is critical for the CPC's legitimacy as it promises the double centenaries—a moderately developed China by 2021 and a fully developed country by 2049—as a part of the China Dream.

A few global and domestic factors in China need consideration here. The first is the global financial crisis of 2008, which exposed the underbelly of the Western financial system. China was deeply affected and in order to pull out of that problem, it invested massively in domestic infrastructure. That created surplus capacities in infrastructure industry. Together with the largest reserves of capital in the world, this surplus capacity is now available for deployment. As a solution to all these domestic issues, China has launched the Belt and Road Initiative. It is a plan that aims at deploying the surplus capital and capacities to create a Sino-centric infrastructure. This will allow China to shift low-value high-volume, environmentally sensitive, energy-intensive industries to its neighbourhood while its own domestic industry scales up the value chain to make high-value low-volume products.

China's intended shifts from manufacturing to services and export to consumption models has had its ripples in the IOR investments. For example, a China-led port city project in Colombo has now become a financial city. With China bequeathing some of its manufacturing and the nations in the IOR becoming part of a resultant Sino-centric value chain, resources including oil, gas, metals and minerals may not traverse all the way to China with the same intensity in future and may partly get processed locally. Such a shift is intrinsic to the Belt and Road Initiative. The BRI has the potential to fragment the present networks creating many hubs and spokes. A case in point is Pakistan, where, the CPEC infrastructure and energy plan has a sequel through industrial investments as revealed by the *Dawn*.[3] At the same time, there are some challenges too. Will developments such as emergence of additive 3D printing disrupt manufacture and logistics networks with just on time, on site printing? Will that shake estimations behind the creation of networks, say of the BRI? Only time can tell.

Physically, the BRI has two branches: the overland Silk Road Economic Belt and the Maritime Silk Road. Between them, they share seven routes of which six head to the West, towards the Indian Ocean and its hinterland. In this westerly bias, the BRI is going along the global grain of growth, in maritime terms, postulated as the 'west line' in Martin Stopford's seminal volume of maritime economics.[4] Taking a long view, he has traced the locus of maritime centres of growth in history for 5000 years and says that it has always shifted westwards, commencing with the Phoenicians, onwards to Greece, Rome, Venice, the Iberian Peninsula, the Netherlands, Britain, America, Japan, Korea, China and in the future, India. That pattern also obliquely states that the maritime centre of gravity will eventually shift west to the Indian Ocean Region where the future scope for growth is. This western bias is also extremely relevant in China's domestic politics—since the western provinces of Xinjiang, Yunnan and Tibet are economically backward and politically volatile. So, the BRI is also a continuum of the Chinese domestic 'go west' policy. It is no coincidence that the maritime centres of growth were also the economic centre of growth. As an economy overheated, the adjacent areas picked momentum spreading that growth. What enabled this growth are critical infrastructure and connectivity networks which is the hard layer of the BRI. Of the two branches of the BRI, the SREB and MSR, the Maritime Silk Road offers tremendous economies of scale.

To illustrate, the largest of container ships carry more than twenty thousand twenty feet containers, which end-to-end, can be 100 kilometres long. However, the gigantic scale possible in MSR is of little use without land routes for hinterland access. Hence, we see the MSR as well as SREB exist complementing each other in the BRI's grand design. The SREB has created a flutter in rail connectivity across Central Asia. It is also a déjà vu moment reminding us of the geopolitician, Mackinder, who saw Eurasia as the 'heartland' which if controlled, can control the globe. It was a similar rail road fever of those times which made him suspect that the Columbian age of the sail is over with the advent and spread of rail roads. The exponential rate at which the maritime networks developed compared to rail networks, did not make Mackinder's prediction a reality. In a rhyme of history, predictions are that the rail routes will carve some share of air freight and not sea freight.[5]

Learning from the current international system, China feels that there is also a need for the creation of alternate economic and financial systems, i.e., organs that equal the formal institutions like the IMF, the World Bank and the WTO and informal ones like the World Economic Forum. Financial institutions like the AIIB, NDB, Silk Road Fund, mega-FTAs such as the RCEP and the Boao Forum, akin to Davos, are harbingers of this process.

Therefore, there are several Sino-centric layers to this aspired structure. First is the hard palpable layer of critical infrastructure network—the continental SREB and Maritime Silk Road. This is the visual One Belt One Road. Then there is a soft, well-known economic, financial and trade institutional layer. Over this comes an inevitable geopolitical layer of which nothing much has been articulated by the Chinese except the Defence White Paper 2015 which said 'maritime over land', 'far seas' and 'open ocean protection'—which are code words which mean more of China's naval presence everywhere. One should endeavour to see these three layers as one structure and not separately, since the Chinese by Leninist training, do so. Politics, to Lenin, was concentrated economics.

Maritime Military Developments in China

The security overlay of China's venture abroad is its Navy, as the flag has historically followed trade. Some discerning patterns emerge from the evolution of the Chinese maritime strategy and the resultant Navy. Under the People's War philosophy, the navy was a coastal force to prevent an invasion from Taiwan. Gen Liu Huaqing, an army general, sensed the relevance of the navy and laid the foundations of the modern avatar in the 1980s. As the military strategy graduated to a pragmatic 'local war' and its technical variants, the navy kept pace. Naval roles transitioned from coastal defence, to offshore defence, far-seas operations and eventually to the current far-seas operations and open-sea protection roles. The old stasis has now given way to a discernible maritime vigour as the largest trading nation when the 2015 Defence White Paper exhorts that "the traditional mentality that land outweighs sea must be abandoned".

It is a navy that has grown quickly in the past twenty-five years to its present form keeping pace with its foreign policy and widening economic footprints and interests. Yet, the primary role of that navy continues to be deterrence enabled by its SSBN fleet and associated command systems. The turn of events in the third Taiwan Straits crisis highlighted anti-access and area denial as a crucial naval role. Being a core issue, this is the second role around which a strong fleet of submarines, missile boats, land-based aircraft and missiles have evolved. The opening up of economy brought to fore the need of a navy that had roles beyond the island chains—for a third role, of 'open sea protection'. The long-legged destroyers, frigates and tankers have been built to fulfil that role. This fleet along with submarines has shown its regular presence in the Indian Ocean since 2008. The base in Djibouti[6] and alliances it forges with its allies, especially Pakistan, Thailand and Bangladesh, has sustenance of this fleet in mind. A rising nationalism viz., the East and South China has necessitated a fourth role, where China wants to act creating adequate space for a calibrated escalation in case of a maritime event. This has resulted in a hybrid fleet with civil and military units acting in concert. The myriad domestic maritime agencies have been integrated under the Coast Guard and the State Oceanic administration for better resource management. This interestingly takes the navy through a full circle, reminiscent of the People's War, with blurred lines of division between the civil and the military.

Nuclear deterrence, denial of access to a superior fleet and territorial assertions in the South and East China Sea have so far kept certain asset classes in the Pacific. As dependence on the Indian Ocean for trade and resources increased, the blue water fleet has maintained a presence in the Indian Ocean consistently since 2008. With a minor staggering of schedules, China is capable of increasing the number of units in IOR substantially surging to double digits. What began a decade ago over an alibi of anti-piracy patrols has also undergone qualitative accretion in this period. For example submarines – a tool for denial – have appeared in the Indian Ocean at least on seven separate occasions. China has also operationalised its base in Djibouti besides the strategic port and rail investments along the Maritime Silk Road (MSR) spanning several countries. The MSR port investments provide more basing options for China as much as they demand the need for a long-legged fleet and bases to protect their interests. All these along with a written strategy about the far-seas operation and open-sea protection point in one direction—the Chinese Navy will be operating in the Indian Ocean routinely in the future. As per a recent publication by the Institute for National Strategic Studies, *Chinese Military Diplomacy, 2003–2016: Trends and Implications*, Pakistan, Thailand and Australia top the list of nations with which China engages in military diplomacy. As regions, South East Asia and South Asia topped the same list with over 31 per cent of interactions with these regions. Most of its naval port calls were in the Middle East and Asia where Oman, Djibouti, Pakistan and Yemen saw the highest port calls. The Anti-Piracy Task Forces port calls came evenly from all three Chinese fleets, whereas the calls from other ships were predominantly from the North Sea Fleet since the training ships are from that fleet.[7]

The recent restructuring of the Chinese military organisation is an important factor to consider. In 2016 China created a Joint Theatre Command system for its military, synergising all services into geographically oriented commands. A continentally oriented China had traditionally given land forces more than their share of control in warfighting. The most telling effect occurred in mid-2017 when its Southern Theatre Command, with the most modern naval assets and bases under its South Sea Fleet, was placed under a Naval Officer, along with its Army and Air Force assets in the region. This development aims to break the silos between the services and enables an appropriate application of air, naval, land, cyber and missile forces under one commander. However, in an Indian Ocean scenario, this may not apply in entirety since the land and air forces facing India are under the Western Theatre Command, which does not have a maritime component. Hence, the coordination is expected to happen at a higher organisation such as the Central Military Commission.

It is to be expected in normal course with such developments that any continental event will eventually have a maritime spill over and vice versa. Not only is the Chinese navy operating in the Indian Ocean, it also plans to raise one lakh marines by converting two amphibious divisions and one armoured brigade to deal with expeditionary roles. That indicates that China not only considers its sea lanes of communication vulnerable but also factors in security of its land-based assets coming up along the Belt and Road, and seeks to protect them through boots on ground.

The creation of PLASSF reinforces new dimensions to warfare including cyber, space and electronic spectrum. The next war will be a multi-dimensional, multi-domain war which will put to test the entire gamut of force including space, cyber, land, air and sea domains. Whether it will it end before firing a shot is a question that needs to be addressed. China is also at the forefront of investments in emerging fields like artificial intelligence and quantum technology, which can be strategically disruptive.

Despite the changes in inventory and organisation, the ideological oversight by the party through a political commissar continues in the PLA and could be a hindrance to the professional latitude available to normal military commanders. That political layer will add to the intellectual challenge posed by the modern battlefield.

The Lessons from the South China Sea

Due to its significance in China's access to the IOR and presence of the US allies in that sea, the SCS is a geographic space that has got affected most by the shifting balance of power. China's conduct in SCS is a bellwether that can hardly be ignored and is an important cog in its IOR strategy. Its late maritime resurgence, the geography that limits its access to open oceans and historical actions in the continent partly answer why China has taken a position different from the UNCLOS it signed in 1996. The SCS is the vital area leading to the Malacca Straits and the Indian Ocean, enabling its two-ocean strategy. This geographic vulnerability was popularly termed the Malacca Dilemma, emphasised by President Hu Jintao in 2003.[8] The US Pivot to East Asia with its allies on the Malacca accentuates that insecurity. Robert D. Kaplan argues that the SCS is key to China's two-ocean strategy just as the Caribbean Sea was key to US's two-ocean presence with the creation of the Panama Canal.[9] Just as it had created a continental buffer around a coastal Han core by annexing Xinjiang, Tibet and Inner Mongolia in the initial days of the PRC, the late maritime power, is in the process of creating a maritime buffer zone in the SCS. The intrinsic economic value of that sea also cannot be ignored. The SCS holds reasonable reserves of natural resources including fisheries, oil and gas. As the largest consumer of fish in the world and with a depleting fish stock in the Chinese EEZ, the SCS is a source of food and livelihood for China.

China therefore has taken steps to convert the buffer of the SCS into zones where it can exert higher control insuring its unimpeded access to the IOR. Its 'nine dashed line', claims to internal waters, archipelagos, island-building and claims based on history are far in excess than what the UNCLOS permits, and aims at appropriating greater control over the South China Sea. The SCS imbroglio tells us a story about China's revisionist position over international law and how China handles the claimant nations individually, deftly using its economic and diplomatic power to alter status on the ground steadily in its favour.

The China Pakistan Economic Corridor

Of all Chinese initiatives in the Indian Ocean, the Pakistan arm of the BRI, the CPEC, is the most significant regional initiative. According to President Xi's statements, the CPEC has four separate areas of focus which are energy, infrastructure, Gwadar and industrial cooperation. What one is witnessing in this initial phase is the first three, with industrial cooperation beyond the present horizon. One major reason for Pakistan's economic woes has been the non-availability of cheap power. The CPEC tries to mitigate that shortage by ushering in coal projects into a fuel mix that hitherto did not use coal. It is thus a bitter package of coal infusion in an energy mix to handhold a crucial ally, deepening the relation with regional implications.

From the large share of energy projects, the CPEC is more about energy than a corridor. The CPEC investments are also in pockets where returns are high—which earns it the sobriquet, the China Punjab Energy Corridor. With such regional biases in project distribution it can accentuate the current fissures within the nation and in the region. For instance, it does not have any major projects in Balochistan. So far the China–Pakistan relationship has had a strategic and elitist nature with military and nuclear cooperation. That has now included common man's issues like electricity and roads. The finances of these projects are at commercial rates which will eventually be borne by the consumers. The impact of Chinese investment when it meets the people, therefore needs consideration. The loans also require to be paid back. Pakistan's capacity to absorb the investments in a given period and pay back is suspect – that is where ports like Gwadar are potential strategic equities which will find military uses. It is a port in wilderness, without rail or proper road connectivity and managed by a little known company with limited experience. In all probability, it will turn out to be a naval base for Chinese foothold in the Indian Ocean. That makes maritime matters complex in the IOR.

Considering economics of transportation, distances, altitudes, terrain and weather, the CPEC may not mitigate the Malacca dilemma as it claims. However, the CPEC is an example of how China picks an existing gap in a country, steps in and gains a strategic foothold, potentially altering the regional dynamics. That gap in Pakistan's case is energy. This is the pattern that the BRI plays out with minor variations in most nations in the Indian Ocean littorals. From fresh revelations, there is a comprehensive Chinese plan as to what industries best work in Pakistan. This has clear zones and corridors of logistics which is a harbinger of Phase II of industrial cooperation mentioned by President Xi in Islamabad but left open-ended thus far. The CPEC is a flagship and a test case for the OBOR and lays an economic weft over strategic warp. Unlike the usual sequence in geopolitics, trade follows flag here.

Just as one focuses on the CPEC, there are several non-CPEC/non-BRI projects that are in fact more strategic in nature, like the nuclear cooperation between China and Pakistan worth $6 billion and the purchase of eight submarines which are equally significant financially and strategically. Such projects in Pakistan as well as other nations get a short shrift due to focus on BRI. Therefore, the BRI is not the only route for the spread of China's interest and investments in the Indian Ocean.

Though India is a major factor in Sino-Pak relations, it also has a target audience in faraway Washington. With a waning US interest in the region, only a closer relation with China will yield Pakistan the necessary leverage in the US–Pakistan relationship. China also uses Pakistan as a useful tool in the region where it may not desire to directly influence events, such as the arms sales to Myanmar and Sri Lanka and for influencing Maldives and Bangladesh. This is also aimed at improving Pakistan's position in the region when compared to India.

A factor to consider is the effect of the CPEC on the democracy in Pakistan. China, with a unitary, authoritarian, totalitarian polity, will possibly find it easier, and prefer to do business with the Pakistan Army, and the effects of such a bias will require further studies just as the effects of the BRI on other nations in the region.

Alternative Access Strategies

Other than Pakistan, countries which can provide or control China's access to the Indian Ocean include Myanmar, Thailand, Malaysia, Indonesia and Singapore. Of these nations, Myanmar, like Pakistan, can offer an alternative land route from China to the Indian Ocean. Myanmar is therefore a key nation in China's Indian Ocean Policy. Unlike in Pakistan, China has already invested in ports, refineries, equity oil and gas as well as pipelines in Myanmar, clearly preferring the Myanmar route over Pakistan. These pipelines feed Myanmarese demand as well as the refineries in Yunnan. This route is not only shorter when compared to the CPEC, but is also all-weather through gentler terrain and touches altitudes of up to 800m unlike 4600m above sea level in the Karakoram Highway. Myanmar is also crucial with high potential for hydropower projects which transfer electricity to China. It is also a significant source for copper, tin and nickel. Together with a high level of arms transfer, investment and political support that go back to the days of its international isolation, China has invested heavily in Myanmar. Myanmar has the highest Chinese investment as a percentage of the GDP in the region. At the same time, China wields influence over the ethnic groups in the periphery of Myanmar, through which it balances the Myanmar government.

The ethnic groups on the northern and eastern borders have well known ties with China through the Wa. It was also underlined during the Panglong Conference 2017, when China played a major role leveraging its influence. China has also offered to mediate in the Rohingya problem in Rakhine, which has been rejected by Myanmar. Kyaukpyu, the port from where the pipelines to China commence, is in the Rakhine province. The access offered by this port has not only motivated influencing a political problem there, but has also made China seek an increased stake of 85 per cent in lieu of the liabilities Myanmar has incurred from a failed dam project at Myitsone.

Ever since the democratisation process began, Myanmar has been trying to wean away from China's influence. The Myitsone Dam, Yangon Kunming Rail and Letpadaung Copper mine are major Chinese projects that have suffered a setback. However, the present government is pragmatic in its relations with China and is reconsidering several stalled projects mentioned previously. The Yunnan province, which benefits from the Myanmarese access route, is not only poorer; it is also energy deficit, unlike Xinjiang which the CPEC connects. Xinjiang is not only the major oil-producing region in China, but it is also the terminal for Central Asian gas and oil pipelines. As an alternative access route to the IOR, Myanmar scores over Pakistan and is higher on the cards in China's access strategy to the Indian Ocean.

Alternative access strategies include the prospect of a canal across the Kra isthmus in Thailand. It can also serve as a land bridge across the oceans. Since the Kra Canal has the potential to separate the Muslim-dominated Southern regions ofThailand, it is doubtful if that deal will ever come through. However, the plans for a canal very much remain active. As an interim measure China has recently signed a deal with Thailand for the transfer of three Yuan-class submarines. Given the shallow seas around Thai bases like Sattahip in the Gulf of Thailand, those submarines may spend more time in Thailand's deeper waters near its Indian Ocean bases close to India's Andaman Islands. Just as Djibouti and Gwadar are located close to chokepoints in the Indian Ocean, Thailand is important to the security of the Malacca Straits. The sale of submarines to Thailand is therefore strategic.

Malaysia, Indonesia and Singapore are key actors in the Straits of Malacca due to their location. The relationship with Singapore has worsened due to its alliance with the USA and touched a low in 2016–17 when Singapore army APCs were confiscated in Hong Kong on their way home after an exercise with Taiwan. The MSR was officially declared in Indonesia in 2013, in recognition of its strategic location. Indonesia is also an emerging economy whom China has been treating with caution unlike other countries with which it has a dispute with in the South China Sea. Indonesia recently named the South China Sea as North Natuna Sea, upping the ante in the SCS. Of these three nations, Malaysia is most suited as a land bridge across the oceans with continental connectivity that can reach all the way to Mainland China. China has therefore invested heavily in that country, especially in ports and a rail line that connects Kuantan and Klang ports on either coast. This is besides plans for port and real-estate investments which are aimed to rival Singapore. China has also docked its submarines more than once in Teluk Sepanggar, Kota Kinabalu, facing the South China Sea, which indicates a growing strategic relationship.

Footholds in the Indian Ocean

Along with strategies of access, China is investing in nations which can offer it pockets of influence in the IOR. China has invested deeply in Bangladesh especially in its military. As far as infrastructure is concerned, China has focussed on critical infrastructure such as bridges, energy projects, ports and shipping. China's Bangladesh strategy reveals the not-so-pleasant intentions in the Indian Ocean Region. A stark feature is the high maritime content in arms sales to Bangladesh, including the sale of submarines. Submarines are purely offensive weapons, with no less-than-war role. China has so far given submarines only to Egypt and North Korea- a privilege now extended to Bangladesh. Pakistan and Thailand too have signed up for submarines. These nations are not only on India's immediate periphery, but such sales also assist China to cultivate a long-term strategic military relationship with them. Submarines are technically intensive platforms that require manufacturers support for a long time. Supply of submarines draws customer nations naturally into China's orbit and infrastructure built for them can serve as plug-and-play facilities for China in the Indian Ocean. As far as the Bangladeshi domestic politics is concerned, the two major parties, the Awami League and the BNP, have won elections roughly in an alternate manner. A strategic visit by President Musharraf in July 2002 and a half-apology for Pakistan's genocides during 1971 preceded the 2002 Defence Agreement with China. This has been a major step in the China–Bangladesh relationship with far-reaching implications for regional security. Unlike Sri Lanka or Maldives which sit astride the maritime sealanes or even Myanmar which offers it a conduit to the IOR, Bangladesh offers no such advantages to China other than being an offensive pawn against India and an opportunity to distract it in the IOR. When seen along with Thailand and Pakistan, the submarine sales have ensured a Chinese military spares logistics chain in the IOR for several decades.

Unlike Bangladesh, which is away from the shipping lines, Sri Lanka is crucial to the Indian Ocean traffic. Its significance hasn't waned through the ages of sail, to steam to contemporary maritime networks. It offers a range of possibilities as a transhipment hub with the highest liner shipping connectivity index in South Asia. It has the capacity to be a regional industrial hub to tap into the emerging economies in the region. Acquisition and creation of assets in such a geographic spot is not only economically attractive, but even strategically significant. As trade in the Indian Ocean grows, the significance of Sri Lankan ports will only grow. Overall $8 billion has been invested by China in Sri Lanka of which a substantial sum has been invested in port and port-related activity. The Colombo International Container Terminal, Hambantota and the reclamation project in Colombo to carve a financial city have been the major projects. Besides ports, China has invested in Sri Lankan critical infrastructure like power, road and rail. The financial capacity of Sri Lanka to pay back has been doubtful from the very beginning.

Unlike Pakistan, Sri Lanka is not an ally sworn to China. It has far lesser reasons to balance India especially after having ended the civil war on its terms. It has better democracy indices than Pakistan. China will also find it harder to play on the internal cleavages of Sri Lanka unlike Myanmar where it has some control over the ethnic groups. The China–Sri Lanka bonhomie bloomed in the murky waters of the civil war. Historic processes threw up a hardliner leader in that circumstance. The opportunity presented by global ire and resultant isolation over human rights violation during the brutal endgames of the civil war allowed China to get a grip on Sri Lanka. However, the field has now shifted to economy. It is today a highly indebted nation with debt at 77 per cent of the GDP, which is the highest in South Asia. It also has a whopping 58 per cent external debt which is again, the highest and three times the normal in South Asia. The repayment of the loans from China will only cause a greater stress on the economy. The plans for land ownership or long-term lease in Hambantota and Colombo Financial City are harbingers of how that debt situation could be ameliorated. It is likely that there will be constant pushes from China to seek strategic equity in the ports which may extend to berthing, basing and logistics rights. This could extend to docking potent platforms like submarines which can worsen the dynamics in the region since India is unlikely to remain a silent bystander to these events.

A likely solution to this financial vortex are hard economic measures and reforms. The strengthening of democracy becomes crucial for political and economic reforms, whereas China has preferred to deal with authoritarian leaders. The US, India and Japan have to act together to ensure that Sri Lanka doesn't slip back into the Chinese economic whirlpool again.

If Sri Lanka is crucial to China as an important cog in the global maritime network, the Maldives which sits astride the shipping lanes is no less important. China is determined to see it have as many favourable footholds available in the IOR, and have thus serenaded the Maldives. Unlike Sri Lanka, the Maldives has no scope for major transhipment ports due to physical limitations of the coral islands. Yet, China finds it valuable enough to be engaged with assiduously since it has the potential to control the eight degree channel. This is free from known navigational dangers and therefore crucial to international sea lanes, between the Minicoy Island and Ihavandiffulu Atoll. This is about 70 miles south of India. Ihavandiffolu also has a major project which has attracted China as an investor.

So far, the China–Maldives relations have no serious military content. Critical infrastructure like bridges and housing has been prime areas of cooperation. A major factor in Maldivian politics today is the influence of hard line Wahhabi Islam and its impacts. Being a low atoll vulnerable to climate change, Maldives is also sensitive to environment. Democracy, which is just taking shape in the island, is another driver. Though Maldives has a large public debt, its external debt is not as bad as Sri Lanka. China is a major factor in the economy, especially in tourism, which earns it the top dollar.

China's Maritime Commercial Network

Shipping by very nature is a global industry with a transnational spread. Even by those liberal standards, the Chinese maritime industry has spread its network fairly wide across geographies and maritime domains. China is a major player in port building, port operation, shipbuilding, shipping operation, providing manpower and has now created shipping indices just for the Maritime Silk Road traffic. China's shipbuilding industry has maintained its top position in the world ahead of South Korea. China has also been in the forefront of building as well as operations of ports across the globe. It is also the largest supplier of seamen to man the ships. The geographic spread of China's port investments extends across continents and oceans. From Panama and Miami in the Americas, to Piraeus in Europe to Tilawa and Colombo in the Indian neighbourhood, this network spreads all the way to the top East Asian Ports. Six of the top container routes had China at one end.[10] 32 out of top 50 container ports were fully or partially owned by China and handled 67 per cent of the containers.[11] Since 2010, Chinese companies have invested USD 45 billion in 40 ports globally.[12] Its quest for access through the Arctic, with a potential to bypass the IOR to connect Europe, has driven investment as far as Archangelsk in Russia. Chinese trade triggers a chain driving up ship sizes due to the economy of scale like the Vale max, leading to port expansions, which China is in a position to finance, create and pick stakes in. Many of these customer nations cannot afford to pay back, yielding strategic concessions. In both Sri Lanka and Malaysia, where China has invested in ports, also have had PLAN submarines on port call. The MSR is expected to give a new direction with a strategic overlay to the existing spread of commercial network.

Resources from Indian Ocean

Links between resources, especially energy and geopolitics, are too well known, and are a crucial factor in the Indian Ocean Region. The Indian Ocean is both a conduit and its littoral lands are a source of commodities for China. In 2015, 47 per cent of China's imports constituted of raw material such as copper, iron ore, etc., that go into infrastructure investment amounting to USD 800 billion.[13] The seabed can also be a source for polymetallic nodules in the future.

Of all the resources, energy is a cardinal factor. As the top importer of oil, and the third largest importer of LNG, China by 2035 will drive one-fourth of the global energy demand. The Indian Ocean littorals are important for China from an energy perspective. Eighty percent of crude oil imports to China are sourced or have to traverse via the Indian Ocean. Nearly thirty percent of LNG imports also traverse the Indian Ocean. This is a trend that will only increase over time as import dependencies only increase with time. The Middle East not only has 47 per cent of global oil reserves, but it also is cheap to extract. As a region, the Middle East's share in China's oil basket has been increasing (Refer Fig. 9.3). China's Middle East Strategy is one that is driven by energy as a core driver in its own words in context of the Arab League. The Indian Ocean is not only a source of these commodities but is also crucial for the transportation of these to China. The Pacific Ocean, where China is situated, is three times as broad as the Atlantic and Indian Oceans at the Equator. This implies that commodities from as far away as the Atlantic Coast of the Americas find the westerly Indian Ocean route viable as an option to China. This option only gets better as ship sizes increase to the very large crude and ore carriers, which cannot use the Panama Canal.

Politically, China has three tracks of relationships in the Middle East, i.e., with the Arab League, Iran and Israel. The former two are driven by energy, whereas the relations with Israel appear to be driven by security, sourcing of high-end technology and of late, investment. Iran is also about balancing US influence in the region. China has to its credit balanced relations with all three nations. The US's waning interest in oil and the Middle East has influenced how countries in the Middle East as well as China, are dealing with each other.

The oil economies want to diversify into other areas and China wants to invest in infrastructure and oil industry in the Middle East, which forms a symbiotic relationship. Religion also plays a role in this relationship with China's large restive Muslim population in Xinjiang with its Turkic connections.

Africa is China's largest source of crude oil after the Middle East, with Angola, Congo and South Sudan leading the list. China has invested deeply in all three oil-rich nations as well as other nations like Nigeria and Ethiopia. Africa is also a supplier of metals and minerals including uranium, which is sourced from Namibia. China's demand for aluminium, nickel, copper and zinc[14] is roughly half the world's demand and that for iron ore was around 70 per cent in 2015. Therefore, China has a motivation for investments in Africa, which direly needs critical infrastructure, especially railways and ports. It is building standard gauge rail lines connecting hinterlands to ports in Kenya, Tanzania, Sudan and Ethiopia with plans to connect landlocked countries to the coast line. Two Indian Ocean islands of Mauritius and Seychelles are being engaged by China as crucial stopovers in its plans for Africa. Relations with Mauritius have not graduated to arms-transfer level unlike that with Seychelles. Mauritius has a small but economically powerful Chinese diaspora but a politically powerful Indian diaspora. China is aiming to make Mauritius a key hub for its Africa Policy, by the creation of financial and industrial hubs. This comes at a crucial time when India–Mauritius relations are entering a new phase with double taxation avoidance agreements. The odd-man-out in the China-dependent resource economies is Australia. It is a liberal democracy of the Western genre and shares its values with the US. However it is geographically close and economically dependent on China. This dependence is for its exports as well as China's investments. This makes that relation tenuous.

The Indian Ocean: Some Common Challenges

The Indian Ocean as a geopolitical space has 38 nations which are diverse in race, religion, economy and political outlook. Majority of the littorals belong to the underdeveloped south. Stakeholders to the region collectively inherit certain natural trends such as climate change and demography. Climate change affects human security, making the population vulnerable to calamities forcing migrations. It is estimated that 50 per cent of global population will face a shortage of water, especially in the Middle East.[15] The low-lying, dense, deltaic littorals and coral islands in South Asia will face climate challenges more than others. An increased risk of natural disasters such as extreme weather, floods and droughts, demand an increased transnational cooperation and consensus.

The sale of weapons as inducements may not exactly help these nations cope with the climate. Sensing that danger, India and the SAARC have created a Humanitarian and Disaster Relief (HADR) ecosystem in the region. To mitigate this challenge, the existing convergence between India and China on climate change, can be extended to low-hanging fruits of cooperation in the Indian Ocean. This is globally significant as the US has pulled out of the Paris Deal.

A large inflow and availability of Chinese capital has the potential to impact domestic politics, foreign policies and political outlook of nations. At a time when democracy has been seen as the end of history,[16] authoritarian China poses some challenges to that theory. As a direct impact, the hard-line authoritarian constituencies in Sri Lanka, Maldives and Bangladesh find a friend in China and its capital. Secondly, its rise and present success motivates an alternate model. Thirdly, liberal capitalist democracies find it hard to match the economic, political and infrastructure inducements that authoritarian capitalism is able to deliver in the region. This is one of the greatest challenges to the future of democracy. As far as governance and democracy are concerned in the Indian Ocean, as per the EIU Democracy Index, Australia, India, South Africa, Malaysia, Sri Lanka, Bangladesh and Indonesia have near-mature democracies, with the rest of the littoral IOR nations having hybrid or authoritarian regimes.[17] The 'China Factor' over democracies in the region needs more data and analysis.

One major challenge in the region will be to synergise multiple critical infrastructure and connectivity projects that are being planned at a frantic pace. Some are domestic plans like the Sagarmala of India. Some are regional initiatives like the BBIN, BIMSTEC, etc. Others are international, like the INSTC, the Ashgabat Agreement, etc. There is also resurgence of the Asia Africa Growth Corridor, the US New Silk Road in Central Asia and the German Marshall Plan for Africa. For unlocking the true potential of these projects, there has to be a cooperative perspective to connectivity. These projects have to offer attractive financing and better implementation, and take the local and regional sensitivities into account, in order to become a viable alternative to China's offers in the region. They may even synergise with China's initiatives for better infrastructure in the region.

China's Strategies for the Indian Ocean

Unlike other Indian Ocean nations, India has an unsettled border with China, whereas the Indian Ocean—where China's economic and maritime interests intersect—is a few thousand miles away from China's shore. Such geography holds true for Indian interests in the South China Sea which is crucial for India's progress. Apart from borders, the issues of river waters and presence of the revered Tibetan spiritual leader the Dalai Lama in India are other significant issues of contention. Due to mature statecraft, the differences have been managed astutely till date by either side. However, there is always the chance of spiralling of incidents over an unsettled continental border. This has the potential to spill over to other domains, especially the Indian Ocean where China's interest and presence are only increasing. At the core of this relationship lies a certain lack of trust which manifests in multiple ways from the border issue to other international fora. Therefore, the need of the hour is for trust-building between India and China.

Apart from these two powers, the US will remain the preeminent power in the IOR, and will continue to play a critical role in the near term. From the IOR littorals, India, Australia, Indonesia and South Africa will be important players. Japan and Korea depend immensely on the Indian Ocean for energy, investments and markets. Russia, through effective roles in Syria, is back on the block, and the UK has returned to the IOR. It is these countries which have to take the lead in funding and leading collective governance and structures in the Indian Ocean which usher in peace.

The Chinese strategy pivots on the access to energy, resources and markets available in the Indian Ocean. Presently, it is focusing on picking political, infrastructure and economic gaps to swing the Indian Ocean nations and systems in favour of it. This creates 'hardwired' infrastructure advantageous to China, with little concern to regional realities, environment, economic and domestic stability. That graph of China's activities and influence is on the rise. This is bound to chafe with Indian interests as China graduates to active intervention in regional politics. Along with building trust, the reality is that only strength respects strength. India must derive that strength from an indigenous military industrial ecosystem. This is as critical as trust-building for meaningful engagement between the two ancient civilisations and the most populous states as they return to the centre stage in the Indian Ocean.

Finally, there is no 'single' Indian Ocean Maritime Strategy of China. It is a series of sub-strategies at work, each tailored to address China's needs, the domestic politics of nations and the regional politics of the Indian Ocean. If it is about access in the eastern Indian Ocean, it is also about the security of sealanes that drives it in Sri Lanka and the Maldives. Pakistan serves as an access as well as client state for balancing and containing India in South Asia.

Resources drive its strategy to the Western littorals of the Indian Ocean. Due to the political and economic diversity amongst the Indian Ocean nations, what works in one nation doesn't work in another. This diversity and economic underdevelopment is also the reason behind the absence of a common security architecture in the IOR unlike other oceans. China with its authoritarian political system and deep pockets is able to muster synergy and scale to serve its interests in the IOR. Offering an alternative is the need of the hour in the Indian Ocean Region. Countries such as the US, Japan, US, EU and India have to provide that much-needed choice before it is late. Notwithstanding the domestic checks and balances, they should keep pace with China's footwork —if not in quantity then in quality. A timely trickle on occasions serves more than a torrent.

NOTES

1. "Why Is World Trade Growth Slowing?," accessed July 22, 2017, https://www.economist.com/blogs/economist-explains/2016/10/economist-explains-5.
2. "The Middle-Income Trap," *The Economist*, accessed May 31, 2017, http://www.economist.com/blogs/graphicdetail/2012/03/focus-3.
3. Khurram Husain, "Exclusive: CPEC Master Plan Revealed," *DAWN.COM*, May 14, 2017, https://www.dawn.com/news/1333101.
4. Martin Stopford, *Maritime Economics 3e*, 3 edition (London/ ; New York: Routledge, 2008).
5. "New Rail Routes between China and Europe Will Change Trade Patterns," accessed September 24, 2017, https://www.economist.com/news/business/21728981-new-silk-railroad-will-challenge-airlines-and-shipping-firms-new-rail-routes-between-china.
6. Jeremy Page, "China Builds First Overseas Military Outpost," *Wall Street Journal*, August 19, 2016, sec. World, http://www.wsj.com/articles/china-builds-first-overseas-military-outpost-1471622690.
7. Chinese Military Diplomacy, 2003–2016: Trends and Implications by Kenneth Allen, Phillip C. Saunders, and John Chen
8. "China's 'Malacca Dilemma,'" *The Jamestown Foundation*, accessed August 2, 2015, http://www.jamestown.org/single/?no_cache=1&tx_ttnews%5Btt_news%5D=3943.
9. Robert D. Kaplan, *Asia's Cauldron: The South China Sea and the End of a Stable Pacific* (Random House Publishing Group, 2014).
10. Ibid.
11. "How China Rules the Waves," accessed April 24, 2017, https://ig.ft.com/sites/china-ports.
12. Ibid.
13. "Global Trends 2030," accessed September 5, 2016, https://www.dni.gov/index.php/about/organization/global-trends-2030.
14. Henry Sanderson, "Commodities Demand and China: An Explainer," *Financial Times*, January 19, 2016, https://www.ft.com/content/56a3dbce-bae6-11e5-bf7e-8a339b6f2164.
15. "Global Trends 2030."
16. Francis Fukuyama," The End of History?", *The National Interest*, Summer 1989
17. "EIU Democracy Index 2016," accessed June 15, 2017, https://infographics.economist.com/2017/DemocracyIndex/.

APPENDICES

APPENDIX 1

Vision and Actions on Jointly Building Silk Road Economic Belt and 21st-Century Maritime Silk Road

Issued by the National Development and Reform Commission, Ministry of Foreign Affairs, and Ministry of Commerce of the People's Republic of China, with State Council authorization

March 2015 *First Edition 2015*

Contents

Preface

More than two millennia ago the diligent and courageous people of Eurasia explored and opened up several routes of trade and cultural exchanges that linked the major civilizations of Asia, Europe and Africa, collectively called the Silk Road by later generations. For thousands of years, the Silk Road Spirit – "peace and cooperation, openness and inclusiveness, mutual learning and mutual benefit" – has been passed from generation to generation, promoted the progress of human civilization, and contributed greatly to the prosperity and development of the countries along the Silk Road. Symbolizing communication and cooperation between the East and the West, the Silk Road Spirit is a historic and cultural heritage shared by all countries around the world.

In the 21st century, a new era marked by the theme of peace, development, cooperation and mutual benefit, it is all the more important for us to carry on the Silk Road Spirit in face of the weak recovery of the global economy, and complex international and regional situations.

When Chinese President Xi Jinping visited Central Asia and Southeast Asia in September and October of 2013, he raised the initiative of jointly building the Silk Road Economic Belt and the 21st-Century Maritime Silk Road (hereinafter referred to as the Belt and Road), which have attracted close attention from all over the world. At the China-ASEAN Expo in 2013, Chinese Premier Li Keqiang emphasized the need to build the Maritime Silk Road oriented towards ASEAN, and to create strategic propellers for hinterland development. Accelerating the building of the Belt and Road can help promote the economic prosperity of the countries along the Belt and Road and regional economic cooperation, strengthen exchanges and mutual learning between different civilizations, and promote world peace and development. It is a great undertaking that will benefit people around the world.

The Belt and Road Initiative is a systematic project, which should be jointly built through consultation to meet the interests of all, and efforts should be made to integrate the development strategies of the countries along the Belt and Road. The Chinese government has drafted and published the Vision and Actions on Jointly Building Silk Road Economic Belt and 21st-Century Maritime Silk Road to promote the implementation of the Initiative, instill vigor and vitality into the ancient Silk Road, connect Asian, European and African countries more closely and promote mutually beneficial cooperation to a new high and in new forms.

I. Background

Complex and profound changes are taking place in the world. The underlying impact of the international financial crisis keeps emerging; the world economy is recovering slowly, and global development is uneven; the international trade and investment landscape and rules for multilateral trade and investment are undergoing major adjustments; and countries still face big challenges to their development.

The initiative to jointly build the Belt and Road, embracing the trend towards a multipolar world, economic globalization, cultural diversity and greater IT application, is designed to uphold the global free trade regime and the open world economy in the spirit of open regional cooperation. It is aimed at promoting orderly and free flow of economic factors, highly efficient allocation of resources and deep integration of markets; encouraging the countries along the Belt and Road to achieve economic policy coordination and carry out broader and more in-depth regional cooperation of higher standards; and jointly creating an open, inclusive and balanced regional economic cooperation architecture that benefits all. Jointly building the Belt and Road is in the interests of the world community. Reflecting the common ideals and pursuit of human societies, it is a positive endeavor to seek new models of international cooperation and global governance, and will inject new positive energy into world peace and development.

The Belt and Road Initiative aims to promote the connectivity of Asian, European and African continents and their adjacent seas, establish and strengthen partnerships among the countries along the Belt and Road, set up all-dimensional, multi-tiered and composite connectivity networks, and realize diversified, independent, balanced and sustainable development in these countries. The connectivity projects of the Initiative will help align and coordinate the development strategies of the countries along the Belt and Road, tap market potential in this region, promote investment and consumption, create demands and job opportunities, enhance people-to-people and cultural exchanges, and mutual learning among the peoples of the relevant countries, and enable them to understand, trust and respect each other and live in harmony, peace and prosperity.

China's economy is closely connected with the world economy. China will stay committed to the basic policy of opening-up, build a new pattern of all-round opening-up, and integrate itself deeper into the world economic system. The Initiative will enable China to further expand and deepen its opening-up, and to strengthen its mutually beneficial cooperation with countries in Asia, Europe and Africa and the rest of the world. China is committed to shouldering more responsibilities and obligations within its capabilities, and making greater contributions to the peace and development of mankind.

II. Principles

The Belt and Road Initiative is in line with the purposes and principles of the UN Charter. It upholds the Five Principles of Peaceful Coexistence: mutual respect for each other's sovereignty and territorial integrity, mutual non-aggression, mutual non-interference in each other's internal affairs, equality and mutual benefit, and peaceful coexistence.

The Initiative is open for cooperation. It covers, but is not limited to, the area of the ancient Silk Road. It is open to all countries, and international and regional organizations for engagement, so that the results of the concerted efforts will benefit wider areas.

The Initiative is harmonious and inclusive. It advocates tolerance among civilizations, respects the paths and modes of development chosen by different countries, and supports dialogues among different civilizations on the principles of seeking common ground while shelving differences and drawing on each other's strengths, so that all countries can coexist in peace for common prosperity.

The Initiative follows market operation. It will abide by market rules and international norms, give play to the decisive role of the market in resource allocation and the primary role of enterprises, and let the governments perform their due functions.

The Initiative seeks mutual benefit. It accommodates the interests and concerns of all parties involved, and seeks a conjunction of interests and the "biggest common denominator" for cooperation so as to give full play to the wisdom and creativity, strengths and potentials of all parties.

III. Framework

The Belt and Road Initiative is a way for win-win cooperation that promotes common development and prosperity and a road towards peace and friendship by enhancing mutual understanding and trust, and strengthening all-round exchanges. The Chinese government advocates peace and cooperation, openness and inclusiveness, mutual learning and mutual benefit. It promotes practical cooperation in all fields, and works to build a community of shared interests, destiny and responsibility featuring mutual political trust, economic integration and cultural inclusiveness.

The Belt and Road run through the continents of Asia, Europe and Africa, connecting the vibrant East Asia economic circle at one end and developed European economic circle at the other, and encompassing countries with huge potential for economic development. The Silk Road Economic Belt focuses on bringing together China, Central Asia, Russia and Europe (the Baltic); linking China with the Persian Gulf and the Mediterranean Sea through Central Asia and West Asia; and connecting China with Southeast Asia, South Asia and the Indian Ocean. The 21st-Century Maritime Silk Road is designed to go from China's coast to Europe through the South China Sea and the

Indian Ocean in one route, and from China's coast through the South China Sea to the South Pacific in the other.

On land, the Initiative will focus on jointly building a new Eurasian Land Bridge and developing China-Mongolia-Russia, China-Central Asia-West Asia and China-Indochina Peninsula economic corridors by taking advantage of international transport routes, relying on core cities along the Belt and Road and using key economic industrial parks as cooperation platforms. At sea, the Initiative will focus on jointly building smooth, secure and efficient transport routes connecting major sea ports along the Belt and Road. The China-Pakistan Economic Corridor and the Bangladesh-China-India-Myanmar Economic Corridor are closely related to the Belt and Road Initiative, and therefore require closer cooperation and greater progress.

The Initiative is an ambitious economic vision of the opening-up of and cooperation among the countries along the Belt and Road. Countries should work in concert and move towards the objectives of mutual benefit and common security. To be specific, they need to improve the region's infrastructure, and put in place a secure and efficient network of land, sea and air passages, lifting their connectivity to a higher level; further enhance trade and investment facilitation, establish a network of free trade areas that meet high standards, maintain closer economic ties, and deepen political trust; enhance cultural exchanges; encourage different civilizations to learn from each other and flourish together; and promote mutual understanding, peace and friendship among people of all countries.

IV. Cooperation Priorities

Countries along the Belt and Road have their own resource advantages and their economies are mutually complementary. Therefore, there is a great potential and space for cooperation. They should promote policy coordination, facilities connectivity, unimpeded trade, financial integration and people-to-people bonds as their five major goals, and strengthen cooperation in the following key areas:

Policy coordination

Enhancing policy coordination is an important guarantee for implementing the Initiative. We should promote intergovernmental cooperation, build a multi-level intergovernmental macro policy exchange and communication mechanism, expand shared interests, enhance mutual political trust, and reach new cooperation consensus. Countries along the Belt and Road may fully coordinate their economic development strategies and policies, work out plans and measures for regional cooperation, negotiate to solve cooperation-related issues, and jointly provide policy support for the implementation of practical cooperation and large-scale projects.

Facilities connectivity

Facilities connectivity is a priority area for implementing the Initiative. On the basis of respecting each other's sovereignty and security concerns, countries along the Belt and Road should improve the connectivity of their infrastructure construction plans and technical standard systems, jointly push forward the construction of international trunk passageways, and form an infrastructure network connecting all sub-regions in Asia, and between Asia, Europe and Africa step by step. At the same time, efforts should be made to promote green and low-carbon infrastructure construction and operation management, taking into full account the impact of climate change on the construction.

With regard to transport infrastructure construction, we should focus on the key passageways, junctions and projects, and give priority to linking up unconnected road sections, removing transport bottlenecks, advancing road safety facilities and traffic management facilities and equipment, and improving road network connectivity. We should build a unified coordination mechanism for whole-course transportation, increase connectivity of customs clearance, reloading and multimodal transport between countries, and gradually formulate compatible and standard transport rules, so as to realize international transport facilitation. We should push forward port infrastructure construction, build smooth land-water transportation channels, and advance port cooperation; increase sea routes and the number of voyages, and enhance information technology cooperation in maritime logistics. We should expand and build platforms and mechanisms for comprehensive civil aviation cooperation, and quicken our pace in improving aviation infrastructure.

We should promote cooperation in the connectivity of energy infrastructure, work in concert to ensure the security of oil and gas pipelines and other transport routes, build cross-border power supply networks and power-transmission routes, and cooperate in regional power grid upgrading and transformation.

We should jointly advance the construction of cross-border optical cables and other communications trunk line networks, improve international communications connectivity, and create an Information Silk Road. We should build bilateral cross-border optical cable networks at a quicker pace, plan transcontinental submarine optical cable projects, and improve spatial (satellite) information passageways to expand information exchanges and cooperation.

Unimpeded trade

Investment and trade cooperation is a major task in building the Belt and Road. We should strive to improve investment and trade facilitation, and remove investment and trade barriers for the creation of a sound business environment within the region and in all related countries. We will discuss with countries and regions along the Belt and Road on opening free trade areas so as to unleash the potential for expanded cooperation.

Countries along the Belt and Road should enhance customs cooperation such as information exchange, mutual recognition of regulations, and mutual assistance in law enforcement; improve bilateral and multilateral cooperation in the fields of inspection and quarantine, certification and accreditation, standard measurement, and statistical information; and work to ensure that the WTO Trade Facilitation Agreement takes effect and is implemented. We should improve the customs clearance facilities of border ports, establish a "single-window" in border ports, reduce customs clearance costs, and improve customs clearance capability. We should increase cooperation in supply chain safety and convenience, improve the coordination of cross-border supervision procedures, promote online checking of inspection and quarantine certificates, and facilitate mutual recognition of Authorized Economic Operators. We should lower non-tariff barriers, jointly improve the transparency of technical trade measures, and enhance trade liberalization and facilitation.

We should expand trading areas, improve trade structure, explore new growth areas of trade, and promote trade balance. We should make innovations in our forms of trade, and develop cross-border e-commerce and other modern business models. A service trade support system should be set up to consolidate and expand conventional trade, and efforts to develop modern service trade should be strengthened. We should integrate investment and trade, and promote trade through investment.

We should speed up investment facilitation, eliminate investment barriers, and push forward negotiations on bilateral investment protection agreements and double taxation avoidance agreements to protect the lawful rights and interests of investors.

We should expand mutual investment areas, deepen cooperation in agriculture, forestry, animal husbandry and fisheries, agricultural machinery manufacturing and farm produce processing, and promote cooperation in marine-product farming, deep-sea fishing, aquatic product processing, seawater desalination, marine biopharmacy, ocean engineering technology, environmental protection industries, marine tourism and other fields. We should increase cooperation in the exploration and development of coal, oil, gas, metal minerals and other conventional energy sources; advance cooperation in hydropower, nuclear power, wind power, solar power and other clean, renewable energy sources; and promote cooperation in the processing and conversion of energy and resources at or near places where they are exploited, so as to create an integrated industrial chain of energy and resource cooperation. We should enhance cooperation in deep-processing technology, equipment and engineering services in the fields of energy and resources.

We should push forward cooperation in emerging industries. In accordance with the principles of mutual complementarity and mutual benefit, we should promote in-depth cooperation with other countries along the Belt and Road in new-generation information technology, biotechnology, new energy technology, new materials and other emerging industries, and establish entrepreneurial and investment cooperation mechanisms.

We should improve the division of labor and distribution of industrial chains by encouraging the entire industrial chain and related industries to develop in concert; establish R&D, production and marketing systems; and improve industrial supporting capacity and the overall competitiveness of regional industries. We should increase the openness of our service industry to each other to accelerate the development of regional service industries. We should explore a new mode of investment cooperation, working together to build all forms of industrial parks such as overseas economic and trade cooperation zones and cross-border economic cooperation zones, and promote industrial cluster development. We should promote ecological progress in conducting investment and trade, increase cooperation in conserving eco-environment, protecting biodiversity, and tackling climate change, and join hands to make the Silk Road an environment-friendly one.

We welcome companies from all countries to invest in China, and encourage Chinese enterprises to participate in infrastructure construction in other countries along the Belt and Road, and make industrial investments there. We support localized operation and management of Chinese companies to boost the local economy, increase local employment, improve local livelihood, and take social responsibilities in protecting local biodiversity and eco-environment.

Financial integration

Financial integration is an important underpinning for implementing the Belt and Road Initiative. We should deepen financial cooperation, and make more efforts in building a currency stability system, investment and financing system and credit information system in Asia. We should expand the scope and scale of bilateral currency swap and settlement with other countries along the Belt and Road, open and develop the bond market in Asia, make joint efforts to establish the Asian Infrastructure Investment Bank and BRICS New Development Bank, conduct negotiation among related parties on establishing Shanghai Cooperation Organization (SCO) financing institution, and set up and put into operation the Silk Road Fund as early as possible. We should strengthen practical cooperation of China-ASEAN Interbank Association and SCO Interbank Association, and carry out multilateral financial cooperation in the form of syndicated loans and bank credit. We will support the efforts of governments of the countries along the Belt and Road and their companies and financial institutions with good credit-rating to issue Renminbi bonds in China. Qualified Chinese financial institutions and companies are encouraged to issue bonds in both Renminbi and foreign currencies outside China, and use the funds thus collected in countries along the Belt and Road.

We should strengthen financial regulation cooperation, encourage the signing of MOUs on cooperation in bilateral financial regulation, and establish an efficient regulation coordination mechanism in the region. We should improve the system of risk response and crisis management, build a regional financial risk early-warning system, and create an exchange and cooperation mechanism of addressing cross-border risks and crisis. We should increase cross-border exchange and cooperation between credit investigation regulators, credit investigation institutions and credit rating institutions. We should give full play to the role of the Silk Road Fund and that of sovereign wealth funds of countries along the Belt and Road, and encourage commercial equity investment funds and private funds to participate in the construction of key projects of the Initiative.

People-to-people bond

People-to-people bond provides the public support for implementing the Initiative. We should carry forward the spirit of friendly cooperation of the Silk Road by promoting extensive cultural and academic exchanges, personnel exchanges and cooperation, media cooperation, youth and women exchanges and volunteer services, so as to win public support for deepening bilateral and multilateral cooperation.

We should send more students to each other's countries, and promote cooperation in jointly running schools. China provides 10,000 government scholarships to the countries along the Belt and Road every year. We should hold culture years, arts festivals, film festivals, TV weeks and book fairs in each other's countries; cooperate on the production and translation of fine films, radio and TV programs; and jointly apply for and protect World Cultural Heritage sites. We should also increase personnel exchange and cooperation between countries along the Belt and Road.

We should enhance cooperation in and expand the scale of tourism; hold tourism promotion weeks and publicity months in each other's countries; jointly create competitive international tourist routes and products with Silk Road features; and make it more convenient to apply for tourist visa in countries along the Belt and Road. We should push forward cooperation on the 21st-Century Maritime Silk Road cruise tourism program. We should carry out sports exchanges and support countries along the Belt and Road in their bid for hosting major international sports events.

We should strengthen cooperation with neighboring countries on epidemic information sharing, the exchange of prevention and treatment technologies and the training of medical professionals, and improve our capability to jointly address public health emergencies. We will provide medical assistance and emergency medical aid to relevant countries, and carry out practical cooperation in maternal and child health, disability rehabilitation, and major infectious diseases including AIDS, tuberculosis and malaria. We will also expand cooperation on traditional medicine.

We should increase our cooperation in science and technology, establish joint labs (or research centers), international technology transfer centers and maritime cooperation centers, promote sci-tech personnel exchanges, cooperate in tackling key sci-tech problems, and work together to improve sci-tech innovation capability.

We should integrate existing resources to expand and advance practical cooperation between countries along the Belt and Road on youth employment, entrepreneurship training, vocational skill development, social security management, public administration and management and in other areas of common interest.

We should give full play to the bridging role of communication between political parties and parliaments, and promote friendly exchanges between legislative bodies, major political parties and political organizations of countries along the Belt and Road. We should carry out exchanges and cooperation among cities, encourage major cities in these countries to become sister cities, focus on promoting practical cooperation, particularly cultural and people-to-people exchanges, and create more lively examples of cooperation. We welcome the think tanks in the countries along the Belt and Road to jointly conduct research and hold forums.

We should increase exchanges and cooperation between non-governmental organizations of countries along the Belt and Road, organize public interest activities concerning education, health care, poverty reduction, biodiversity and ecological protection for the benefit of the general public, and improve the production and living conditions of poverty-stricken areas along the Belt and Road. We should enhance international exchanges and cooperation on culture and media, and leverage the positive role of the Internet and new media tools to foster harmonious and friendly cultural environment and public opinion.

V. Cooperation Mechanisms

The world economic integration is accelerating and regional cooperation is on the upswing. China will take full advantage of the existing bilateral and multilateral cooperation mechanisms to push forward the building of the Belt and Road and to promote the development of regional cooperation.

We should strengthen bilateral cooperation, and promote comprehensive development of bilateral relations through multi-level and multi-channel communication and consultation. We should encourage the signing of cooperation MOUs or plans, and develop a number of bilateral cooperation pilot projects. We should establish and improve bilateral joint working mechanisms, and draw up implementation plans and roadmaps for advancing the Belt and Road Initiative. In addition, we should give full play to the existing bilateral mechanisms such as joint committee, mixed committee, coordinating committee, steering committee and management committee to coordinate and promote the implementation of cooperation projects.

We should enhance the role of multilateral cooperation mechanisms, make full use of existing mechanisms such as the Shanghai Cooperation Organization (SCO), ASEAN Plus China (10+1), Asia-Pacific Economic Cooperation (APEC), Asia-Europe Meeting (ASEM), Asia Cooperation Dialogue (ACD), Conference on Interaction and Confidence-Building Measures in Asia (CICA),

China-Arab States Cooperation Forum (CASCF), China-Gulf Cooperation Council Strategic Dialogue, Greater Mekong Sub-region (GMS) Economic Cooperation, and Central Asia Regional Economic Cooperation (CAREC) to strengthen communication with relevant countries, and attract more countries and regions to participate in the Belt and Road Initiative.

We should continue to encourage the constructive role of the international forums and exhibitions at regional and sub-regional levels hosted by countries along the Belt and Road, as well as such platforms as Boao Forum for Asia, China-ASEAN Expo, China-Eurasia Expo, Euro-Asia Economic Forum, China International Fair for Investment and Trade, China-South Asia Expo, China-Arab States Expo, Western China International Fair, China-Russia Expo, and Qianhai Cooperation Forum. We should support the local authorities and general public of countries along the Belt and Road to explore the historical and cultural heritage of the Belt and Road, jointly hold investment, trade and cultural exchange activities, and ensure the success of the Silk Road (Dunhuang) International Culture Expo, Silk Road International Film Festival and Silk Road International Book Fair. We propose to set up an international summit forum on the Belt and Road Initiative.

VI. China's Regions in Pursuing Opening-Up

In advancing the Belt and Road Initiative, China will fully leverage the comparative advantages of its various regions, adopt a proactive strategy of further opening-up, strengthen interaction and cooperation among the eastern, western and central regions, and comprehensively improve the openness of the Chinese economy.

Northwestern and northeastern regions. We should make good use of Xinjiang's geographic advantages and its role as a window of westward opening-up to deepen communication and cooperation with Central, South and West Asian countries, make it a key transportation, trade, logistics, culture, science and education center, and a core area on the Silk Road Economic Belt. We should give full scope to the economic and cultural strengths of Shaanxi and Gansu provinces and the ethnic and cultural advantages of the Ningxia Hui Autonomous Region and Qinghai Province, build Xi'an into a new focus of reform and opening-up in China's interior, speed up the development and opening-up of cities such as Lanzhou and Xining, and advance the building of the Ningxia Inland Opening-up Pilot Economic Zone with the goal of creating strategic channels, trade and logistics hubs and key bases for industrial and cultural exchanges opening to Central, South and West Asian countries.

We should give full play to Inner Mongolia's proximity to Mongolia and Russia, improve the railway links connecting Heilongjiang Province with Russia and the regional railway network, strengthen cooperation between China's Heilongjiang, Jilin and Liaoning provinces and Russia's Far East region on sea-land multi-modal transport, and advance the construction of an Eurasian high-speed transport corridor linking Beijing and Moscow with the goal of building key windows opening to the north.

Southwestern region. We should give full play to the unique advantage of Guangxi Zhuang Autonomous Region as a neighbor of ASEAN countries, speed up the opening-up and development of the Beibu Gulf Economic Zone and the Pearl River-Xijiang Economic Zone, build an international corridor opening to the ASEAN region, create new strategic anchors for the opening-up and development of the southwest and mid-south regions of China, and form an important gateway connecting the Silk Road Economic Belt and the 21st-Century Maritime Silk Road. We should make good use of the geographic advantage of Yunnan Province, advance the construction of an international transport corridor connecting China with neighboring countries, develop a new highlight of economic cooperation in the Greater Mekong Sub-region, and make the region a pivot of China's opening-up to South and Southeast Asia. We should promote the border trade and tourism and culture cooperation between Tibet Autonomous Region and neighboring countries such as Nepal..

Coastal regions, and Hong Kong, Macao and Taiwan. We should leverage the strengths of the Yangtze River Delta, Pearl River Delta, west coast of the Taiwan Straits, Bohai Rim, and other areas with economic zones boasting a high level of openness, robust economic strengths and strong catalytic role, speed up the development of the China (Shanghai) Pilot Free Trade Zone, and support Fujian Province in becoming a core area of the 21st-Century Maritime Silk Road. We should give full scope to the role of Qianhai (Shenzhen), Nansha (Guangzhou), Hengqin (Zhuhai) and Pingtan (Fujian) in opening-up and cooperation, deepen their cooperation with Hong Kong, Macao and Taiwan, and help to build the Guangdong-Hong Kong-Macao Big Bay Area. We should promote the development of the Zhejiang Marine Economy Development Demonstration Zone, Fujian Marine Economic Pilot Zone and Zhoushan Archipelago New Area, and further open Hainan Province as an international tourism island. We should strengthen the port construction of coastal cities such as Shanghai, Tianjin, Ningbo-Zhoushan, Guangzhou, Shenzhen, Zhanjiang, Shantou, Qingdao, Yantai, Dalian, Fuzhou, Xiamen, Quanzhou, Haikou and Sanya, and strengthen the functions of international hub airports such as Shanghai and Guangzhou. We should use opening-up to motivate these areas to carry out deeper reform, create new systems and mechanisms of open economy, step up scientific and technological innovation, develop new advantages for participating in and leading international cooperation and competition, and become the pace-setter and main force in the Belt and Road Initiative, particularly the building of the 21st-Century Maritime Silk Road. We should leverage the unique role of overseas Chinese and the Hong Kong and Macao Special Administrative Regions, and encourage them to participate in and contribute to the Belt and Road Initiative. We should also make proper arrangements for the Taiwan region to be part of this effort.

Inland regions. We should make use of the advantages of inland regions, including a vast landmass, rich human resources and a strong industrial foundation, focus on such key regions as the city clusters along the middle reaches of the Yangtze River, around Chengdu and Chongqing, in central Henan Province, around Hohhot, Baotou, Erdos and Yulin, and around Harbin and Changchun to propel regional interaction and cooperation and industrial concentration. We should build Chongqing into an important pivot for developing and opening up the western region, and make Chengdu, Zhengzhou, Wuhan, Changsha, Nanchang and Hefei leading areas of opening-up in the inland regions. We should accelerate cooperation between regions on the upper and middle reaches of the Yangtze River and their counterparts along Russia's Volga River. We should set up coordination mechanisms in terms of railway transport and port customs clearance for the China-Europe corridor, cultivate the brand of "China-Europe freight trains," and construct a cross-border transport corridor connecting the eastern, central and western regions. We should support inland cities such as Zhengzhou and Xi'an in building airports and international land ports, strengthen customs clearance cooperation between inland ports and ports in the coastal and border regions, and launch pilot e-commerce services for cross-border trade. We should optimize the layout of special customs oversight areas, develop new models of processing trade, and deepen industrial cooperation with countries along the Belt and Road.

VII. China in Action

For more than a year, the Chinese government has been actively promoting the building of the Belt and Road, enhancing communication and consultation and advancing practical cooperation with countries along the Belt and Road, and introduced a series of policies and measures for early outcomes.

High-level guidance and facilitation. President Xi Jinping and Premier Li Keqiang have visited over 20 countries, attended the Dialogue on Strengthening Connectivity Partnership and the sixth ministerial conference of the China-Arab States Cooperation Forum, and met with leaders of relevant countries to discuss bilateral relations and regional development issues. They have used these opportunities to explain the rich contents and positive implications of the Belt and Road Initiative, and their efforts have helped bring about a broad consensus on the Belt and Road Initiative.

Signing cooperation framework. China has signed MOUs of cooperation on the joint development of the Belt and Road with some countries, and on regional cooperation and border cooperation and mid- and long-term development plans for economic and trade cooperation with some neighboring countries. It has proposed outlines of regional cooperation plans with some adjacent countries.

Promoting project cooperation. China has enhanced communication and consultation with countries along the Belt and Road, and promoted a number of key cooperation projects in the fields of infrastructure connectivity, industrial investment, resource development, economic and trade cooperation, financial cooperation, cultural exchanges, ecological protection and maritime cooperation where the conditions are right.

Improving policies and measures. The Chinese government will integrate its domestic resources to provide stronger policy support for the Initiative. It will facilitate the establishment of the Asian Infrastructure Investment Bank. China has proposed the Silk Road Fund, and the investment function of the China-Eurasia Economic Cooperation Fund will be reinforced. We will encourage bank card clearing institutions to conduct cross-border clearing operations, and payment institutions to conduct cross-border payment business. We will actively promote investment and trade facilitation, and accelerate the reform of integrated regional customs clearance.

Boosting the role of cooperation platforms. A number of international summits, forums, seminars and expos on the theme of the Belt and Road Initiative have been held, which have played an important role in increasing mutual understanding, reaching consensus and deepening cooperation.

VIII. Embracing a Brighter Future Together

Though proposed by China, the Belt and Road Initiative is a common aspiration of all countries along their routes. China is ready to conduct equal-footed consultation with all countries along the Belt and Road to seize the opportunity provided by the Initiative, promote opening-up, communication and integration among countries in a larger scope, with higher standards and at deeper levels, while giving consideration to the interests and aspirations of all parties. The development of the Belt and Road is open and inclusive, and we welcome the active participation of all countries and international and regional organizations in this Initiative.

The development of the Belt and Road should mainly be conducted through policy communication and objectives coordination. It is a pluralistic and open process of cooperation which can be highly flexible, and does not seek conformity. China will join other countries along the Belt and Road to substantiate and improve the content and mode of the Belt and Road cooperation, work out relevant timetables and roadmaps, and align national development programs and regional cooperation plans.

China will work with countries along the Belt and Road to carry out joint research, forums and fairs, personnel training, exchanges and visits under the framework of existing bilateral, multilateral, regional and sub-regional cooperation mechanisms, so that they will gain a better understanding and recognition of the contents, objectives and tasks of the Belt and Road Initiative.

China will work with countries along the Belt and Road to steadily advance demonstration projects, jointly identify programs that accommodate bilateral and multilateral interests, and accelerate the launching of programs that are agreed upon by parties and ready for implementation, so as to ensure early harvest.

The Belt and Road cooperation features mutual respect and trust, mutual benefit and win-win cooperation, and mutual learning between civilizations. As long as all countries along the Belt and Road make concerted efforts to pursue our common goal, there will be bright prospects for the Silk Road Economic Belt and the 21st-Century Maritime Silk Road, and the people of countries along the Belt and Road can all benefit from this Initiative.

APPENDIX 2

Responding to a Query on the Participation of India in OBOR/BRI Forum, the Official Spokesperson Said

We had received formal invitation to participate in the 6 separate forums that China is organizing as part of the Belt and Road Forum being held in Beijing on May 14-16, 2017.

We are of firm belief that connectivity initiatives must be ***based on universally recognized international norms, good governance, rule of law, openness, transparency and equality***. Connectivity initiatives must follow principles of financial responsibility to avoid projects that would create **unsustainable debt burden for communities; balanced ecological and environmental protection and preservation standards; transparent assessment of project costs; and skill and technology transfer** to help long-term running and maintenance of the assets created by local communities. Connectivity projects must be pursued in a manner that respects ***sovereignty and territorial integrity***.

India shares international community's desire for enhancing physical connectivity and believes that it should bring greater economic benefits to all in an equitable and balanced manner. We are working with many countries and international institutions in support of physical and digital connectivity in our own immediate and near neighbourhood.

Expansion and strengthening of connectivity is an integral part of India's economic and diplomatic initiatives. Under the 'Act East' policy, we are pursuing the Trilateral Highway project; under our 'Neighbourhood First' policy we are developing multimodal linkages with Myanmar and Bangladesh; under our 'Go West' strategy, we are engaged with Iran on Chabahar Port and with Iran and other partners in Central Asia on International North South Transport Corridor. BBIN initiative is aimed at enhancing logistics efficiencies in South Asian region. We are also actively considering acceding to TIR Convention.

Guided by our principled position in the matter, we have been urging China to engage in a ***meaningful dialogue on its connectivity initiative***, 'One Belt, One Road' which was later renamed as 'Belt and Road Initiative'. We are awaiting a positive response from the Chinese side.

Regarding the so-called '***China-Pakistan Economic Corridor***', which is being projected as the flagship project of the BRI/OBOR, the international community is well aware of India's position. No country can accept a project that ignores its core concerns on sovereignty and territorial integrity.

New Delhi
13 May 2017

APPENDIX 3

China's Military Strategy (Full Text)

Updated: May 27, 2015, 10:55 AM *Xinhua*: The Information Office of the State Council on Tuesday published a White Paper on China's military strategy. The following is the full text:

China's Military Strategy, The State Council Information Office of the People's Republic of China, May 2015, Beijing

Contents

Preface

The world today is undergoing unprecedented changes, and China is at a critical stage of reform and development. In their endeavor to realize the Chinese Dream of great national rejuvenation, the Chinese people aspire to join hands with the rest of the world to maintain peace, pursue development and share prosperity.

China's destiny is vitally interrelated with that of the world as a whole. A prosperous and stable world would provide China with opportunities, while China's peaceful development also offers an opportunity for the whole world. China will unswervingly follow the path of peaceful development, pursue an independent foreign policy of peace and a national defense policy that is defensive in nature, oppose hegemonism and power politics in all forms, and will never seek hegemony or expansion. China's armed forces will remain a staunch force in maintaining world peace.

Building a strong national defense and powerful armed forces is a strategic task of China's modernization drive and a security guarantee for China's peaceful development. Subordinate to and serving the national strategic goal, China's military strategy is an overarching guidance for blueprinting and directing the building and employment of the country's armed forces. At this new historical starting point, China's armed forces will adapt themselves to new changes in the national security environment, firmly follow the goal of the Communist Party of China (CPC) to build a strong military for the new situation, implement the military strategic guideline of active defense in the new situation, accelerate the modernization of national defense and armed forces, resolutely safeguard China's sovereignty, security and development interests, and provide a strong guarantee for achieving the national strategic goal of the "two centenaries" and for realizing the Chinese Dream of achieving the great rejuvenation of the Chinese nation.

I. National Security Situation

In today's world, the global trends toward multi-polarity and economic globalization are intensifying, and an information society is rapidly coming into being. Countries are increasingly bound together in a community of shared destiny. Peace, development, cooperation and mutual benefit have become an irresistible tide of the times.

Profound changes are taking place in the international situation, as manifested in the historic changes in the balance of power, global governance structure, Asia-Pacific geostrategic landscape, and international competition in the economic, scientific and technological, and military fields. The forces for world peace are on the rise, so are the factors against war. In the foreseeable future, a world war is unlikely, and the international situation is expected to remain generally peaceful. There are, however, new threats from hegemonism, power politics and neo-interventionism. International competition for the redistribution of power, rights and interests is tending to intensify. Terrorist activities are growing increasingly worrisome. Hotspot issues, such as ethnic, religious, border and territorial disputes, are complex and volatile. Small-scale wars, conflicts and crises are recurrent in some regions. Therefore, the world still faces both immediate and potential threats of local wars.

With a generally favorable external environment, China will remain in an important period of strategic opportunities for its development, a period in which much can be achieved. China's comprehensive national strength, core competitiveness and risk-resistance capacity are notably increasing, and China enjoys growing international standing and influence. Domestically, the Chinese people's standard of living has remarkably improved, and Chinese society remains stable. China, as a large developing country, still faces multiple and complex security threats, as well as increasing external impediments and challenges. Subsistence and development security concerns, as well as traditional and non-traditional security threats are interwoven. Therefore, China has an arduous task to safeguard its national unification, territorial integrity and development interests.

As the world economic and strategic center of gravity is shifting ever more rapidly to the Asia-Pacific region, the US carries on its "rebalancing" strategy and enhances its military presence and its military alliances in this region. Japan is sparing no effort to dodge the post-war mechanism, overhauling its military and security policies. Such development has caused grave concerns among other countries in the region. On the issues concerning China's territorial sovereignty and maritime rights and interests, some of its offshore neighbors take provocative actions and reinforce their military presence on China's reefs and islands that they have illegally occupied. Some external countries are also busy meddling in South China Sea affairs; a tiny few maintain constant close-in air and sea surveillance and reconnaissance against China. It is thus a long-standing task for China to safeguard its maritime rights and interests. Certain disputes over land territory are still smoldering. The Korean Peninsula and Northeast Asia are shrouded in instability and uncertainty. Regional terrorism, separatism and extremism are rampant. All these have a negative impact on the security and stability along China's periphery.

The Taiwan issue bears on China's reunification and long-term development, and reunification is an inevitable trend in the course of national rejuvenation. In recent years, cross-Taiwan Straits relations have sustained a sound momentum of peaceful development, but the root cause of instability has not yet been removed, and the "Taiwan independence" separatist forces and their activities are still the biggest threat to the peaceful development of cross-Straits relations. Further, China faces a formidable task to maintain political security and social stability. Separatist forces for "East Turkistan independence" and "Tibet independence" have inflicted serious damage, particularly with escalating violent terrorist activities by "East Turkistan independence" forces. Besides, anti-China forces have never given up their attempt to instigate a "color revolution" in this country. Consequently, China faces more challenges in terms of national security and social stability. With the growth of China's national interests, its national security is more vulnerable to international and regional turmoil, terrorism, piracy, serious natural disasters and epidemics, and the security of overseas interests concerning energy and resources, strategic sea lines of communication (SLOCs), as well as institutions, personnel and assets abroad, has become an imminent issue.

The world revolution in military affairs (RMA) is proceeding to a new stage. Long-range, precise, smart, stealthy and unmanned weapons and equipment are becoming increasingly sophisticated. Outer space and cyber space have become new commanding heights in strategic competition among all parties. The form of war is accelerating its evolution to informationization. World major powers are actively adjusting their national security strategies and defense policies, and speeding up their military transformation and force restructuring. The aforementioned revolutionary changes in military technologies and the form of war have not only had a significant impact on the international political and military landscapes, but also posed new and severe challenges to China's military security.

II. Missions and Strategic Tasks of China's Armed Forces

China's national strategic goal is to complete the building of a moderately prosperous society in all respects by 2021 when the CPC celebrates its centenary; and the building of a modern socialist country that is prosperous, strong, democratic, culturally advanced and harmonious by 2049 when the People's Republic of China (PRC) marks its centenary. It is a Chinese Dream of achieving the great rejuvenation of the Chinese nation. The Chinese Dream is to make the country strong. China's armed forces take their dream of making the military strong as part of the Chinese Dream. Without a strong military, a country can be neither safe nor strong. In the new historical period, aiming at the CPC's goal of building a strong military in the new situation, China's armed forces will unswervingly adhere to the principle of the CPC's absolute leadership, uphold combat effectiveness as the sole and fundamental standard, carry on their glorious traditions, and work to build themselves into a people's military that follows the CPC's commands, can fight and win, and boasts a fine style of work.

In the new circumstances, the national security issues facing China encompass far more subjects, extend over a greater range, and cover a longer time span than at any time in the country's history. Internally and externally, the factors at play are more complex than ever before. Therefore, it is necessary to uphold a holistic view of national security, balance internal and external security, homeland and citizen security, traditional and non-traditional security, subsistence and development security, and China's own security and the common security of the world.

To realize China's national strategic goal and implement the holistic view of national security, new requirements have been raised for innovative development of China's military strategy and the accomplishment of military missions and tasks. In response to the new requirement of safeguarding national security and development interests, China's armed forces will work harder to create a favorable strategic posture with more emphasis on the employment of military forces and means, and provide a solid security guarantee for the country's peaceful development. In response to the new requirement arising from the changing security situation, the armed forces will constantly innovate strategic guidance and operational thoughts so as to ensure the capabilities of fighting and winning. In response to the new requirement arising from the worldwide RMA, the armed forces will pay close attention to the challenges in new security domains, and work hard to seize the strategic initiative in military competition. In response to the new requirement coming from the country's growing strategic interests, the armed forces will actively participate in both regional and international security cooperation and effectively secure China's overseas interests. And in response to the new requirement arising from China's all-round and deepening reform, the armed forces will continue to follow the path of civil-military integration (CMI), actively participate in the country's economic and social construction, and firmly maintain social stability, so as to remain a staunch force for upholding the CPC's ruling position and a reliable force for developing socialism with Chinese characteristics.

China's armed forces will effectively perform their missions in the new historical period, resolutely uphold the leadership of the CPC and the socialist system with Chinese characteristics, safeguard China's sovereignty, security and development interests, safeguard the important period of strategic opportunities for China's development, maintain regional and world peace, and strive to provide a strong guarantee for completing the building of a moderately prosperous society in all respects and achieving the great rejuvenation of the Chinese nation.

China's armed forces mainly shoulder the following strategic tasks:

- To deal with a wide range of emergencies and military threats, and effectively safeguard the sovereignty and security of China's territorial land, air and sea;

- To resolutely safeguard the unification of the motherland;
- To safeguard China's security and interests in new domains;
- To safeguard the security of China's overseas interests;
- To maintain strategic deterrence and carry out nuclear counterattack;
- To participate in regional and international security cooperation and maintain regional and world peace;
- To strengthen efforts in operations against infiltration, separatism and terrorism so as to maintain China's political security and social stability; and
- To perform such tasks as emergency rescue and disaster relief, rights and interests protection, guard duties, and support for national economic and social development.

III. Strategic Guideline of Active Defense

The strategic concept of active defense is the essence of the CPC's military strategic thought. From the long-term practice of revolutionary wars, the people's armed forces have developed a complete set of strategic concepts of active defense, which boils down to: adherence to the unity of strategic defense and operational and tactical offense; adherence to the principles of defense, self-defense and post-emptive strike; and adherence to the stance that "We will not attack unless we are attacked, but we will surely counterattack if attacked."

Shortly after the founding of the PRC in 1949, the Central Military Commission (CMC) established the military strategic guideline of active defense, and later, in line with the developments and changes in the national security situation, had made a number of major revisions of it. In 1993 the military strategic guideline of the new era was formulated, which took winning local wars in conditions of modern technology, particularly high technology, as the basic point in making preparation for military struggle (PMS). In 2004, the guideline was further substantiated, and the basic point for PMS was modified to winning local wars under conditions of informationization.

China's socialist nature, fundamental national interests and the objective requirement of taking the path of peaceful development all demand that China unswervingly adhere to and enrich the strategic concept of active defense. Guided by national security and development strategies, and required by the situation and their tasks in the new historical period, China's armed forces will continue to implement the military strategic guideline of active defense and enhance military strategic guidance as the times so require. They will further broaden strategic vision, update strategic thinking and make strategic guidance more forward-looking. A holistic approach will be taken to balance war preparation and war prevention, rights protection and stability maintenance, deterrence and warfighting, and operations in wartime and employment of military forces in peacetime. They will lay stress on farsighted planning and management to create a favorable posture, comprehensively manage crises, and resolutely deter and win wars.

To implement the military strategic guideline of active defense in the new situation, China's armed forces will adjust the basic point for PMS. In line with the evolving form of war and national security situation, the basic point for PMS will be placed on winning informationized local wars, highlighting maritime military struggle and maritime PMS. The armed forces will work to effectively control major crises, properly handle possible chain reactions, and firmly safeguard the country's territorial sovereignty, integrity and security.

To implement the military strategic guideline of active defense in the new situation, China's armed forces will innovate basic operational doctrines. In response to security threats from different directions and in line with their current capabilities, the armed forces will adhere to the principles of flexibility, mobility and self-dependence so that "you fight your way and I fight my way." Integrated combat forces will be employed to prevail in system-vs-system operations featuring information dominance, precision strikes and joint operations.

To implement the military strategic guideline of active defense in the new situation, China's armed forces will optimize the military strategic layout. In view of China's geostrategic environment, the security threats it faces and the strategic tasks they shoulder, the armed forces will make overall planning for strategic deployment and military disposition, in order to clearly divide areas of responsibility for their troops, and enable them to support each other and act as an organic whole. Threats from such new security domains as outer space and cyber space will be dealt with to maintain the common security of the world community. China's armed forces will strengthen international security cooperation in areas crucially related to China's overseas interests, to ensure the security of such interests.

To implement the military strategic guideline of active defense in the new situation, China's armed forces will uphold the following principles:

- To be subordinate to and in the service of the national strategic goal, implement the holistic view of national security, strengthen PMS, prevent crises, deter and win wars;

- To foster a strategic posture favorable to China's peaceful development, adhere to the national defense policy that is defensive in nature, persevere in close coordination of political, military, economic and diplomatic work, and positively cope with comprehensive security threats the country possibly encounters;
- To strike a balance between rights protection and stability maintenance, and make overall planning for both, safeguard national territorial sovereignty and maritime rights and interests, and maintain security and stability along China's periphery;
- To endeavor to seize the strategic initiative in military struggle, proactively plan for military struggle in all directions and domains, and grasp the opportunities to accelerate military building, reform and development;
- To employ strategies and tactics featuring flexibility and mobility, give full play to the overall effectiveness of joint operations, concentrate superior forces, and make integrated use of all operational means and methods;
- To make serious preparations to cope with the most complex and difficult scenarios, uphold bottom-line thinking, and do a solid job in all aspects so as to ensure proper responses to such scenarios with ease at any time and in any circumstances;
- To bring into full play the unique political advantages of the people's armed forces, uphold the CPC's absolute leadership over the military, accentuate the cultivation of fighting spirit, enforce strict discipline, improve the professionalism and strength of the troops, build closer relations between the government and the military as well as between the people and the military, and boost the morale of officers and men;
- To give full play to the overall power of the concept of people's war, persist in employing it as an ace weapon to triumph over the enemy, enrich the contents, ways and means of the concept of people's war, and press forward with the shift of the focus of war mobilization from human resources to science and technology; and
- To actively expand military and security cooperation, deepen military relations with major powers, neighboring countries and other developing countries, and promote the establishment of a regional framework for security and cooperation.

IV. Building and Development of China's Armed Forces

In the implementation of the military strategic guideline in the new situation, China's armed forces must closely center around the CPC's goal of building a strong military, respond to the state's core security needs, aim at building an informationized military and winning informationized wars, deepen the reform of national defense and the armed forces in an all-round way, build a modern system of military forces with Chinese characteristics, and constantly enhance their capabilities for addressing various security threats and accomplishing diversified military tasks.

Development of the Services and Arms of the People's Liberation Army (PLA) and the People's Armed Police Force (PAPF).

In line with the strategic requirement of mobile operations and multi-dimensional offense and defense, the PLA Army (PLAA) will continue to reorient from theater defense to trans-theater mobility. In the process of building small, multi-functional and modular units, the PLAA will adapt itself to tasks in different regions, develop the capacity of its combat forces for different purposes, and construct a combat force structure for joint operations. The PLAA will elevate its capabilities for precise, multi-dimensional, trans-theater, multi-functional and sustainable operations.

In line with the strategic requirement of offshore waters defense and open seas protection, the PLA Navy (PLAN) will gradually shift its focus from "offshore waters defense" to the combination of "offshore waters defense" with "open seas protection," and build a combined, multi-functional and efficient marine combat force structure. The PLAN will enhance its capabilities for strategic deterrence and counterattack, maritime maneuvers, joint operations at sea, comprehensive defense and comprehensive support.

In line with the strategic requirement of building air-space capabilities and conducting offensive and defensive operations, the PLA Air Force (PLAAF) will endeavor to shift its focus from territorial air defense to both defense and offense, and build an air-space defense force structure that can meet the requirements of informationized operations. The PLAAF will boost its capabilities for strategic early warning, air strike, air and missile defense, information countermeasures, airborne operations, strategic projection and comprehensive support.

In line with the strategic requirement of being lean and effective and possessing both nuclear and conventional missiles, the PLA Second Artillery Force (PLASAF) will strive to transform itself in the direction of informationization, press forward with independent innovations in weaponry and equipment by reliance on science and technology, enhance the safety, reliability and effectiveness of missile systems, and improve the force structure featuring a combination of both nuclear and conventional capabilities. The PLASAF will strengthen its capabilities for strategic deterrence and nuclear counterattack, and medium- and long-range precision strikes.

In line with the strategic requirement of performing multiple functions and effectively maintaining social stability, the PAPF will continue to develop its forces for guard and security, contingency response, stability maintenance, counter-terrorism operations, emergency rescue and disaster relief, emergency support and air support, and work to improve a force structure which highlights guard duty, contingency response, counter-terrorism and stability maintenance. The PAPF will enhance its capabilities for performing diversified tasks centering on guard duty and contingency response in informationized conditions.

Force Development in Critical Security Domains

The seas and oceans bear on the enduring peace, lasting stability and sustainable development of China. The traditional mentality that land outweighs sea must be abandoned, and great importance has to be attached to managing the seas and oceans and protecting maritime rights and interests. It is necessary for China to develop a modern maritime military force structure commensurate with its national security and development interests, safeguard its national sovereignty and maritime rights and interests, protect the security of strategic SLOCs and overseas interests, and participate in international maritime cooperation, so as to provide strategic support for building itself into a maritime power.

Outer space has become a commanding height in international strategic competition. Countries concerned are developing their space forces and instruments, and the first signs of weaponization of outer space have appeared. China has all along advocated the peaceful use of outer space, opposed the weaponization of and arms race in outer space, and taken an active part in international space cooperation. China will keep abreast of the dynamics of outer space, deal with security threats and challenges in that domain, and secure its space assets to serve its national economic and social development, and maintain outer space security.

Cyberspace has become a new pillar of economic and social development, and a new domain of national security. As international strategic competition in cyberspace has been turning increasingly fiercer, quite a few countries are developing their cyber military forces. Being one of the major victims of hacker attacks, China is confronted with grave security threats to its cyber infrastructure. As cyberspace weighs more in military security, China will expedite the development of a cyber force, and enhance its capabilities of cyberspace situation awareness, cyber defense, support for the country's endeavors in cyberspace and participation in international cyber cooperation, so as to stem major cyber crises, ensure national network and information security, and maintain national security and social stability.

The nuclear force is a strategic cornerstone for safeguarding national sovereignty and security. China has always pursued the policy of no first use of nuclear weapons and adhered to a self-defensive nuclear strategy that is defensive in nature. China will unconditionally not use or threaten to use nuclear weapons against non-nuclear-weapon states or in nuclear-weapon-free zones, and will never enter into a nuclear arms race with any other country. China has always kept its nuclear capabilities at the minimum level required for maintaining its national security. China will optimize its nuclear force structure, improve strategic early warning, command and control, missile penetration, rapid reaction, and survivability and protection, and deter other countries from using or threatening to use nuclear weapons against China.

Military Force Building Measures

Strengthening ideological and political work. China's armed forces always treat ideological and political building as the first priority, and have endeavored to reinforce and improve their political work in the new situation. They will continue to practice and carry forward the Core Socialist Values, cultivate the Core Values of Contemporary Revolutionary Service Personnel, and carry forward their glorious traditions and fine styles. Moreover, the armed forces will uphold a series of fundamental principles for and institutions of the CPC's absolute leadership over the military, enhance the creativity, cohesion and combat effectiveness of their CPC organizations at all levels, make great efforts to cultivate a new generation of revolutionary service personnel of noble soul, competence, courage, uprightness and virtue, and ensure that the armed forces will resolutely follow the commands of the CPC Central Committee and the CMC at all times and under all conditions, and consistently retain the nature and purpose of the people's armed forces.

Pushing ahead with logistics modernization. China's armed forces will deepen logistics reform in relevant policies, institutions and support forces, and optimize strategic logistics deployment. They will innovate the modes of support, develop new support means, augment war reserves, integrate logistics information systems, improve rules and standards, and meticulously organize supply and support, so as to build a logistics system that can provide support for fighting and winning modern wars, serve the modernization of the armed forces, and transform towards informationization.

Developing advanced weaponry and equipment. Persevering in information dominance, systems building, independent innovation, sustainable development, overall planning, and emphasis on priorities, China's armed forces will speed up to upgrade weaponry and equipment, and work to develop a weaponry and equipment system which can effectively respond to informationized warfare and help fulfill the missions and tasks.

Cultivating new-type military personnel. China's armed forces will continue with the strategic project for personnel training and perfect the system for military human resources. They will deepen the reform of military educational institutions and improve the triad training system for new-type military personnel—institutional education, unit training and military professional education, so as to pool more talented people and cultivate more personnel who can meet the demands of informationized warfare.

Intensifying efforts in running the armed forces with strict discipline and in accordance with the law. Aiming at strengthening the revolutionization, modernization and regularization of the armed forces in all respects, China will innovate and develop theories and practice in relation to running the armed forces in accordance with the law, establish a well-knit military law system with Chinese characteristics, so as to elevate the level of rule by law of national defense and armed forces building.

Innovating military theories. Under the guidance of the CPC's innovative theories, China's armed forces will intensify their studies of military operations, probe into the mechanisms of winning modern wars, innovate strategies and tactics featuring mobility and flexibility, and develop theories on military building in the new situation, so as to bring into place a system of advanced military theories commensurate with the requirement of winning future wars.

Improving strategic management. It is necessary to optimize the functions and institutions of the CMC and the general headquarters/departments, improve the leadership and management system of the services and arms, and adhere to demand-based planning and plan-based resource allocation. China's armed forces will set up a system and a working mechanism for overall and coordinated programming and planning. They will also intensify overall supervision and management of strategic resources, strengthen the in-process supervision and risk control of major projects, improve mechanisms for strategic assessment, and set up and improve relevant assessment systems and complementary standards and codes.

In-depth Development of Civil-Military Integration (CMI)

Following the guiding principle of integrating military with civilian purposes and combining military efforts with civilian support, China will forge further ahead with CMI by constantly bettering the mechanisms, diversifying the forms, expanding the scope and elevating the level of the integration, so as to endeavor to bring into place an all-element, multi-domain and cost-efficient pattern of CMI.

Accelerating CMI in key sectors. With stronger policy support, China will work to establish uniform military and civilian standards for infrastructure, key technological areas and major industries, explore the ways and means for training military personnel in civilian educational institutions, developing weaponry and equipment by national defense industries, and outsourcing logistics support to civilian support systems. China encourages joint building and utilization of military and civilian infrastructure, joint exploration of the sea, outer space and air, and shared use of such resources as surveying and mapping, navigation, meteorology and frequency spectra. Accordingly, military and civilian resources can be more compatible, complementary and mutually accessible.

Building a mechanism for operating CMI. At the state level, it is necessary to establish a mechanism for CMI development, featuring unified leadership, military-civilian coordination, abutment of military and civilian needs, and resource sharing. Furthermore, it is necessary to improve the management responsibilities of relevant military and civilian institutions, improve the general standards for both the military and the civilian sectors, make studies on the establishment of a policy system in which the government makes the investment, offers tax incentives and financial support, and expedites legislation promoting military-civilian coordinated development, so as to form a pattern featuring overall military-civilian planning and coordinated development. It is also necessary to push forward with the shared utilization of military capabilities and those of other sectors, and establish a mechanism for joint civil-military response to major crises and emergencies.

Improving the systems and mechanisms of national defense mobilization. China will enhance education in national defense and boost the awareness of the general public in relation to national defense. It will continue to strengthen the building of the reserve force, optimize its structure, and increase its proportion in the PLAN, PLAAF and PLASAF as well as in combat support forces. The ways to organize and employ reserve forces will be more diversified. China will devote more efforts to science and technology in national defense mobilization, be more readily prepared for the requisition of information resources, and build specialized support forces. China aims to build a national defense mobilization system that can meet the requirements of winning informationized wars and responding to both emergencies and wars.

V. Preparation for Military Struggle

Preparation for military struggle (PMS) is a basic military practice and an important guarantee for safeguarding peace, containing crises and winning wars. To expand and intensify PMS, China's armed forces must meet the requirement of being capable of fighting and winning, focus on solving major problems and difficulties, and do solid work and make relentless efforts in practical preparations, in order to enhance their overall capabilities for deterrence and warfighting.

Enhancing capabilities for system-vs-system operations based on information systems. China's armed forces will quicken their steps to transform the generating mode of combat effectiveness, work to use information systems to integrate a wide range of operational forces, modules and elements into overall operational capacity, and gradually establish an integrated joint operational system in which all elements are seamlessly linked and various operational platforms perform independently and in coordination. China's armed forces will endeavor to address the pressing problems constraining the capabilities for system-vs-system operations. They will make further exploration and more efficient utilization of information resources, strengthen the building of the systems of reconnaissance, early-warning and command and control, develop medium- and long-range precision strike capabilities, and improve the comprehensive support systems. In accordance with the requirement of being authoritative, streamlined, agile and efficient, they will strive to establish and improve the CMC command organ and theater-level command systems for joint operations.

Pushing ahead with PMS in all directions and domains. Due to its complex geostrategic environment, China faces various threats and challenges in all its strategic directions and security domains. Therefore, PMS must be carried out in a well-planned, prioritized, comprehensive and coordinated way, so as to maintain the balance and stability of the overall strategic situation. China's armed forces will make overall planning for PMS in both traditional and new security domains, and get ready to safeguard national sovereignty and security, protect the country's maritime rights and interests, and deal with armed conflicts and emergencies. To adapt to the upgrading of weaponry and equipment as well as changes of operational patterns, China's armed forces will further optimize battlefield disposition and strengthen strategic prepositioning.

Maintaining constant combat readiness. China's armed forces will continue to improve its routine combat readiness, maintain a posture of high alertness, and conscientiously organize border, coastal and air defense patrols and guard duties. The PLAA will improve its combat readiness system with inter-connected strategic directions, combined arms and systematized operational support, so as to ensure agile maneuvers and effective response. The PLAN will continue to organize and perform regular combat readiness patrols and maintain a military presence in relevant sea areas. The PLAAF will continue to observe the principles of applicability in peacetime and wartime, all-dimensional response and full territorial reach, and maintain vigilant and efficient combat readiness. The PLASAF will continue to keep an appropriate level of vigilance in peacetime. By observing the principles of combining peacetime and wartime demands, maintaining all time vigilance and being action-ready, it will prefect the integrated, functional, agile and efficient operational duty system.

Enhancing realistic military training. The PLA will continue to attach strategic importance to combat training in realistic conditions, and strictly temper the troops according to the Outline of Military Training and Evaluation (OMTE). It will constantly innovate operational and training methods, improve military training criteria and regulations, and work to build large-scale comprehensive training bases in an effort to provide real-combat environments for training. The PLA will continue to conduct live-setting training, IT-based simulated training, and face-on-face confrontation training in line with real-combat criteria, and strengthen command post training and joint and combined training. It will intensify training in complex electro-magnetic environments, complex and unfamiliar terrains, and complex weather conditions. It will also set up a training supervision and inspection system, so as to incorporate real-combat requirements into training.

Preparing for military operations other than war (MOOTWs). As a necessary requirement for China's armed forces to fulfill their responsibilities and missions in the new period as well as an important approach to enhancing their operational capabilities, the armed forces will continue to conduct such MOOTWs as emergency rescue and disaster relief, counter-terrorism and stability maintenance, rights and interests protection, guard duty, international peacekeeping, and international humanitarian assistance and disaster relief (HADR). They will work to incorporate MOOTW capacity building into military modernization and PMS, and pay special attention to establishing emergency command mechanisms, building emergency forces, training professionals, supporting task-specific equipment, and formulating relevant policies and regulations. Military emergency-response command systems will be tuned into state emergency management mechanisms. China's armed forces will persist in unified organization and command, scientific employment of forces, rapid and efficient actions, and strict observation of related policies and regulations.

VI. Military and Security Cooperation

Pursuing a security concept featuring common, comprehensive, cooperative and sustainable security, China's armed forces will continue to develop military-to-military relations that are non-aligned, non-confrontational and not directed against any third party. They will strive to establish fair and effective collective security mechanisms and military confidence-building measures (CBMs), expand military and security cooperation, and create a security environment favorable to China's peaceful development.

Developing all-round military-to-military relations. China's armed forces will further their exchanges and cooperation with the Russian military within the framework of the comprehensive strategic partnership of coordination between China and Russia, and foster a comprehensive, diverse and sustainable framework to promote military relations in more fields and at more levels. China's armed forces will continue to foster a new model of military relationship with the US armed forces that conforms to the new model of major-country relations between the two countries, strengthen defense dialogues, exchanges and cooperation, and improve the CBM mechanism for the notification of major military activities as well as the rules of behavior for safety of air and maritime encounters, so as to strengthen mutual trust, prevent risks and manage crises. In the spirit of neighborhood diplomacy of friendship, sincerity, reciprocity and inclusiveness, China's armed forces will further develop relations with their counterparts in neighboring countries. Also, they will work to raise the level of military relations with European counterparts, continue the traditional friendly military ties with their African, Latin American and Southern Pacific counterparts. China's armed forces will work to further defense and security cooperation in the Shanghai Cooperation Organization (SCO), and continue to participate in multilateral dialogues and cooperation mechanisms such as the ASEAN Defense Ministers' Meeting Plus (ADMM+), ASEAN Regional Forum (ARF), Shangri-La Dialogue (SLD), Jakarta International Defence Dialogue (JIDD) and Western Pacific Naval Symposium (WPNS). The Chinese military will continue to host multilateral events like the Xiangshan Forum, striving to establish a new framework for security and cooperation conducive to peace, stability and prosperity in the Asia-Pacific region.

Pushing ahead with pragmatic military cooperation. On the basis of mutual respect, equality, mutual benefit and all-win cooperation, China's armed forces will continue to carry out pragmatic cooperation with their counterparts in various countries of the world. In response to the changing situation, China's armed forces will constantly explore new fields, new contents and new models of cooperation with other militaries, so as to jointly deal with a diverse range of security threats and challenges. Extensive dialogues and exchanges will be conducted with foreign militaries on defense policy, services and arms building, institutional education, logistics and other subjects to promote mutual understanding, mutual trust and mutual learning. The Chinese military will also strengthen cooperation with related countries in personnel training, material assistance, equipment and technology, so as to strengthen mutual support and enhance respective defensive capabilities. Bilateral and multilateral joint exercises and training, involving various services and arms, will be conducted at multiple levels and in various domains to enhance joint operational capabilities. The Chinese military will work to extend the subjects of such training and exercises from non-traditional to traditional security areas. It will actively participate in international maritime security dialogues and cooperation, and jointly deal with traditional and non-traditional maritime security threats.

Fulfilling international responsibilities and obligations. China's armed forces will continue to participate in UN peacekeeping missions, strictly observe the mandates of the UN Security Council, maintain its commitment to the peaceful settlement of conflicts, promote development and reconstruction, and safeguard regional peace and security. China's armed forces will continue to take an active part in international disaster rescue and humanitarian assistance, dispatch professional rescue teams to disaster-stricken areas for relief and disaster reduction, provide relief materials and medical aid, and strengthen international exchanges in the fields of rescue and disaster reduction. Through the aforementioned operations, the armed forces can also enhance their own capabilities and expertise. Faithfully fulfilling China's international obligations, the country's armed forces will continue to carry out escort missions in the Gulf of Aden and other sea areas as required, enhance exchanges and cooperation with naval task forces of other countries, and jointly secure international SLOCs. China's armed forces will engage in extensive regional and international security affairs, and promote the establishment of the mechanisms of emergency notification, military risk precaution, crisis management and conflict control. With the growth of national strength, China's armed forces will gradually intensify their participation in such operations as international peacekeeping and humanitarian assistance, and do their utmost to shoulder more international responsibilities and obligations, provide more public security goods, and contribute more to world peace and common development.

BIBLIOGRAPHY

Books

Agnihotri, Kamlesh K. *Strategic Direction of the Chinese Navy: Capability and Intent Assessment*. Bloomsbury India, 2016.

Aiyar, Pallavi. *Smoke and Mirrors*. Harper Collins, 2012.

Bhatia, Rajiv. *India—Myanmar Relations: Changing Contours*. Routledge, 2015.

Blasko, Dennis J. *The Chinese Army Today: Tradition and Transformation for the 21st Century*. Routledge, 2013.

Buzan, Barry and Ole Wæver. *Regions and Powers: The Structure of International Security* (Cambridge University Press, 2003).

Cole, Bernard D. *Sea Lanes and Pipelines Energy Security in Asia*. Westport, Conn: Pentagon Energy Press, 2008.

Cole, Bernard D. *The Great Wall at Sea: China's Navy in the Twenty-First Century*. Naval Institute Press, 2010.

Cullinane, Kevin. *International Handbook of Maritime Economics*. Edward Elgar Publishing, 2011.

Dalvi, J. P. *Himalayan Blunder: The Curtain-Raiser to the Sino-Indian War of 1962*. Natraj Publishers, 1997.

Economy, Elizabeth and Michael Levi. *By All Means Necessary: How China's Resource Quest Is Changing the World*. OUP USA, 2014.

Fairbank, John King. *China—A New History 2e Enlarged Edition OISC*. 2nd Enlarged edition. Cambridge, Mass: Harvard University Press, 2006.

Finkelstein, David M. and Kristen Gunness. *Civil-Military Relations in Today's China: Swimming in a New Sea*. Routledge, 2015.

Garver, John W. *Protracted Contest: Sino-Indian Rivalry in the Twentieth Century*. University of Washington Press, 2011.

Global Trends 2030. Accessed November 12, 2015. http://www.dni.gov/index.php/about/organization/global-trends-2030.

Hayton, Bill. *The South China Sea: The Struggle for Power in Asia*. Yale University Press, 2014.

Holmes, James R. and Toshi Yoshihara. *Chinese Naval Strategy in the 21st Century: The Turn to Mahan*. Routledge, 2012.

Joffe, Ellis. *The Chinese Army after Mao*. Weidenfeld and Nicolson, 1987.

Kaplan, Robert D. *Asia's Cauldron: The South China Sea and the End of a Stable Pacific*. Random House Publishing Group, 2014.

Kaplan, Robert D. *Monsoon: The Indian Ocean and the Future of American Power*. Random House Publishing Group, 2010.

Keay, John. *China: A History*. HarperCollins UK, 2010.

Khilnani, Sunil. *Non-Alignment 2.0: A Foreign and Strategic Policy for India in the 21st Century*. Penguin UK, 2014.

Kroeber, Arthur R. *China's Economy: What Everyone Needs to Know*. Oxford University Press, 2016.

Kumar, Anand. *Multi-Party Democracy in Maldives and the Emerging Security Environment in the Indian Ocean Region*, 2016.

Lewis, John Wilson and Litai Xue. *China's Strategic Seapower: The Politics of Force Modernization in the Nuclear Age*. Stanford University Press, 1996.

Lintner, Bertil. *Great Game East – India, China, and the Struggle for Asia's Most Volatile Frontier.* New Haven: Yale University Press, 2015.

Madhav, Ram. *Uneasy Neighbours: India and China after 50 Years of the War*. Har-Anand Publications, 2014.

Mahan, A. T. *The Influence of Sea Power upon History, 1660-1783*, n.d.

Mattis, Peter. *Analyzing the Chinese Military: A Review Essay and Resource Guide on the People's Liberation Army*. CreateSpace Independent Publishing Platform, 2015.

Maxwell, Neville. *India's China War*. Natraj Publishers, 2013.

Menon, Rear Admiral K. Raja. *Maritime Strategy and Continental Wars*. Routledge, 2013.

Menon, Shivshankar. *Choices: Inside the Making of Indian Foreign Policy*. Penguin UK, 2016.

Miller, Tom. *China's Asian Dream: Empire Building along the New Silk Road*. Zed Books, 2017.

Mohan, C. Raja. *Samudra Manthan: Sino-Indian Rivalry in the Indo-Pacific*. Carnegie Endowment for International Peace, 2012

Office, U.S. Government Printing. Global Trends: Paradox of Progress. Government Printing Office, 2017.

Palat, Madhavan. *Geopolitics or Dominion of the Globe*. Nehru Memorial Museum and Library, n.d.

Paret, Peter, Gordon A. Craig and Felix Gilbert. *Makers of Modern Strategy from Machiavelli to the Nuclear Age*. Princeton University Press, 2010.

Pearson, Michael. *The Indian Ocean*. Routledge, 2007.

Peng, Guangqian and Youzhi Yao. *The Science of Military Strategy*. Military Science Publishing House, 2005.

Rajesh, M. H., and Raj Kumar Sharma, eds. *Strategic Balance in the Indo-Pacific Region: Challenges and Prospects*. New Delhi, India: VIJ Books, 2017.

Ranganathan, C. V. and Vinod C. Khanna. *India and China: The Way Ahead after "Mao's India War"*. Har-Anand Publications, 2000.

Rodrigue, Jean-Paul, Claude Comtois and Brian Slack. *The Geography of Transport Systems*. 3 edition. Abingdon, Oxon: Routledge, 2013.

Saran, Shyam. *How India Sees The World: From Kautilya to the 21st Century*. S.l.: Juggernaut, 2017.

Saunders, Stephen. *Jane's Fighting Ships, 2014-2015*. Jane's Information Group, 2015.

Shambaugh, David. *China's Future*. John Wiley & Sons, 2016.

Sharma, B.K., and Dr Nivedita Das Kundu. *China's One Belt One Road: Initiative, Challenges and Prospects*. Vij Books India Pvt Ltd, 2016.

Shourie, Arun. *Self-Deception: India's China Policies*. HarperCollins Publishers India, 2013.

Small, Andrew. *The China-Pakistan Axis: Asia's New Geopolitics*. Oxford University Press, 2015.

Stopford, Martin. *Maritime Economics 3e*. 3 edition. London/ ; New York: Routledge, 2008.

Till, Geoffrey. *Seapower: A Guide for the Twenty-First Century*. Routledge, 2013.

Tse-tung, Mao. *Selected Military Writings of Mao Tse-Tung*. Praetorian Press Llc, 2011.

Articles or other work in a journal, papers in think tanks

Blasko, J. Dennis, "China's Merchant Marine" *A paper for the China as "Maritime Power" Conference*, July 28-29, 2015 CNA Conference Facility Arlington, Virginia

Collins, Gabriel and Grubb, Michael. "A Comprehensive Survey of China's Dynamic Shipbuilding Industry-Commercial Development and Strategic Implications", n.d.

"China in Africa." *Council on Foreign Relations*. Accessed May 20, 2017. https://www.cfr.org/backgrounder/china-africa.

"China's 'Malacca Dilemma.'" *The Jamestown Foundation*. Accessed August 2, 2015. http://www.jamestown.org/single/?no_cache=1&tx_ttnews%5 Btt_news%5 D=3943.

"Chinese Dam Incurs KIO Wrath. Institute for Defence Studies and Analyses." Accessed May 8, 2017. http://www.idsa.in/TWIR/9_5_2008_KIO.

"Chinese Investments in Sri Lanka." *Gateway House*, December 1, 2016. http://www.gatewayhouse.in/chinese-investments-sri-lanka/.

"Chinese Submarines in Sri Lanka Unnerve India: Next Stop Pakistan?," Jamestown. Accessed August 12, 2017. https://jamestown.org/program/chinese-submarines-in-sri-lanka-unnerve-india-next-stop-pakistan/.

Christopher Dunn, Lin Ji and Kui Peng. "Chinese Investments in Myanmar - A Scoping Study", Global Environmental Institute.

Francis Fukuyama. "The End of History?", *The National Interest*, Summer 1989.

Goldstein, Lyle J. "Five Dragons Stirring Up the Sea: Challenge and Opportunity in China's Improving Maritime Enforcement Capabilities". PN, 2010.

"Israel-China Arms Trade and the US Factor." *International Strategic and Security Studies Programme, NIAS, India*, April 11, 2014. http://isssp.in/israel-china-arms-trade-and-the-us-factor/.

Johannes F. Linn. "Economic (Dis)Integration Matters: The Soviet Collapse Revisited." The Brookings Institution, October 2004. http://www.brookings.edu/views/papers/200410linn.pdf.

Kelegama, Saman. "China–Sri Lanka Economic Relations: An Overview." *China Report* 50, no. 2 (May 1, 2014): 131–49. doi:10.1177/0009445514523646.

Lintner, Bertil. "The People's Republic of China and Burma: Not Only Pauk-Phaw", Project 2049 May 9, 2017

"Lubricated With Oil: Iran-China Relations in a Changing World," Middle East Policy Council. Accessed May 20, 2017. http://www.mepc.org/lubricated-oil-iran-china-relations-changing-world.

Mackinder, Halford John. "The Geographical Pivot of History". Royal Geographical Society, 1904.

"Map: China's West-East Electricity Transfer Project." *Wilson Center*, February 19, 2013. https://www.wilsoncenter.org/article/map-chinas-west-east-electricity-transfer-project.

"One Belt One Road in Malaysia: China's Strategic Enabler?" *The Strategist*, April 20, 2017. https://www.aspistrategist.org.au/one-belt-one-road-malaysia-chinas-strategic-enabler/.

"Pakistan-Sri Lanka Relations." *The Lakshman Kadirgamar Institute*. Accessed April 16, 2017. http://www.lki.lk/publication/speech-prime-minister-nawaz-sharif/

"PLAN Officers to Train on Brazilian Aircraft Carrier," Jamestown. Accessed August 7, 2017. https://jamestown.org/program/plan-officers-to-train-on-brazilian-aircraft-carrier/.

Rajesh, M.H. "China Pakistan Economic Corridor – Current Status with Focus on Energy Sector", *Journal of the United Service Institution of India*,Vol. CXLVII, No. 607, Jan-Mar 2017

Rajesh, M.H. "Continuing Evolution of Chinese Armed Forces-A Review of Recent Organisational Changes", *Journal of the United Service Institution of India*, Vol. CXLVI, No. 603, Jan-Mar 2016

Rajesh, M.H. "Indian Ocean Regional Security: Mechanisms Problems and Prospects", *Journal of Indian Ocean*, Vol.24, No.3, Dec 2016

Rajesh, M.H. "India-South Korea Relations: An Indian Perspective". Sharma, B.K. and Rajesh, M.H. ed. *Geopolitics, Security and Bilateral Relations: Perspectives from India and South Korea.* New Delhi (India): VIJ Books, 2016.

Rajesh, M.H. "Maritime Silk Road: An Indian Perspective", Sharma, B.K., and Dr Nivedita Das Kundu ed. *China's One Belt One Road: Initiative, Challenges and Prospects.* Vij Books India Pvt Ltd, 2016.

Rajesh, M.H. "South China Sea in Retrospect", *Journal of the United Service Institution of India,* Vol. CXLVI, No. 605, Jul-Sep 2016

Rajesh, M.H. "The Party's Maritime Power: Four Roles and Three-and-a-Half Fleets". *China Report 53*, no. 1 (February 2017): 46–58. doi:10.1177/0009445516677363.

"Rethinking Australia's Relationship with China." *East Asia Forum*, April 13, 2017. http://www.eastasiaforum.org/2017/04/13/rethinking-australias-relationship-with-china/.

Roberts, James M. and Huma Sattar. "Pakistan's Economic Disarray and How to Fix It". *The Heritage Foundation*. Accessed October 4, 2016. http://www.heritage.org/research/reports/2015/06/pakistans-economic-disarray-and-how-to-fix-it.

Rory Medcalf, "The Indo-Pacific: What's in a Name?". Lowy Institute for International Policy," accessed November 12, 2015, http://www.lowyinstitute.org/publications/indo-pacific-whats-name.

Sareen, Sushant. "Corridor Calculus China Pakistan Economic Corridor & China's Comprador Investment Model in Pakistan". April 22, 2016. http://www.vifindia.org/monograph/2016/april/22/corridor-calculus-china-pakistan-economic-corridor-and-china-s-comprador-investment-model-in-pakistan.

"Taming the Five Dragons? China Consolidates Its Maritime Law Enforcement Agencies." *The Jamestown Foundation*. Accessed May 15, 2016.http://www.jamestown.org/programs/chinabrief/single/?tx_ttnews%5Btt_news%5D=40661&cHash=c3c1a5a4ce04d29db680c8a092843afd.

University, National Defense. *A Low-Visibility Force Multiplier: Assessing China's Cruise Missile Ambitions*. LULU Press, 2015.

Government Statements, White Papers, International Organisations and NGO Publications

"5 Things to Know about China and Australia's Economic Ties." *World Economic Forum*. Accessed July 3, 2017. https://www.weforum.org/agenda/2016/04/5-things-to-know-about-china-and-australia-s-economic-ties/.

"Aid to Pakistan by the Numbers." *Center For Global Development.* Accessed January 8, 2017. http://www.cgdev.org/page/aid-pakistan-numbers.

"Burma (Myanmar) - International - Analysis - U.S. Energy Information Administration (EIA)." Accessed May 7, 2017. https://www.eia.gov/beta/international/analysis.cfm?iso=MMR.

"China - International - Analysis - U.S. Energy Information Administration (EIA)." Accessed August 23, 2017. https://www.eia.gov/beta/international/analysis.cfm?iso=CHN.

"China and India Hold First Round of Dialogue on Maritime Cooperation." Accessed August 28, 2017. http://www.fmprc.gov.cn/mfa_eng/wjbxw/t1339176.shtml.

"China to Explore Civilian Ships' Great Potential for National Defense." Accessed March 25, 2016. http://eng.mod.gov.cn/TopNews/2015-06/12/content_4590018.htm.

"China, Import Trade & Tariff, by Country 2015, WITS, Data." Accessed July 8, 2017. http://wits.worldbank.org/CountryProfile/en/Country/CHN/Year/2015/TradeFlow/Import/Partner/by-country/Show/Partner%20Name;mprt-shr-ttl-prdct;mprt-trd-vl;mprt-prtnr-shr;ahs-wghtd-avrg;mfn-wghtd-avrg;trf-nmbr-aggrmnt;/sort/mprt-trd-vl/Chart/top10.

"China's Arab Policy Paper." Accessed May 20, 2017. http://www.fmprc.gov.cn/mfa_eng/wjdt_665385/2649_665393/t1331683.shtml.

"Chinese Naval Base at Seychelles Island." Accessed May 20, 2017. http://pib.nic.in/newsite/PrintRelease.aspx?relid=119836.

"Contribution to GDP - Financial Services Commission - Mauritius." Accessed May 20, 2017. https://www.fscmauritius.org/en/media-publications/contribution-to-gdp.

"CPEC, China-Pakistan Economic Corridor (CPEC) Official Website." Accessed February 17, 2017. http://cpec.gov.pk/#.

"Digital India, MyGov.in." Accessed November 13, 2015. https://mygov.in/group/digital-india/.

"Full Text of Chinese Gov't Statement on China's Territorial Sovereignty and Maritime Rights and Interests in S. China Sea ," *Xinhua, English.news.cn.* Accessed September 9, 2016. http://news.xinhuanet.com/english/2016-07/12/c_135507754.htm.

"Full Text: China Adheres to the Position of Settling Through Negotiation the Relevant Disputes Between China and the Philippines in the South China Sea," *Xinhua, English.news.cn.* Accessed September 9, 2016. http://news.xinhuanet.com/english/china/2016-07/13/c_135509153.htm.

"Full Text: China's Military Strategy." Accessed August 7, 2017. http://eng.mod.gov.cn/Press/2015-05/26/content_4586805.htm.

"Global Trends 2030." Accessed November 12, 2015. http://www.dni.gov/index.php/about/organization/global-trends-2030.

"Home - Make In India." Accessed November 13, 2015. http://www.makeinindia.com/home.

"IEA - Report." Accessed October 18, 2016. http://www.iea.org/statistics/statisticssearch/report/?year=2014&country=PAKISTAN&product=Coal.

"IMF Survey/ : Sri Lanka to Reboot Economic Policies." Accessed February 26, 2017. http://www.imf.org/external/pubs/ft/survey/so/2016/car061416a.htm.

"Inaugural India-China Maritime Affairs Dialogue." Accessed March 10, 2016. http://www.mea.gov.in/press-releases.htm?dtl/26317/Inaugural+ IndiaChina +Maritime+Affairs+Dialogue.

"Indian Ocean Rim Association for Regional Co-Operation (IOR-ARC)," accessed November 10, 2015, http://mea.gov.in/in-focus-article.htm?20707/Indian+Ocean+Rim+Association+for+Regional+ Cooperation+IORARC.

"Iran - International - Analysis - U.S. Energy Information Administration (EIA)." Accessed May 20, 2017. https://www.eia.gov/beta/international/analysis.cfm?iso=IRN.

"Is China Pivoting towards the Middle East?" *World Economic Forum*. Accessed May 20, 2017. https://www.weforum.org/agenda/2017/04/is-china-pivoting-towards-the-middle-east/.

"Joint Communiqué of the 14th Meeting of the Foreign Ministers of the Russian Federation, the Republic of India and the People's Republic of China." Accessed August 10, 2017. http://mea.gov.in/bilateral-documents.htm?dtl/26628/Joint_Communiqu_of_the_ 14th_ Meeting_of_ the_Foreign_Ministers_of_the_ Russian_Federation _the_ Republic_of_India_and_ the_Peoples_Republic_of_China.

"Joint Statement Of The People's Republic Of China And The People's Republic Of Bangladesh On Establishing Strategic Partnership Of Cooperation 14 October 2016, Dhaka, Welcome to MOFA Website." Accessed September 1, 2017. http://www.mofa.gov.bd/media/joint-statement-people%E2%80%99s-republic-china-and-people%E2%80%99s-republic-bangladesh-establishing.

"Keynote Address by Prime Minister at India-China Business Forum in Shanghai (May 16, 2015)." Accessed November 22, 2015. http://mea.gov. in/Speeches-Statements.htm?dtl/25247/Keynote_Address_by_ Prime_Minister_at_IndiaChina_Business_Forum_in_Shanghai_May_ 16_2015.

"Myanmar, International Hydropower Association." Accessed June 30, 2017. https://www.hydropower.org/country-profiles/myanmar.

"NAB Statement 1-17 – Northern Alliance (Burma)." Accessed June 4, 2017. http://northernalliance.today/nab-statement-1-17/.

"Norochchole Coal Power Project (3X300MW)." *Ministry of Power and Energy*. Accessed February 25, 2017. http://powermin.gov.lk/english/?page_id=1517.

"Official Spokesperson's Response to a Query on Participation of India in OBOR/BRI Forum." Accessed July 11, 2017.http://mea.gov.in/media-briefings.htm?dtl/28463/Official+Spokespersons+response+to+a+query+ on+participation+of+India+in+OBORBRI+Forum.

"OPEC/ : OPEC Share of World Crude Oil Reserves." Accessed July 5, 2017. http://www.opec.org/opec_web/en/data_graphs/330.htm.

National Bureau of Statistics of China, http://www.stats.gov.cn/tjsj/ndsj/2016/indexeh.htm

"Pakistan, Data." Accessed October 3, 2016. http://data.worldbank.org/country/pakistan.

POCS. "Singapore-Kunming Rail Link Project to Sync with Master Plan on ASEAN Connectivity, one vision one identity one community." *ASEAN, one vision one identity one community*, August 12, 2011. http://asean.org/singapore-kunming-rail-link-project-to-sync-with-master-plan-on-asean-connectivity/.

"Railway-Network-of-CPAC_newjpg.jpg (962×722)." Accessed August 30, 2016. http://www.pc.gov.pk/wp-content/uploads/2016/01/Railway-Network-of-CPAC_newjpg.jpg.

"Republic of Mauritius- China-Mauritius: China Writes off Debts Amounting to Rs 450 Million." Accessed May 20, 2017. http://www.govmu.org/English/News/Pages/China-writes-off-debts-amounting-Rs-450-million-for-Mauritius.aspx.

"Sagarmala: Concept and Implementation towards Blue Revolution." Accessed August 20, 2015. http://pmindia.gov.in/en/news_updates/sagarmala-concept-and-implementation-towards-blue-revolution/.

"Skill India Portal." Accessed November 13, 2015. http://skillindia.gov.in/.

"SmartCities.gov.in." Accessed November 13, 2015. http://smartcities.gov.in/

"Statement of the Government of the People's Republic of China on China's Territorial Sovereignty and Maritime Rights and Interests in the South China Sea." Accessed July 17, 2016. http://www.fmprc.gov.cn/mfa_eng/zxxx_662805/t1379493.shtml.

"The IMF's Extended Fund Facility (EFF)." Accessed October 3, 2016. https://www.imf.org/en/About/Factsheets/Sheets/2016/08/01/20/56/Extended-Fund-Facility.

The United Nations Convention on the Law of the Sea." Accessed June 12, 2017. http://www.un.org/depts/los/convention_agreements/texts/unclos/part4.htm.

"The World Factbook — Central Intelligence Agency." Accessed June 15, 2017. https://www.cia.gov/library/publications/the-world-factbook/geos/xo.html.

"Transcript of Media Briefing by Foreign Secretary in Beijing on Prime Minister's Ongoing Visit to China (may 15, 2015)." Accessed November 22, 2015.

http://www.mea.gov.in/search-result.htm?25245/Transcript+ of+Media+ Briefing+ by+Foreign+Secretary+in+Beijing+on+Prime+ Ministers+ ongoing+ visit+to+ China+may+15+2015.

"Transcript of Prime Minister's Interaction with Chinese Media Organizations." Accessed November 22, 2015. http://mea.gov.in/interviews.htm?dtl/24011/ Transcript_of_Prime_Ministers_ Interaction_ with_ Chinese_media_organizations.

UNCTAD. "UNCTADstat - Maritime Profile: Sri Lanka." *UNCTADstat*. Accessed March 26, 2017. http://unctadstat.unctad.org/CountryProfile/ MaritimeProfile/en-GB/144/index.html.

"Vision and Actions on Jointly Building Silk Road Economic Belt and 21st-Century Maritime Silk Road." Accessed July 30, 2015. http:// www.fmprc.gov.cn/mfa_eng/zxxx_662805/t1249618.shtml.

"Vision and Actions on Jointly Building Silk Road Economic Belt and 21st-Century Maritime Silk Road." Accessed July 30, 2015. http:// www.fmprc.gov.cn/mfa_eng/zxxx_662805/t1249618.shtml.

"Wang Yi: China Will Advance Connection in Two Fields, Explore Expansion in Two Sectors and Deepen Cooperation in Two Aspects with Mauritius." Accessed May 20, 2017.http://www.fmprc.gov.cn/mfa_eng/zxxx_662805/ t1337829.shtml.

"Welcome to the Board of Investment." Accessed October 5, 2016. http:// boi.gov.pk/foreigninvestmentinpakistan.aspx.

"Which Are the World's Fastest-Growing Economies?" *World Economic Forum*. Accessed June 15, 2017. https://www.weforum.org/agenda/2016/04/worlds-fastest-growing-economies/.

WTO, 2015 Press Releases - Accessed September 8, 2016. https://www.wto.org/ english/news_e/pres15_e/pr739_e.htm.

Public Lectures

Public Lectures, webcasts and Broadcast during the period 2013-17 by diplomats, journalists, analysts and scholars as Amb. Shivshankar Menon, Amb. Shyam Saran, Prof. David Shambaugh, Prof. Madhavan Palat, Prof.Alka Acharya, Amb. Ashok Kantha, Gen Narasimhan, Andrew Small, Srinath Raghavan, Dr Manoj Joshi, Dr Raja Mohan, Amb. S. Jaishankar, Amb. K.S. Bajpai, Amb. Kanwal Sibal, Amb. Nirupama Rao, Jayadeva Ranade, Andrew Yang, Srikanth Kondapalli, Jabin Jacob, Lt Gen Prakash Menon, John Garver, Mohan Guruswami, B.R. Deepak, Amb. Phunchak Stobdan, Claude Arpi, Amb. Nalin Surie, Amb. Ranjit Kalha, D.S. Rajan, Ruchir Sharma (Broadcast), Arun Shourie, Prof. Manoranjan Mohanty, Prof. Patricia Uberoi, Barry Buzan, Ashok Behuria, VAdm A.K. Singh, R Adm Raja Menon.

Legal Case

Award of PCA Case N° 2013-19, in the matter of the South China Sea arbitration-before - an arbitral tribunal constituted under annex VII to the 1982 United Nations Convention On The Law Of The Sea between The Republic Of The Philippines and The People's Republic Of China Arbitral Tribunal: Judge Thomas A. Mensah (Presiding Arbitrator), Judge Jean-Pierre Cot Judge Stanislaw Pawlak, Professor Alfred H.A. Soons, Judge Rüdiger Wolfrum, Registry: Permanent Court of Arbitration, 12 July 2016.

"PH-CN-20160712-Award.pdf." Accessed July 18, 2016. https://pca-cpa.org/wp-content/uploads/sites/175/2016/07/PH-CN-20160712-Award.pdf.

Internet Sources

"ADMM, ASEAN Defence Ministers Meeting," accessed November 12, 2015, https://admm.asean.org/.

"ADMM-Plus - ASEAN Defence Minister's Meeting (ADMM)," accessed November 12, 2015, https://admm.asean.org/index.php/about-admm/about-admm-plus.html.

"Airpower in the South China Sea." *Asia Maritime Transparency Initiative*. Accessed July 25, 2017. https://amti.csis.org/airstrips-scs/.

"Background - IORA - Indian Ocean Rim Association," accessed November 12, 2015, http://www.iora.net/about-us/background.aspx.

"Bangladesh Signs US$13.6bn Investment Package with China." Accessed June 26, 2017. http://country.eiu.com/article.aspx?articleid=1544727338&Country=Bangladesh&topic=Economy.

"BIMSTEC Convention on Cooperation in Combating International Terrorism, Transnational Organised Crime And Illicit Drug Trafficking," accessed November 12, 2015, http://mea.gov.in/bilateral-documents.htm?dtl/5070/BIMSTEC+Convention+on+Cooperation+in+Combating+International+Terrorism+Transnational+Organised +Crime+ And+Illicit+Drug+Trafficking.

"BRICS Bank Opens for Business in China - IBNLive." Accessed November 13, 2015. http://www.ibnlive.com/news/world/brics-bank-opens-for-business-in-china-1023400.html.

"China and India Hold First Round of Dialogue on Maritime Cooperation," accessed August 28, 2017, http://www.fmprc.gov.cn/mfa_eng/wjbxw/t1339176.shtml.

"China Military Online." Accessed May 13, 2016. http://english.chinamil.com.cn/.

"Chinese Government Continues to Provide Emergency Assistance to the Maldives," accessed June 15, 2017, http://www.fmprc.gov.cn/mfa_eng/zxxx_662805/t1217941.shtml.

"Communiqué - IORA - Indian Ocean Rim Association," accessed November 12, 2015, http://www.iora.net/documents/communique.aspx.

"COPHC Pakistan." Accessed June 22, 2017. http://cophcgwadar.com.192-185-11-8.pss19.hgwin.temp.domains/about.aspx.

"COSCO SHIPPING Ports Limited." Accessed June 27, 2017. http://www.coscopac.com.hk/en/about_us.php?class_id=5.

"Current Myanmar Hydro-Electric Power Projects List." Accessed May 6, 2017. http://www.oilseedcrops.org/2012/11/30/current-myanmar-hydro-electric-power-projects/.

"Current Status of Dam Projects on Burma's Salween River." *International Rivers*. Accessed September 2, 2017. https://www.internationalrivers.org/resources/current-status-of-dam-projects-on-burma%E2%80%99s-salween-river-7867.

"Dialogue with Prof. Ahsan Iqbal On CPEC - YouTube." Accessed January 5, 2017. https://www.youtube.com/watch?v=9dkQxmycuu8&t=1045s.

"Doraleh Multi-Purpose Port," Port De Djibouti. Accessed July 8, 2017. http://www.portdedjibouti.com/doraleh-multi-purpose-port/.

"Drug Trafficking and the Financing of Terrorism," accessed November 8, 2015, https://www.unodc.org/unodc/en/frontpage/drug-trafficking-and-the-financing-of-terrorism.html.

"EIU Democracy Index 2016." Accessed June 15, 2017. https://infographics.economist.com/2017/DemocracyIndex/.

"Gwadar Port City, China-Pakistan Economic Corridor (CPEC)." Accessed August 5, 2016. http://www.cpecinfo.com/gwadar-port-city.php.

"Hutchison Ports PPC – Balboa, Hutchison Ports." Accessed June 13, 2017. /en/ports/world/panama-ports-company-port-of-balboa-ppc-balboa/.

"Hutchison Ports." Accessed June 27, 2017./en/.

"Ihavanddhippolhu Integrated Development Project (iHavan), Invest Maldives." Accessed September 1, 2017. http://investmaldives.org/investmaldives/strategic-investment-guide/strategic-investment-projects/ihavanddhippolhu-integrated-development-project-ihavan/.

"Interview – Barry Buzan," accessed November 12, 2015, http://www.e-ir.info/2013/03/27/interview-barry-buzan-2/.

"Irrawaddy Myitsone Dam." *International Rivers*. Accessed May 6, 2017. https://www.internationalrivers.org/campaigns/irrawaddy-myitsone-dam-0.

"Julie Bishop MP Speeches - IORA - Indian Ocean Rim Association," accessed November 10, 2015, http://www.iora.net/documents/speeches.aspx.

Lawfare, https://www.lawfareblog.com

"Malaysia Cuts Defence Budget by 12%," *Jane's 360*. Accessed July 3, 2017. http://www.janes.com/article/64867/malaysia-cuts-defence-budget-by-12.

"Member's Country, Indian Ocean Naval Symposium," accessed November 12, 2015, http://ions.gov.in/member_country.

"Myanmar Wanbao Mining Copper." *Myanmar Wanbao Copper Mining Limited.* Accessed May 5, 2017. http://www.myanmarwanbao.com.mm/.

"NDRRM-South Asian Disaster Knowledge Network," accessed November 12, 2015, http://saarc-sadkn.org/ndrrm.aspx.

"NSA Level Meeting on Trilateral Maritime Security Cooperation between India, Sri Lanka and Maldives," accessed November 12, 2015, http://mea.gov.in/in-focus-article.htm?23037/NSA+level+meeting+on+trilateral+Maritime+Security+Cooperation+ between+ India+Sri+Lanka+and+Maldives.

Octaviano, Trishia P., and Researcher. "Popular Economics: Economic Corridors Boost Markets, Living Conditions," Business World Research. Accessed December 19, 2016. http://research.bworldonline.com/popular-economics/story.php?id=350&title=Economic-corridors-boost-markets,-living-conditions.

Project 2049, http://project2049.net/

"Qinglong's Letter to King George." Accessed June 23, 2016. http://academics.wellesley.edu/Polisci/wj/China/208/READINGS/qianlong.html.

"Shareholders – Newcastle Port." Accessed July 9, 2017. http://www.portofnewcastle.com.au/Company-Information/Shareholders.aspx.

"Silk Road and Indian Ocean Traders: Connecting China and the Middle East, The Oriental Institute of the University of Chicago." Accessed August 20, 2017. https://oi.uchicago.edu/museum-exhibits/special-exhibits/silk-road-and-indian-ocean-traders-connecting-china-and-middle-east.

"Terminals, CMA CGM Group Activities." Accessed June 27, 2017. https://www.cma-cgm.com/the-group/activities/shipping/terminals.

"The Economic History of the Last 2000 Years: Part II - The Atlantic." Accessed November 11, 2015. http://www.theatlantic.com/business/archive/2012/06/the-economic-history-of-the-last-2000-years-part-ii/258762/.

"The Silk Road and Arab Sea Routes." Accessed July 30, 2015. http://people.hofstra.edu/geotrans/eng/ch2en/conc2en/silkroad.html.

UNCTAD Review of Maritime Transport

Encyclopaedia Article

"Sergey Georgyevich Gorshkov, Soviet Admiral," *Britannica.com.* Accessed September 17, 2016. https://www.britannica.com/biography/Sergey-Georgyevich-Gorshkov.

Periodicals, Magazines, Webzines

ABC News, http://www.abc.net.au

ABC News, http://www.abc.net.au

African Business Magazine, http://africanbusinessmagazine.com

Al Jazeera, http://www.aljazeera.com
Apanews.net, http://apanews.net
Asiatimes, http://www.atimes.com
Bangladesh News, 24 http://bdnews24.com
BBC News, http://www.bbc.com
Bloomberg, https://www.bloomberg.com
Business Standard India, http://www.business-standard.com
Channel NewsAsia, http://www.channelnewsasia.com
China Daily, http://chinadaily.com.cn
CNN, http://www.cnn.com
Daily News, http://dailynews.lk
Dawn, http://www.dawn.com
Deutsche Welle, DW, http://www.dw.com
Dhaka Tribune, http://www.dhakatribune.com
Dhaka Tribune, http://www.dhakatribune.com
DNA, http://www.dnaindia.com
Eleven Myanmar, Accessed May 9, 2017. http://elevenmyanmar.com
Eurasia Review, http://www.eurasiareview.com
Financial Times, https://ig.ft.com
Financial Times, http://www.ft.com
Forbes, http://www.forbes.com
Foreign Affairs, https://www.foreignaffairs.com
Foreign Affairs, https://www.foreignaffairs.com
Foreign Policy, https://foreignpolicy.com
Foreign Policy, https://foreignpolicy.com
Frontier Myanmar, https://frontiermyanmar.net
Global Times, http://www.globaltimes.cn
Hellenic Shipping News Worldwide, http://www.hellenicshippingnews.com
http://www.theindependentbd.com
IHS Fairplay, http://fairplay.ihs.com
IHS Jane's, 360, http://www.janes.com
India Today, http://indiatoday.intoday.in
Mihaaru, http://en.mihaaru.com
NDTV.com, http://www.ndtv.com
Newsweek, http://www.newsweek.com
Reuters, http://www.reuters.com
Sawarajya, http://swarajyamag.com
South China Morning Post, http://www.scmp.com
States Times Review, http://statestimesreview.com
Stratfor, https://www.stratfor.com

Taipei Times, http://www.taipeitimes.com
The Australian, http://at.theaustralian.com.au/
The Bangladesh Post, http://www.thebangladeshpost.com
The Daily Mirror, http://www.dailymirror.lk
The Daily Star, http://www.thedailystar.net
The Diplomat, http://thediplomat.com
The Economic Times, http://economictimes.indiatimes.com/
The Economist, http://www.economist.com
The Express Tribune, http://tribune.com.pk
The Financial Express, http://www.thefinancialexpress-bd.com
The Guardian, http://www.theguardian.com
The Hindu, http://www.thehindu.com
The Independent Barents Observer, https://thebarentsobserver.com
The Independent, http://www.independent.co.uk
The Indian Express, http://indianexpress.com
The Irrawaddy, https://www.irrawaddy.com
The Myanmar Times, Accessed May 9, 2017. http://www.mmtimes.com
The National, http://www.thenational.ae
The New York Times, https://www.nytimes.com/
The Star Online, http://www.thestar.com.my
The Straits Times, http://www.straitstimes.com
The Telegraph , http://www.telegraphindia.com
The Times of India, http://timesofindia.indiatimes.com
The Washington Post, http://www.washingtonpost.com
The Wire, http://thewire.in
USNI News, https://news.usni.org
Wall Street Journal, http://www.wsj.com
WION (World Is One News), http://www.wionews.com/
Wired, https://www.wired.com
Xinhua, http://news.xinhuanet.com

Databases

AidData, http://china.aiddata.org/projects/33184.
British Petroleum Statistical Review of World Energy
China Global Investment Tracker. *AEI*. https://www.aei.org/china-global-investment-tracker/
EIU Democracy Index 2016. https://infographics.economist.com/2017/DemocracyIndex/.
International Energy Agency, https://www.iea.org/
National Bureau of Statistics of China, http://www.stats.gov.cn/tjsj/ndsj/2016/indexeh.htm

Notre Dame University -GAIN Index, http://index.gain.org/.
SIPRI Arms Transfers Database — www.sipri.org.http://www.sipri.org/databases/armstransfers.
World Bank Database, http://data.worldbank.org

Documents

British Petroleum. "BP Energy Outlook 2017 Edition," n.d. https://www.bp.com/content/dam/bp/pdf/energy-economics/energy-outlook-2017/bp-energy-outlook-2017.pdf.
"Maritime Transportation: Drivers for the Shipping and Port Industries - Transport Research International Documentation - TRID." Accessed November 22, 2015. http://trid.trb.org/view.aspx?id=1085868#.
"Statistical Review of World Energy, Energy Economics," BP. Accessed August 28, 2017. http://www.bp.com/en/global/corporate/energy-economics/statistical-review-of-world-energy.html.

Television Series

The Rise of the Great Powers (*TV Mini-Series 2006–*). Accessed June 9, 2017. http://www.imdb.com/title/tt2802874/.

INDEX